AGING IN SOCIETY:
Selected Reviews of Recent Research

AGING IN SOCIETY:
Selected Reviews of Recent Research

Edited by
Matilda White Riley
Beth B. Hess
Kathleen Bond

With a Foreword by
ROBERT N. BUTLER, M.D.

LEA LAWRENCE ERLBAUM ASSOCIATES, PUBLISHERS
1983   Hillsdale, New Jersey   London

Lawrence Erlbaum Associates, Inc. Publishers
365 Broadway
Hillsdale, New Jersey 07642

Library of Congress Cataloging in Publication Data

Main entry under title:

Aging in society.

  Bibliography: p.
  Includes index.
  1. Aging—United States—Psychological aspects.
2. Aging—Social aspects—United States.   I. Riley,
Matilda White, 1911–   II. Hess, Beth B., 1928–
III. Bond, Kathleen.
HQ1064.U5A6346   1983   305.2'6'0973   82-21083
ISBN 0-89859-267-4

35,253

Printed in the United States of America
10 9 8 7 6 5 4 3 2 1

Contents

Authors and Advisers

4. AGING AND WORK ORGANIZATIONS

Harris T. Schrank
Joan M. Waring
The Equitable Life Assurance Society

Adviser

W. Richard Scott
Department of Sociology, Stanford University

5. WORK AND RETIREMENT IN A CHANGING SOCIETY

Anne Foner
Department of Sociology, Rutgers University
Karen Schwab
Office of Research and Statistics, Social Security Administration

Advisers

Lenore E. Bixby
Consultant on Social Security
Gordon F. Streib
Department of Sociology, University of Florida

6. RECENT TRENDS IN THE GEOGRAPHICAL DISTRIBUTION OF THE ELDERLY POPULATION

Tim B. Heaton
Family and Demographic Research Institute, Brigham Young University

Adviser

Karl E. Taeuber
Department of Sociology and Rural Sociology, University of Wisconsin, Madison

7. MINORITY AGING

Kyriakos S. Markides
Department of Preventive Medicine and Community Health, University of Texas Medical Branch, Galveston.

Adviser

John Santos
Department of Psychology, University of Notre Dame

8. WOMEN AND MEN: MORTALITY AND HEALTH OF OLDER PEOPLE
Lois M. Verbrugge
Survey Research Center, Institute for Social Research, University of Michigan
Advisers
Helena Z. Lopata
Department of Sociology, Loyola University, Chicago
George C. Myers, Director
Center for Demographic Studies, Duke University

9. AGE, PSYCHOSOCIAL STRESS, AND HEALTH
James S. House
Cynthia Robbins
Survey Research Center and Department of Sociology, Institute for Social Research, University of Michigan
Adviser
George L. Maddox
Center for the Study of Aging and Human Development, Duke University Medical Center

10. SOCIAL CHANGE AND FOOD HABITS OF THE ELDERLY
Maradee A. Davis
Department of Preventive Medicine and Community Health, University of Texas Medical Branch, Galveston
Elizabeth Randall
Human Nutrition Center, University of Texas School of Public Health
Adviser
Doris Howes Calloway
Provost, Professional Schools and Colleges, University of California, Berkeley

11. LEARNING AND MEMORY THROUGH ADULTHOOD
Marion Perlmutter
Institute of Child Development, University of Minnesota
Advisers
Jack Botwinick
Department of Psychology, Washington University
Fergus I. M. Craik
Erindale College, Ontario, Canada
Elizabeth Loftus
Department of Psychology, University of Washington

12. BEYOND AGEISM: POSTPONING THE ONSET OF DISABILITY
Matilda White Riley
Kathleen Bond
National Institute on Aging

POSTWORD: WHERE WE ARE AND WHERE WE MIGHT GO
Beth B. Hess
Department of Sociology, County College of Morris

Foreword

Robert N. Butler, M.D.

The history of this volume is quickly told. In anticipation of the 1981 White House Conference on Aging—and the key role to be played by the Conference committee on research—the National Institute on Aging (NIA) was asked to provide a series of background papers on various aspects of psychosocial aging. The objective of this task was to broaden scientific understanding of the psychosocial components of the aging process, to contribute more accurate information on the place of older people in society, and to call attention to a number of "leading edges" in research on aging.

The importance of this task was monumental. Although past White House Conferences on Aging have recognized the potential impact of aging research on the development of public policy, this was the first time that research was allotted committee stature. We at the NIA considered it necessary that the delegates understand the vital role of research on psychosocial aging in the context of Conference objectives. We hear a good deal about the "graying of America." What we need to know is how the striking changes in the age composition of our society will affect labor, housing, health care, and other areas of concern, and how we can plan and promote an effective national policy on aging.

Leading Edges: Recent Research on Psychosocial Aging (NIH Publication No. 81-2350) was published in November 1981 for purposes of the White House Conference on Aging. This limited edition was almost immediately exhausted. Now, for a wider audience, the papers appear under a new title—reformatted, reordered and reedited.

Had the NIA been able to update Volume I of *Aging and Society: An Inventory of Research Findings* (Riley, Foner, and associates, Russell Sage Foundation, 1968) it would have more than met the Institute's obligation to the White House

Conference. But that pioneering work with its demanding scientific standards could not readily be revised to reflect the enormous production of research findings on psychosocial aging during the past 15 years. It seems fitting, however, that the present volume carry a title closely related to *Aging and Society* since each essay attempts, as in the original work, to review critically selected inventories of the recent literature.

Thus, the enterprise of preparing this book was not launched *de novo*. It rests upon several decades of psychosocial research on age and aging. Most recently, it has been informed, stimulated, and sponsored by NIA, which is supporting, directly or indirectly, the work of the contributors.

In 1974, Congress created the NIA for the "conduct and support of biomedical, social, and behavioral research and training related to the aging process and the diseases and other special problems and needs of the aged." Under this mandate, the program in behavioral sciences is developing new and sometimes radical approaches to the study of basic aging processes. The program demonstrates that aging is not entirely biologically determined, but also contains significant behavioral components. People do not grow old in laboratories; rather, they grow old in social situations that are constantly changing. We believe that a new paradigm for research on aging is in the making and that new breakthroughs may be in the offing.

In order to avoid the risk of parochialism in preparing this book, Matilda White Riley* and her colleague, Kathleen Bond at the NIA enlisted the aid of a distinguished "outsider." Beth B. Hess, a widely recognized sociologist and social gerontologist, was the senior editor of the original edition and her overview, which now appears as a POSTWORD, offers a glimpse of possibilities for the future. In addition, a number of established experts in the field provided guidance and suggestions for the preparation of each paper and critically read earlier drafts of each manuscript. The NIA takes this opportunity to thank them publicly for their expertise, their wisdom, and their patience.

As Director of the National Institute on Aging,† however, I would be remiss if I failed to acknowledge the superb efforts of Matilda White Riley and her associates for having moved our understanding of the behavioral and psychosocial aspects of aging so far ahead in such a relatively short period of time.

---

*Matilda White Riley is Associate Director, Behavioral Sciences Research, National Institute on Aging, National Institutes of Health, U.S. Department of Health and Human Services.

†Robert N. Butler is now Chairman, Department of Geriatrics and Adult Development, Mt. Sinai School of Medicine.

1 Introduction: A Mosaic of Knowledge

Matilda White Riley
National Institute on Aging

This book is concerned with the social, cultural, economic, and psychological factors that affect both the process of growing old and the place of older people in society. Research already shows the power of these factors; it shows that aging and the status of the elderly are not inevitably fixed but are subject to social modification and change. But more research is needed on how these factors operate. In order to enhance the quality of life for older people and to contain the personal and social costs of health care and dependency, more knowledge is required to strengthen the scientific basis for professional practice and public policy.

Bit by bit, the necessary science base—a mosaic of knowledge—is being established. For example, we already know that individuals differ widely in the ways they experience aging: some are "old" at 40, while others find the passage of time of little consequence. We know that chronological age produces quite different "markers" for racial and ethnic minorities than for the so-called majority populations: blacks, like Hispanics, have comparatively short lives on the average, although some blacks live to an extraordinarily old age. We know that historical time is not unrelated to age and aging: to have been 65 in 1881 was very different from being 65 in 1981, and becoming 65 in 2081 will be unimaginably different. We know that the life course varies with the characteristics of the birth cohort into which people happen to have been born: on the whole, the chances of a good life have been better for people in small cohorts than for those born during a "baby boom." We know from the classic anthropological studies that growing up in Samoa or New Guinea is very different from growing up in the United States. We know that the life course is experienced not in a vacuum, but in societies that are continually changing. In myriad ways aging reflects alterations in dietary habits, changing sex roles, shifting minority group relations, cultural variability, and the many imperious forces inherent in historical change.

We also know a great deal about the place of older people in society. We know that—chronologically speaking—people can only grow older, whereas because of changing age composition, societies can grow either older or younger. We know something about age inequalities of income distribution; differential access to political participation; age constraints on work opportunities; age segregation in living arrangements, family relationships, and social support systems; the status of minority elderly; the relative social positions of older women and older men; and the changing norms and patterns of retirement.

In short, we know a good deal about the ways in which people grow up and grow old and about the place of older people in society. Yet what we know is only a beginning. Each of the papers that follows, especially written for this book, makes its own contribution to the understandings now being forged into a new scientific specialty. Indeed, it is our view that *Aging in Society* may set the stage for a later volume to deal with such topics as the relationship of age and aging to the law, to wisdom and creativity, to political attitudes, to vision and hearing, and to many more aspects of society. Moreover, fuller attention needs to be paid to age-related phenomena in other countries (most papers here are limited to the United States) and to societies at earlier points in historical time.

The book has no overarching plan. It is a collection of papers on topics where important work is under way, written by scholars aiming to contribute new scientific perspectives on each topic. The authors were asked to reflect critically on recent research findings and to discuss dimensions of what is known and what needs to be known. It was our wish that each paper be selective rather than comprehensive, critically analytic rather than neutrally descriptive, interpretative and reflective rather than merely authoritative. The book is designed for scientists (though not necessarily specialists in the particular fields under review) who are interested in being brought up to date on the nature and status of rival points of view and on the variety of empirical work on these topics.

Yet we do not seek knowledge for the sake of knowledge. We are impatient to see the knowledge put to work. The signs are favorable, for already many feasible types of interventions are beginning to be specified. For example, research described in the last substantive paper in the book reports that:

- Intellectual decline with aging (when it occurs) can often be slowed or reversed by relatively simple training interventions.
- Older people can learn to compensate through research-tested mnemonic strategies for declines in reaction time, memory, and other age-related deficits.
- Although many older people suffer visual impairments, particular styles and sizes of type facilitate reading, and improved environmental design can offset their inability to see large objects in low contrast.

- To counter the serious malnutrition suffered by many older people, research has demonstrated ways in which food preparation can be adapted to age-related changes in taste and smell.
- Through relatively simple changes in daily regimens, patients in nursing homes can often attain a new sense of independence and improved levels of health in general.

Along such lines, research now in place is beginning to identify those behavioral and social factors that interact with biological factors to extend the productive middle years of life, prevent and postpone old age disability, and contain the costs to individuals and society of health care or dependency.

Taken together with such current research, the several papers in this book contribute to the emerging mosaic of our knowledge of basic aging. In themselves, the papers suffer the shortcomings intrinsic to most research reports. They are sometimes difficult to read, sometimes inconsistent, and sometimes frustratingly inconclusive. The order in which they are presented is arbitrary. Yet, read as a whole, they tell a story. People do not grow old alone; they live in a net of family relationships. Their economic well-being is closely linked to organizations which themselves grow younger or older. The health of older people is affected by the kinds of stress they have experienced. The ways in which women and men or members of minority groups grow old reflect social change. The places where older people live change around them, as people of all ages move in and out. Age-related losses in memory, learning, and physical functioning are open to intervention and remediation. Work life and retirement life are socially constructed, and their future patterns can be made to serve human needs and values.

What of the future? By the turn of the century, armed with progressively distilled scientific knowledge about age and aging, we should be able to tell people with ever greater assurance that the aging process is not necessarily characterized by an inevitable accumulation of decrements, deficits, and other reductions in the quality of life.

In the meantime, research is providing guideposts that, if we can manage to discern and follow them, point to brighter prospects for older people and their place in society.

2 A Sense of History: Recent Research on Aging and the Family[1]

Andrew Cherlin
Johns Hopkins University

Prior to 1960, most students of the contemporary family paid little attention to history, and most historians paid little attention to the family. The dominant sociological perspective on the family—the structural-functionalism of Talcott Parsons—was an attempt to construct a general model of family structure that would be valid in diverse historical situations. Historians, conversely, were much less concerned with the family life of ordinary people than with studying political and economic events. But in the 1960's, these orientations began to change as historians discovered the family and family sociologists discovered history. In the 1970's, the interests of historians converged with the interests of other social scientists to produce an important new body of research on family life (Elder, 1980). What has happened to the study of the family in general has also happened to the study of aging and the family in particular: A new, historically oriented body of research has emerged in recent years. Some of this scholarship is the work of historians who have provided comparative information on the family life of the elderly in past time. The rest has been produced by sociologists, psychologists, and demographers, who have shown a heightened awareness of the importance of an individual's life history and of changing historical conditions affecting family relations in later life.

This essay summarizes these recent developments in the study of aging and the family and discusses their implications for the family relations of the men and women who will be entering old age in the near future. I will try to be wide-ranging in my discussion, but it is impossible to consider all aspects of a topic in

[1] In addition to Vern Bengtson, the author is grateful to Margaret Bright, Doris Entwisle, and Judith Treas for their critical reading of an earlier version of this paper.

a short treatment such as this. Of necessity, the presentation will be limited in several ways. First, I will discuss only research and writing on American families, although a great deal of important work has been done recently on family life elsewhere in the world. Second, my comments will focus on one major aspect of the family life of older people—their relations with their children and, to a lesser extent, with their grandchildren. Intergenerational relations certainly are the most widely discussed and debated aspect of the family life of the elderly, and many observers would argue that they constitute the most problematic aspect. Furthermore, several recent trends will be discussed that have the potential to alter intergenerational relations in significant ways. Thus, I will restrict my attention to intergenerational relations. This restriction also means that not much will be said about the one out of five noninstitutionalized older persons who do not have living children (Shanas, 1980). Finally, I will be unable to consider a great deal of valuable recent research that is not directly related to my theme. This is not, then, an attempt to assemble a comprehensive bibliography of recent work on aging and the family; rather, it is an attempt to illuminate what is, in my judgment, the most useful and exciting direction in recent scholarship.

LONG-TERM TRENDS IN OLDER PARENT-ADULT CHILD RELATIONS

What has been the long-term trend in the relations between older Americans and their children? To this question, most scholars until very recently would have responded quite simply and emphatically that family relations have deteriorated. The conventional wisdom among commentators has been that the position of the aged was most advantageous in the preindustrial era and that the coming of industrialization and urbanization resulted in a slow, steady decline. Once powerful, revered, and integrated into family and society, according to this view, the aged are now powerless, scorned, and isolated. In the past two decades, to be sure, a number of social scientists have produced evidence that the aged are not nearly as cut off from kin as prevailing beliefs suggested. Yet even these revisionist scholars were helpless to combat the argument that, however serviceable intergenerational ties are today, the family life of the aged was far superior in olden days. The revisionist social scientists were helpless because there had been almost no historical research on old age in America, and thus the prevailing view was as difficult to refute as it was to prove.

Since the mid-1970's, however, we have witnessed the birth and rapid growth of historical scholarship on the life of the aged in America. Two book-length studies have appeared—*Growing Old in America,* by David Hackett Fischer (1978), and *Old Age in the New Land,* by W. Andrew Achenbaum (1978)—along with numerous articles, most of which have been published since 1976. The emergence of a body of research on the history of old age is one of the most important recent developments in the study of aging and the family because it has provided us with a much-needed perspective on the current situation. From these fresh historical writings, we can gain considerable insight into the long-term trends in aging, and we can use this insight to ascertain the most useful directions for contemporary research.

The historians of old age have confirmed the widely held view that the elderly of colonial times were venerated by their family members and their communities. In part, they were respected because there were so few of them—to have lived to old age was itself an accomplishment, perhaps even a sign that a person was one of the elect. But in addition, older people were respected because they controlled most of the valuable resources, especially land. Philip J. Greven, Jr. (1970), has documented the reluctance of first-generation settlers in 17th century Andover, Mass., to relinquish control of their property to their sons. Since the young men of Andover needed farm land to start their own families, the reluctance of fathers to part with their land sometimes meant that sons were forced to postpone marrying until a relatively late age. In fact, parents exerted substantial control over their children's marriage patterns in pre-Revolutionary America. For example, Daniel Scott Smith's (1973) study of Hingham, Mass., demonstrated that the daughters in a family were more likely to marry in the order of their birth—an indicator of parental influence—before the Revolution than afterward. And sons in Hingham whose fathers died before age 60 married earlier than sons whose fathers survived to 60, reflecting, presumably, the influence of a living father on his son's marriage plans. Thus, older people-and, in particular, older men—in pre-Revolutionary America exerted substantial control over their families, much of it rooted in their command of resources, and they were accorded the respect due those in authority.

This great respect for the elderly, however, was apparently not matched by an outpouring of affection. Recent historical work suggests, to the contrary, that intergenerational relations in colonial days may have been colder and more distant than in modern times. Much of the writing on this issue is impressionistic; it is a question on which more historical research needs to be done. Still, several scholars have concluded that the unequal, rigid, and sometimes authoritarian relations between generations often resulted in considerable tension between older people and their adult children (Fischer, 1978; Demos, 1979; Smith, 1978). The dependence of the young on the old seems to have worked against the expression of warm, affectionate sentiments. Fischer's (1978:72) analysis is representative of this point of view:

> Even as most (though not all) elderly people were apt to hold more power than they would possess in a later period, they were also apt to receive less affection, less love, less sympathy from those younger than themselves. The elderly were kept at an emotional distance by the young. If open hostility between the generations was not allowed, affection was not encouraged either. Veneration, after all, is a cold emotion. The elderly often complained that they had lived to become strangers in their own society, aliens in their own time. And so they were, in a psychic

sense—strangers in the hearts of their own posterity, aliens from the affection of their own kin.

If this new perspective is correct, then we must question the widespread assumption that the preindustrial era was a "Golden Age" in the family relations of older Americans. We must, instead, begin to consider the possibility that the family life of the elderly may have improved in some ways over the course of American history. In colonial America, the elderly controlled most of the resources, and intergenerational relations were correct but cold. As the young and the middle-aged gained more independence from their parents, however, relations between the generations may have grown closer-provided that the elderly retained sufficient resources to avoid dependence on their children. In fact, my reading of the recent historical research suggests the following hypothesis: that relations between the elderly and their adult children tend to be more emotionally satisfying—closer, warmer, more loving, and more affectionate—when neither generation is economically dependent on the other. And I would suggest that this condition for emotionally satisfying relations is better realized today than in much of our Nation's past.

Trends in Income and Well-Being

Some might argue that the elderly *have* become increasingly dependent on their children; certainly there is a great deal of scholarly and popular commentary suggesting as much. But recent trends suggest otherwise. For example, national statistics and recent research indicate that the economic conditions and the health of the elderly have improved dramatically in this century, with most of the improvement occurring in the last few decades. As recently as 1959, the elderly were disproportionately poor: 35.2 percent of persons aged 65 and over had incomes below the federally defined poverty level in 1959, compared with 22.4 percent of the total population. By 1979, the difference had diminished sharply: 14.0 percent of those aged 65 and over were poor, compared with 11.4 percent of the total population (Bureau of the Census, 1980a, b). Much of the improvement is the result of the increasing coverage of the aged under Social Security, the rising level of Social Security benefits, and the growth of private pension plans.

Actually, Social Security is a system in which some of the earnings of young and middle-aged workers are transferred to the elderly, and it does, in fact, increase the economic dependence of the aged on the young. But we maintain a fiction about Social Security, a myth that the recipients are only drawing out money that they put into the fund earlier in their lives. Thus, the economic dependence of the elderly is ignored, and the elderly are allowed to believe that they are just receiving what they are entitled to by virtue of their own hard work. The tenacity of this myth—witness the resistance to supporting Social Security with general tax revenues—shows its importance. It allows the elderly to accept assistance without compromising their autonomy, and it allows children to support their parents partially without either generation openly acknowledging as much.

The elderly also have benefited from a general improvement in life expectancy. At the turn of the century, a white woman aged 60 could expect to live an average of 15.2 more years; in 1975, a comparable woman could expect to live 21.9 more years. For white men aged 60, life expectancy rose from 14.4 years in 1900 to 16.8 in 1975. The gains for blacks have been even greater. Most of the increase in life expectancy at older ages has occurred since the Depression, and it appears to be continuing (Bureau of the Census, 1980b; National Center for Health Statistics, 1980). However, as increasing proportions of people survive to very old age, the health implications are still unclear (see the essay in this book by Verbrugge). To be sure, the elderly are more likely than young people to have chronic illnesses or conditions which limit their activities, but it is not known whether a person of, say, 65 is healthier today than a person of 65 was a few decades ago (Riley and Foner, 1968:204). The limited data available for recent decades show little change in disability for the 95 percent of people 65 and over who are noninstitutionalized (National Center for Health Statistics, 1978). For example, among the noninstitutionalized elderly in a 1975 national survey, 14 percent had restrictions on their mobility, an increase from 11 percent in a similar 1962 survey (Shanas, 1978). Yet 7 out of 10 elderly respondents in the 1975 survey reported that they were not restricted in carrying out a set of six common activities of daily living. Moreover, about half of the elderly rated their health as "good" (even among those aged 80 and over), about one-third said their health was "fair," and about one-fifth responded that their health was "poor" (Shanas, 1978).

Many older persons, of course, are still poor, many more are struggling to stay just above the poverty level, and others are ill and in need of assistance. But the evidence suggests that the material welfare of the aged has improved in recent decades and that it is sufficient to allow many of them considerable independence from their children. It also seems clear that both generations prefer to be largely independent of each other. Most of the elderly, for example, prefer to live physically apart from their children, but nearby (Troll et al., 1979). Currently, then, intergenerational relations are based on cooperation and on the mutual exchange of emotional and material support, and neither generation need be subject to the authority of the other. I suspect that this situation is more conducive to the establishment and maintenance of warm, close, and affectionate relations between the elderly and their adult children than was the case earlier in American history.

For Better and for Worse

My point is not to create a new myth of a contemporary "Golden Age" in intergenerational relations. Nor do I wish to claim that the material situation of the elderly is adequate in all respects. Rather, I wish to demonstrate why the belief that intergenerational relations have deteriorated steadily since preindustrial times is much too simplistic to be of use in analyzing the contemporary situation. To be sure, the family situation of the elderly has become worse in some respects, notably in the degree to which they wield authority and command respect. Some elderly persons, moreover, may be in desperate need of support from family members-due to an inadequate income or to poor health—and they may be unable to receive this help, for reasons we will discuss later.

I would suspect, however, that the family lives of the aged may have changed for better as well as for worse during our Nation's history. The aged are more independent of their children because more of them live to old age than in the past and because in the last few decades their economic situation has improved. Moreover, they no longer control their adult children's lives to the extent they once did. The greater mutual independence of older people and their adult children, I believe, may have made it easier than in the past for parents and children to maintain emotionally satisfying relationships. If we accept this argument, then we must revise our overall view of aging and the family. Specifically, we must reject the notion that the relations between the aged and their kin today are inherently problematic—that the family life of the elderly necessarily constitutes a growing "social problem" in a generic sense, like adolescent pregnancy or drug abuse. Moreover, we should keep this more balanced perspective in mind when we choose topics for future research; it implies that it is not productive to search for new ways of demonstrating the dubious proposition that there has been a general decline in the family relations of the elderly. Instead, we should be alert for more specific social trends that could be affecting particular aspects of intergenerational relations. And we should watch for and investigate the ways in which parent-offspring relationships either are improving or are exhibiting the potential for improvement.

A shift in scholarly orientation from a general "social problems" approach to a search for more specific trends affecting the family life of the elderly both positively and negatively will, I suspect, lead to a more useful and stimulating body of research in the future. The next section examines some recent scholarship that can help identify some of the specific trends whose implications are worthy of future research.

THE EMERGENCE OF THE LIFE-COURSE PERSPECTIVE ON THE FAMILY

One important recent development has been the emergence of the "life-course" perspective on the study of the family. The body of research that now goes by this name is the result of the efforts of scholars in a number of disciplines over the past decade or so. Glen H. Elder, Jr., a sociologist, has provided major theoretical statements (Elder, 1978a; 1978b) and a thorough empirical treatment (Elder,

1974). More general pioneering work has been contributed by Paul B. Baltes (Baltes and Schaie, 1973) in developmental psychology, Tamara K. Hareven (1978) in history, Matilda White Riley (Riley, Johnson, and Foner, 1972) in the sociology of age, and Bernice Neugarten (1968) in gerontology. Indeed, the collaboration of sociologists, developmental psychologists, social historians, social gerontologists, demographers, and economists has made the life-course perspective one of the liveliest interdisciplinary enterprises in the social sciences.

In sociology, at least, the popularity of the lifecourse perspective can be seen as a reaction to earlier approaches to the study of the family. In the 1930's and 1940's, Ernest Burgess and other influential writers studied the family as if it were isolated from other social institutions such as the economy and the state. Burgess urged researchers to focus on relationships internal to the nuclear family household, especially the relationship between husband and wife. The family, according to Burgess, had changed from "an institution to a companionship" (Burgess and Locke, 1945), and it should be studied as a "unity of interacting personalitie" (Burgess, 1926) as well as an institution subject to outside influences. In the 1950's, scholars such as Talcott Parsons, as I noted earlier, sought universal principles that they could apply to the family within broad historical limits (Parsons and Bales, 1955).

The Parsonian study of the family concentrated on structure rather than process and on social stability rather than social change. Moreover, the "family lifecycle" approach developed by Paul C. Glick (1947) and others presented a series of stages in family life that were defined independently of individual life histories or changing historical conditions.

These approaches to the family produced writings which downplayed the variations in family life that can be produced by differences in the earlier experiences of family members and by changing historical conditions. In response, life-course scholars are now emphasizing the importance of studying the biographies of family members and the historical context of family life. Moreover, they are focusing interest on studying social change. The life-course perspective fits well with the writings of C. Wright Mills, who urged, in his critique of Parsonian structural-functionalism, that social scientists undertake "the study of biography, of history, and of the problems of their intersection within the social structure" (Mills, 1959:143).

Cohort Analysis

The orientation of the life-course scholars has led many of them to make heavy use of the concept of a "cohort" in their studies. A "cohort" consists of people who experience some event in the same time period. Most often, it refers to people who were born in the same time period, and that is the sense in which the term is used here. We can examine the lifetime experiences of the members of a cohort, watch their progress through stages of family life, and see how these earlier experiences affect their later lives. In addition, by comparing the lifetime experiences of successive cohorts, we can study how patterns of family life appear to have changed.

Some of the difficulties of cohort analysis arise from its failure to distinguish between a cohort and a generation. By a "generation," I mean the members of a kinship group who stand in the relationship of ascendants or descendants to others in the group, such as the grandparents, parents, and grandchildren who compose three generations in a family. To study intergenerational relations, we often assume that the characteristics of successive generations can be approximated by the characteristics of successive cohorts. For example, we might assume that the members of the parental generation of the postwar Baby Boom belonged to the cohort that was born in the 1930's, and the grandparental generation during the postwar Baby Boom belonged to the cohort that was born about 25 years earlier. Yet, as Gunhild O. Hagestad (1979) has argued, there is considerable overlapping in the age distribution of the members of a given generation: "People do not file into generation by cohort." Many of the people who became parents in the 1950's, for instance, were born in the 1920's. A small proportion were born earlier, and a handful were born in the early 1940's. Thus, any analogy between a particular generation—say, the parents of the 1950's-and a particular cohort is only approximate. Moreover, the term generation is sometimes used to denote a group of people of approximately the same age who develop a distinct group identity as a result of their shared experiences. Some commentators, for example, wrote about the "sixties generation" of young adults who opposed the Vietnam War and explored alternative lifestyles. Yet such a generation included only some of the young adults in the 1960's. (See Bengtson and Cutler [1976] for a discussion of the ways social scientists have used the term generation.) If these limitations are kept in mind, the study of cohorts can be quite useful in identifying trends in intergenerational relations.

Childbearing

Consider, for instance, cohort trends in childbearing. The number of living children an older person has is one of the most important determinants of that person's ties with his or her kin. We know that since the early 19th century the average number of children borne by each successive cohort of women has been falling. This long-term decline in fertility has been cited often as an indicator of the decreasing ability of the aged to rely on their children for support. But we also know that the fertility of the cohorts of women whose prime child-bearing years occurred during the postwar Baby Boom rose sharply and unexpectedly. Women born in the late 1920's and the early and mid-1930's, for example, averaged more than three births, a higher level than is found among cohorts of women born 10 or 20 years earlier or later (Ryder, 1980). Furthermore, much of this rise in fertility was not due to a return to the large family; rather, more women married, and more had at least one or two children (Ryder, 1980).

What these statistics mean is that the declining number of living children per elderly person—a steady trend during this century which has accelerated recently because of the low fertility among the women who are now elderly whose prime childbearing years occurred during the Depression—is now reversing direction. Between now and the end of the century, women from the high fertility cohorts of the 1920's and 1930's will be entering old age. Thus, at the turn of the 21st century, the chances that an elderly person will have at least one living child will be substantially greater than is the case today. After the turn of the century, however, the long-term decline will resume because of the entrance into old age of the low fertility cohorts born after the war (unless, of course, another unexpected baby boom takes place).

A cohort analysis of trends in fertility, consequently, alerts us that future cross-sectional studies are likely to show a changing pattern of intergenerational relations. It would not be surprising, for instance, if studies performed in the 1980's or 1990's were to show an increase in the proportion of the elderly who are in frequent contact with their adult children or who receive support from children. But before concluding that there has been a new breakthrough in intergenerational relations, future researchers should remember that trends in cohort fertility may well produce temporary changes as the Baby Boom cohorts work their way through the age structure. Richard A. Easterlin's aphorism about the societal consequences of trends in cohort sizes for the next 20 years may apply to patterns of contact between the elderly and their children: "The good news is that things will get better; the bad news, it won't last" (Easterlin, 1980: 131).

Mortality

Cohort trends in mortality also have altered the family situation of the elderly. As I mentioned above, the life expectancy of a person reaching age 60 has increased greatly in this century. In fact, the "old old," those aged 75 and over, constitute the fastest growing segment of the elderly population: in 1900, 29 percent of the elderly (65 and over) were 75 or over; in 1975, 38 percent were 75 or over; and in 2000, some 44 percent will be 75 or over, according to projections (Bureau of the Census, 1976a). And, as I also noted, the average length of life for women has increased much more than that of men. In 1900, there were 102 males aged 65 and over for every 100 females 65 and over; in 1975, there were only 69 males for every 100 females (Bureau of the Census, 1976a). As is well-known, one result of this differential is an increase in the number of elderly widows. During the 1980's, researchers undoubtedly will devote more attention to widowhood (Lopata, 1973).

But perhaps the most interesting family-related consequence of the increase in life expectancy of the aged is the emergence of the four-generation family. Almost half of all persons aged 65 and over have great-grandchildren (Shanas, 1980). In these families, it is often the case that the children of the oldest generation are themselves elderly or nearing old age—about 10 percent of all elderly persons have children aged 65 or over (Troll et al., 1979). The members of the grandparental generation, then, may face obligations not only to their children and grandchildren, but to their aged parents as well (Bengtson and Treas, 1980; Hagestad, 1979). As Shanas (1980) has observed, the strain resulting from these multiple demands may be considerable. In addition, these middle-aged and "young-old" grandparents may be undergoing stress related to deteriorating health or the transition to retirement; they may be subject to what Hagestad (1979) has labeled the "generation crunch." This is a new phenomenon made possible by the continuing increases in life expectancy. We know very little about it, and it should be high on the research agenda for the 1980's.

Divorce and Remarriage

While observers of the situation of the elderly have long paid attention to trends in fertility and mortality, other social demographic trends in the lives of successive cohorts have received much less attention. One of these is the trend in divorce and remarriage. The divorce rate has been rising in the United States for at least the past century, but a sharp rate of increase after 1960 caused much concern. Between 1963 and 1976, the divorce rate more than doubled in the United States, although the rate of increase has slowed since 1975 (Cherlin, 1981). The sharpest increases in the 1960's and 1970's occurred among persons in their twenties and thirties, however, so that the divorce rate among the elderly is still relatively low. Nevertheless, the current high rate of divorce among young and middle-aged adults portends a large increase in the proportion of the elderly of the future who will have been divorced. Peter Uhlenberg and Anne P. Myers (1980) estimate that, currently, 10 to 13 percent of the elderly have ever experienced divorce—a not inconsiderable proportion. My own estimates, which assume that the divorce rate will not fall, indicate that the lifetime percentage of those who have ever divorced will reach 15 percent for the 1910–14 cohort, 25 percent for the 1930–34 cohort, and 45 percent for the 1950–54 cohort (Cherlin, 1981). Thus, it is reasonable to expect that by the turn of the century, one-fourth of all persons reaching old age will have experienced divorce. What's more, if the divorce rate continues its long-term rise, this projection will prove too low. In addition, the recent rise in divorce among young married couples means that there has been a sharp rise in the number of elderly persons who currently are witnessing the divorce of one or more of their adult children. About one-fourth of all persons who married in 1970, for example, had already ended their marriages in divorce by 1977 (Weed, 1978).

These two aspects of the rise in divorce—the current jump in the number of young adults who have ever divorced and the imminent jump in the number of older persons who have ever divorced—may have important implications for the family relations of the elderly. Let us consider first the implications of the more immediate concern: the increasing number of elderly persons whose children are divorcing. We know that divorce is a traumatic experience for those going through it, and we might expect that many adult children who are ending their marriages will turn to their parents for emotional support. We also know that the economic situation of mothers often deteriorates after a divorce (Espenshade, 1979), so that daughters may turn to their parents for financial support. Consequently, divorce should strengthen the ties between elderly persons and their divorcing children, as the children turn to their parents for comfort and assistance. But what if the parents are unable to meet these new demands? What if, for instance, the parents do not have the financial resources to assist their child or if they disapprove of the child's divorce? What if many middle-aged grandmothers must choose between achieving personal goals or helping to care for their grandchildren? In these cases, relations between parents and divorcing children might become more strained and distant. A divorce, moreover, could greatly limit the ability of adult offspring to provide either emotional or material support to an aging parent. Precisely because divorce is a traumatic experience, a divorcing adult may be too distraught and preoccupied to attend to a parent's needs. Because divorce often leaves women in a worsened economic position, daughters may no longer have the financial resources to care for their parents.

It is not clear, then, what the net effect of rising levels of divorce among the young and middle-aged will be on the relations between older persons and their adult children. It may be that divorce will strengthen intergenerational ties in some instances and weaken them in others. Even less clear is the effect of divorce on the relations between grandparents and their grandchildren. Because divorces tend to occur soon after marriage, more than half of all divorces involve children under the age of 18 (National Center for Health Statistics, 1979). Consider the situation of an elderly person whose son divorces 5 years after the birth of a grandchild. In most such cases, the daughter-in-law would keep custody of the grandchild. What, then, will happen to the relationship between the elderly person and his or her grandchild? We might expect that, in general, the ties between grandparents and grandchildren will be attenuated, but there are hints in the sparse literature on grandparenting that in many instances the relationship remains intact (Furstenberg and Spanier, 1980). The custodial parent may feel an obligation to maintain the tie between her former in-laws and her children. In some cases, the custodial parent herself may maintain kin-like ties to the former in-laws. Almost no research has been done on this aspect of grandparenting, and until more is known, we can only speculate.

When considering studies of divorce, we must also consider remarriage. Most people who divorce also remarry, although the remarriage rate has declined somewhat in recent years (Norton and Glick, 1980). About half of all divorced persons who will ever remarry do so within 3 years of their divorce (Bureau of the Census, 1976b). Consequently, a divorce in the family will often involve all generations in a complex and expanded set of kin relations. Once again, we know very little about what these complex families will mean for the relations between older people and their kin. An elderly man who divorced earlier in life and subsequently saw little of his children, for example, may not be able to rely on these children for assistance in his old age; but he may well have remarried a woman with children from a previous marriage—children who will fulfill their filial obligations to their stepfather. An elderly woman who lost touch with her grandchildren after her son was divorced may become a stepgrandmother to the children of her son's second marriage. Children whose parents have divorced and then both remarried may find themselves with four sets of "grandparents": two sets of biological grandparents, the parents of their stepfather, and the parents of their biological father's new wife. All four of these sets of grandparents are likely to play a role in family life.

Thus, while divorce may disrupt and contract the family relationships of older people, remarriage may reconstitute and expand them. Some elderly persons will experience a diminution of family ties as a result of their own divorce or the divorce of their child; others will find that a divorce brings them closer to some of their kin. Many will find that remarriage enlarges the pool of kin who can provide emotional and material support. At the moment, we cannot be precise in stating the magnitudes of these positive and negative effects of increasing divorce and remarriage on intergenerational relations because there has been virtually no research on the subject. In the last year or two, a number of papers have appeared, but most are preliminary statements of the issues rather than reports of empirical research. (See, for example, Furstenberg, 1979; Hagestad, 1979; Smyer, 1979; Uhlenberg and Myers, 1980.) This topic is ripe for research, and we should learn much more about it during the present decade.

Women's Labor Force Participation

Another trend worthy of more attention from students of the elderly is the rising labor force participation of women. Between 1900 and 1940, the percentage of all women who were in the labor force increased gradually, but since 1940 the percentage has risen dramatically. The rise has been especially pronounced for married women. In 1940, only one out of seven married women was working outside the home or looking for work; by 1979, one out of two was working or looking for work (Oppenheimer, 1970; Bureau of Labor Statistics, 1979). The women who first brought about this sharp increase were in their prime working years in the 1950's and 1960's, and they are currently entering old age. As a result, elderly women are increasingly likely to have extensive employment histories.

The rising labor force participation of women could alter intergenerational relations in a number of ways. The independence of many older women will be enhanced by added income and the development of skills for dealing with the world outside the home (Treas, 1979). If my earlier hypothesis about mutual independence and satisfying intergenerational relations has any validity, then this increased independence might encourage the establishment and maintenance of warm, affectionate ties between elderly women and their offspring. Yet the rise in labor-force participation means that many of the daughters of these elderly women will be employed, leaving the daughters less time in which to attend to the needs of their aged parents. If so, then some of the elderly could find that their daughter's employment leads to less satisfactory relations. In addition, women who have a lifelong history of employment may find the transition to retirement more difficult than women who have worked infrequently. There are some suggestions in the literature—although not much hard evidence—that the transition to retirement currently is less difficult for women than for men. According to this argument, there is greater continuity between the pre- and postretirement lives of women than of men because women's lives traditionally revolve around the home, while men's lives center more on work. If there is merit to this position, then the new cohorts of elderly women may find retiring more difficult than in the past, and they may need more support from their kin. (See Bengtson and Treas, 1980.)

As with the trends in divorce and remarriage, the trend toward greater female labor-force participation probably will have both positive and negative effects on the relations between older people and their families. And as with research on divorce, only a few articles-largely programmatic—address the implications for the aged of increasing female labor-force participation (for example, Treas, 1979). We need—and we will undoubtedly see—empirical research on this topic.

TRENDS IN THE FUNCTIONS OF INTERGENERATIONAL TIES

These, then, are some of the trends in aging and the family that have been identified in the recent, historically oriented research. They imply that we may be in the midst of a period of considerable change in some aspects of intergenerational relations. The lifetime experiences of the cohorts reaching old age currently and in the next few decades will differ in significant ways from the life histories of the elderly earlier in the century. Some of these differences could lead to improvements in intergenerational relations, but others may cause difficult problems. We should not exaggerate the uniqueness of the current situation; concern about the relations betweeen parents and children is nothing new. Yet, taken together, the recent trends suggest a need to step back and rethink some of our fundamental assumptions about the nature of parent-offspring relationships in advanced industrial societies (Hess and Waring, 1978).

Traditionally, material obligations cemented the ties between older parents and their adult children. In colonial America, as I noted, many children remained dependent on their parents' support well into adulthood. Conversely, earlier in this century, many of the aged, although not all, were dependent on their children for support. Yet today the growth of institutional supports such as Social Security and the improvements in health status have allowed many more of the elderly to provide for their own basic needs themselves. With much of the economic underpinning gone, one might conclude hastily that the importance of intergenerational ties has diminished. But studies of the elderly suggest that this is not the case. Most older parents see their children often and turn to them for assistance in times of difficulty (Shanas, 1978).

The Function of Intergenerational Ties

What, then, is the major function of intergenerational relations between the elderly and their children? I would suggest, following Ethel Shanas (1980) and others, that the major function is as follows: family ties provide the primary means by which older people are integrated into societies such as ours. With the decline of other roles for the elderly—their loss of prestige and authority in the community, for example, and their earlier retirement from the labor force—the elderly have fewer opportunities to maintain their links to society. Family relations provide a way for the elderly to reinforce those links continually. Thus, although the material significance of family relations may have declined, family relations may be more important now than in the past as a way for the elderly to reaffirm the purpose and meaning of their lives.

Shanas seems to assume that families are fulfilling this role well, but others disagree. Family and kinship ties, she has written, may change in the future, "but [families] will continue to provide safe harbor for their members however long they may live" (Shanas, 1980: 15). Yet the assertion that families are doing well at the task of integrating older people into society is open to question. Let us briefly examine a more general, current debate about the adequacy of family functioning to see the kinds of questions one could raise about the quality of intergenerational relations.

In the 1950's, Talcott Parsons and other social scientists argued that the family's one remaining function for adults in our society was the provision of an emotional refuge in an increasingly rational, bureaucratic society (see, for example, Parsons and Bales, 1955). Parsons conceded that the family had lost many of its other functions, but he claimed that it had become the one institution specializing in emotional support. Thus, according to Parsons, the family's importance may actually have increased, even though the number of functions it performs has decreased. Recently, social critic Christopher Lasch led an attack on the predominant Parsonian view. Lasch's argument is that the family's functions are interdependent; if most of them are taken away, then the family is unable to perform those that remain. Therefore, Lasch would state, the reduction of the family's sphere of autonomy—a result of the growing intervention of the liberal state—means that the family cannot fulfill its remaining function as a "haven in a heartless world" (Lasch, 1977).

Lasch's argument could be extended directly to the family's role in providing a "safe harbor" for the elderly. If one accepts Lasch's premises, then one might imagine that the family will be unable to shoulder the entire burden of integrating the elderly into society. Lasch, of course, has many critics, and I do not mean to suggest that he is necessarily correct. Rather, I wish to point out that students of aging and the family should devote more time to considering some broader issues concerning the functioning of the family before they conclude that the family will be able to perform its important tasks adequately in the near future. Specifically, I would suggest that the relationship between the family and state—one of the themes of Lasch's work and of similar writings by French philosopher Michel Foucault (1978) and his colleague Jacques Donzelot (1979)—should be examined for its relevance to the aged. To what extent, researchers might ask, is state intervention in the lives of the elderly strengthening or weakening intergenerational ties? What are the consequences of different degrees of intervention by the state? Some interesting writing has appeared on these issues (see the volume edited by Shanas and Sussman (1977)), but we have only begun to explore them.

Normative Considerations

These kinds of questions border on the normative—on considerations, for example, of what the proper roles of the family and the state should be with regard to the elderly. Most social scientists are reluctant to consider normative issues, choosing instead to follow Max Weber's dictum that "an empirical science cannot tell anyone what he *should* do—but rather what he *can* do—and under certain circumstances—what he wishes to do" (Weber, 1949:54). Although I grant that social scientific research cannot resolve questions about what the roles of the family and the state should be, I do not think that students of aging and the family can avoid such questions entirely. Most of the issues studied by researchers interested in aging and the family relate ultimately to matters of public policy; indeed, many of the leading scholars in the field clearly are motivated by their advocacy of the cause of the elderly. Under these circumstances, the normative stance scholars take will influence the topics they choose to study and the perspectives they choose to apply.

Some observers would claim that scholars need not take a normative stance to work in this field. For example, Beth B. Hess and Joan M. Waring (1978:267) wrote recently:

> Let us eschew prescriptions about what intergenerational relations should be and instead respond to the diversity by encouraging the broadest spectrum of social sup-

ports and services to aging parents and their offspring, so that they may work out their singular solutions to singular problems in the best way possible.

But Hess's and Waring's remarks show how difficult it is for social scientists to stake out a neutral position on these issues. Their call for "encouraging the broadest spectrum of social supports and services to aging parents and their offspring" would itself be seen as a "prescription" by conservative "pro-family" groups and by radicals such as Lasch. Both of these factions would claim—correctly, I think—that Hess's and Waring's views constitute a tacit endorsement of large-scale state intervention in the provision of services to the elderly. And both factions believe that such intervention should be severely limited for the good of the family. In policyrelevant fields such as aging and the family, then, the views of social scientists are rarely as value-free as they would like to believe. I think, consequently, that social scientists in the field of aging and the family need to think more about normative issues to make clear to their audience (and to themselves) the values that underlie their research.

Emerging Roles

In addition to considering these larger issues, researchers should be sensitive to the emergence of new family roles for the elderly and their children. Recently, for example, a number of scholars have suggested that adult children may be needed as intermediaries between their aged parents and the bureaucracies that serve the elderly. Such was the thrust of an international conference sponsored by the Gerontological Society in 1973 and reported in a volume edited by Ethel Shanas and Marvin B. Sussman (1977). But there seems to be no empirical evidence as yet that the intermediary role has, in fact, emerged. Instead, the popularity of this idea appears to reflect little more than the hope of many observers that the institutionalization of the provision of services to the elderly will create a new role for family members. We need empirical research in the 1980's to determine whether hypothetical new family roles such as this one will or will not become common.

Overall, our thinking about the changing relationship between the elderly and their children should be influenced in the 1980's by the continuation of the recent research developments I have noted. In surveying work in this field, one is struck by how much the scope of inquiry has broadened in recent years. What was once the bailiwick of a small number of sociologists and psychologists has now become the province of a large, diverse group of social scientists. I have attempted to demonstrate how in the 1970's the expansion and diversification of research on aging and the family has deepened our understanding and stimulated our curiosity. It has also provided us with something that was lacking in much previous research: a sense of history.

REFERENCES

Achenbaum, W. Andrew 1978. Old Age in the New Land. Baltimore: Johns Hopkins University Press.

Baltes, Paul B., and K. Warner Schaie (eds.) 1973. Life-Span Developmental Psychology: Personality and Socialization. New York: Academic Press.

Bengtson, Vern L., and Neal E. Cutler 1976. "Generations and intergenerational relations: perspectives on age groups and social change." Pp. 130–159 in Robert H. Binstock and Ethel Shanas (eds.), Handbook of Aging and the Social Sciences. New York: Van Nostrand Reinhold.

Bengtson, Vern L., and Judith Treas 1980. "The changing family context of mental health and aging." Pp. 400–428 in James E. Birren and Bruce Sloane (eds.), Handbook of Mental Health and Aging. Englewood Cliffs, N.J.: Prentice-Hall.

Bureau of the Census 1976a. Current Population Reports, Series P-23, No. 59, "Demographic aspects of aging and the older population in the United States." Washington: U.S. Government Printing Office.

———. 1976b. Current Population Reports, Series P-20, No. 297, "Number, timing, and duration of marriages and divorces in the United States: June 1975." Washington: U.S. Government Printing Office.

———. 1980a. Current Population Reports, Series P-60, No. 124, "Characteristics of the population below the poverty level: 1978." Washington: U.S. Government Printing Office.

———. 1980b. Statistical Abstract of the United States: 1979. Washington: U.S. Government Printing Office.

Bureau of Labor Statistics 1979. "Multi-earner families increase." Press Release USDL 79–747, October 31.

Burgess, Ernest W. 1926. "The family and a unity of interacting personalities." Family 7:3–9.

Burgess, Ernest W., and Harvey J. Locke 1945. The family: From Institution to Companionship. New York: American Book.

Cherlin, Andrew J. 1981. Marriage, Divorce, Remarriage: Changing Patterns in the Postwar United States. Cambridge: Harvard University Press.

Demos, John 1979. "Old age in early New England." Pp. 115–164 in David D. Van Tassel (ed.), Aging, Death, and the Completion of Being. Philadelphia: University of Pennsylvania Press.

Donzelot, Jacques 1979. The Policing of Families. New York: Pantheon.

Easterlin, Richard A. 1980. Birth and Fortune: The Impact of Numbers on Personal Welfare. New York: Basic Books.

Elder, Glen H., Jr. 1974. Children of the Great Depression. Chicago: University of Chicago Press.

———. 1978a. "Family history and the life course." Pp. 17–64 in Tamara K. Hareven (ed.), Transitions: The Family and the Life Course in Historical Perspective. New York: Academic Press.

———. 1978b. "Approaches to social change and the family." Pp. S1–S38 in John Demos and Sarane Spence Boocock (eds.), Turning Points: Historical and Sociological Essays on the Family. Chicago: University of Chicago Press.

———. 1980. "History and the family." Burgess Award Lecture, National Council on Family Relations, Portland, Ore., October.

Fischer, David Hackett 1978. Growing Old in America. Expanded Edition. New York: Oxford University Press.

Foucault, Michel 1978. The History of Sexuality. Vol. I: An Introduction. New York: Vintage.

Furstenberg, Frank F., Jr. 1979. "Remarriage and intergenerational relations." Paper presented at the Workshop on Stability and Change in the Family, National Academy of Sciences, Annapolis, Md., March.

Furstenberg, Frank F., Jr., and G. B. Spanier 1980. "Marital dissolution and generational ties." Paper presented at the Annual Meeting of the Gerontological Society, San Diego, Calif.

Glick, Paul C. 1947. "The family cycle." American Journal of Sociology 12:164–174.

Greven, Phillip J., Jr. 1970. Four Generations: Population, Land, and Family in Colonial Andover, Massachusetts. New York: Cornell University Press.

Hagestad, Gunhild O. 1979. "Problems and promises in the social psy chology of intergenerational relations." Paper presented at the Workshop on Stability and Change in the Family, National Academy of Sciences, Annapolis, Md., March.

Hareven, Tamara K. (ed.) 1978. Transitions: The Family and the Life Course in Historical Perspective. New York: Academic Press.

Hess, Beth B., and Joan M. Waring 1978. Parent and child in later life: rethinking the relationship." Pp. 241–273 in R.M. Lerner and G.B. Spanier (eds.), Child In fluences on Marital and Family Interaction: A Life-Span Perspective. New York: Academic Press.

Lasch, Christopher 1977. Haven in a Heartless World: The Family Besieged. New York: Basic Books.

Lopata, Helen Z. 1973. Widowhood in an American City. Cambridge, Mass.: Schenkman.

Mills, C. Wright 1959. The Sociological Imagination. New York: Oxford University Press.

National Center for Health Statistics 1978. Health, United States, 1976–77. Washington: U.S. Government Printing Office.

_____. 1979. Vital and Health Statistics of the United States, 1975, Vol. III—Marriage and Divorce. Washington: U.S. Government Printing Office.

_____. 1980. Vital and Health Statistics of the United States, 1975, Vol. II—Mortality, Part A. Washington: U.S. Government Printing Office.

Neugarten, Bernice L. (ed.) 1968. Middle Age and Aging: A Reader in Social Psychology. Chicago: University of Chicago Press.

Oppenheimer, Valerie K. 1970. The Female Labor Force in the United States. Berkeley, Calif.: Institute of International Studies.

Parsons, Talcott, and Robert F. Bales 1955. Family, Socialization, and the Interaction Process. New York: Free Press.

Riley, Matilda White, and Anne Foner 1968. Aging and Society: An Inventory of Research Findings, Vol. I. New York: Russell Sage Foundation.

Riley, Matilda White, Marilyn Johnson, and Ann Foner 1972. Aging and Society. Vol. III: A Sociology of Age Stratification. New York: Russell Sage Foundation.

Ryder, Norman B. 1980. "Components of temporal variations in American fertility." Pp. 15–54 in Robert W. Hiorns (ed.), Demographic Patterns in Developed Societies. London: Taylor and Francis.

Shanas, Ethel 1978. "A national survey of the aged." Final Report to the Administration on Aging. Washington: U.S. Department of Health, Education, and Welfare.

_____. 1980 "Old people and their families: the new pioneers." Journal of Marriage and the Family 42:9–15.

Shanas, Ethel, and Marvin B. Sussman 1977. Family, Bureaucracy, and the Elderly. Durham: Duke University Press.

Smith, Daniel S. 1973. "Parental power and marriage patterns: an analysis of historical trends in Hingham, Massachusetts," Journal of Marriage and the Family 35:419–428.

_____. 1978. "Old age and the 'Great Transformation': a New England case study," Pp. 285–302 in Stuart F. Spicker, Kathleen M. Woodward, and David D. Van Tassel (eds.), Aging and the Elderly: Humanistic Perspectives in Gerontology. Atlantic Highlands, N.J.: Humanities Press.

Smyer, Michael A. 1979. "Divorce and family support in later life: emerging trends and issues." Paper presented at the 87th Annual Convention, American Psychological Association, New York, September.

Treas, Judith 1979. "Women's employment and its implication for the status of the elderly of the future." Paper presented at the Workshop on Stability and Change in the Family, National Academy of Sciences, Annapolis, Md., March.

Troll, Lillian E., Sheila J. Miller, and Robert C. Atchley 1979. Families in Later Life. Belmont, Calif: Wadsworth.

Uhlenberg, Peter, and Anne P. Myers 1980. "Divorce and the elderly." Manuscript, Department of Sociology, University of North Carolina at Chapel Hill.

Weber, Max 1949. The Methdology of the Social Sciences. New York: Free Press.

Weed, James A. 1978. "Trends in divorce: implications for family health." Paper presented at the 1978 Annual Meeting of the American Sociological Association, San Francisco, Calif.

3 Economic Aspects of an Aging Population and the Material Well-Being of Older Persons[1]

Thomas J. Espenshade
Rachel Eisenberg Braun
The Urban Institute

Demographic aging can be viewed from two perspectives. At the level of the individual, aging in a chronological sense begins at the moment of birth and continues without interruption until the individual dies. We can also think of a collection of individuals as composing a population, and we can speak of the population as a whole growing older. Both types of aging are associated with distinct economic effects, and this paper focuses on those effects about which our knowledge is insufficient. We begin by discussing demographic aging at both the societal and the individual level, drawing distinctions between the two processes and showing how they are related, using data from the United States. We then proceed to reflect critically on what is known concerning the economic implications of an aging population and the economic well-being of older persons.

TWO VIEWS OF DEMOGRAPHIC AGING

Macro-Aging

A change in the age of a population as a whole occurs when there has been a change in the age structure or age composition of the collectivity of individuals composing that population. Changes in an age structure are in turn caused by past

[1] In addition to James H. Schulz, the authors are grateful to June O'Neill for her critical reading of an earlier version of this essay. The research assistance of Carolyn Taylor O'Brien and the cooperation of the staff of the Urban Institute library are gratefully acknowledged. The views expressed here are those of the authors and do not necessarily represent those of the Urban Institute or any of its sponsors.

and current trends in fertility, mortality, and international migration—the three driving forces behind the growth and shape of national populations. Of these three, fertility rates usually have the greatest impact on the age of a population. Increases in fertility tend to make the population younger because there is a higher ratio of children to parents and of parents to grandparents. Reductions in fertility have the opposite effect, making the population older. The effects of changes in death rates on age composition are more complex, depending often on the initial level of mortality. When mortality declines from a high level, the population is usually made younger because the most significant reductions in death rates frequently occur at the youngest ages. More children survive through infancy and early childhood, so that the ratio of children to parents increases. On the other hand, if mortality is already low, further improvements will typically increase the age of the population because the greatest declines in death rates tend to be concentrated at the older ages. In economically advanced nations today, mortality reduction can be equated with an increase in the age of a population. Finally, since transnational migrants tend to be relatively young heads of families between the ages of 20 and 30, international migration lowers the age of populations in the receiving countries.[2]

There are several techniques for measuring the age of national populations. Two of the most common involve using an indicator of central tendency such as the mean or median age of all individuals in the population or, alternatively, using the proportion of the population under or over a particular age (e.g., 15). In the former case, increases in either the mean or median age correspond to an aging of the population, and vice versa. In the latter case, declines in the proportion of youth or increases in the proportion of older persons lead to population aging, and vice versa. One problem with these measures is that they sometimes convey ambiguous information regarding the changing age composition of the population. In the United States, for example, the maturation of the Baby Boom cohort is currently raising the median age of the population, with little or no commensurate increase in the proportion of the population over age 65.

Viewed from this societal or macro level, a population can either age or grow younger. During the demographic transition in more developed countries, fertility levels have fallen dramatically, contributing in a major way to the gradual aging of these populations. These secular declines in birth rates, however, have occasionally been interrupted by short-term increases in fertility that temporarily halt or even reverse the long-term aging of a national population. The capacity of large aggregates of people to alter the tempo and direction of trends in population aging is in marked contrast to the ability of individuals to slow the speed of their own chronological aging processes.

---

[2]The interested reader is encouraged to see Coale (1964) for an expanded nontechnical account of the influence that fertility and mortality changes have on age composition. A complete and more mathematical discussion can be found in Coale (1972).

The Experience in the United States

The data in Table 1 show that the United States Table 1 has undergone a progressive aging of its population since the beginning of the 20th century. This trend is primarily the result of a decline in the total fertility rate, which stood at 3.56 for the white population in 1900 and was half that in 1978.[3] The small departure from the upward direction of the median age registered in 1970 reflects the aftereffects of the Baby Boom, a period during which fertility rates rose from a low of 2.2 during the Depression to a maxium of nearly 3.7 in the late 1950's before falling again to a current value of about 1.85.

What can we expect for the future? Projections of the U.S. population to the year 2050 prepared by the Bureau of the Census (1977) and shown in Table 2 provide some tentative answers to this question. The Bureau of the Census has prepared three alternative projections, each characterized by different assumptions about the future course of fertility. In series I, it is postulated that fertility will move gradually from a total fertility rate in 1975 of 1.77 to an average number of lifetime births per woman of 2.7. A value of 2.1 is assumed for series II and 1.7 for series III. Taken together, these estimates are thought to provide a realistic range of future fertility patterns in the United States.

The projections show that continued aging is expected, although the high fertility assumption (series I) causes the population to become somewhat younger after the year 2000. On the other hand, if series III prevails, the median age is projected to reach 43.7 years by 2050, when almost one out of every four people will be 65 or older. The expansion of this older group will be especially noteworthy between 2005 and 2030, when the number of persons 65 years of age and older grows from 32 million to 55 million as the Baby Boom children of the 1940's and 1950's reach old age. This projected increase of 23 million in a 25-year span equals the 1976 population 65 and over. Of increasing interest is the comparative growth of age groups within the 65 and over category. The fastest percentage increase is expected to take place among the "old-old," or those in the 85 and over category.

Micro-Aging

Chronological aging is an irreversible and monotonic process that begins at birth and continues until death. In describing micro-level aging and how it differs from social mobility, Riley (1976:475) says, "But mobility through the age strata is, of course, universal, undirectional, and irreversible. Everybody ages. Everybody changes over his or her life course as personality develops, experience accumu-

---

[3]The period total fertility rate is the average number of births a woman would have by the end of her childbearing years if she were subject at each age to the birth rates observed among women of different ages in a given year. Data for 1900–16 on the total fertility rates of the white population are contained in Coale and Zelnik (1963:36).

TABLE 1
Estimates of the Population of the United States
in Selected Age Groups: 1900-1978 (in thousands)

Year	All Ages	Under 5	5-13	14-17	18-24	25-44	45-64	65 and Over	Median Age
1900	76,094	9,181	15,402	6,132	10,383	21,434	10,463	3,099	22.9
1930	123,077	11,372	22,266	9,370	15,482	36,309	21,573	6,705	26.5
1960	179,323	20,321	32,726	11,155	15,604	46,899	36,057	16,560	29.5
1970	203,235	17,163	36,675	15,851	23,714	48,024	41,837	19,972	28.0
1978	218,059	15,361	31,378	16,637	28,687	58,097	43,845	24,054	29.7
Percentage Distribution									
1900	100.0	12.1	20.2	8.1	13.6	28.2	13.8	4.1	—
1930	100.0	9.2	18.2	7.6	12.6	29.5	17.5	5.4	—
1960	100.0	11.3	18.2	6.2	8.7	26.2	20.1	9.2	—
1970	100.0	8.4	18.0	7.8	11.7	23.6	20.6	9.9	—
1978	100.0	7.0	14.4	7.6	13.2	26.6	20.1	11.0	—

SOURCE: For 1900 and 1930, U.S. Bureau of the Census, *Current Population Reports*, Series P-25, No. 311, "Estimates of the Population of the United States by Single Years of Age, Race, and Sex. 1900 to 1959." July 1976; for 1960 to 1978, U.S. Bureau of the Census, *Statistical Abstract of the United States: 1979* (100th edition), Washington, D.C., 1979, Table 29.

TABLE 2

Projections of the Population of the United States
in Selected Age Groups: 1985–2050
(in thousands)

Year	All Ages	Under 5	5–13	14–17	18–24	25–44	45–64	65 and Over	65–74	75–84	85 and Over	Median Age
1985												
Series I	238,878	22,887	31,012	14,392	27,853	71,235	44,194	27,305	16,545	8,172	2,588	30.7
Series II	232,880	18,803	29,098	14,392	27,853	71,235	44,194	27,305	16,545	8,172	2,588	31.5
Series III	228,879	16,235	27,665	14,392	27,853	71,235	44,194	27,305	16,545	8,172	2,588	32.0
2000												
Series I	282,837	23,638	44,725	19,698	28,029	75,794	59,132	31,822	17,436	10,630	3,756	32.5
Series II	260,378	17,852	35,080	16,045	24,653	75,794	59,132	31,822	17,436	10,630	3,756	35.5
Series III	245,876	14,158	28,915	13,831	22,225	75,794	59,132	31,822	17,436	10,630	3,756	37.3
2025												
Series I	373,053	32,931	58,767	24,976	38,336	97,609	69,516	50,920	30,946	15,003	4,971	31.5
Series II	295,742	19,495	36,639	16,356	26,978	77,669	67,686	50,920	30,946	15,003	4,971	37.6
Series III	351,915	12,700	25,016	11,669	20,348	64,956	66,306	50,920	30,946	15,003	4,971	42.4
2050												
Series I	488,230	44,378	77,006	32,372	51,587	127,555	95,096	60,235	33,609	17,103	9,523	30.9
Series II	315,622	20,917	38,486	17,128	29,123	81,379	73,096	55,494	28,867	17,103	9,523	37.8
Series III	230,998	11,404	22,074	10,314	18,474	57,078	59,342	52,312	25,686	17,103	9,523	43.7

(continued)

TABLE 2 (cont.)

Year	All Ages	Under 5	5–13	14–17	18–24	25–44	45–64	65 and Over	65–74	75–84	85 and Over	Median Age
					Percentage Distribution							
1985												
Series I	100.0	9.6	13.0	6.0	11.7	29.8	18.5	11.4	6.9	3.4	1.1	—
Series II	100.0	8.1	12.5	6.2	12.0	30.6	18.9	11.7	7.1	3.5	1.1	—
Series III	100.0	7.1	12.1	6.3	12.2	31.1	19.3	11.9	7.2	3.6	1.1	—
2000												
Series I	100.0	8.4	15.8	7.0	9.9	26.8	20.9	11.3	6.2	3.8	1.3	—
Series II	100.0	6.9	13.5	6.2	9.5	29.1	22.7	12.2	6.7	4.1	1.4	—
Series III	100.0	5.8	11.8	5.6	9.0	30.8	24.1	12.9	7.1	4.3	1.5	—
2025												
Series I	100.0	8.8	15.8	6.7	10.3	26.2	18.1	13.6	8.3	4.0	1.3	—
Series II	100.0	6.6	12.4	5.5	9.1	26.3	22.9	17.2	10.5	5.1	1.7	—
Series III	100.0	5.0	9.9	4.6	8.1	25.8	26.3	20.2	12.3	6.0	2.0	—
2050												
Series I	100.0	9.1	15.8	6.6	10.6	26.1	19.5	12.3	6.9	3.5	2.0	—
Series II	100.0	6.6	12.2	5.4	9.2	25.8	23.2	17.6	9.1	5.4	3.0	—
Series III	100.0	4.9	9.6	4.5	8.0	24.7	25.7	22.7	11.1	7.4	4.1	—

SOURCE: U.S. Bureau of the Census, *Current Population Reports*, Series P-25, No. 704, "Projections of the Population of the United States: 1977 to 2050," July 1977.

lates, and adjustments are made to new roles. Nobody can ever go back, although individuals may age in different ways and at different rates."[4]

The average length of life, however, is variable and can be lengthened or shortened. Thus changes in mortality provide the link between our two concepts of aging. Table 3 shows selected data on life expectancy in the United States between 1920 and 1977. It is immediately clear that not everyone survives to old age, although the chances of living to old age have increased as life expectancy improved. For example, between 1940 and 1977, life expectancy at birth for white males rose from 62.8 years to 70.0 years, corresponding to an increase from 0.58 to 0.71 in the probability of surviving to age 65.[5] Life expectancy beyond age 65 has also risen, but much more slowly for men than for women. It is likely that mortality reductions will continue, thereby contributing both to length of life and to population aging. For example, in the most recent set of population projections prepared by the Bureau of the Census (1977), life expectancy at birth in the year 2050 is projected to be 71.8 years for both white and black males and 81.0 years for white and black females.

Implications of These Two Perspectives on Aging

Our discussion of macro-aging has shown us that changes in a population's age usually arise from changes in the number of people at *each* age and not simply from changes in the number of elderly. Moreover, micro-aging can be viewed as an ongoing process that starts at birth and characterizes individuals at each point in the age structure. Therefore, aging or its consequences is *not* something that can be studied by focusing only on the aged. Rather, each age group must be studied in relation to others, and if the data permit, we should follow cohorts of individuals over time as they move through a sequence of successively older age categories. In addition, different research questions are raised depending on the type of demographic aging under consideration. Potentially dissimilar economic effects are associated with each kind of aging. Yet the two sets of outcomes need to be assessed simultaneously because the impact of an aging population on the economy may have a critical effect on the Nation's capacity to provide for its elderly.

---

[4]In fact, if society changes, individuals *must* age—socially, psychologically and biologically—in different ways (cf. Riley, 1979).

[5]In other words, if a hypothetical cohort of 1,000 newborn babies were subject at each age to the mortality risks experienced in 1939–41 by white males in the United States, 583 would be expected to survive to age 65. The same experiment using 1977 death rates would imply an expected 707 survivors at age 65.

TABLE 3
Expectation of Life at Birth and Selected Life Table Values for the U.S. White Population: 1920–1977

Item	Males							Females						
	1920	1930	1939–1941	1949–1951	1959–1961	1969–1971	1977	1920	1930	1939–1941	1949–1951	1959–1961	1969–1971	1977
Average expectation of life in years:														
At birth	54.4	59.7	62.8	66.3	67.6	67.9	70.0	55.6	63.5	67.3	72.0	74.2	75.5	77.7
Age 20	(NA)	(NA)	47.8	49.5	50.3	50.2	51.9	(NA)	(NA)	51.4	54.6	56.3	57.2	59.1
Age 40	(NA)	(NA)	30.0	31.2	31.7	21.9	33.4	(NA)	(NA)	33.3	35.6	37.1	38.1	39.8
Age 50	(NA)	(NA)	22.0	22.8	23.2	23.3	24.7	(NA)	(NA)	24.7	26.8	28.1	29.1	30.7
Age 65	(NA)	(NA)	12.1	12.8	13.0	13.0	13.9	(NA)	(NA)	13.6	15.0	15.9	16.9	18.4
Number surviving to specified age per 1,000 born alive:														
Age 20	(NA)	(NA)	923	951	959	964	972	(NA)	(NA)	940	965	971	976	982
Age 40	(NA)	(NA)	869	912	924	925	937	(NA)	(NA)	898	941	953	957	967
Age 50	(NA)	(NA)	805	856	874	877	895	(NA)	(NA)	853	907	925	929	943
Age 60	(NA)	(NA)	583	635	658	652	707	(NA)	(NA)	687	768	807	809	838

NA = Not available.
SOURCE: U.S. Bureau of the Census, *Statistical Abstract of the United States: 1979* (100th edition), Washington, D.C., 1979, Tables 100 and 101.

ECONOMIC EFFECTS OF AN AGING POPULATION[6]

Despite recent scholarly and policy interest in the economic consequences of an aging population, much of the current discussion is based more on reasoned speculation than on empirical evidence. The major task now is to test these unexamined hypotheses scientifically with the available data.

Labor Force

The labor force is one of the most direct channels through which changes in population size and composition affect the economy. Economic efficiency depends on the willingness of workers to change jobs and sometimes move their place of residence when economic forces require it. But since an aging population also means an older work force, it has been suggested that three aspects of worker mobility will be adversely affected—the geographical mobility of labor, occupational mobility, and upward mobility through hierarchical organizations. Leibenstein (1972), Shabecoff (1978), Spengler (1976), and Wander (1978), all have expressed concern over a prospective shortage of younger workers in developed countries. According to Spengler, labor's mobility, both occupational and geographical, may be hindered by an aging labor force and by the relative depletion of the "mobile labor reserve," or younger workers. This argument also implies the possibility of higher structural unemployment if the composition of consumer demand is significantly altered by a shift in the age distribution of the population. Wander (1972) suggests that a proportional reduction in younger workers might diminish wage differentials between younger and older workers (or between less experienced and more experienced workers) and thus weaken incentives for younger workers to upgrade their occupational skills. In addition to these demographic effects, wages also depend on the amount of human capital workers possess in the form of education, skills, and work experience, as well as on physical capital accumulation and how much physical capital younger and older workers have at their disposal. Moreover, during the 1950's, younger workers were scarce, but they nevertheless invested heavily in formal education.

Spengler warns of increased "stickiness" in terms of mobility between occupations. A trend toward lifelong learning, however, might overcome some of the reluctance of older workers to change jobs. In addition, since geographic mobility tends to decline beyond age 30, an older work force may inhibit the role of migration in correcting interregional imbalances in labor supply and demand. Nevertheless, these effects would be offset to some extent because successive generations tend to have more education and higher incomes, factors with which migration is positively correlated.

---

[6]Portions of this section draw on work by Espenshade (1978b).

A further issue is the effect of an older age distribution on the probability of individual advancement. Since most hierarchical organizations have a pyramid shape, population age compositions that more nearly resemble a rectangle produce demographic incongruities that could retard individual promotion. As Keyfitz (1973:335) has said, "An increasing population facilitates individual mobility. One of the consequences of moving toward the inevitable stationary population is that mobility will be more difficult." Although it is plausible that such a situation, if left uncorrected, may add to worker disgruntlement and have a negative effect on labor productivity, it is perhaps equally likely that lengthening the period over which workers must compete for promotions might augment productivity. Raising the mandatory retirement age would take advantage of the skills and experience of older workers, provide some buffer against the impact of inflation on those facing fixed-income pensions, and ease the financing problems of the Social Security system. On the other hand, it would exacerbate the situation of slower promotions for many individuals.

Among the many suggestions for alleviating these problems are such ideas as financial incentives to increase labor's willingness to migrate and replacing the steplike process of economic and social advancement with a mechanism more akin to a ramp. Yet these proposed strategies are offered as remedies to problems whose actual severity is unknown. Few if any empirical studies have been conducted to see how sensitive any of these aspects of labor mobility is to changes in the age composition of the labor force. Research on this topic should begin by analyzing past situations.

Patterns of Consumer Spending

A similar picture emerges for analyses of the effects of a changing age structure on patterns of consumer expenditure, where effects have been hypothesized but only partially and inadequately measured. Because the types and quantities of goods and services purchased vary by age group and because a transition to an older population restructures the relative proportions of successive age groups in the population, it is widely believed that sustained low fertility would result in a redistribution in the pattern of consumer expenditures away from those items used by the young and toward those consumed primarily by older persons. Lionel Robbins (1929) refers to the eventual desire for fewer toys and more footwarmers, and Ansley Coale (1960) foresees the necessity for fewer baby buggies and more false teeth.

Despite the common sense appeal of these hypotheses, empirical measurement suggests the effects are not marked. The question of how alternative rates of population growth affect the pattern of consumption has been studied empirically for the United States by Eilenstine and Cunningham (1972), Resek and Siegel (1974), Ridker (1978), and Espenshade (1978a). Looking at rather broad categories of consumption in the Bureau of Labor Statistics' 1960–61 Survey of Consumer Expenditures, Eilenstine and Cunningham (1972:230) conclude: "The consumption patterns of a stationary population are sufficiently like those associated with a growing population, so that there is no real reason to fear economic disorder from this source with the cessation of population growth." Resek and Siegel (1974:290) report similar findings, but they note that lower population growth brings "a change in the distribution of the sectors toward durables at the expense of services with little effect in the relative share of nondurables." Increased expenditures for furniture and reduced consumption of housing services account for most of the observable differences. Ridker finds some influence, with slower growth signifying a somewhat reduced proportion of expenditures on food, fuel, rent, and transportation and relatively greater spending for beverages, clothing, household operations, medical care, recreation, and private schools. In no case, however, are the effects pronounced, and they may be explained, perhaps, by the failure to incorporate age composition and household size variables into the analysis. Finally, Espenshade analyzed annual consumption data in 11 categories from the U.S. national income and product accounts for the period 1929–70 and, assuming both threechild and two-child families, projected the results to the year 2020. Negligible differences were found in the pattern of consumer expenditures between the two series.[7]

In each of these four studies, the extent of aggregation into expenditure categories is rather broad, and further disaggregation may uncover demographic influences that have thus far been obscured. Moreover, available data have been inadequately exploited. The 1972–73 Consumer Expenditure Survey from the Bureau of Labor Statistics offers numerous advantages over the 1960–61 study in the coding of household composition. In addition, a continuing consumer expenditure survey with richer data at yearly intervals will soon be available. Finally, the growing body of literature under the rubric of complete systems of demand equations offers an improved theoretical framework within which to conduct empirical investigations.

Relative Cost of Youthful and Elderly Dependents

When birth rates fall from high or moderate levels, the age distribution is affected in such a way as to lower the overall economic dependency ratio.[8] But there is also a shift in the composition of the dependent population as elderly dependents make up a larger share and youth a declining share. Whether economic welfare increases as a result of these age structural changes depends on the relative costs

---

[7]The 11 categories of personal consumption expenditure include automobiles and parts, furniture and household equipment, other durables, food and drink, clothing and shoes, gasoline and oil, other nondurables, housing, household operations, transport, and other services.

[8]This ratio is usually defined as the population under age 15 or 20 plus the population over age 60 or 65 divided by the number of people in the central age groups.

of maintaining youthful dependents compared with elderly dependents. In much of the economicdemographic growth model literature inspired by the early work of Coale and Hoover (1958), it is assumed that young and old dependents are equally costly, so that a reduction in fertility leads to an increase in per capita income. More recent work challenges this assumption. Based on her research with German data, Hilde Wander (1978:57–58) states: "It is seldom realized that a child absorbs more resources than an old person, on the average. At current mortality and current standards of consumption, educational performance, and social security in the Federal Republic of Germany, it costs society about one-fourth to one-third more to bring up an average child from birth to the age of 20 than to support an average person of 60 years over the rest of his or her life. This estimate is based on national accounts statistics of the Federal Republic of Germany of 1973 and refers to final private and public consumption expenditure as well as to fixed capital formation for internal use." Based on these calculations, Wander concludes: "Therefore, the secular decline to near replacement fertility and the continuation of this level over several decades, although provoking rapid aging of the population, was a basic condition for the release of funds necessary to raise educational standards, skills, and labor productivity and, in turn, to support larger proportions of old people."

Clark and Spengler (1977) estimate that in the United States the public cost of financing transfers to the aged is three times greater than is such financing for children. They also point out that a large proportion of the dependency costs of the young are for education, which creates human capital and influences future earnings and productivity, whereas expenditures on the aged are primarily maintenance costs and do not add to the productive potential of the economy.

One reason why the Wander and Clark and Spengler conclusions do not agree is that different countries-and therefore different institutional arrangements—are being considered. Another is that Wander includes both public and private expenditures, while Clark and Spengler emphasize public transfers. In the past several years, there has been growing interest in the cost of rearing American children. Techniques have been developed that permit estimates of the dollar volume of parental expenditures on children disaggregated by the age of the child. These methods could be applied to consumer expenditure data to estimate levels of private consumption for individuals of any age. If it were also possible to allocate public expenditures at all levels of government to individuals according to the age of the individual, private and public costs could then be combined into an age profile of total consumption costs. This approach should lead to more definitive information on the relative costs of dependents.

Savings and Investment

The potential effects of an aging population on savings and investment are important to consider because these are basic to economic growth. Much speculation has centered on the sensitivity of household savings to numbers of dependent children and thus to alternative population growth rates and age compositions. Winger (1976) contends that a stationary population would have two favorable effects on the household sector: First, there would be proportionately fewer families whose ability to save is lessened due to an excessive number of children, and second, periods favorable to saving over the family life cycle would be lengthened. Eversley (1976) points out that declining fertility, compression of the reproductive period, and greater labor force participation of married women would reduce the period (to less than 10 years) over the family life cycle when the typical family would be characterized by the one-earner multidependent model that has been prevalent in developed countries until quite recently. Furthermore, the number of dependents even during this brief span would be less than in the past.

On the other hand, Ridker (1978) suggests a number of ways in which the generally presumed negative impact of children on parents' ability to save might be mitigated: Expenditures on children may be made at the expense of other consumption goods rather than savings; children may contribute to family income or may spur their parents to work harder and longer; and children may encourage the amassing of estates. Further, Kelley's (1972, 1976) work casts doubt on the validity of some widely applied generalizations on children's negative impact on household savings rates. He finds that these rates actually increase with the first and second child. Maillat (1976:16), however, claims that this hypothesis does not stand up "if it is accepted that a reduction in family size is the result of a choice (substitution) made by the parents between the number of children and the acquisition of other consumer durables as and when family income rises." Espenshade (1975) concludes that family savings are more a function of the average age of children than of their number.

Finally, Neal (1978) claims that most models of household savings rely on the level of per capita income as the crucial factor and not on the number of children per se. An interesting variant is the Modigliani-Ando (1963) life cycle model, which posits that savings are a function of an individual's age or point in the life cycle. Under this formulation, people maximize their lifetime consumption by saving during their working years and dissaving (or consuming more than their current income) during retirement. If this model is correct, the increasingly older character of a population undergoing a transition to zero population growth would depress aggregate savings if the rise in the proportion of elderly is considerable. However, in examining the relationship between wealth and age among the elderly, Thad Mirer (1979,1980) finds that elderly persons tend to dissave far more slowly than would be expected on the basis of simple life cycle savings theory and that some even increase their wealth over time. How the wealth-age relation is influenced by Social Security is also the subject of some debate (see, for example, Feldstein and Pellechio, 1979; and Barro, 1978). Kotlikoff's (1979) econometric results, however, give mixed support to the notion that the microeconomic mechanisms of the life cycle model are at work. He finds, for example, that the savings of the old may have increased to offset the reduced savings of the young, leaving a net impact of zero on aggregate savings.

Of course, household savings represent only a small, and declining, fraction of the economy's total savings. For the United States, Ridker (1978) reports that over 80 percent of the new funds in the private sector are generated out of firms' retained earnings. He argues that, whereas these savings may be influenced by the effect of population growth rates on aggregate demand and on profit rates, they are also amenable to monetary and fiscal policy. If it is assumed that the Federal Government pursues policies to maintain full employment, this process will tend to offset any changes in aggregate demand and profit rates induced by population changes. Thus, in making projections for the American economy, Ridker believes that not enough is yet known to warrant any assumption except that savings do not depend on the rate of population growth.

Proponents of the stagnation thesis—a view that was fashionable among some academic economists in the United States and Western Europe during and after the Great Depression—believed that the low fertility levels that were producing a slowdown in population growth and an aging of the population would also slow the growth of aggregate consumption, unsold goods would accumulate in warehouses, and employers would lay off increasing numbers of workers and would have no need to invest in expanding their productive plants and equipment. Eventually, it was thought, the economy would stagnate at a level of less than full employment. Yet no one has systematically analyzed the level and composition of investment demand under alternative agestructured scenarios. In his study for the United States, Neal (1978:103–104) claims, "Neither in the short run of the next two to three years nor in the long run of 20 to 30 years . . . is it likely that the adverse effects of declining population growth upon investment demand will also lower the rate of growth of per capita income. Since investment demand is only important insofar as it helps maintain per capita income through full employment and continued technical progress, the theme of secular stagnation will not play well under these circmstances."

In the absence of better knowledge about how population growth and composition affect savings, many authors simply assume the savings rates are invariant with respect to population changes (see, for example, Ridker, 1978). Research on the impact of fertility changes and age-compositional effects on household savings behavior could profitably take advantage of existing microsimulation modeling capabilities. Investment behavior is perhaps better understood with time-series data relating investment changes to population age distribution, interest rates, prior levels of investment, and the like. Cross-country comparisons would also be useful.

As a postscript to the first four topics considered in this section, it should be pointed out that many previous investigations of these issues have compared a population growing at a rate equivalent to three children per family with a population growing at a rate consistent with two children per family. However, fertility rates in the United States have fallen below the replacement level since the early 1970's, and we need to take seriously the possibility that they may remain there for many decades to come. The implication of this reasoning is that future empirical studies should postulate fertility rates permanently below replacement as one alternative.

Aging of the Baby Boom Cohort

One aspect of the future aging of the U.S. population deserves special attention. The major fertility swings of the past 30 years—the post-World War II rise in birth rates coupled with the decline in birth rates over the past 10 years—have produced an unprecedentedly large bulge in the age distribution of this country. Measured in terms of the annual number of births, the postwar increase in fertility was most evident between 1955 and 1964, when more than 4 million children were born each year. This group of Americans, now aged 16 to 25, is larger than any other 10-year birth cohort in U.S. history. As time passes and as this cohort continues to age, institutions and programs that respond to the needs of particular age groups will be differentially affected.

To use Norman Ryder's imagery, the pictorial representation of the movement of the Baby Boom generation through the age structure will be much like that of a boa constrictor swallowing a pig, and we can speculate on some of the likely societal effects of this form of demographic peristalsis. During the decade of the 1980's, a number of effects are likely to be felt as the largest of the Baby Boom cohorts passes through its late teens and twenties. First, unemployment rates are typically highest for persons in this age group, primarily due to high rates of labor force turnover (entrances and exits). Thus, a decline in the number of people 16 to 24 would probably result in lower levels of frictional unemployment. A continued demand for workers in high-turnover jobs (e.g., fast-food chains) could increase wages for such jobs and income opportunities for older persons.

Second, during the 1980's, the traditional age group from which college students are drawn (18 to 24) will be getting smaller. Persons in this age group numbered 28.2 million in 1976, but are expected to fall to 27.8 million by 1985 and possibly to 24.7 million by the year 2000. These demographic developments increasingly threaten enrollment in higher educational institutions. More and more schools that prospered during the 1960's face the prospect of shutting their doors unless markedly higher proportions of high school graduates decide to continue their education.

Third, demand for new housing should continue strong throughout the coming decade. This conclusion follows from the entry of the Baby Boom cohorts into the years of peak household formation. During the decade of the 1970's, 32 million Americans reached age 30; for the current decade, the projected figure is 42 million. Some economists project an average of slightly more than 2 million new housing starts each year over the next decade, or an increase of 300,000 new houses annually compared with the past 10 years.

Fourth, one of the emerging concerns for the U.S. economy is the slowdown in productivity growth since the late 1960's, especially since 1973. Indeed, in the past year or two, output per worker has actually declined. To some extent, these productivity changes may be demographically related. The rate of savings, which is near an all-time low today, might be expected to accelerate during the 1980's as the Baby Boom children establish their households and enter the higher income-earning years. Levels of investment in capital equipment may increase, too, as the declining number of youthful entrants to the labor market makes it more economically advantageous for firms to begin investing in laborsaving equipment. Thus, productivity growth may also accelerate during this decade.

Looking ahead to the 21st century, the first wave of Baby Boom children will begin to reach retirement sometime after the year 2005, and the annual number of persons retiring will continue at a high level until the year 2030. Unless the birth rate is suddenly revived, the first quarter of the next century will see a substantial increase in the reliance on persons of working age to provide for the economic security of their elders.

We have touched only quickly on some of the possible effects of the maturation of the Baby Boom cohort. One research priority is to quantify some of these potential influences. For example, if a serious labor shortage occurs in the coming years arising from the recent decline in the birth rate and the subsequent movement of smaller birth cohorts into the labor market, and if this shortage cannot be compensated for by increases in female labor force participation, by a postponement in the customary age of retirement, or by greater substitution of capital for labor, then U.S. employment policy may require close coordination with immigration policy. Second, although much can be surmised about the implications of the Baby Boom generation passing through its twenties and about what is likely to be its effect on the Social Security system once the Baby Boom adults reach retirement age, the social and economic effects of the Baby Boom cohorts between age 30 and age 65 represent a vast black box about which we know practically nothing. This terrain requires mapping as well.

THE MATERIAL WELL-BEING OF OLDER PEOPLE

The economic well-being of older people is of interest and concern regardless of the shape of the age distribution. Economic well-being will acquire even greater significance as the proportion of older persons (especially the "old-old") rises and as longevity increases.

Expanded Measures of Economic Well-Being

The concept of "material well-being" is fundamental to our consideration of the economic implications of micro-aging. Previous research on the economic wellbeing of older persons has been handicapped by equating it with money income, ignoring such considerations as net worth, home equity, leisure, and possession of durable goods.

Moon and Smolensky (1977:46) suggest that a more comprehensive measure is needed: "Indexes of economic welfare ought to capture a family's command over all goods and services: it should measure neither actual levels of consumption nor actual levels of income, but, rather the resource constraint faced by the family. Attainable rather than attained consumption is what is appropriate to measure." The measure Moon and Smolensky suggest is consistent with the Modigliani-Ando (1963) life-cycle hypothesis, whereby individuals maximize their utility by smoothing consumption over both current and future periods. A measure of material well-being based on this hypothesis would reduce the effect of yearto-year fluctuations in current money income, which give a distorted picture of what a family could consume in any one year.

Property income, for example, is only partly reflective of net worth because some kinds of net worth yield no income. Thus, the authors include in their measure an annuitized portion of net worth. Home equity, the largest component of assets for the elderly, yields an "imputed rent" that should not be ignored in the measurement of well-being. It would be misleading, however, to include the full value of annuitized net worth. Imperfect capital markets, such as the lack of liquidity of home ownership and high transaction costs, discourage the inclusion of full annuitization.

Human capital is included in the measure, not as education or experience but as the capitalized value of expected future earnings. Younger families generally have more human capital and consequently can consume more out of current income or borrow on expected lifetime income. As the individual ages, however, net worth holdings are increasingly important relative to human capital in determining material well-being. Moon and Smolensky include both variables to prevent an age bias in their measure. For the elderly, public policy through the Social Security system discourages work by imposing a stiff implicit marginal tax rate on earnings. This effect is reinforced by the private pension system since pension receipt is contingent on retirement from the associated job. Although an elderly person can supplement pension income by getting a new job, the loss of seniority and the possible inapplicability of the person's experience, knowledge, and training specific to the previous firm may lessen the level of pay at the new firm. Hence, future earnings are reduced, and the opportunity cost of leisure, which rightly belongs in the measure, is substantially below the wage rate, complicating its valuation.

Intrafamily in-kind transfers are another important but often neglected component of economic welfare (e.g., elderly parents living in an extended family arrangement). Moon and Smolensky also include in-kind transfers (e.g., Medicare, Medicaid, food stamps, and rent subsidies) available from the Government, noting that the value of these transfers is hard to define. They point out that many economists feel that recipients value their in-kind transfers at an amount less than their costs, essentially because in-kind transfers, unlike cash, do not substitute for other goods.

Moon and Smolensky's comprehensive measure of economic well-being overcomes the restrictions caused by equating cash income with well-being. It also takes the significant step of including living arrangements, recognizing that the elderly are not a homogeneous group. At the same time, their measure raises issues that both clarify the concept of well-being and complicate its valuation.

A major debate revolves around the components of a broader index and the method of giving value to each. Robin Walther (1977:63) criticizes Moon and Smolensky for their failure to specify a theoretical definition of well-being: "This lack of specificity in their theoretical concept of economic well-being is not unusual in this area of research. However, the lack of specificity means that there is no one standard by which to judge their suggestions about the appropriate methods for the incorporation of various resources into the measure of economic well-being." This is not a trivial matter, for as Walther points out, the methods that one uses to incorporate such assets as home ownership or in-kind transfers into a measure of well-being turn on the specific theoretical measure of economic well-being that is being approximated.

Walther argues that the first step in developing an empirical measure of economic well-being is to determine why the measure is needed. Ideally, the motivation for the measure will suggest an appropriate theoretical definition that will, in turn, guide the empirical specification of variables. Since measures have usually been developed to frame and evaluate equitable social policies, we must decide on some criterion by which an equitable social distribution can be defined. Walther (1977:62) suggests two possibilities: "If an endowment-based criterion is adopted, then the appropriate definition of economic well-being is an objective measure in which the value of assigned family resources is determined by a market price. If a utilitarian or economic welfare criterion is adopted, the appropriate definition of economic well-being is a subjective measure in which the value assigned resources is dependent on individual preferences."

Thad Mirer (1979) is critical of the use of the simple life-cycle theory of savings to help construct a comprehensive measure of economic welfare. Other motives for holding wealth, Mirer suggests, are to provide for bequests and emergencies, to hold power and prestige, and to prepare for an old age of unknown length and uncertain health. His findings have implications for apportioning net worth in the measurement of economic well-being.

James Morgan (1965) provides another measure of the economic welfare of the aged that also incorporates noncurrent resources such as assets and intrafamily transfers. Because of valuation problems, he excludes a number of components from his measure. One such component is leisure. Traditional economic theory equates the marginal utility of leisure, when voluntary, with the marginal rewards from extra work. Yet for some elderly persons, leisure is often excessive, imposed, and even distasteful due to mandatory retirement, age, disability, or disincentives created by the implicit Social Security tax on wages (but see Foner and Schwab in this book). Morgan also notes that while it is so difficult to place a value on leisure that its inclusion may misrepresent economic wellbeing, international comparisons are distorted by the failure to take account of differences in leisure time.

The value of housing is another component of economic welfare that is difficult to assess. Many older persons who own their homes have far more housing than they need, and inclusion of imputed rent on extra rooms tends to overstate the level of economic wellbeing. Morgan suggests that among the reasons for maintaining an oversized house are the costs of moving, both monetary and psychological, and the acceptability of dissaving through letting a house depreciate and run down. Resistance to change, uncertainty as to the length of remaining lifetime, lack of suitable alternatives, and the desire to remain in familar surroundings are other considerations that may prevent elderly persons from moving, taking in boarders, or refinancing. Hope for the "house rich, cash poor" elderly may lie in newly developing equity conversion plans that allow elderly persons to free some of the equity frozen in their homes. With "reverse-mortgages," banks pay out an annuity based on a percentage of the home value and recoup their payments, plus interest, upon sale of the house or estate. "Sale and leaseback" arrangements allow elderly homeowners to sell their houses with contractual rights to remain in them while the buyers pay for their investments with monthly installments.

Other obstacles to constructing a comprehensive measure include incorporating the differential effects of tax laws, finding a suitable theory or definition in which to frame our understanding of material well-being, evaluating the worth of the components of the measure, and even deciding if the property of being a "good"-something that contributes to economic well-being—is age-specific (as may be the case with extra housing and leisure). Morgan (1965:13-14) tells us: "The most important next step in assessing the adequacy of the economic status of the aged (or indeed of any other group) is to recognize that financial resources are not perfectly substitutable for one another. Having devoted most of this paper to the attempt to include all resources, we must admit that we have not gone too far in adding them up or assuming that one was as good as another."

Thus a number of problems and research issues arise in constructing measures of economic well-being. Mirer's work on the wealth-age relation suggests several research questions. What are the motivations for holding wealth? Concerning income support programs for the elderly, should we expect the elderly to run down their wealth or should there be a wealth criterion for eligibility? Unfortunately, the lack of good data on wealth accumulation and the gross underreporting that is typical of such data frustrate attempts to study the relationships between wealth and other variables. Further investigation requires both finer breakdowns of the data on changes in the components of wealth over time and cohort data that disaggregate the elderly population by age group. Similarly, longitudinal data on lifetime earnings, Social Security, and private accumulation of wealth will improve our ability to test hypotheses on savings behavior throughout the life cycle and to investigate how, if at all, people change savings and transfer behavior in the presence of a Government-imposed Social Security system. Other promising directions include looking at the wealth of the elderly according to their labor force status or considering the income-mortality relationship that may, through selectivity, bias our results when looking at cohorts of elderly persons at only one point in time.

Subjective Perceptions of Well-Being

How do the elderly's subjective perceptions of their material well-being correlate with the traditional objective measures of economic status? Liang and Fairchild (1979) are concerned with the subjective meanings older people attach to their finances. A central assumption of their work is that the connection between a person's observed economic status and his or her perceived financial well-being is mediated by subjective interpretations of the situation in terms of "relative deprivation." According to Liang and Fairchild (1979:747), "The concept of relative deprivation . . . refers to the way reality may be matched against expectation to induce an attitude of satisfaction or dissatisfaction . . . assumes that people evaluate themselves and orient their behavior by reference to values or standards of other individuals and groups."

A modified definition of relative deprivation allows a comparison of one's present circumstance with the previous situation. These concepts can help us interpret the disparity between objective and perceived economic wellbeing. Liang and Fairchild analyzed six national samples of elderly persons and found that feelings of relative deprivation were more important than variables such as social status and current income in their effects on financial satisfaction. Moreover, intrapersonal relative deprivation—a comparison with one's own previous circumstances—was found to have more impact than deprivation with respect to others.

Similarly, James Schulz (1976:569) identifies a group of aged persons who may have incomes above an official poverty line but are poor in some respects: "If an individual's income drops sharply, his ability to maintain his accustomed standard of living also drops—unless savings are utilized or borrowing takes place. A great many elderly persons have found that this is exactly what happens when they retire: the pensions they receive are much less than their prior earnings and cause a dramatic change in the standard of living which can be maintained without supplementation. Such persons—confronted with a substantial drop in their living standard—can be characterized as experiencing relative poverty."

Juanita Kreps (1970) also makes this distinction between relative and absolute poverty, considering particularly the effect of technology and growth. Technological advances raise the incomes of all families. Nevertheless, since the benefits of advances in technology accrue mainly to persons in the labor force, the incomes of retired persons gradually deteriorate relative to the incomes of the working population. This problem is accentuated if the retirement span is long and the economic growth rate high. Furthermore, there is a differential impact on age groupings within the elderly population. The young elderly, those aged 65 to 69, are more likely to be in the labor force (though with more obsolete skills relative to the younger population) than those in their seventies and eighties. The older aged also rely more heavily on pensions accrued in an earlier, less productive time. Hence, technological growth heightens the disparity between the nonworking elderly and the working population, generating feelings of relative economic deprivation. This trend has been reversed in recent years with the indexing of Social Security payments, which has actually increased the money incomes of the elderly faster than those of the working population.

Budget Standards and Replacement Ratios

The concept of relative deprivation affects our definition of who is in poverty. In a society as visible and as above subsistence as ours, the specification of technical physical standards as a dividing line between poverty and minimum well-being is insufficient and no longer corresponds to the notion of adequacy. Budget standards and, in particular, poverty thresholds have been estimated based on the amount of money needed for adequate housing, food, and other items or according to a subsistence food budget based on family size and composition, multiplied by a factor representing the share of income spent on food by a poor family. It is difficult, however, to apply these poverty standards to the elderly. The types of foods on which the estimates are based—more grains, beans, etc., and less meat—often deviate from lifelong family food patterns and require a considerable amount of skill in cooking and home preparation, rendering these measures inappropriate to elderly householders. Marilyn Moon (1979) notes that budget standards for the elderly must be careful to establish levels of consumption that could sustain a person for an extended period of time, because poverty is seldom temporary among the elderly. The Expert Committee on Family Budget Revisions (1980:ii) suggests a criterion for budget standards more in line with the concept of relative deprivation: "The acceptability and usefulness of explicitly stated standards depends, in our opinion, on how successfully such statements capture the popular notion of what it takes to live moderately or comfortably, or at any other specific level."

In calculating benefit levels in programs such as Social Security, absolute measures (e.g., budget standards and poverty thresholds) are needed to ensure the minimum adequacy of retirement income. Relative measures, the subject of much policy debate, are another means for judging the level of benefits. A frequently used relative measure consists of wage replacement ratios, which are used to determine the amount of preretirement disposable income that must be replaced to prevent a drop in standard of living. According to the President's Commission on Pension Policy (1980), it may seem at first glance that 100 percent replacement is needed to maintain a given standard of living. Changes in consumption patterns, tax liabilities, and savings rates of retired persons, however, reduce the necessary replacement ratio. For example, the commission notes that an estimate of 13.6 percent is often used to show the drop in work-related expenses. Acknowledging that it is difficult to measure the adjustments in postretirement expenses, the commission suggests replacement ratios ranging from 51 percent to 79 percent for single persons and 55 percent to 86 percent for married couples, with the highest earners receiving the lowest replacement rates.

The derivation of replacement ratios is sensitive not only to estimates of changes in postretirement expenses, but also to policy objectives concerning the amount of preretirement earnings to be replaced and the desired level of benefits available given the cost constraints. Applebaum and Faber (1979) discuss the many issues associated with developing practical definitions of replacement ratios. For example, several criteria are available to determine the appropriate level of preretirement earnings that must be replaced. According to one criterion—recency—the measure of lost earnings should reflect amounts earned near the initial receipt of benefits to represent preretirement standard of living. According to another criterion—stability—the measure should be relatively insensitive to fluctuations in the worker's earnings history, since the most recent wages may reflect poor health or downgrading of a job. Hence, some pension systems choose the highest year's earnings as the wage base for calculating benefits, in case the final earnings record does not reflect the usual standard of living. On the basis of another criterion—uniformity—the measure of the amount of earnings replaced should not reflect options exercised by beneficiaries, such as delayed or early retirement.

Applebaum and Faber note that no definition of replacement ratios is optimal for these and other criteria. Some criteria are somewhat conflicting, as in the case of recency and stability. Consequently, certain policy choices are reflected in the definition of replacement ratios used to compute actual benefits. The President's Commission on Pension Policy, for example, questions whether it is appropriate to replace the highest standard of living ever achieved by an indivdual, and recommends that unless preretirement earnings are indexed by the inflation rate, only recent earnings should be used to determine the amount of lost earnings to be replaced.

Research in this area should be aimed at outlining for policymakers the implications of each set of criteria that shape a definition of replacement ratios. In addition, collection and analysis of longitudinal data documenting changes in consumption and savings patterns would allow more precise measurements in the calculation of these rates. The findings on relative deprivation and relative poverty also have implications for Government income maintenance programs. Liang and Fairchild (1979) suggest that elderly well-being will be strengthened by maintaining the incomes of elderly people at levels commensurate with their peers and with their own previous incomes through the use of high replacement ratios. A high replacement ratio, however, does not necessarily imply a high benefit, depending on the minimum absolute measure used to determine retirement income adequacy. Applebaum and Faber (1979:6) conclude that "the reality is that the general level of benefits under Social Security is determined by how much our society is willing to pay for this program."

Dynamic Analyses of Intertemporal Linkages

In studies of aging, we would be remiss to concentrate exclusively on the elderly population, particularly when analyzing or formulating policy. Since aging is a process occurring throughout the lifetime, we should consider how economic behavior at all points in the life cycle influences later outcomes. What is the relationship between economic well-being at younger ages and in old age, and how do Government policies impinge on this link?

Viscusi (1979) examines these questions at a fairly abstract level, with an eye toward isolating effects over the entire lifetime of Government policies aimed at the elderly. In the absence of Government policies, two types of difficulties are likely to arise: People are unlikely to save enough for retirement, and market imperfections work against the welfare of the elderly, particularly where there are uncertainties. Among the problems in savings markets, Viscusi cites the existence of middlemen, driving a wedge between interest earned and interest paid, and indivisibilities, such as requiring a minimum to purchase high interest-bearing bonds. While the availability of other savings and investment options suggests that these difficulties are not insurmountable, the practical impact is that individuals have an incentive to allocate too much of their resources to their preelderly years.

On the other hand, those who try to allocate resources for their elderly years are faced with uncertainties about the length of life remaining, inflation, medical costs, etc. In the absence of private or public insurance, welfare of the elderly would be reduced because of the need to provide for contingencies. This situation would result in a less than optimal consumption stream throughout the lifetime.

Apart from these market imperfections, individuals may misallocate for old age. One of the most important reasons for this is changing utility functions (i.e., shifts in a person's preferences over a period of time). A common example is "temporal myopia," or a failure to weigh one's future needs and desires heavily enough.

Viscusi contends that much of the support for aid programs for the elderly results from their alleged influence in alleviating market imperfections and individual misallocations. Ordinarily, Government programs operate by identifying a needy group and providing assistance. For the future elderly, however, the most effective means may not be to boost aid to the aged, but to concentrate on preelderly behavior and policies so that when younger cohorts grow older they have the characteristics conducive to a productive life.

Linkages over time between individual action and Government policy for elderly welfare operate in both forward and reverse directions. Forward temporal linkages, says Viscusi, are critical determinants of elderly welfare. For example, the tax subsidy for savings through pension plans acts as an incentive for individuals to set aside for old age. According to Viscusi (1979:66), ''The conjunction of these factors makes it evident that a coherent policy to assist the elderly must recognize and be structured in response to the important links between preelderly actions and policies and welfare in the elderly years.'' Reverse linkages work through anticipatory behavior on the preelderly. ''Individuals who have not yet reached their elderly years may recognize the impact that their present actions will have on their welfare in old age, and will choose accordingly.''

The magnitude of the influence of policy across time may be difficult to estimate. Empirical analysis is hampered by the absence of long-term controlled experiments and variations in policies that produce observable results for lifetime allocations. Viscusi suggests that with such comprehensive longitudinal data, the problem could be studied using an optimization technique-dynamic programming—to handle complicated intertemporal linkages. This process involves looking forward at the implications of current actions and then tracing backward to select the most appropriate mode of behavior.

SUMMARY AND CONCLUSIONS

This paper has suggested that there are two different ways of viewing demographic aging. Individuals can only get older as time passes. Societies, on the other hand, can age or grow younger, depending on changes in their age structures. Each perspective on aging raises a different set of research issues. At the macro level, unanswered questions about the economic implications of societal aging include effects in such areas as labor mobility, consumption patterns, the relative economic cost of younger versus older dependents, and savings and investment. Special attention ought to be given to economic consequences related to the aging of the Baby Boom generation. At the micro level, as a result of increases in life expectancy and a steady growth in the proportion of elderly in the population, the economic well-being of older people is acquiring greater importance. There is a need to expand traditional notions of what constitutes material well-being and to find some way to integrate each of the components, as well as to ask the extent to which older people's perceptions of their well-being are congruent with the assessments of outsiders. Regardless of the direction from which one approaches these issues, it is important not to confuse a study of aging with a study of the aged. Economic effects of aging—whether at the micro level or macro level—are best understood when all age groups are considered simultaneously.

REFERENCES

Applebaum, Joseph A., and Joseph F. Faber 1979. "The concept of replacement ratios under Social Security." Actuarial Note Number 96. Washington, D.C.: Social Security Administration.

Barro, Robert J. 1978. "The impact of Social Security on private savings—evidence from the U.S. time series." Washington, D.C.: American Enterprise Institute.

Bureau of the Census 1977. "Projections of the Population of the United States: 1977–2050." Current Population Reports, Series P-25, No. 704.

Clark, Robert L., and J.J. Spengler 1977. "Changing demography and dependency costs: the implications of future dependency ratios." Pp. 55–89 in Barbara R. Herzog (ed.), Aging and Income: Essays on Policy Prospects. New York: Human Sciences Press.

Coale, Ansley J. 1960 "Population change and demand, prices and the level of employment." Pp. 352–371 in National Bureau of Economic Research, Demographic and Economic Change in Developed Countries. Princeton, N.J.: Princeton University Press.

———. 1964. "How a population ages or grows younger." Pp. 47–58 in Ronald Freedman (ed.), Population: The Vital Revolution. Garden City, N.Y.: Doubleday.

———. 1972. The Growth and Structure of Human Populations. Princeton, N.J.: Princeton University Press.

Coale, Ansley J., and Edgar M. Hoover 1958. Population Growth and Economic Development in Low-Income Countries. Princeton, N.J.: Princeton University Press.

Coale, Ansley J., and Melvin Zelnik 1963. New Estimates of Fertility and Population in the U.S. Princeton, N.J.: Princeton University Press.

Eilenstine, Donald L., and James P. Cunningham 1972. "Projected consumption demands for a stationary population." Population Studies 26:223–231.

Espenshade, Thomas J. 1975. "The impact of children on household saving: age effects versus family size." Population Studies 29:123–125.

———. 1978a. "How a trend toward a stationary population affects consumer demand." Population Studies 32:147–158.

———. 1978b. "Zero population growth and the economies of developed nations." Population and Development Review 4:645–680.

Eversley, David 1976. "Demographic aspects of welfare policies." Paper presented at the Council of Europe Seminar on the Implications of a Stationary or Declining Population in Europe, Strasbourg, September.

Feldstein, Martin, and Anthony Pellechio 1979. "Social Security and household wealth accumulation: new microeconomic evidence." Review of Economics and Statistics 61:361–368.

Harney, Kenneth R. 1980. "Some homeowners cashing in without having to move out." The Washington Post, December 6:F13.

Kelley, Allen C. 1972. "Demographic changes and American economic development." Pp. 9–48 in Elliot R. Morss and Ritchie H. Reed (eds.), Economic Aspects of Population Change. Washington, D.C.: U.S. Government Printing Office.

———. 1976. "Savings, demographic change, and economic development." Economic Development and Cultural Change 24:683–693.

Keyfitz, Nathan 1973. "Individual mobility in a stationary population." Population Studies 27:335–352.

Kotlikoff, Laurence J. 1979. "Testing the theory of Social Security and life cycle accumulation." American Economic Review 69:396–410.

Kreps, Juanita M. 1970. "Economics of aging: work and income through the lifespan." American Behavioral Scientist 14:81–90.

Leibenstein, Harvey 1972. "The impact of population growth on the Ameri can economy." Pp. 49-69 in Elliot R. Morss and Ritchie H. Reed (eds.), Economic Aspects of Population Change. Washington, D.C.: U.S. Government Printing Office.

Liang, Jersey, and Thomas J. Fairchild 1979. "Relative deprivation and perception of financial adequacy among the aged." Journal of Gerontology 34:746–759.

Maillat, Denis 1976. "Population growth and economic growth." Paper presented at the Council of Europe Seminar on the Implications of a Stationary or Declining Population in Europe, Strasbourg, September.

Mirer, Thad W. 1979. "The wealth-age relation among the aged." American Economic Review 69:435–443.

———. 1980. "The dissaving behavior of the retired aged." Southern Economic Journal 46:1197–1205.

Modigliani, Franco, and Albert Ando 1963. "The 'life-cycle' hypothesis of savings." American Economic Review 53:55–84.

Moon, Marilyn 1979. "The incidence of poverty among the aged." Journal of Human Resources 14:211–221.

Moon, Marilyn, and Eugene Smolensky 1977. "Income, economic status, and policy toward the aged." Pp. 45–60 in G.S. Tolley and Richard Burkauser (eds.), Income Support Policies for the Aged. Cambridge, Mass.: Ballinger Publishing Company.

Morgan, James N. 1965. "Measuring the economic status of the aged." International Economic Review 6:1–17.

Neal, Larry 1978. "Is secular stagnation just around the corner? A survey of the influences of slowing population growth upon investment demand." Pp. 101–125 in Thomas J. Espenshade and William J. Serow (eds.), The Economic Consequences of Slowing Population Growth. New York: Academic Press.

President's Commission on Pension Policy 1980. An Interim Report. Washington, D.C.: U.S. Government Printing Office.

Resek, Robert W., and Frederick Siegel 1974. "Consumption demand and population growth rates." Eastern Economic Journal 1:282–290.

Ridker, Ronald G. 1978. "The effects of slowing population growth on long-run economic growth in the U.S. during the next half century." Pp. 127–155 in Thomas J. Espenshade and William J. Serow (eds.), The Economic Consequences of Slowing Population Growth. New York: Academic Press.

Riley, Matilda White 1976. "Social gerontology and the age stratification of society." Reprinted in Beth Hess (ed.), Growing Old in America. New Brunswick, N.J.: Transaction Books.

Riley, Matilda White (ed.) 1979. Aging from Birth to Death: Multidisciplinary Perspectives. Boulder, Colo.: Westview Press.

Robbins, Lionel 1929. "Notes on some probable consequences of the advent of a stationary population in Great Britain." Economica 9:71–82.

Schulz, James H. 1976. "Income distribution and the aging." Pp. 561–591 in Robert H. Binstock and Ethel Shanas (eds.), Handbook of Aging and the Social Sciences. New York: Van Nostrand & Reinhold.

Shabecoff, Philip 1978. "A fast-aging population." The New York Times, July 30:F16.

Spengler, Joseph J. 1976. "Stationary populations and changes in age structure: Implications for the economic security of the aged." Durham, N.C.: Duke University, Center for the Study of Aging and Human Development.

Viscusi, W. Kip 1979. Welfare of the Elderly: An Economic Analysis and Policy Prescription. New York: Wiley.

Walther, Robin Jane 1977. "Comment on Moon and Smolensky." Pp. 336–351 in G.S. Tolley and Richard V. Burkhauser (eds.), Income Support Policies for the Aged. Cambridge, Mass.: Ballinger Publishing.

Wander, Hilde 1972. "The decline of the birth rate in Western Europe: economic implications." Bloomington, Ind.: International Development Research Center, Indiana University.

———. 1978. "Zero population growth now: the lessons from Europe." Pp. 41–69 in Thomas J. Espenshade and William J. Serow (eds.), The Economic Consequences of Slowing Population Growth. New York: Academic Press.

Winger, Max 1976. "Demographic aspects of sociology and family microeconomics." Paper presented at the Council of Europe Seminar on the Implications of a Stationary or Declining Population in Europe, Strasbourg, September.

4 Aging and Work Organizations[1,2]

Harris T. Schrank
Joan M. Waring
The Equitable Life Assurance Society

Several kinds of aging take place within a work organization. Members age in the usual sense as they grow older. Members age in an organizational sense as the length of their affiliation with the institution increases. Members age in the particular jobs they hold as their tenure in them is extended. The membership of the organization grows older (or perhaps younger) as a result of internal demographic processes affecting age composition. All the while, the organization itself grows older as it moves away from newness toward or even beyond maturity.

These various aging processes and the points at which they intersect could form a research agenda to occupy a generation of scholars. Unfortunately, too few such studies are now available to make their review and synthesis a major purpose of this paper. But the lack of empirical studies has far more serious implications. Over the past few years, legislation related to aging and organizations has been proposed—and resisted—without the benefit of pertinent data. For example, the effort to extend the age of mandatory retirement was championed and opposed with, at best, anecdotal data on the effect the policy would have on businesses and other organizations (Rosenblum, 1977). A body of laws, cases, and administrative regulations continues to grow—gravely uninformed by empirical research (Yale Law Journal, 1979). Recent judicial dicta and observations about how age affects decisions within organizations or how age relates to career prog-

[1] In addition to W. Richard Scott, we thank Anne Foner and John W. Riley, Jr., for their their cogent criticisms of an earlier draft of this paper.

[2] This paper grew out of analyses within the Equitable Life Assurance Society initiated by these authors in association with John W. Riley, Jr., Matilda White Riley, Seymour Spilerman, and Burton Singer.

ress demonstrate clearly how little is known about such matters and how consequential that lack of knowledge can be.

The objectives of this paper, therefore, are to raise questions regarding the adequacy of conventional understandings about the workings of the age-
organization nexus and to raise consciousness about the need for empirical studies of age and workplace issues. By suggesting some different perspectives, we
hope to stimulate lines of research that can inform policy development in the
public and private sectors and that can contribute to theory development in the
sociology of age and organizations.

Our approach applies the age stratification paradigm of Riley, Johnson, and
Foner (1972) to work organizations in order to identify and examine how age
factors and aging processes operate in these contexts. First, we look at the relationship of the workplace to the age stratification of the larger society; we view
firms as part of the societal age-grading structure. Then, we consider firms as
places that create and maintain their own age stratification systems; we discuss
age norms, the age structure of rewards, and the relationship between age and
innovation. Next, we look at the way people age in work organizations; emphasis
is on the mobility-age relationship and on ways in which employee cohorts might
age and succeed one another in organizational contexts.

WORK ORGANIZATIONS AND AGE
STRATIFICATION

Nearly all societies come to some sort of consensus about the social roles and
rewards appropriate to individuals of certain ages. That is, inevitably societies
develop norms that stratify people and roles by age. The resulting age structures
of people and of roles, while implicit, are also dynamic (Riley, Johnson, and
Foner, 1972; Riley and Waring, 1976). The age structure of people, for example,
continually changes as the individuals in it grow older and as it is reshaped by
outcomes of demographic processes. The age structure of roles likewise continually changes as roles are added, withdrawn, and revised or as age requirements
are altered because of historical and environmental events. Since age criteria are
used to allocate roles not always equally desirable, people of some ages rather
than others have greater access to roles with greater financial rewards, power,
and prestige. We argue that in work organizations the age structures of people
and positions and the propensities to age inequalities are similar to those that pre-
vail in the larger society.

Firms as Components of the Age Stratification System

Like schools, voluntary associations, and many other formal organizations, business firms are an integral part of the age stratification structure. Defining as well
as providing the activities agreed upon as appropriate for people within particular

age boundaries, work organizations collectively serve as a societal age grade. For example, joining a firm is tantamount to joining the ranks of adulthood. Moving up the hierarchy of the firm is virtually the measure of success as an adult. Leaving the work organization-and concomitantly the labor force—is for some an announcement that middle age is over and that old age has begun. Not only do business firms represent a significant set of age-graded institutions, but also they are the locus of some of the most highly valued roles modern societies have to offer. Business firms, furthermore, control the access routes to these roles.

In common with other components of the age stratification system, work organizations use age criteria-formal and informal—to specify appropriate times of entry to and exit from their system. These criteria can be quite idiosyncratic. Some business firms, for example, provide opportunities for a sequence of roles that can cover the entire span of what is usually considered adulthood, while other firms, by design or chance, are only short-stay institutions. Some, positioned in the secondary labor market, have jobs sought primarily by the young and old who, because of low skills and status, cannot compete for more desirable roles elsewhere (Spilerman, 1977). Still other work organizations are viewed as transitory places for apprenticeship or skill improvement before a more permanent niche is sought—for example, training hospitals and some government posts. Some firms tend to have young employee populations because they offer mostly entry positions or because expansions have led to the hiring of young people. Similarly, organizations in decline tend to have relatively old employee populations.

While firms may simply let labor market forces dictate the age composition of employee populations, it appears that, legally, they can no longer deliberately favor certain age categories. It is as if government recognized the crucial function of the firm as an adult age grade and has, through law, ensured that whatever role opportunities exist must be made available to all age strata ordinarily thought to constitute adulthood.

That work organizations are restricted to people in various stages of adulthood raises a critical issue. Unlike the larger society, where the age range goes from neonate to centenarian, the age boundaries of a work organization typically go from "young," meaning the late teens, to "old," meaning late middle age. That firms are age-truncated in this way has important implications. For example, organizations are thereby deprived of the experience, advice, and wisdom of old or very long-service members. Lost are the positive benefits that can accrue from the continued inclusion of older people in the firm (Schrank and Riley, 1976).

Firms as Age Stratification Systems

Work organizations are not only a component of the societal age stratification structure, but are also a microcosm—maybe even a caricature—of it. Replicated within a firm, for example, are an age structure of people and a corresponding age structure of roles. Like their counterparts in the larger society, these structures are far more complex than the simplicity of the model would imply. In the firm's age structure of people, for example, sometimes organizational age (length of time with the firm) or job age (tenure in a particular job) may be more significant than chronological age in qualifying for roles. At other times, chronological age may be the chief determinant (legal or not) of eligibility for a valued role.

Similarly, the structure of work roles within a firm is seldom neatly hierarchical or unambiguously stratified by age. In fact, there may be a large number of roles—elevator operators or cafeteria workers—for which no age norms exist at all. Or, access to certain other roles could depend on seniority or on age-irrelevant subjective evaluations (Halaby, 1978). Moreover, the age structure of roles within a firm may have a different configuration for women than for men—with women of disparate ages eligible for entry-level positions. Or, the age markers for success may be different for a professional track than for a managerial track.

Again, as in its societal counterpart, the age structures of people within firms are dynamic. They change as employees age, are hired, are terminated, take leaves, become disabled. Just a management decision to prefer or require college degrees for a set of jobs that previously required only a high school diploma can have dramatic effects on the age structure—both immediately and over the long term. The age structure changes in response to events external to the organization as well as to companywide or more local internal policy. The age structure, for example, can change as a result of national policies and events. The number of employees over 65 may inch upward now that retirement at that age can no longer be made mandatory by the firm. At the other end of the age spectrum, a military draft, higher college enrollments, or desires for a large family could empty the firm of young men or women.

The age structure of roles in a firm is likewise dynamic—a fact often overlooked (at considerable peril) by students of formal organizations, career trajectories, and job mobility. The role structure of work organizations changes with remarkable frequency. New roles are created, and old ones are temporarily or permanently abandoned. Roles are merged and roles are divided, changing critical counts. Roles are upgraded and occasionally downgraded. Job descriptions are revised as new skills are needed or some duties become obsolete. These shifts affect other roles. When new jobs are created, the role of manager of these jobs may be upgraded because of the added responsibility of managing additional jobs. Sometimes a whole new stratum in the hierarchy may be added as technology or a new product creates an entire set of jobs at a particular level. As the role structure shifts, new age criteria are generated for allocating people of various ages-chronological, organizational, and job—to the roles available.

Age Norms and Work Roles

Despite their complexity and flux, the age structures of people and roles in work organizations yield recognizable and fairly stable strata. Minimally, people in a firm can be stratified along such dimensions as newcomer, veteran, and senior—with each stratum having more or less understood age boundaries. Typically, norms exist to suggest that kinds of jobs are seemly and "only fair" for newcomers, veterans, and seniors or for employees of given ages.

Of course, the way roles are stratified in a firm may be complex. Some companies have devised systems with 10, 20, and even 65 designated ranks between the lowest entry point and officer levels. Various age norms develop around these strata. For example, placement in the bottom 10 percent of grades could be deemed inappropriate or "behind schedule" for all employees except those of young chronological or organizational age. Arrival in a specific grade band, say, somewhere in the middle, may have to be attained by a given age (in years or tenure) to ensure remaining "on schedule" throughout the rest of a career. Moving close to the upper ranks while of low chronological age, however, signals being "ahead of schedule." Indeed, such a violation of the norms is considered newsworthy, as when the election of a relatively young person to a presidency or chairmanship is given special journalistic attention. Nonetheless, according to Sofer (1979), businessmen tend to equate success with being on or ahead of schedule. This is an aspect of aging within formal organizations that has received attention in the sociological literature (Neugarten and Hagestad, 1976).

Age norms not only measure and make career progress, but also can inhibit such progress. For example, there may be bias against starting an older worker in a longterm developmental career path or even a short-term training program. Organizational gatekeepers might believe that the amount of time in which the organization can profit from the investment is too short to warrant starting the process (Becker, 1964; Mincer, 1974). This sort of calculation could be especially misguided now that the age for mandatory retirement has been extended. Middle-aged or older workers are more likely than younger ones to remain with the firm, thus increasing the likelihood of eventual organizational benefit (Waring, 1978).

Age and the Allocation of Organizational Rewards

Social roles have differential social value because there are different amounts of money, prestige, and power attached to them. Translated into the context of a firm, jobs are differentially valued by virtue of their salaries, titles, and authority to command people or company resources. Jobs can be hierarchically ranked on the basis of these characteristics—either separately or in combination. In terms of the stratification system based on age—where norms typically specify approximate time intervals between moves up the hierarchy—higher ranks should be available only to the most senior members of the company. And in fact, that is most often the case. Incumbents in roles having the greatest financial rewards, power, and prestige tend to be chronologically old (Rosenbaum, 1979a; Davis, 1979).

Although digressive, it probably should be reiterated at this point what "old" or "gerontocratic" generally means in the context of a firm. In terms of chronological age, the lower boundary of "old" hovers about the mid- to late fifties and in organizational age probably two to three decades with the firm. Historical trends toward earlier retirement and withdrawals from the work force reportedly for health reasons, however, have meant that today in the United States relatively few people are in the older age strata of firms (Schwab, 1974). Firms are "age truncated" at the upper age levels. Indeed, the discovery of this fact by the business community helps explain its lack of vigorous opposition to the 1978 amendment to the Age Discrimination in Employment Act.

The important questions therefore becomes why age remains a criterion for the allocation of higher organizational rewards. In part, age has such legitimacy because it can be used as an index or surrogate for characteristics thought to be important for top management positions. For example, age may serve as a rough index of knowledge and experience, and organizational age ties this knowledge and experience to the specific history of the firm. Age—and especially organizational age—may also be seen as an index of insider knowhow: how things are best done and who knows how to get them done. The importance of age as a surrogate for particular characteristics, however, may vary from one organization to another. Davis (1979) observes that in new firms requiring "knowledge," youthful management appears to be more successful, whereas in mature firms, where experience is important, older leadership seems more successful.

It appears that age stratification also solves problems for the work organization. To have older members of the firm in the higher ranks, for example, ensures turnover at the top ranks. By contrast, a younger incumbent in these ranks could lock up a leadership position for several decades, blocking mobility for some and perhaps courting stagnation in the role (Jennings, 1976). In addition, it has been argued that the greater rewards for senior employees serve to motivate younger workers to improve present performance in the hope of such eventual status (Hall, 1976). The relationship between greater age and greater reward may also serve as an inducement to workers to stay with the company. The age stratification system of the work organization can be said to facilitate socialization of new recruits as it replicates the pattern of age-hierarchical socialization found in the familiar settings of the family and school (Parsons and Platt, 1972).

Maintaining the Age Stratification System

Several organizational practices support or maintain the age stratification system. For example, insisting that workers go through various positions, levels, educational training, credential gathering, or otherwise "put in time" before moving ahead assures that some age ranking is maintained. Whether the skills or talents developed through these long socialization processes are necessary (or even useful) as background experience for a high-level position may often be difficult to ascertain. But the existence of a career path, virtually any career path, as long as it takes up time and prevents very young people from assuming—or feeling they can assume—high-level positions, is functional for maintaining the age-grading system within the organization (Schrank, 1972).

Other structures and practices also preserve a system in which increments in age typically bring increments in organizational rewards. The stratification structure itself, for example, can contribute to its continuance. Like its counterpart in the larger society, the organization's social stratification system has three dimensions: wealth, prestige, and power (or, as represented within the work context, salary, title, and command over people and resources). This tripartite structure of rewards, however, is more easily discerned and distinguished within the social microcosm of the work organization than in the society at large.

While advances in age ordinarily would lead to improvements in position within each of the three structures simultaneously, this is not necessarily the case. Movement in one structure is certainly not independent of movement in the others; neither is it contingent. Status inconsistency is, of course, common in the social stratification system of the larger society (Lenski, 1966). For example, an outstanding employee may be given a role with power that is extraordinary for his or her chronological or organizational age. However, salary and prestige levels may not be made commensurate with level of power. The partibility of rewards allows this "violation" of the age-reward system. If the young incumbent should prove inadequate, then power can be withdrawn. Since advances in the other structures were withheld earlier, the three rewards would again fall back into alignment. Conversely, an ineffective executive need not be formally demoted to make way for a more capable replacement. Only power needs to be removed; prestige can be kept intact by a title suggestive of a high position on the organizational chart, and even remuneration can be increased. This action, obviously, is the operational definition of being "kicked upstairs." Although this solution is costly in terms of compensation to an older employee, it resolves the problem of who should perform in a role (the power question) while preserving the semblance of integrity of the other two components of the reward structure.

This is not to say, of course, that the organization's "power structure" is always able to manipulate the tripartite reward system in clearly preordained ways. Nor does our argument imply that only those at the top of the power hierarchy are the source of these rewards (though they probably exercise substantial control over allocations of money and titles). Individuals may have (or lack) power and prestige because of differential access to crucial information or because of having (or lacking) scarce and valued skills. Nonetheless, the tripartite reward system appears to ensure flexibility. It allows rewards to be given and taken back in accord with organizational needs while simultaneously supporting an age stratification system in which rewards manifestly accrue with increasing age.

Age and Innovation

Two common stereotypes about organizational life are that age of leadership is inversely related to innovation and that "new blood" (typically young) serves to invigorate and restore. Given that top management positions in firms are usually held by executives who are older in both years and organizational age, it seems useful to explore the contention that they would be a less innovative set of leaders than younger people. Our guess is that older executives are probably *not* less innovative than younger subordinates or even equals. Contrary to the conventional wisdom, the greater likelihood is that the firm will be made up of young fogies and old Turks.

Consider the situation of new, typically young recruits to the company. For the most part, their concerns necessarily focus on learning the norms, definitions, and rules that allow them to gain recognition and rewards. If they are ambitious and aspire to high positions, they will be especially anxious to do things well, avoid risks, follow instructions, and learn the accepted way of doing things (Hall, 1976). If they fail at this early point, hopes for a future position of responsibility could fade or separation from the firm could become a possibility (Schein, 1971). The little research on behavioral correlates of organizational age and job age suggests that autonomy produces uneasiness among newcomers during the first stages of job socialization and that providing competence in a new position is a foremost concern of organizational veterans being resocialized to new jobs (Katz, 1978). In short, the risks and time associated with innovation make it an unlikely undertaking for young or upwardly mobile employees.

To be sure, older members of the corporation are likely to be thoroughly steeped in the rules, norms, and mores as a result of long association with the firm and, perhaps, because they have contributed to the emergence and preservation of these traditions. It is even possible that, in some circumstances, older workers prefer to reward behavior that is consistent with the internal culture. Extensive knowledge of the company's ways, however, does not necessarily stifle innovative effots but may instead foster them. For example, successful innovations typically require familiarity with existing procedures and methods. Such familiarity, a result of long association with the firm, helps identify the areas where the introduction of change could be the most useful, how it might be done, and with what results. Thus the three kinds of age—years, length of affiliation with the firm, and tenure on the job—can combine to provide older executives, work group leaders, secretarial supervisors, etc., opportunities to make novel interventions in work life that can enhance organizational goals.

Older members of the firm also tend to have more organizational power than do younger members. Innovative ideas are more likely to be taken seriously and implemented when proposed from a position of power. Similarly, older innovators can expedite as well as smooth the course of change through their access to a range of company resources or because they can command compliance with new sets of rules throughout the hierarchy. Older innovators are less likely than younger innovators to experience frustration in having their ideas accepted.

Older employees may be more likely to be innovative than younger ones for still another reason. Many older people have a fairly clear retirement date in mind. For some, this means they face little risk in proposing something they had refrained from suggesting earlier because it could be embarrassing to a superior. Before leaving the firm, some employees may seek to create a memorial by inventing new ways of governing or organizing the company to ensure orderly succession, instituting a new program, developing a new product, and so forth. Of course, not all older people will be innovative or more innovative than in their younger years. Some will feel threatened by suggestions to do something differently, especially if there is an emotional stake in a process that they developed earlier.

Our line of reasoning about the possibility of a positive relationship between age and innovation is not widely accepted, but neither this nor the other, negative, position has been put to a credible test.

WORK ORGANIZATIONS AND AGING PROCESSES

So far the look at age and organizations has been largely cross-sectional: how firms fit into the agegrading system, how age is a criterion for organizational roles, how age determines the allocation of organizational rewards, the salience of the age of leaders, and so forth. Next we look at what the age stratification paradigm calls age dynamics—the processes of aging and cohort flow as they are expressed in employing organizations.

Aging in Organizations

Several kinds of individual aging take place within the firm—with the organization itself shaping and defining how that process takes place. The roles people assume, the environment in which they work, and the opportunities they seize are all relevant to the aging process. For example, it is likely that if a job has sufficient complexity, intellectual flexibility will be maintained as the worker grows older (Kohn and Schooler, 1979); or, if the environment is noxious, physical decline is likely to be accelerated; or, if work is not particularly satisfying, a decision will be made to retire early (Barfield and Morgan, 1969). However, there are too few longitudinal studies involving more than one age cohort to say much about how ordinary aging in the context of a firm is expressed. One cross-sectional study, however, asserts the longitudinal conclusion that successive co-horts of young workers can be expected to have low job satisfaction relative to older workers because young workers simply are given the unattractive jobs while older workers are given the better jobs. In time the young will grow older and obtain the jobs that give satisfaction.

The lack of longitudinal data also hinders the effort to describe organizational aging, that is, the attitudes and behaviors associated with increasing amounts of time spent with the firm. Studies are needed of organizational cohorts—employ-ees recruited in a certain period of time such as a calendar year. Such studies are rare; however, there is some evidence from one analysis of successive cohorts that as organizational age increases the likelihood of staying with the firm in-creases while the likelihood of a promotion decreases (Rosenbaum, 1979b). However, a persistent failure to get a promotion appears to be an impetus to leave (Equitable Life Assurance Society, unpublished data).

A major longitudinal study by Bray and associates (1974) focuses on two co-horts of Bell System managers of similar chronological age and identical organi-zational age. Although representing a small and select population, Bray's find-ings may have more general significance. For example, in the earlier cohort the managers, regardless of level of success, became more "independent, achieve-ment oriented, unaffiliative, and hostile" over the 20-year period of the study.

Bray recently began studying the second cohort, which had a roughly similar "starting profile" of psychological dimensions as the original cohort. Thus Bray's method could counter the possibility that the longitudinal change he dis-covered typifies only a single and unique cohort. This study could serve as a prototype for future kinds of research relating to aging and organizations.

Similar problems of inappropriate methodology arise in the effort to indicate the salience of job age—the time spent in a particular role. Whereas some evi-dence indicates that tenure increases commitment to a role (Price, 1977), other social scientists are beginning to challenge the idea of the "one life, one career imperative" (Sarasan, 1977). These data, however, are largely anecdotal.

Mobility

In the age stratification paradigm, aging is viewed as a form of mobility. Effortlessly and automatically, the passage of time propels people through suc-cessive age strata—childhood, adulthood, old age—and thus through the roles the social norms have allocated to these strata. Indeed, moving through the ex-pected sequence of roles is how social aging is mainly defined.

Although age advancement—chronological, organizational, and job—is simi-larly inevitable for anyone staying with a work organization, mobility through the role structure is not assured; nonetheless, there is a strong relationship be-tween aging and mobility. The literature available as well as several sources of unpublished data indicate that it is virtually axiomatic that age and the probability of being promoted are inversely related (Rosenbaum, 1979a). In a firm, promo-tions are granted with the greatest frequency to the young and with least fre-quency to the old—both in chronological and organizational age. Several expla-nations have been offered for this phenomenon.

One conventional explanation is that departures from the firm occur at much higher rates among young people occupying the lower ranks than among older employees in the higher ranks of the organization. Opportunities for mobility are therefore made more plentiful for the young for whom these "vacancies" could be a step up. Moreover, managers wanting to increase retention may promote relative newcomers often because of the tendency of young people to leave the firm for a variety of reasons—including the belief that rewards are inadequate. Evidence suggests that those who have been upwardly mobile are less likely to leave their employers than those not promoted (Equitable Life Assurance Soci-ety, unpublished data; Bray, 1979). In contrast, neither vacancies nor threats of departure—because of their rarity—create many mobility opportunities for older workers.

Some analysts explain the age-mobility relationship by the simple observation that most hierarchies are shaped so that there are fewer positions at the top than at the bottom. Therefore, moves are less frequent at or near the top, and since older workers are at higher levels of the organization they would necessarily have fewer mobility chances. The mobility rate by position level is an empirical issue, of course, but some studies indicate that even when promotion rates are higher at high levels of the organization than at low levels, the negative age-mobility rela-tionship still seems to hold (Equitable Life Assurance Society, unpublished data). Moreover, the negative age-mobility relationship seems to hold *at all lev-els* of corporate hierarchies. Hence, the argument based on numbers of positions at various levels, while intuitively satisfying to some, is not adequate.

Still another explanation for the differential frequency of upward mobility be-tween the young and old may reside in the structure of the job hierarchy itself. The distance between two adjacent grade levels could be different at different locations in the grade structure. For example, crossing the boundary from one low-level grade to the next may be a relatively routine matter. The next level job may have little more complexity or responsibility than the one left behind. Higher in the grade hierarchy, however, there may be threshold or barrier grades; that is, there may be some grades for which the qualifications are especially strin-gent and, if met, mean further mobility or, if not met, a stalled career. For exam-ple, the step from grade 19 to 20 could be a matter of great moment for both the individual and the organization. The point is that the increments in power, money, prestige, and promise probably would be greater at the higher reaches of the hierarchy. In this sense, the youth preference in mobility argument is some-what attenuated; for older people, mobility tends to mean more—both to them-selves and to the organization—because it occurs at higher levels.

While neither incorrect nor implausible, none of these explanations provides the basis for a satisfying theory of the relationship between accelerated mobility and youth or, of larger concern here, of the relationship between age and organizations. In the interest of stimulating research, we propose a new conceptualization of the issue that we call the "gap hypothesis." Young people, upon entering a firm, are ordinarily assigned a rank or level far below that which they are expected to attain and even below that in which they might give a good accounting of themselves. The practice is widely in force in work organizations and widely accepted by the new recruits.

There appear to be two major reasons this practice is given such legitimacy. One is that the recruit has not yet had a chance to demonstrate his or her capabilities, however substantial and valuable they may prove to be. Roles with high rewards are not usually given merely because of potential. The other reason is motivational. Recruits see older workers—perhaps with less potential and not fully adequate performances—receiving rewards. Thus, rewards are perceived as available in the future for adequate performance in the present. In addition, veteran workers probably would lose motivation if newcomers were given equivalent rewards without first "putting in the time."

Since the age-based reward deficit is set at the outset, we need to ask: When and how is the gap eradicated so that rewards finally become commensurate with performance regardless of age? The answer is most likely a long time.

The hypothesis here is that the discrepancy between performance and reward is largest at young chronological and organizational ages. Therefore, to prevent the gap from reducing worker motivation, the pace of reward improvement needs to be fastest when the gap is greatest: early in the career. Moreover, since the gap is most obvious at that time, persuading institutional allocators to award a promotion becomes easier as the imbalance of reward and effort clearly justifies redress.

As the gap between earnings (rewards) and contributions narrows with increasing age, promotions become less frequent. For an organizational age cohort of older people, this means not only that a smaller proportion is promoted within a given year, but also that those who are mobile wait longer between promotions because it takes longer for a "gap" to build up. Indeed, some people will have reached a point where they no longer receive any promotions because no discrepancy is perceived between their rewards and their contributions. Others will have a "negative" gap where rewards are perceived as exceeding the contributions made. Sometimes a "negative" gap may be justified or tolerated within the organization as recognition for an essential past contribution or as compensation for past inequitable treatment. This situation where people are promoted to their level of incapacity or incompetence, which probably occurs only occasionally, has been humorously elevated to a general principle by Lawrence Peter (1969) and seriously pursued by several researchers (e.g., Schaefer, Massey, Hermanson, 1980).

The "gap theory" seems a plausible supplement to human capital theory (Mincer, 1974; Becker, 1964), providing an additional set of variables to describe earnings over a life course. The theories are similar in that each makes estimates of the value of human work to organizations (or within labor markets). The extent to which "human capital" calculations are actually made by those allocating rewards, however, is an empirical question. Our sense is that such calculations are not ordinarily made at all; calculations based on the agereward gap, however, are commonplace and often in rather explicit terms. Hence, though the two theoretical approaches are not inconsistent, empirical tests reflecting the "real life" of firms might prove illuminating.

Organizations and the Succession of Cohorts

Work organizations, like other social systems, need a continual replenishment of their ranks in order to survive. Each year (or some other period), therefore, they bring into their boundaries a new cohort of recruits to replace those who have moved up or out or to fill recently created positions. Together the members of this new cohort begin the process of organizational aging-and perhaps in the course of such aging introduce organizational change (Waring, 1976).

The number and characteristics of the people brought into the firm at the same time can have far-reaching consequences. For example, bringing a large and youthful cohort into the organization—nearly all at entry positions—probably means that considerable resources are needed for training, orientation, and socialization. The members of the large cohort may put extraordinary pressure upon the corporation's reward and mobility system as more than the usual number would be seeking next level positions. As a result, new positions may have to be created or the customary age criteria relaxed to ensure that the talented and able members of the cohort will remain with the firm. The interaction of numbers and mobility pressures may also press management to give special attention to early and frequent performance appraisal and other kinds of evaluations—perhaps to skim the cream.

It should be emphasized, however, that having an unduly large and unwieldy employee cohort in a firm need not occur except as a planned response to business needs. Unlike a society which has limited influence on the size of birth cohorts, corporate management can set limits on the number of entrants it admits. Nonetheless, an unanticipated cohort explosion can occur in much the same way a population explosion might occur—by a fall in the rate of attrition, especially in the first years of employment when departure rates are highest. In many ways, it is the size of the cohort in its second year of organizational age that best suggests what its aging patterns and impact on the firm will be.

It should also be noted that the composition of new employee cohorts can vary widely from one year to the next. The diversity of the cohort tends to indicate that many aging patterns will be traced by its members. For example, some cohorts may include large numbers of older people who arrive at the firm with "advanced standing"—those who, in a demographic analogy, are more like migrants than newborns (Waring, 1973). That is, because of previous experience, education, and chronological age, they start at intermediate or high levels in the firm rather than at low-level entry positions. In doing so, they not only have a substantial spread between chronological and organizational age, but can also expect to have mobility patterns and socialization requirements different from others in the cohort. By contrast, there might be large numbers of older women in the cohort who start at the bottom and expect an aging pattern like that of younger women—but possibly not of younger men—in the cohort.

In our discussion, we have alluded to some parallels and interactions of social trends and the internal demography of the organization. A cautionary note, however, is in order. It is fallacious to assume that events or trends found at the societal level are prevalent or even present at the organizational level. An age-related phenomenon occurring in the larger society need not have a counterpart or parallel in the organization. For example, a large influx of young people into the societal labor force might not be paralleled by an increase of young people in a particular organization or set of organizations. Trends occurring at the societal level are likely to be expressed differently and to have different consequences in organizational contexts. Therefore, to understand age-related phenomena within an organization, direct examination of the organization—not deductions from social trends—is necessary.

It seems likely that the study of the experience of single cohorts of employees and of a succession of these cohorts will most enrich our understanding of aging processes within a work organization. To discover how and with what consequences each cohort—as an aggregate and in terms of its subpopulations—fashions career paths, interacts with organizational rules, challenges customary policies, and responds to environmental events could be a major contribution to the theoretical foundations of this area of a discipline.

Aging in an organization is not unlike walking through the cars of a moving train. Individual walkers change position at the same time that the train moves on and changes position in its environment. Nothing will ever be exactly the same again for successive cohorts of newcomers or veterans or seniors or the firm itself. What impact the aging of the firm has on careers or the stratification structure of rewards has only been briefly alluded to here. A body of literature is developing, however, on the demography and aging of organizations themselves. Eventually, the study of organizational aging and human aging within an organization may be integrated (Kimberly and Miles, 1980). This development will enhance our understanding of what age and aging means in the context of a firm.

REFERENCES

Barfield, Richard, and James Morgan 1969. Early Retirement: The Decision and the Experience. Ann Arbor, Mich.: Institute for Social Research, University of Michigan.

Becker, Gary S. 1964. Human Capital: A Theoretical and Empirical Analysis with Special Reference to Education. New York: National Bureau of Economic Research.

Bray, Douglas W., Richard J. Campbell, and Donald L. Grant 1974. Formative Years in Business: A Long-Term AT&T Study of Managerial Lives. New York: Wiley.

Bray, Douglas W., and Ann Howard 1978. "Career success and life satisfaction in middle-aged managers." Paper presented at the Fourth Vermont Conference on the Primary Prevention of Psychopathology, June 23.

————. 1979. "Keeping in touch with success: a midcareer portrait at AT&T." The Wharton Magazine: 28–33.

Cann, Kenneth T., and Joseph J. Cangemi 1971. "Peter's principal principle." Personnel Journal: 872–877.

Chandler, Alfred D., Jr. 1977. The Visible Hand: The Managerial Revolution in American Business. Cambridge and London: Belknap Press of Harvard University Press.

Churchill, Betty C. 1955. "Age and life expectancy of business firms." Survey of Current Business: 15–19.

Davis, Stanley, M. 1979. "Ideas for action: no connection between executive age and corporate performance." Harvard Business Review: 6–8.

Doeringer, Peter B, and Michael J. Piore 1971. Internal Labor Markets and Manpower Analysis. Lexington: Heath Lexington.

Farkas, George 1977. "Cohort, age, and period effects upon the employment of white females: evidence for 1957–1968." Demography 14:33–42.

Freeman, John, and Michael T. Hannan 1975. "Growth and decline processes in organizations." American Sociological Review 40:215–228.

Halaby, Charles N. 1978. "Bureaucratic promotion criteria." Administrative Science Quarterly 23:466–484.

Halaby, Charles N., and Michael E. Sobel 1979. "Mobility effects in the workplace." American Journal of Sociology 85.

Hall, Douglas T. 1976. Careers in Organizations. Santa Monica: Goodyear Series in Management and Organizations.

Jennings, Eugene E. 1976. Routes to the Executive Suite. New York: McGraw-Hill.

Katz, Ralph 1978. "Job longevity as a situational factor in job satisfaction," Administrative Science Quarterly 23:204–223.

Kaufman, Robert L., and Seymour Spilerman (no date). "The age structure of occupations and jobs." Unpublished paper.

Kimberly, John R., Robert H. Miles, and Associates 1980. The Organizational Life Style. San Francisco: Jossey-Bass.

Kohn, Melvin L., and Carmi Schooler 1979. "The reciprocal effects of the substantive complexity of work and intellectual flexibility: a longitudinal assessment." Pp. 47–75 in Matilda White Riley (ed.), Aging from Birth to Death: Interdisciplinary Perspectives. Washington, D.C.: American Association for the Advancement of Science.

Konda, Suresh L., and Shelby Stewman 1980. "An opportunity labor demand model and Markovia labor supply models: comparative tests in an organization." American Sociological Review 45:276–301.

Lenski, G. 1966. Power and Privilege: A Theory of Social Stratification. New York: McGraw-Hill.

March, James G., and Herbert A. Simon 1958. Organizations. New York: Wiley.

Merton, Robert K. 1968. Social Theory and Social Structure. New York: Free Press, MacMillan.

Meyer, Marshall W., and Associates 1978. Environments and Organizations. San Francisco: Jossey-Bass.

Mincer, Jacob 1974. Schooling, Experience and Earnings. New York: National Bureau of Economic Research.

Neugarten, Bernice L., and Gunhild O. Hagestad 1976. "Age and the life course." Pp. 35–55 in Robert H. Binstock and Ethel Shanas (eds.), Handbook of Aging and the Social Sciences. New York: Van Nostrand Reinhold.

Ouchi, William G., and Alfred M. Jaeger 1978. "Type Z organization: stability in the midst of mobility." Academy of Management Review 3:305–314.

Parsons, Talcott, and Gerald M. Platt 1972. "Higher education and changing socialization. Pp. 236–291 in Matilda White Riley, Marilyn Johnson, and Ann Foner (eds.), Aging and Society: Volume III: A Sociology of Age Stratification. New York: Russell Sage Foundation.

Peter, Laurence, and Raymond Hull 1969. The Peter Principle. New York: William Morrow and Co.

Price, James 1977. The Study of Turnover. Ames, Iowa: Iowa State University Press.

Riley, Matilda White (ed.) 1979a. Aging from Birth to Death: Interdisciplinary Perspectives. Washington, D.C.: American Association for the Advancement of Science.

———. 1979b. "Aging, social change and social policy." Aging from Birth to Death: Interdisciplinary Perspectives. Washington, D.C.: American Association for the Advancement of Science.

Riley, Matilda White, Marilyn Johnson, and Anne Foner (eds.) 1972. Aging and Society: Volume III: A Sociology of Age Stratification." New York: Russell Sage Foundation.

Riley, Matilda White, and Joan Waring 1976. "Age and aging." Pp. 355–410 in Robert K. Merton and Robert Nisbet (eds.), Contemporary Social Problems, 4th Edition. New York: Harcourt Brace Jovanovich.

Rosenbaum, James E. 1979a. "Organizational career mobility: promotion chances in a corporation during periods of growth and contraction." American Journal of Sociology 85:21–47.

———. 1979b. "Tournament mobility: career patterns in a corporation." Administrative Science Quarterly 24:220–241.

Rosenblum, Marc 1977. The Next Steps in Combating Age Discrimination in Employment: With Special Reference to Mandatory Retirement Policy. A working paper prepared for use by the Special Committee on Aging, United States Senate, 95th Congress, 1st Session. Washington, D.C.: U.S. Government Printing Office.

Sarason, Seymour B. 1977. Work, Aging and Social Change. New York: Free Press.

Schaefer, Mark E., Fred A. Massey, and Roger H. Hermanson 1980. "The Peter Principle revisited." Across the Board: 3–7.

Schein, Edgar H. 1971. "The individual, the organization and the career: a conceptual scheme." Journal of Applied Behavioral Science 7.

Schrank, Harris T. 1972. "The Work Force." Pp. 160–197 in Matilda White Riley, Marilyn Johnson, and Anne Foner, Aging and Society: Volume III: A Sociology of Age Stratification. New York: Russell Sage Foundation.

Schrank, Harris T., and John W. Riley, Jr. 1976. "Women in work organizations." In Juanita M. Kreps (ed.), Women in the American Economy: A Look to the 1980s. Englewood, N.J.: American Assembly, Columbia University, Prentice-Hall.

———. 1978. "Retirees who don't retire: their contribution to work groups." Paper prepared for the 11th International Congress of Gerontology, Tokyo, Japan, August 20–25.

Schwab, Karen 1974. "Early labor force withdrawal of men: participants and nonparticipants aged 58-63." Pp. 43–56 in Almost 65: Baseline Data from the Retirement History Study. U.S. Department of Health, Education, and Welfare, Social Security Administration, Office of Research and Statistics, Research Report No. 49. Washington, D.C.: U.S. Government Printing Office.

Smith, John M. 1974."Age and occupation." Industrial Gerontology:42–57.

Sofer, Cyril 1979. Men in Mid-Career: A Study of British Man agers and Technical Specialists. London and New York: Cambridge University Press.

Spilerman, Seymour 1977. "Careers, labor market structure, and socioeconomic achievement." American Journal of Sociology 83:551–593.

Staw, Barry M., and Greg R. Oldham 1978. "Reconsidering our dependent variables: a critique and empirical study." Academy of Management Journal 21:539–559.

Stewman, Shelby 1980. "The aging of work organizations: impact on organization and employment practice." Unpublished paper.

Swinyard, Alfred W., and Floyd A. Bond 1980. "Probing opinions: who gets promoted?" Harvard Business Review (Sept.-Oct.): 6–8, 12, 14, 18.

Tuma, Nancy Brandon 1976. "Rewards, resources, and the rate of mobility: a nonstationary multivariate stochastic model." American Sociological Review 41:338–360.

Waring, Joan M. 1973. Some Approaches to the Study of Cohort Flow. Unpublished Master's Essay, New Brunswick, N.J.: Rutgers University.

———. 1976. "Social replenishment and social change: the problem of disordered cohort flow." In Anne Foner (ed.), Age in Society. Beverly Hills: Sage Contemporary Social Science Issues 30.

———. 1978. The Middle Years: A Multidisciplinary View. Summary of the Second Annual Conference on Major Transitions in the Human Life Course, sponsored by the Schweppe Research and Education Fund. New York: Academy for Educational Development.

Wise, David A. 1975. "Academic achievement and job performance." The American Economic Review 65:350–366.

Work in America Institute, Inc. 1980. The Future of Older Workers in America: New Options for an Extended Working Life. Policy Study directed by Jerome M. Rostow and Robert Zager. Scarsdale, N.Y.: Work in America Institute.

Yale Law Journal 1979. "The cost of growing old: business necessity and the Age Discrimination in Employment Act." Yale Law Journal 88:565–595.

5 Work and Retirement in a Changing Society[1]

Anne Foner
Rutgers University
Karen Schwab
Social Security Administration

Retirement from the labor force at age 65 or earlier is a well-established pattern in the United States today. In 1978, only about 20 percent of the men and 8 percent of the women 65 and over were working or looking for work (Bureau of the Census, 1979). According to common stereotypes, however, most workers do not retire willingly. They are instead the victims of mandatory retirement rules and would be eager to return to work if they were given the opportunity. Further, according to stereotypes, retired people are not satisfied with retired life. Some retirees are so unhappy that retirement results in illness and early death.

Although solid research challenges some of these stereotypes and finds others are oversimplifications, unfounded beliefs about retirement die hard. In this paper, we review evidence on some widely held beliefs about retirement, and we explore why myths about retirement persist—even among gerontologists and professional practitioners. We also review studies which suggest that misleading perceptions about the abilities of older workers are common. We propose that one source of unfounded beliefs is the narrow focus of paradigms guiding much work in the field. A more comprehensive approach that recognizes the impact of trends in society and dynamic age-related processes on older people is important for interpreting data about work and retirement of older people today and for developing policies for the future.

[1]In addition to Lenore E. Bixby and Gordon F. Streib, the authors are grateful to John W. Riley, Jr., and Joan Waring for their critical reading of an earlier version of this paper. Many of the guiding ideas for our analysis have grown out of discussions and earlier collaboration with Matilda White Riley. Some of the themes in this paper are further developed in Foner and Schwab (1981).

71

EVIDENCE ON STEREOTYPES OF RETIREMENT

Fortunately, a great deal of research on current cohorts of retirees and those approaching retirement-including two major longitudinal surveys following workers from their preretirement to postretirement years[2] is available to shed light on the retirement process. Our summary of relevant aspects of this research indicates that there is little support for the image of retirement as an affliction imposed on older workers. Let us consider the evidence.

Have most workers been forced to retire because of mandatory retirement rules? The data indicate that most workers do not retire because of rules on mandatory retirement. For one thing, most older workers are not covered by mandatory retirement provisions. According to 1971 data from the Retirement History Study and the National Longitudinal Surveys (referred to as RHS and NLS, respectively), less than half the workers aged 60 to 65 are subject to mandatory retirement regulations (Clark et al., 1979; Parnes and Nestel, 1979).

Even among those covered by mandatory retirement regulations, many retire before the mandatory age. A study of one cohort of white male wage earners aged 62 to 63 in 1969 found, for example, that by 1973 about half of those covered by mandatory retirement rules—about 20 percent of the whole cohort-retired early (Clark et al., 1979). These data, shown in Figure 1, parallel patterns of early retirement among all workers. For several decades, increasing proportions of workers have retired before age 65. As recently as 1970, for example, 75 percent of the males and 36 percent of the females aged 60 to 64 were in the labor force; by 1978 this proportion was reduced to 62 percent and 33 percent, respectively (Bixby, 1976; Department of Labor, 1979).

In addition, many of those who retire at the mandatory retirement age do so willingly. According to reports from male retirees 65 to 69 who had been subject to mandatory retirement (1976 NLS data), 15 percent were forced out by the mandatory plan, 21 percent retired because of poor health, 39 percent retired early, and 25 percent retired at the normal age but had indicated previously they had no desire to work beyond the mandatory age (Parnes and Nestel, 1979). According to these researchers, only about 3 percent of the total retirements in their sample of male workers over the period 1966–76 could be classified as the unwilling victims of mandatory retirement plans.

How eager are retirees to reenter the labor force? Retirees do not appear to be eager to reenter the labor force. Studies carried out in the mid-1970's found that relatively few retirees were either able or wanted to return to the labor force (Harris, 1975; Motley, 1978). The NLS found that in 1976, only 2 percent of the

---

[2]Articles and books reporting on various phases of these surveys cited here are: Bixby, 1976; Clark et al., 1979; Fox, 1976, 1979; Motley, 1978; Quinn, 1978; Schwab, 1976, on the Retirement History Study, and Andrisani, 1977; Chirikos and Nestel, 1979; Parnes, 1979; Parnes and Nestel, 1979, on the National Longitudinal Surveys.

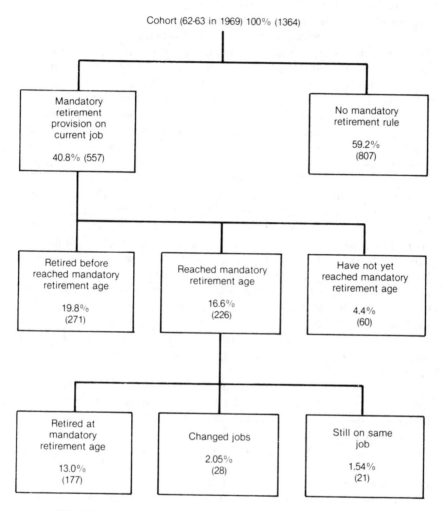

FIG.   5.1   The incidence of mandatory retirement 1969–73 in a cohort of white male wage-earners age 62–63 in 1969. Source: Clark et al., 1979, p. 12. Based on Retirement History Study.

white male retirees and 5 percent of the of the retired black men would accept a job unconditionally; 12 percent of the whites and 13 percent of the blacks would accept a job under certain conditions (Parnes and Nestel, 1979). Even in 1978, when inflation pressures were a concern, a majority (though slim) of retirees in a Louis Harris (1979) survey said they preferred not to work for pay. The salience of economic considerations is demonstrated by the fact that those receiving pension benefits were less likely than those without benefits to say they preferred to work (40 percent vs. 52 percent).

Are most retired people dissatisfied with their lives in retirement? According to most survey data, retired people are satisfied with their lives. When they are dissatisfied, the cause is usually not lack of employment per se. As early as the mid-1950's, Streib and his colleagues found that the vast majority of retired respondents felt that retirement was mostly good for a person (Streib and Schneider, 1971). According to nationwide surveys carried out from 1965 to 1978, no less than 55 percent and as many as 75 percent of the retired respondents expressed some type of positive reaction to retirement—for example, that it had fulfilled their expectations, it was enjoyable, they were glad they retired when they did, these were the best years of their lives, or that they felt good about their lives since retiring (Foner and Schwab, 1981).

Even when retirees are compared with older people still in the labor force or when retirees compare their lives before and after retirement, they appear to be relatively satisfied. Several nationwide studies have found that the morale of retired men and women 65 and over was only slightly lower than that of their employed counterparts once income, age, and health were controlled in the analysis (Jaslow, 1976; Thompson, 1973). Similarly, older people in the labor force were just somewhat more satisfied with their lives than those who had retired, according to another national study, once race, marital status, sex, income, education, and health were held constant (Campbell et al., 1976). As for life before and after retirement, in 1978 two-thirds of the retirees in a national survey said that retired life was the same as or better than working life, with 40 percent saying it was better (Harris, 1979).

Of course, as these data indicate, some retirees are not satisfied with retirement. The two most important correlates of satisfaction with retirement are health and money. Those who perceive themselves to be in poor health and those who do not have adequate incomes are less likely than their healthier and wealthier counterparts to feel positive about retirement. Interview data suggest, however, that the dissatisfaction of those in poor health may not be due primarily to nonwork, but to limitations on activity and the pain they experience. They might be just as happy, if not more so, if they had to work 8 hours a day 5 days a week. Similarly, much of the unhappiness of those with low incomes may be due less to the frustrations of not working than to concerns about maintaining their standard of living and the lack of funds to finance interesting and meaningful activities.

In short, a majority of retirees profess to be satisfied with life in retirement, but a minority, especially those who are ill or who have low incomes, do not have the personal and economic resources to lead the good life in retirement.

Does retirement lead to ill health and premature death? There is no unequivocal answer to the question of the effect of retirement on health. Rates of illness not only increase with age, but retirees' health is poorer than that of the their age peers in the labor force. Early studies, however, indicated that retirement in itself did not appear to have a direct effect on health or longevity (Riley and Foner, 1968).

One reason for the relatively poor health of retirees compared with older people in the labor force is the tendency of persons who report illness or work limitations to elect to retire as soon as possible. Studies consistently report that both planning for early retirement and the actual event of retirement are strongly related to the individual's perception of poor health (Barfield and Morgan, 1970; Parnes and Nestel, 1979; Schwab, 1976). To be sure, poor health may not be the only reason for retiring early; assurance of an adequate income, one the one hand, and unpleasant job conditions, on the other, are also considerations (Quinn, 1978).

If poor health is a factor motivating some people to retire, it is important to consider whether poor health is the key factor in their early retirement. Some people retiring early—particularly those imbued with a strong work ethic—may exaggerate health conditions as a more legitimate reason for leaving the work force than simply not wanting to work any longer. Available survey data suggest that health status *is* poorer among early retirees than among their employed age peers. In addition, small studies indicate that there is a correlation between perceived health and physicians' ratings; in some cases, the perceptions are more positive than the physicians' ratings (Riley and Foner, 1968). Further, male Social Security beneficiaries aged 58 to 63 who had chosen early retirement were more likely than their age peers in the labor force to have visited a physician or to have been hospitalized in the year preceding the interviews, according to an RHS analysis (Schwab, 1976). Similarly, men aged 45 to 59 in the NLS sample who reported work limitations in 1966 were more likely to have died by 1971 than their healthier counterparts (Andrisani, 1977). Analysis by NLS researchers of interviews conducted in 1976 showed a correlation between self-reported work limitations and an index of impairment based on such items as ability to walk up and down stairs, lift heavy or light objects, and hear without difficulty (Chirikos and Nestel, 1979).

Much work on the relationship between retirement and health remains to be done. On the basis of available evidence, a case can be made that the link between poor health and retirement is more in the direction of health status as an influence on the decision to retire rather than a physical decline when individuals are removed from the labor force.

EXPLAINING THE PERSISTENCE OF MYTHS:
GUIDING PARADIGMS

In the light of such consistent findings, what sustains negative views of retirement? For one thing, important works in gerontology, developmental psychology, and sociology have called attention to potential and real difficulties in the retirement process. The mass media as well as many physicians and other professionals in the field have tended to dwell on these problems and disregard factors that offset transition difficulties. Certainly, there are problematic aspects to retirement, and we discuss some of the critical problems below. But, we will argue, a one-sided emphasis on the troublesome aspects of retirement is inadequate for a full understanding of retirement and the retirement process.

An important assumption about life transitions at any point in the life course is that such transitions will be accompanied by stress, especially if they entail major changes in the person's life. The evidence indicates that many types of changes can effect mental and physical functioning. Events as joyous as the birth of a child or a promotion in a job or as sad as the death of a family member or the loss of a job have been found to be related to a variety of physical and psychological malfunctions (Liem and Liem, 1978).

The transition to retirement is thought to be beset by special problems. The shift to retirement is fairly abrupt (Morgan, 1980), and the retirement role is markedly different from the work role. At the same time, mechanisms that might reduce the trauma of such discontinuities are typically absent. Few employers are flexible enough to permit employees to ease into retirement gradually, and only a small percentage of today's older workers are self-employed and therefore able to set their own pace. Only limited opportunities are available to prepare for the retirement role. Very few companies offer preretirement counseling that goes beyond discussions of financial matters such as pensions, Social Security, and insurance (O'Meara, 1977). The mass media do not provide many positive images upon which a "retirement self" can be patterned. Moreover, the content of the retirement role lacks clear definition. Is retirement simply an extension of leisure time—a week full of Saturdays, so to speak? Does a person begin some new style of living? Is it a time for fulfilling secret ambitions? And how do others expect the retiree to behave?

Perhaps even more important, retirement, unlike many other life-course transitions, involves losses-of income, esteem, and for many, the power attached to their former work roles. Consider the financial status of retirees. Based on their relatively low incomes alone, we might expect retirees to be dissatisfied with retirement. Whether retirees compare their financial condition with that of their age peers, with younger adults in the labor force, or with their own situation before retirement, they are, on the average, relatively deprived. For example, in 1972, among men aged 61 to 66 and their wives, 20 percent of those who had retired since 1968 had annual incomes of $10,000 or more compared with 51 percent of those who were still employed. Those who retired before 1968 were even less likely to have annual incomes of this size (Fox, 1976). Further, couples retiring in 1973-74 had retirement incomes of roughly 55 percent of their preretirement earnings, on the average (Fox, 1979).

Of course, a minority of retirees have relatively high incomes. The incomes of some 10 percent of Social Security beneficiaries, however, are so low that they require public assistance of some sort, usually Supplemental Security Income (Grad and Foster, 1979). Recipients of Supplementary Security Income are disproportionately female, black, widowed, and less well-educated than their peers (Sherman, 1979).

Given these negative features of the transition to retirement and of the retirement role itself—lack of opportunities for anticipatory socialization, of positive public role models, and of clear role definitions and the relative deprivations of retirees—it is not surprising that retirement is assumed to be a time of stress and discontent. Yet, as we have shown, increasing numbers of workers have been choosing to retire before age 65, few retirees seem eager to return to the labor force, and most are reasonably content with their lives in retirement. In short, there seems to be a gap between theory and fact.

TOWARD A BROADER THEORETICAL
PERSPECTIVE

We suggest that the paradox just noted is more apparent than real. Assumptions about the deleterious consequences of retirement emphasize only certain aspects of the retirement process; they do not take into account society-wide changes and age-related processes that affect retirees and the retirement role. In the first place, societal "inputs" in the past decade have helped to make retirement a rewarding rather than an unhappy experience. Second, mechanisms associated with aging and the unique background of current cohorts of retirees have operated to mitigate difficulties that have materialized.

The Changing Social Context

Retirees do not react to change in their lives at retirement in isolation from the social and economic context in which retirement occurs; they are affected by the climate of opinion in the society and by the economic, political, and social environment. True, decisions are made by individuals, but calculations of costs and benefits and attitudes regarding work and leisure are developed within a field of influence that is itself continuously changing. And, in general, the social environment has become increasingly favorable to retirees.

Attitudes

Since the 1950's, attitudes toward retirement have changed dramatically as workers have increasingly come to define retirement as a right earned after a lifetime of employment. In a 1950 study of steelworkers aged 55 and over, for example, over half felt that retirement was only for the physically impaired; by 1960, less than 25 percent of older workers in the same company agreed with that assessment (Ash, 1966). The proportions defining retirement as a well-earned rest or reward rose commensurately.

Positive orientations to retirement—as reflected in the proportions of people saying they looked forward to retirement—have also increased. According to a recent Harris survey (1979), the percentage of adult employees who personally looked forward to retirement rose from 43 percent to 54 percent between 1974 and 1978. In 1978, among those aged 50 to 64 for whom retirement was imminent, almost two-thirds said they looked forward to retirement (Harris, 1979).

Economic Resources

A crucial factor in retirees' positive reactions to retirement is the ability to maintain a comfortable standard of living. As recently as 1978, 46 percent of a national sample of retirees said their present income provided them with an adequate standard of living; another 12 percent said it was more than adequate (Harris, 1979). An adequate standard of living among retirees—at least until recent periods of double-digit inflation—can be attributed to demographic and economic trends in the past several decades. The period of economic growth following World War II, despite spells of instability, facilitated the expansion of the Social Security system, which provides the foundation of economic support for most retirees. As employment grew and wages increased, so did Social Security revenues. In addition, the number of people of working age increased, thereby widening the tax base for Social Security funds. With growing revenues, Social Security coverage was broadened and benefits raised. As of 1980, about 90 percent of all workers were covered by Social Security, and benefits were indexed to the inflation rate. Further, private pension coverage was also enlarged.

In addition to these income-maintenance supports, a host of other programs enhance the economic position of retirees. Perhaps most important, Medicare has lifted the threat of crushing medical costs, although more than one-third of all health-related expenses are still borne by the older patient. At local, State, and Federal levels, tax burdens have been eased for older people: Property tax relief is provided to older homeowners, home sellers over age 55 can exclude the first $100,000 realized from the sale of their residence from capital gains liability, older people are relieved of the tax on prescriptions, Social Security benefits are exempt from income taxes, and a double personal exemption for Federal taxes is allowed (Schulz, 1976). Discounts for transportation, entertainment, and shopping are common, and many municipalities provide subsidized transportation, recreation, and meals. The sharp drop in income with retirement is to some extent offset by these programs and by reductions in work-related outlays, although health costs generally rise in old age.

Perhaps as important as the manifest income-maintenance function of Government programs is their latent function in legitimating retirement. There can be little question that the existence of a wide-ranging system of direct benefits constitutes an imprimatur of respectability—if not encouragement—of the retirement role. In the 1970's and early 1980's, public opinion was strongly in favor of the right to retire and the responsibility of the Government to provide adequate resources (Harris, 1975; Hart, 1980).

Social Supports

A number of other societal factors enhance the attraction of retirement. Most obviously, the sheer increase in numbers of retired people makes adjustment to the role easier. The more people who do anything, the greater the pressures to define that behavior as normal. At the interpersonal level, of course, there will be more status peers with whom to interact—for pure sociability and for the creation of norms.

As the number of retired persons has grown, so has a "retirement industry." Products and services oriented toward this market are increasingly common. Especially active are builders of retirement housing, travel services, and promoters of leisure pursuits. Locally, beauty parlors, movie houses, pharmacies, and restaurants offer discounts to this specialized clientele, usually during hours when working people do not patronize the facilities.

Another type of senior citizen industry is organizational. There are mass membership organizations such as the National Retired Teachers Association and American Association of Retired Persons (NRTA-AARP), which had a combined dues-paying membership in 1979 of over 11 million persons aged 55 and over. NRTA-AARP provides information through its journal *Modern Maturity,* a discount mail order prescription service, vacation discounts, tax assistance, group tours, and various types of insurance policies for the elderly.

At the local level, clubs and centers for the elderly are quite common today. In addition, Government-sponsored programs—Foster Grandparents, Senior Companions, Retired Senior Volunteer Program (RSVP), the Service Corps of Retired Executives (SCORE), Volunteers in Service to America (VISTA), and the Peace Corps-provide retirees with opportunities to serve others. In sum, a network of formal and informal groups is available to those retired persons who are willing and able to participate. To date, only a minority of old people participate regularly. The percentage of attendees at special clubs for older people, however, has doubled, from about 10 percent in the 1960's (Riley and Foner, 1968) to almost 20 percent in the mid-1970's (Harris, 1975).

Over the past two decades, then, major changes have occurred in the social context of retirement. Increased acceptance of the role, defining retirement as a right, and the presence of other retirees have made the transition less difficult for today's workers than was the case in the recent past. An array of supports—material and social—have been constructed to make retirement a relatively attractive alternative to working. Of course, this situation is subject to change. Given the importance of a favorable economic climate for positive feelings about retirement, continued inflation and recession could alter retirees' reactions. Further, we do not mean to imply that retirement has ceased to be problematic for some, even in the best of times; instead, we suggest that there are age-related dynamic processes that affect the way an individual deals with those problems that do arise.

Dynamic Age-Related Processes: Aging Over the Life Course

The biological, psychological, and social processes that affect aging and coping ability over the life course are interdependent. Changes along any dimension interact with and influence the others. Growing older—and the transition to retirement in particular—involves losses. But individuals are not only acted *upon* by social forces; they respond to and deal with their life situations. The old person, no less than the child or adult, is an active interpreter and coper, although the manner in which problems are dealt with is likely to vary by age. In other words, aging may promote particular ways of coping with loss.

Lowered Expectations

Although the evidence is not in, it may be that the elderly, especially the very old, tend to lower their expectations and limit their goals compared with their own earlier standards. For example, Campbell, Converse, and Rodgers (1976) found that "satisfaction" is not always equated with "happiness"; among their older respondents, high levels of satisfaction were combined with relatively low levels of happiness, suggesting lowered expectations in old age. The aged may be "satisfied" because they do not have very high hopes. Many old people are content to be alive (in Maurice Chevalier's famous quip, being very old "is OK, when you consider the alternative"). Some feel that surviving to old age is a noteworthy accomplishment in itself.

Actually, adjustment to declining capacities and role loss typically begins before retirement. Most workers will be resigned to accomplishing less than they might have hoped (there is only so much room at the top); parents will have launched their offspring, the probability of death will have been faced through the purchase of a cemetery plot and the writing of a will, and small accommodations made to flagging energy, changed appearance, memory lapses, unaccustomed aches, etc.—not that all such changes are inevitable, but that they can seem reasonable.

Redefinition of Rewards

To the sociologist, "rewards" refer to three types of scarce resources in a society: wealth or material goods, prestige (respect from others), and power (the ability to impose one's will upon others). In retirement, certain tradeoffs apparently are made; that is, other social "goods" are reevaluated in terms of what is available. Leisure becomes as important as, and perhaps more important than, money, at least beyond the subsistence level. Freedom and release from onerous obligations give retirees a sense of power over their own lives, rather than the power over others that they may have exercised in their former roles. Many if not most newly retired persons welcome the opportunity to slow down (Atchley, 1976; Riley and Foner, 1968; Streib and Schneider, 1971). Among retirees in the 1978 Harris survey who indicated that retirement was preferable to working, almost half mentioned freedom from scheduling, and another 37 percent mentioned being able to take it easy and not having to push or worry (Harris, 1979).

In this regard, it is well to remember that many jobs are not intrinsically satisfying; they do not enhance feelings of self-worth, encourage autonomy, or permit the exercise of independent judgment. Many jobs—in factories, mines, and some types of institutions—are actually harmful. The proportion of workers expressing satisfaction with their jobs decreases as the occupational prestige level declines (Andrisani, 1977). Dissatisfied workers are also among those most likely to retire early. Conversely, professionals and managers-individuals with high levels of autonomy in intrinsically satisfying employment—are less likely to retire early, even though, presumably, they have the financial resources to do so (Bixby, 1976).

Thus, especially for those with unpleasant employment, retirement can be a rewarding experience for what it does *not* entail. Failure to appreciate this factor may be a result of the relatively privileged positions of those who write about retirement—reporters, professors, and physicians, for example, all of whom have some degree of control over the pace and direction of their work. Indeed, generalizations about work and retirement on the basis of such work experiences may have contributed to myths about retirement.

Strain Toward Continuity

A third technique for actively coping with the changes caused by retirement is to minimize the extent of lifestyle changes by maintaining familiar patterns of activity in spheres other than work. Data from RHS permit comparison of activity levels in persons before and after retirement (respondents were 64 to 69 when interviewed in 1975). Unfortunately, the information on activities in 1970 is retrospective, because respondents were asked in 1975 how their current activity compared with 5 years before. Comparisons between the two times and between retired and still-working respondents are presented in Table 1.

Clearly, most respondents perceived that their activity levels remained stable over the 5 years, although some retirees report a reduction in certain activities. It is possible that income and health constraints account for many such changes in activity levels. All in all, there is little evidence in these data that retired people put added energy and time into activities that might substitute for work, but neither is there support for the disengagement thesis among these relatively young retirees. Continuity and stability appear to be the dominant tendencies.

TABLE 1
Five-Year Changes in Activities Among One Cohort
of Retired and Employed Persons
Aged 64–69 in 1975

	Frequency with Which Engaged in Each Activity in 1975 and 5 Years Previously (Self-Reports in 1975)							
	Retired Between 1971 and 1975 Interviews				Worked at the Time of the 1971 and 1975 interviews			
	Same %	Less %	More %	Total %	Same %	Less %	More %	Total %
Watches television	84	3	13	2,999*	89	4	7	2,403*
Gets together with neighbors	60	21	19		70	19	11	
Gets together with relatives	62	19	19		71	17	12	
Reads books, magazines, or newspapers	89	6	5		93	4	3	
Works on hobbies	62	10	27		77	10	13	
Works on home maintenance or small repairs around house	63	16	20		78	12	11	
Goes outside	95	4	1		98	1	1	
Goes for walk	66	15	19	2,982†	83	9	7	2,398†
Participates in sports or exercise	80	12	7		86	11	4	
Goes to club meetings or other organizational activity	70	20	10		79	15	6	
Goes to restaurant	56	34	10		73	16	10	
Goes to church or temple services	80	14	5		87	10	4	
Goes to grocery store	79	9	12		86	7	8	
Goes to concert, play, movie, sports events, or opera	72	21	7		77	17	5	
Does volunteer work	83	8	8		87	8	5	
Takes trip lasting longer than one day	71	18	11		78	15	7	

*Actual number reporting on each item varies slightly since small number of individuals did not report on each item.

†Interviewers were instructed to skip this and the following items if the respondent was obviously unable to walk. Slight variations on each item with nonreporting.

SOURCE: Unpublished data from Retirement History Study, Social Security Administration.

To summarize, certain processes associated with growing older can reduce the stress of status transition and contribute to well-being in retirement. These include lowering expectations, reevaluating what is rewarding, and maintaining activities and relationships over which the person can exercise some control.

Dynamic Age-Related Processes: Cohort Succession

Not only are reactions to retirement—indeed, any life-course transition—influenced by social forces prevailing at the time when transitions are made, but

retirees' reactions are affected by their collective histories and the social, economic, and political environment in which they grew up and grew older. Since
the physical and social environment varies over time, no two cohorts have exactly the same life experiences, nor are they socialized to the same values, beliefs, and expectations. Because no two cohorts age in exactly the same way,
there is no one "natural" reaction to retirement. It seems likely that the unique
backgrounds of current cohorts of retirees have contributed to their adjustment to
the retirement role.

Table 2 presents data on selected characteristics of three birth cohorts: those
born in 1870, none of whom is still alive; those born in 1900, who were about 65
to 75 at the time of the research reported here; and those born in 1930. The bulk
of current retirees were born around the turn of the century and in the period
before World War I. Large numbers were born abroad, many spent their earliest
years in rural areas, and a good number experienced the death of a parent before
they were 15. Only about one-fourth graduated from high school or went on to
higher education.

We can only speculate about the effects of this type of background on their
attitudes toward retirement, since there are few data on basic orientations of these

TABLE 2
Demographic Perspective on Three Cohorts

Cohort characteristics	Cohorts of		
	1870	1900	1930
Select childhood characteristics			
Percent rural when 5–9	78	59	51
Percent distribution by number of siblings			
0–1	6	14	29
2–3	14	25	34
4+	80	61	37
Percent with parent who died before child reached age 15	27	22	11
Percent distribution by number of school years completed			
less than 8	44	28	8
8 - H.S. 3	42	45	25
H.S. 4+	14	27	67
Select adult characteristics			
Percent rural when age 25–29	47	37	28
Percent distribution of males by occupation when age 35–39			
white collar	NA	31	44
blue collar	NA	52	53
farm	NA	17	3

SOURCE: Adapted from Uhlenberg, P., Demographic Change and Problems of the Aged, pp.
153–165 in *Aging from Birth to Death,* edited by M.W. Riley. Published for the American Association for the Advancement of Science by Westview Press, 1979. Copyright 1979 by the American
Association for the Advancement of Science. Reprinted by permission.

cohorts or on how such dispositions are related to responses to retirement. It is not farfetched, however, to suggest that people who spent their childhood in settings where traditional values were important, who were familiar with death in the family at early ages, and who have limited educational attainments might be encouraged to accept whatever happens to them as fate or God's will or somehow inevitable. Hence, they tend to become resigned to those deprivations that seem unavoidable and to be satisfied with what they have.

Given the different backgrounds of future cohorts of retirees—markedly better educated, more likely to have had jobs offering autonomy and opportunities to exercise judgment, and more likely to have spent their formative years in an urban environment, to name a few important characteristics—their retirement attitudes and behavior will undoubtedly differ from those found among today's retirees, a point to which we will return later.

So far our focus has been on retirement. We turn now to review evidence about the competence of older workers, a topic that is not only of intrinsic interest, but also has important implications for patterns of retirement.

EVIDENCE ON STEREOTYPES OF OLDER WORKERS

Just as there are stereotypes about retirement, the capabilities of older workers are subject to misleading assumptions. Table 3, for example, from the 1974 Harris survey of the general public, illustrates differences between the way younger respondents perceive the abilities of old people and the way the elderly perceive themselves. Qualities associated with work performance-getting things done, adaptability, brightness, and physical activity—are generally not associated with the elderly by younger respondents. Yet when also asked whether "older people can continue to perform as well on the job as they did when they were younger," 59 percent of those 18 to 64 answered "yes." Nevertheless, two-fifths thought the contrary (Harris, 1975).

Personnel officers are similarly dubious regarding the abilities of older workers (Harris, 1975). Since personnel officers are often the gatekeepers of employment opportunities, it seems logical to suspect that some older workers have been denied promotions, new jobs, or chances to remain at their current jobs because of such opinions. Several studies of employers' hiring practices (carried out before the Age Discrimination in Employment Act) suggest that belief in a worker's inability to meet the physical or educational requirements of a job accounted for many failures to hire an older worker (Wirtz, 1965; Sheppard, 1976). Despite legislation enacted since these studies were done, stereotypes about older workers' abilities may still influence personnel practices.

At best, these beliefs are only half-truths; at worst, they have little basis in fact. Misinterpretations of data have contributed to the plausability of these beliefs. To be sure, studies have shown that, on the average, older people do not

TABLE 3
Perceptions of Older Persons Held by the Public,
Self-Image of Persons 65 and Over,
and Self-Image of Persons 18 to 64 Years of Age

	Column A Image of "most People Over 65" held by persons 18–64 %	Column B Self-Image of People 65 and Over %	Difference between A and B %	Column C Self-Image of Persons 18–64 %	Difference between B and C %
Very good at getting things done	35	55	−20	60	+ 5
Very open minded and adaptable	19	63	−44	67	+ 4
Very bright and alert	29	68	−39	73	+ 5
Very physically active	41	48	− 7	65	+17
Very wise from experience	66	69	− 3	54	−15
Very friendly and warm	82	72	+10	63	− 9

SOURCE: Adapted from Harris, 1975.

perform as well as younger people on tests of strength, intellectual functioning, and speed of response. However, much of this research is based on cross-sectional observations comparing *different* people—young and old—at one particular time (for a review of relevant cross-sectional studies, see Botwinick, 1973; Barton et al., 1975; Welford, 1977). As Riley (1973) has shown, it is misleading to make inferences about aging processes from such data. Available longitudinal studies that follow the *same* individuals over a period of time do *not* find universal and inevitable declines with aging. For example, longitudinal evidence does not support inferences from cross-sectional data that intellectual functioning peaks in the twenties and declines thereafter (Riley and Foner, 1968; Schaie, 1979; Barton et al., 1975). Rather, measured intelligence, on the average, is maintained at least up to age 60 or so, while studies of different kinds of intellectual abilities suggest that reliable decrements on all abilities do not appear until the eighth decade. Longitudinal analyses of several cohorts indicate that cross-sectional differences in intelligence are in good part due to cohort differences in educational attainment. For example, older people's lower educational attainments or their inexperience in taking tests compared with younger cohorts are thought to affect the performance of the elderly on IQ tests (Baltes and Schaie, 1974; Schaie, 1979). Similarly, age differences in strength that have been observed at one time may partly reflect cohort differences in height and weight and the particular nutrition patterns or other relevant experiences of the several cohorts.

It should be noted that even in cross-sectional studies there are great individual differences among older people, with some old people outperforming some young people; frequently, observed age differences are not great. Unless a direct relationship can be shown between a given task and the particular abilities of a specific older worker, the blanket exculsion of older employees is unjustified on the basis of the best evidence available today.

The ultimate question, then, is: What effect do age differences in abilities and capacities have on the productivity and creativity of older workers? Again, the data are primarily from cross-sectional research, and the subjects, drawn from the minority of older workers who are still in the labor force, are likely to be healthier and possibly more competent than older people who have retired. Depending upon the specific tasks involved, declines in productivity by age vary from nonsignificant to slight. Even when experience is held constant—greater experience having been cited as a factor in older people's ability to do the job—older workers' performance continues to approximate that of younger workers (Walker, 1964; Bureau of Labor Statistics, 1960; Canadian Department of Labor, 1959; Schwab and Heneman III, 1977).

As for creativity, creative output among scholars, scientists, artists, and composers who lived to advanced ages continued into old age in some fields and declined moderately in others. In all fields, people have performed a considerable part of their total creative work in their older years (Dennis, 1966). Examples include Bach, Haydn, Stravinsky, O'Keeffe, Picasso, Freud, and G. Stanley Hall, to name a few.

Perhaps it is not accidental that beliefs about older people's incompetence have been compatible with trends towards mass retirement. Such beliefs facilitate employer decisions about who shall stay and who shall go, rationalizing the extrusion of older workers from the labor force where they can be replaced by somewhat less costly, younger employees. The stereotypes also accord well with interests of younger workers. In turn, those older workers who have internalized the stereotypes may be more accepting of retirement.

A renewed emphasis on the authentic capabilities of older workers—and such an emphasis seems to be emerging—could benefit those older workers who are reluctant to retire. On the other hand, it might also lead to exaggerated claims supporting the retention of employees whether or not they wish to remain at work.

WORK AND RETIREMENT IN THE FUTURE

Failure to consider the impact of social forces and age-related dynamic processes has helped to perpetuate misleading conceptions of the meaning of retirement and the responses of retirees to this relatively new phase in the life course. This failure has also contributed to incorrect assumptions about the capabilities of older workers. Those who fashion retirement policies for the future or who need to predict individual reactions, then, will have to look carefully at both societal changes and personal characteristics of potential retirees if they are to construct viable policies. An enormous range of societal changes can affect work and retirement in the future—changes in levels of employment, productivity, and prices and changes in occupational structure, political climate, and foreign relations, to name a few. Here we will focus on demographic changes—on the societal level—and just a few of the changing characteristics of members of new cohorts—on the personal level—as such developments begin to suggest problems policymakers will have to deal with.

Demographic Change and Social Policy

In looking to the future of work and retirement of older people, changes in the age structure of the population are critical. The age structure of the population—the proportion of young, middle-aged, and old in the population—affects the worker-to-retiree ratio, a rough estimate of the number of retirees who have to be supported directly and indirectly by each worker. As the number of workers to retirees declines, the financial burden of each worker increases.

What, then, is the future worker-to-retiree ratio likely to be? The number of older people in the first quarter of the next century can be predicted with some confidence, since they are alive now. Of particular interest is the impact of the Baby Boom cohorts, who will be reaching age 60 and starting to retire about three decades from now. These extra large cohorts, born from 1946 to about 1960, were followed by relatively small cohorts. If future birth rates continue to be low-most demographers do not expect another baby boom-there will be relatively small cohorts of workers to support the Baby Boom cohorts in retirement.

The relationship between fertility levels, the age structure of the population, and the worker-to-retiree ratio is illustrated in Table 4, which looks still farther into the future, at the midpoint of the next century. Table 4 shows three different projections of the age structure of the population in the year 2050 based on three alternative sets of assumptions about birth and mortality rates. Whichever estimates are used, these projections indicate that future workerto-retiree ratios will be lower than they are today.

Indeed, one need not look ahead to 2050; the high old-age dependency ratios shown in Table 4 could emerge as early as the 2020's. Note, incidentally, that the *total* dependency ratio does not change greatly; it combines *both* old and young. What does change is the composition of the dependency group—a smaller proportion of children and a higher proportion of old people.

Clearly, such changes will create problems in financing the retirements of older people in the years ahead. Spurred by inflationary pressures that have increased pension expenditures, policymakers have already turned their attention

TABLE 4

Age Structure of the Population and Dependency Ratios in 1979 and 2050
Under Three Sets of Economic and Demographic Assumptions

		2050		
	1979	Alternative I	Alternative II	Alternative III
Ultimate fertility (average number of babies born per woman, projected)		2.5	2.1	1.5
Percent of population aged:				
Under 20	32%	32%	26%	16%
20–64	57%	54%	54%	51%
65 and over	11%	15%	20%	33%
Aged dependency ratio*	.194	.270	.370	.644
Total dependency ratio*	.763	.858	.847	.962
Number of working age people for each aged person	5.15	3.71	2.70	1.55

*The total dependency ratio is based on the number of people under age 20 plus the number of people 65 and over divided by the number of people of working age 20 to 64. It provides a rough estimate of the number of people to be supported by people of working age. The age dependency ratio is the population 65 and over as a ratio to the population 20 to 64.

SOURCE: Adapted from Board of Trustees, 1980, p. 94.

to these funding problems. Since the major mechanism by which workers in the United States support retirees is the Social Security system, which uses current tax receipts from self-employed persons and from wage earners and their employers to pay for pension benefits to retirees, much discussion has focused on proposals for maintaining the viability of the Social Security system. Among the major proposals for assuring the strength of the Social Security system are the following: raising payroll taxes, lowering benefits, financing some benefits from general revenues accrued through other taxes, and raising the age at which workers would be entitled to benefits. National surveys conducted in 1978 and 1980 indicated little sentiment for reducing benefits (Harris, 1979; Hart, 1980), nor was there much support for financing Social Security pensions by income taxes or a national sales tax rather than payroll taxes. Most respondents did not favor a proposal for delaying retirement age either (Hart, 1980). However, despite antitax sentiment in the country at the time, when asked to choose between higher payroll taxes and lower retirement benefits in the future, 62 percent of nonretired respondents and 66 percent of the retired respondents chose higher taxes (Hart, 1980).

Whether or not the various proposals for dealing with the financial problems of the Social Security system would be effective, each of the "solutions" could give rise to other problems. Attempts to reduce benefits or even use sales or income taxes to finance pensions would not be popular politically. Although people may be resigned to an increase in payroll taxes, there is likely to be a limit on the size of a tax increase that would be politically acceptable. Further, higher payroll taxes could place an unwelcome burden on low-income workers, and such tax increases might induce employers to scale down private pension plans. Delaying retirement age is likely to frustrate workers who looked forward to retiring at age 65 or earlier and those who are unable to work beyond age 62. (According to Hart's 1980 survey, only about one-fifth of a cross-section of the adult population in the United States felt that later retirement was appealing.) A later retirement age could affect firms that want to hire younger and more recently educated workers, and it might limit job openings and delay promotions for young and middle-aged workers. Indeed, such a solution might generate a good deal of hostility between young and old workers.

Whatever course is taken, the decision to retire and the nature of retirement will be affected, regardless of other economic and political changes. As the nature and timing of retirement change, societal attitudes toward retirement, business practices, and younger people's work patterns and work histories are all likely to be affected.

Changes in the Characteristics of Retirees

As indicated in Table 2, retirees of the future will differ from those currently retired along a number of dimensions: place of birth, education, rural-urban residence, occupation, family size, and experience of death in family. Given better nutrition and health practices, it is possible that the health of future retirees will be improved, at least among those under age 75. Increasing numbers of retirees will be women who qualify for pension benefits on their own work records. At this date, over half of all working-age women are in the labor force, and most have full-time jobs in employment covered by Social Security (Bureau of the Census, 1979). In addition, higher proportions of retirees in coming years will be over 75 compared with today's retirees. The proportion of the population 65 and over that is 75 and older increased from 31.5 percent in 1950 to 37.8 percent in 1980, and it is expected to increase to 43.2 percent by 2010 (Johnston, 1981).

In addition to these personal characteristics, future cohorts of retirees will have shared a unique history. The "me" generation of the 1970's will become the retirees of the early 21st century. Many have had experience with political dissent. They spent their youth and early adulthood in a period of an expanding economy. They have observed a steady increase in social welfare entitlements. In short, they were socialized to expect more—material *and* personal fulfillment.

Considering such backgrounds as well as the changing societal context, societal attitudes and the reactions of retirees today may not be an accurate guide to the way future cohorts of older people and the wider society will deal with and react to work and retirement of older people.

IMPLICATIONS

Studying and predicting the future is always a precarious enterprise. Although it may not be possible to predict exactly how incoming cohorts of retirees and society will respond to changing circumstances, there are some safe general conclusions. The retirement process involves a reciprocal interaction between societal conditions and individual responses, each changing the context in which further action takes place. For example, the decision for early retirement was made singularly by thousands of older workers. These separate choices constituted a trend that eventually put additional strains on pension systems, thus contributing to an unfavorable climate for those who would prefer to retire early in the years ahead. Society-wide changes such as expanded coverage and benefits under Social Security, the spread of private pensions, and more favorable attitudes toward retirement encouraged today's older cohorts to look forward to retirement as a reward for hard work. Yet for many, continued inflation threatens their enjoyment of retired life. In short, individual and societal agendas do not always agree.

Given the uncertainties of the future and the often unexpected consequences of societal programs, it is crucial to have an accurate and continuous mapping of new developments in both individual and societal actions and reactions, building on existing studies and devising new and better research methods. There are predictable changes that already suggest new issues and dilemmas. Constant monitoring of such trends and of individual and societal responses can lead to deeper understanding and can alert policymakers to emerging problems. Indicators of social change must be complemented by continuing longitudinal studies of successive cohorts of aging individuals.

Trends in women's work patterns provide an example. We know all too little about women retirees today, since many studies have focused only on male retirees and workers. The increase in women's participation in the labor force raises new questions. Will the retirement process be the same for men and women? How will husbands and wives, both of whom have had a lifetime of work, reach a consensus on their retirement plans? Will the pressure be toward retiring at the same time? If so, will having relatively high lifetime family earnings encourage wives—typically younger than their husbands-to retire early? Will husbands remain at work because wives want to continue employment? Or will it be wives who continue to work after husbands retire or die? How will widowed retirees—most likely to be women, since women typically outlive men—face retirement without a spouse?

The retired population of the future will also be an older population than that of 1980. Yet the longitudinal data at hand, excellent as they are, have focused on the transition to retirement and on the immediate consequences of retirement. But what of the consequences of prolonged retirement? How will retirees in their eighties and nineties deal with mounting physical disabilities? How will older retirees—especially women, who have had lower average earnings than men, who are less likely than men to be covered by private pensions, and who are more likely to have no spouse—manage with low incomes? How will older retirees deal with the long-term separation from mainstream institutions of the society? Will lack of stimulation affect their intellectual functioning?

Demographic changes noted previously will not only affect the funding of older people's retirement, but will also have an impact on the social environment of future retirees. Low birth rates mean that the family support system of older people in the future will be smaller than in the past. Rising divorce rates will produce a number of unmarried retirees (primarily female). It appears that many old people will be unable to count on the emotional support and services of offspring and spouse, necessitating the expansion of social services to the unmarried and childless. Will sufficient social resources be available to provide such services, and will there be a willingness to use these resources for older people? Indeed, will the political and economic climate permit the maintenance of existing social welfare programs at present levels?

Even the apparent advantages of new cohorts of retirees may create dilemmas. Cohorts in the future will be more educated and better prepared for retirement, yet they may find that the rules have changed in the direction of encouraging *continued* labor force participation, delaying or displacing their retirement plans. Rather than experiencing an expanding world of leisure activities, opportunities for enjoyment of nonwork could be curtailed. Ironically, people who followed the advice of experts and made the most careful long-term plans may be the most frustrated with these unexpected obstacles. When they do retire, will people who are relatively well-educated and healthy and who have a sense of personal and political efficacy be resigned to losses associated with retirement? Will self-help groups flourish among the retired, as they have among other groups of people sharing a common problem? Will these future retirees engage in organized political action to further their interests?

If increasing numbers of older workers delay retirement, how will the relationship between young and older workers be affected? Can measures be devised that might utilize the skills of older workers without penalizing younger workers? For example, how viable is job sharing between older, experienced workers and younger female or male workers with major childrearing responsibilities?

Another issue concerns the population growth in the Sunbelt areas and the population loss in many large cities in the Northeast. Older people tend to have lower residential mobility rates than younger people. Will older people maintain these patterns? If so, what will be the consequences for older people living in the older cities and suburbs and for these areas themselves? Alternatively, is the slogan "Go West, Old People" a realistic or desirable policy?

All such questions, and many that are now unforeseen, will have to be addressed against the background of larger dilemmas facing the society, such as problems of economic growth, issues of social justice, or potential shortages of natural resources. And the way older people themselves deal with all these developments will play a role in shaping the future of work and retirement.

REFERENCES

Andrisani, Paul 1977. "Effects of health problems on the work experience of middle-aged men." Industrial Gerontology 4:97–112.

Ash, Philip 1966. "Pre-retirement counseling." The Gerontologist 6:97–99.

Atchley, Robert C. 1976. The Sociology of Retirement. New York: Halsted/Wiley.

Baltes, Paul B., and K. Warner Schaie 1974. "Aging and IQ: the myth of the twilight years." Psychology Today 7:35–40.

Barfield, Richard E., and James N. Morgan 1970. Early Retirement: The Decision and the Experience and a Second Look. Ann Arbor, Mich.: Institute for Social Research, University of Michigan.

Barton, Elizabeth M., Judy K. Plemons, Sherry L. Willis, and Paul B. Baltes 1975. "Recent findings on adult and gerontological intelligence: changing a stereo type of decline." American Behavioral Scientist 19:224–236.

Bixby, Lenore E. 1976. "Retirement patterns in the United States: research and policy interaction." Social Security Bulletin 39:3–19.

Board of Trustees 1980. 1980 Annual Report of the Board of Trustees of the Federal Old-age and Survivors Insurance and Disability Insurance Trust Funds. Washington, D.C.: U.S. Government Printing Office.

Botwinick, Jack 1973. Aging and Behavior. New York: Springer.

Bureau of the Census 1979. Statistical Abstract of the United States. Washington, D.C.: U.S. Government Printing Office.

Bureau of Labor 1979. Special Labor Force Reports, No. 218.

Bureau of Labor Statistics 1960. Comparative Job Performance by Age: Office Workers. Bulletin No. 1273.

Campbell, Angus, Philip E. Converse, and Williard L. Rodgers 1976. The Quality of American Life. New York: Russell Sage Foundation.

Canadian Department of Labor, Economics and Research Branch 1959. Age and Performance in Retail Trade. Ottawa: The Queen's Printer and Controller of Stationery.

Chirikos, Thomas N., and Gilbert Nestel 1979. "Impairment and labor market outcomes: a cross-sectional and longitudinal analysis." Pp. 89–166 in H.S. Parnes, G. Nestel, T.N. Chirikos, T.N. Daymont, F.L. Mott, D.O. Parsons and Associates, From the Middle to the Later Years: Longitudinal Studies of the Preretirement and Postretirement Experiences of Men. Columbus, Ohio: Center for Human Resources, Ohio State University.

Clark, Robert L., David T. Barker, and R. Steven Cantrell 1979. Outlawing Age Discrimination: Economic and Institutional Responses to the Elimination of Mandatory Retirement. Final Report for Administration on Aging Grant No. 90-A-1738. Mimeo.

Dennis, Wayne 1966. "Creative productivity between the ages of 20 and 80 years." Journal of Gerontology 21:1–8.

Foner, Anne, and Karen Schwab 1981. Aging and Retirement. Monterey, Calif.: Brooks/Cole.

Fox, Alan 1976. "Work status and income change, 1968–72: Retirement History Study preview." Social Security Bulletin 39:14–30.

———. 1979. "Earnings replacement rates of retired couples: findings from the Retirement History Study." Social Security Bulletin 42:17–39.

Grad, Susan, and Karen Foster 1979. Income of the Population 55 and Older, 1976. Staff Paper No. 35. U.S. Department of Health, Education, and Welfare, Social Security Administration, Office of Policy/Office of Research and Statistics.

Harris, Louis, and Associates 1975. The Myth and Reality of Aging in America. Washington, D.C.: National Council on the Aging.

———. 1979. 1979 Study of American Attitudes Toward Pensions and Retirement: A Nationwide Survey of Employees, Retirees and Business Leaders. New York: Johnson and Higgins.

Hart, Peter D., Research Associates 1980. A Nationwide Survey of Attitudes Toward Social Security. A report prepared for the National Commission on Social Security. Mimeo.

Jaslow, Philip 1976. "Employment, retirement, and morale among older women." Journal of Gerontology 31:212–218.

Johnston, Denis F. 1981. "Social indicators of aging." Paper presented at the Annual Meeting of the American Association for the Advancement of Science. Toronto.

Liem, Ramsay, and Joan Liem 1978. "Social class and mental illness reconsidered: the role of economic stress and social support." Journal of Health and Social Behavior 19:139–156.

Morgan, James N. 1980. "Retirement in prospect and retrospect." Pp. 73–105 in Greg J. Duncan and James N. Morgan (eds.), Five Thousand American Families—Patterns of Economic Progress. Ann Arbor, Mich.: Institute of Social Research, University of Michigan.

Motley, Dena K. 1978. "Availability of retired persons for work: findings from the Retirement History Study." Social Security Bulletin 41:1–12.

O'Meara, J. Roger 1977. Retirement: Reward or Rejection? New York: The Conference Board.

Parnes, Herbert S. 1979. "Summary and conclusions." Pp. 257–269 in H.S. Parnes, G. Nestel, T.N. Chirikos, T.N. Daymont, F.L. Mott, D.O. Parsons and Associates, From the Middle to the Later Years: Longitudinal Studies of the Preretirement and Postretirement Experiences of Men. Columbus, Ohio: Center for Human Resources, Ohio State University.

Parnes, Herbert S., and Gilbert Nestel 1979. "The retirement experience." Pp. 167–255 in H.S. Parnes, G. Nestel, T.H. Chirikos, T.N. Daymont, F.L. Mott, D.O. Parsons and Associates, From the Middle to the Later Years: Longitudinal Studies of the Preretirement and Postretirement Experiences of Men. Columbus, Ohio: Center for Human Resources, Ohio State University.

Quinn, Joseph F. 1978. The Early Retirement Decision: Evidence from the 1969 Retirement History Study. U.S. Department of Health, Education and Welfare, Social Security Administration, Office of Research and Statistics, Staff Paper No. 29. Washington, D.C.: U.S. Government Printing Office.

Riley, Matilda White 1973. "Aging and cohort succession: interpretations and misinterpretations." Public Opinion Quarterly 37:35–49.

Riley, Matilda White, and Ann Foner 1968. Aging and Society, Volume I: An inventory of Research Findings. New York: Russell Sage Foundation.

Schaie, K. Warner 1979. "The primary mental abilities in adulthood: an exploration in the development of psychometric intelligence." Pp. 68–115 in R.H. Binstock, E. Shanas and Associates (eds.), Handbook of Aging and the Social Sciences. New York: Van Nostrand Reinhold.

Schulz, James H. 1976. "Income Distribution and the Aging." Pp. 561–591 in Robert H. Binstock, Ethel Shanas, and Associates, (eds.), Handbook of Aging and the Social Sciences, New York: Van Nostrand and Reinhold.

Schwab, Donald P., and Herbert G. Heneman III. 1977. "Effects of age and experience on productivity." Industrial Gerontology 4:113–117.

Schwab, Karen 1976. "Early labor force withdrawal of men: participants and non-participants aged 58–63." Pp. 43–56 in Almost 65: Baseline Data from the Retirement History Study. U.S. Department of Health, Education and Welfare, Social Security Administration, Office of Research and Statistics, Research Report No. 49. Washington, D.C.: U.S. Government Printing Office.

Sheppard, Harold L. 1976. "Work and retirement." Pp. 286–309 in Robert H. Binstock, Ethel Shanas, and Associates (eds.), Handbook of Aging and the Social Sciences. New York: Van Nostrand Reinhold.

Sherman, Sally R. 1979. "Comparision of aged OASDI and SSI recipients, 1974." Social Security Bulletin 42:40–44.

Streib, Gordon, and J. Clement Schneider 1971. Retirement in American Society: Impact and Process. Ithaca, N.Y: Cornell University Press.

Thompson, Gayle B. 1973. "Work versus leisure roles: an investigation of morale among employed and retired men." Journal of Gerontology 28:399–344.

Uhlenberg, Peter 1979. "Demographic change and problems of the aged." Pp. 153–166 in Matilda W. Riley (ed.), Aging from Birth to Death. Boulder, Colo.: Westview Press.

Walker, James 1964. "The job performance of federal mail sorters by age." Monthly Labor Review 87:296–301.

Welford, A.T. 1977. "Motor performance." Pp. 450–496 in J. Birren and K.W. Schaie (eds.), Handbook of the Psychology of Aging. New York: Van Nostrand Reinhold.

Wirtz, W. Willard 1965. The Older American Worker: Age Discrimination in Employment I and II (Report of the Secretary of Labor). Washington, D.C.: U.S. Government Printing Office.

6 Recent Trends in the Geographical Distribution of the Elderly Population[1]

Tim B. Heaton
Brigham Young University

One of the most significant demographic changes of the 20th century in the United States has been the resurgence of the population in small towns and rural areas. The 1970's were characterized by new patterns of population deconcentration to smaller places, to nonmetropolitan areas, and to the South. Compared with past trends, the shift toward nonmetropolitan residence is greater than either the shift to smaller places or regional shifts, with regional shifts being the smallest of the three (Heaton and Fuguitt, 1980).

These shifts in population distribution have sparked increased interest in the spatial distribution of the elderly population. The growth in the number of elderly persons, coupled with changes in their residential locations, has apparently played an important part in these redistribution trends. Older people are responding as well as contributing to the turnaround in the longterm trend toward urbanization. In fact, the movement of elderly people to nonmetropolitan areas, beginning in the 1950's, preceded the general trend, which did not appear until after 1970.

Although this turnaround phenomenon is extremely complex (both the data and analysis are highly technical), the significance of changes in population redistribution for the elderly can scarcely be questioned. The well-being and qual-

---

[1]In addition to Karl E. Tauber, the author is grateful to William Clifford, Glenn Fuguitt, Bill Heaton, and Dan Lichter for their critical reading of an earlier version of this essay. A portion of the analysis cited herein is part of an ongoing project involving Glenn Fuguitt, William Clifford, Dan Lichter, and the author, and has been supported by the Economic Development Division, Economic Research Service, U.S. Department of Agriculture, and by the College of Agriculture and Life Sciences, University of Wisconsin, Madison, through cooperative agreement. The author remains solely responsible for any errors in the text.

ity of life of older people reflect the communities in which they live, and the meaning of "home" is especially poignant for people in their later years.

On the other hand, this shift from the cities to smaller places and nonmetropolitan areas should not be exaggerated. Old people are not predominantly isolated in semirural towns. In 1980, approximately 11.5 percent of metropolitan central city residents were 65 or older, as were about 8.5 percent of residents in metropolitan suburbs, compared with 12.6 percent in nonmetropolitan areas. Mapping the location of the elderly reveals comparatively heavy concentrations in nonmetropolitan sections of the Midwest and Great Plains, in peninsular Florida, in the northern Midwest, and in Appalachia. Scattered counties with high concentrations also appear along the eastern seaboard and in the West (Graff and Wiseman, 1978). These patterns, however, are continuously being modified by population redistribution.

Table 1 summarizes some of the recent trends in the geographical redistribution of the elderly population. The first four columns show that the general rise since 1950 in the proportion of the population who are aged 65 and over appears in every category. The three columns at the right demonstrate the turnaround in migration. Since 1950, the large metropolitan "core" areas have consistently experienced a net outmigration of the elderly, and the trend has been most pronounced during the past decade. By contrast, the small metropolitan areas (with

TABLE 1
Percentage of Elderly and Net Migration by Metropolitan Status: 1950–1980*

Type of County	Percentage Age 65+				Net Migration (000) of Persons Age 65+		
	1950	1960	1970	1980*	1950–60	1960–70	1970–80*
SMSA**	7.8	8.8	9.2	10.5	47	−91	−172
1,000,000+:core	8.0	9.4	10.1	11.5	−198	−364	−604
1,000,000+:fringe	7.6	7.5	7.5	8.5	131	111	65
<1,000,000	7.7	8.5	9.1	10.6	115	163	387
Nonmetropolitan†	8.7	10.4	11.5	12.6	−109	159	454
Adjacent to SMSA	9.0	10.5	11.3	12.4	−28	112	280
Nonadjacent:							
Largest place 10,000+	8.2	9.4	10.3	11.5	−4	13	69
Largest place <10,000	8.7	11.1	12.8	14.0	−77	33	106

*Numbers are adjusted to estimate change between 1970 and 1980 based on annualized rates of net migration for the 1970–75 period.

**Standard Metropolitan Statistical Area, defined by the Census Bureau generally as a county or group of counties containing at least one city (or twin cities) having a population of 50,000 or more plus adjacent counties which are metropolitan in character and are economically and socially integrated with the central city.

†Places not included as part of SMSA's. Includes small cities and towns as well as rural areas.

SOURCE: Lichter et al., 1981.

fewer than 1 million inhabitants) have gained substantial numbers of older people over the same period. Nonmetropolitan areas have experienced even greater gains in the numbers of elderly inmigrants, especially in those areas adjacent to the large metropolitan centers.

This paper reviews some of the recent literature on residential patterns among the elderly. It also suggests some ways in which existing research might be extended to provide a more adequate understanding of the processes that determine where the elderly live and the consequences of these processes. Three major topics will be considered: 1) What are the demographic dynamics of change in the relative size of the elderly population in particular geographical areas? 2) How well do existing models of migration fit the elderly population? and 3) What are the consequences for the individuals and communities involved?

DEMOGRAPHIC PROCESSES AND THE SPATIAL DISTRIBUTION OF THE ELDERLY

What accounts for the spatial variation in age structure? In principle, the age structure of a closed population (a population unaffected by migration) is a function of patterns of fertility and mortality. Changes in this age structure result from changes in fertility and mortality in conjunction with the inevitable aging-in-place of the existing population. When a spatial dimension is added to the analysis, migration also becomes an important determinant of age structure.[2]

This section describes these underlying demographic processes. It outlines some actual studies and quantitative approaches, and concludes with the emphasis on migration as the major determinant of spatial variation in age structure.

Some Analyses of Recent Trends

In their analysis of the changing distribution of older persons, Graff and Wiseman (1978) describe the way in which these components can operate. Aging-in-place, in combination with outmigration of young cohorts, produces high percentages of older persons in the nonmetropolitan Midwest and Great Plains. A similar outmigration of youth leaves an older, agingin-place population in central cities. In contrast, elderly inmigration accounts for concentrations of elderly in peninsular Florida. Yet another pattern is observed in many Northeast-

---

[2]It is important to note how the relative importance of these components varies according to the size of the geographical units utilized. As smaller geographic subunits are taken into consideration, more residential moves are counted, and the relative importance of migration increases. This empirical generalization must be remembered when we compare the relative magnitude of components of change in the age structure, since the outcome of our comparison will depend, in part, on the geographical units being considered.

ern and Western States, where inmigration of younger cohorts has produced a decline in the proportion of elderly people.

The dynamics of these components of change are evident in the historical development of the United States (Graff and Wiseman, 1978). Initial settlement by younger migrants is followed by aging-in-place, and increases in the percentage of elderly lag behind growth by several decades. This aging-in-place is inevitably followed by dying-in-place. In the past, aging-in-place and young migration have been the dominant components of change. In the future, however, aging-inplace and dying-in-place will be of major importance, while migration of the elderly will become more salient.

In a similar vein, Golant (1979) has noted that growth of the aged in central cities has slowed recently because of extensive suburban migration of younger families in earlier decades. This suburbanization has depleted the size of the group left behind that is now aging-in-place. Correspondingly, there is now a large suburban cohort aging-in-place, which, along with sharp declines in fertility, is leading to a higher percentage of older people in the suburbs. In a comparison of young and elderly migration, he shows that the patterns of migration are similar, although elderly migrants appear to have more of a preference for nonmetropolitan areas than for suburbs and central cities when compared with younger migrants. Because the size of the elderly migration stream is small, however, the migration flows of elderly people are unlikely to influence substantially the future shifts in their metropolitan-nonmetropolitan distributions.[3]

Components of Change

Some researchers have attempted to quantify these components of change, going beyond simple recognition to their existence. Golant et al. (1978) partitioned change in the size of the cohort aged 55 and over in central cities into net migration, death, and annexation. (Annexation does not entail actual relocation of persons and consequently will be ignored in this paper.) Between 1960 and 1970, only the smallest central cities (under 50,000) had net migration gains of white persons aged 55 and over. In cities over 50,000, the larger the central city the greater was the net white migration loss. For older nonwhites, however, the larger the central city, the greater the net gain in population from migration. For whites and nonwhites alike, the net migration component was dwarfed by the death component, which varied little across regions or sizes of central cities. The

---

[3]As a cautionary note, Golant (1979) makes an erroneous statement that in the 1970–75 period, nonmetropolitan areas became younger. The source for this error appears to be an incorrect usage of denominators. The number of nonmetropolitan elderly in 1970 is based on a report using the 1960 nonmetropolitan classification, whereas the denominator or total population in 1970 is based on a report using the 1970 nonmetropolitan classification. Since many counties were reclassified as metropolitan in the 1960's, his percentage of elderly in 1970 is inflated, and as a result he misstates the direction of change in the 1970-75 period.

magnitude of the death component is, perhaps, a little deceptive, since the elderly population is continually replenished by aging-in-place of younger cohorts.

Taking a different approach, VanEs and Bowling (1979) predict a change in the elderly over two successive decades on the basis of net migration of a young cohort (aged 15 to 19 at the beginning of the decade) and measures of urbanization, economic conditions, and initial size of the elderly population. In the Illinois counties studied, net inmigration of the young had a strong negative association with aging, while elderly migration had a small positive effect in one decade and a small negative effect in the other. A negative association between elderly migration and aging of the population seems counterintuitive. Perhaps inclusion of the entire age distribution in the migration rates would yield more consistent results. In any event, this study documents the importance of young migration and, in fact, shows that young migration has a substantially larger impact on population aging than elderly migration. Moreover, the study notes that a reversal in migration trends may have resulted in a change in the parameters for particular variables, a point which will be developed later.

Yet another approach is taken by Stahura (1980) in an analysis of the aging of suburban populations. Change in the ratio of the elderly population (65 and over) to children (0 to 15) is separated into change in the proportion of aged and change in the proportion of children. Of the two, change in the aged is found to have by far the largest effect on the aged-to-child ratio. But the reader is left wondering what roles migration and aging of the local population play in the observed aging of suburbs. As with the preceding approaches, this study, while providing new insights, presents an incomplete picture of the processes that generate variance in the age structure among different geographical areas.

The most complete and detailed analysis to date derives two components of change in the absolute size of the elderly population: 1) natural increase (includes deaths and aging-in-place) and net migration among the elderly, and 2) four additive components of change in the relative size of the elderly population. These four components are the natural increase among the elderly, net migration among the elderly, natural increase (includes births, deaths, and aging-in-place) among the young, and net migration among the young (Fuguitt, 1980). Analysis of change in these components for counties at various levels of urbanization over the period 1950–75 demonstrates the rather complex demographic processes that affect the age structure (Lichter et al., 1981). There has been an increase in the contribution of net migration to the growth of the elderly population in nonmetropolitan counties and small Standard Metropolitan Statistical Areas (see Table 1 for definition), a reversal in the previous movement toward metropolitan areas for the young and old alike, and a slowing of growth of the elderly population in remote nonmetropolitan areas. This analysis agrees with earlier findings that the demographic components of the young exercise an important effect on the rate of increase in the elderly proportion. Although the natural increase components of change in the relative size of the elderly population tend to be larger than the migration components within each type of county, the migration components exhibit greater variance across types of counties than do natural increase components.[4]

Demographic Dynamics of the Aging Process

The complex details of such studies may be simplified by a more formal demographic analysis. Formal analysis has shown that regardless of the initial age structure, fixed mortality and fertility schedules will generate a fixed age structure (i.e., the proportion in each age group remains constant over time) in a matter of a few generations (Coale, 1957). Extending this logic to the spatial dimension, if the fertility and mortality schedules are fixed and remain constant from one area to the next, then each area will eventually attain the same age structure, given that no migration occurs. In such a system, the combination of births, deaths, and aging creates spatial units that are homogeneous with respect to age structure. Differences in fertility, mortality, and migration are the only factors that can create spatial variance in the age structure, and therefore, any existing spatial variance is a product of the history of these demographic processes.

In low fertility and low mortality societies such as the United States, migration is the major process of population redistribution (Goldstein, 1975). In such societies, much of the spatial variation in age structure may be due to migration. Because spatial differences in fertility and mortality are not large enough to generate extreme differences in age composition, migration can be thought of as a disturbance that creates spatial differences in age structure. Fertility, mortality, and aging act, albeit slowly, to reestablish spatial homogeneity. In such a society, the impact of any migration that occurs during one time interval will eventually be erased by other demographic processes. The effects of elderly migration are particularly short lived. In the short term, areas of outmigration will have fewer deaths in subsequent years because there are fewer older people. In contrast, areas of inmigration will have more deaths because of increases in the number older people. Once the migrant cohort dies off, however, spatial balance is restored, assuming no additional migration occurs.

The consequences of younger migration are more complex. Initially, areas experiencing young outmigration are left with an older age structure, and destination areas get a younger population. But as the migrant cohort ages, these patterns reverse. The areas of outmigration will, at a later date, become younger than they were before the migration occurred because of a small cohort entering old age. The opposite will be true of inmigration areas. Eventually, however, mortality will reestablish spatial homogeneity. Thus, young migration creates somewhat of a "pendulum" effect as areas of outmigration shift from old to young and then back to normal and areas of inmigration shift from young to old

---

[4]As was noted earlier, a finer distinction between types of counties would yield even greater variance in the migration components.

and back to normal. These processes become more complex if births to migrants are taken into account. Aging of migrants' children at the destination and the death of children at the origin create an echo effect, but this too will eventually dissipate.

If a migration pattern is to have a long-lasting effect on the age structure, then the migration must persist over long periods of time. Indeed, recent evidence of rural-urban differences in aging suggests that the effects of historically salient migration trends are already being eroded. In the past, the movement of young families to the suburbs has been a major factor in the aging of central cities, but since the 1950's, the gap in percentage increases of elderly persons between large central cities and their surburbs has narrowed substantially (Lichter et al., 1981). In addition, although the exodus of young people from nonmetropolitan areas continues but at a slower pace (Tucker, 1976), nonmetropolitan areas, especially the remote rural counties, are not aging to the same degree that they were in the 1950's (Lichter et al., 1981). Evidence reported by Beale (1969) also indicates a homogenizing trend. Areas that have experienced outmigration in the past had an excess of deaths over births in the 1960's because of the distorted age structures resulting from selective young outmigration.

The exact contributions of spatial variation in fertility, mortality, and migration to spatial variation in age structure remain to be demonstrated. This demonstration would require data covering longer periods of time than have been reported in the preceding research. Nevertheless, the evidence considered here suggests that migration has played a greater role than either fertility or mortality and that migration will play an even greater role in the future.

MODELS OF MIGRATION

Migration of both young and old can affect spatial variation in the proportion of elderly. In fact, an analysis of U.S. counties for 1950–60, 1960–70, and 1970–75 indicates that young migration, rather than elderly migration, accounts for the larger share of between-county variance in the percentage change in the elderly population. This is not surprising when we consider that the young are much more mobile than the old. Uhlenberg (1973) suggests that explanations of why people do not move may be at least as appropriate as explaining why they do move. This is especially true in a discussion of the elderly because their mobility rates are much lower than rates for the rest of the population.

Why Don't Old People Move?

Many authors have questioned the relevance of economic theory for explaining elderly migration. Economic cost-benefit models of migration, however, offer some insights into why the elderly do not move. The cost of moving is likely to be greater for older people. Over time, they have probably invested more in housing and other material possessions that must be moved, sold, or otherwise disposed of. Moreover, they have had longer to develop social ties and patterns of interaction that might bind them to their place of residence. They have also had longer to find the type of community in which they feel comfortable. In economic terms, they have had longer to accrue location-specific capital which acts as a deterrent to migration (DaVanzo, 1982).

On the benefit side of the economic equation, the elderly may have less to gain from migration. For those who have withdrawn from the labor force, no income returns can be expected to result from migration. Even for those who work, the expected time period over which gains are acquired is much shorter than for younger migrants, thus minimizing the cumulative expected gain from migration. In fact, employment at older ages is a deterrent to migration (Chevan and Fischer, 1979; Goldstein, 1976; Barsby and Cox, 1975; Heaton et al., 1980). About the only means available to those on a fixed income to improve their financial situation through moving is to find a destination with a lower cost of living.

These are some reasons why older people are less likely to migrate than younger people. The lack of literature in this area is surprising, however, given the number of articles that focus on elderly migration. The number of questions remaining unanswered represents a serious gap in migration research.

Why Do Old People Move?

Local residential mobility for the elderly is often necessitated by increased dependency or by negative aspects of one's neighborhood or housing (Goldschieder, 1967; Wiseman and Virden, 1977). In such cases, moves are less voluntary than in cases where attractions at the destination motivate the move. Unlike migration between communities, local residential mobility is negatively associated with socioeconomic status among the elderly (Goldscheider, 1966). Thus, the profile of a migrant and theories of migration provide a more positive view of movers than would be the case if we were analyzing purely local residential mobility, which is outside the scope of this discussion.

For reasons cited previously, the elderly are less responsive than younger migrants to formal economic considerations, at least when conceived in terms of getting better jobs or a higher salary. What factors do the elderly respond to? What is the relative importance of these factors? What theories might explain the observed relationships?

A brief survey of the literature indicates that progress is being made along these lines of inquiry. Beale (1977) and Fuguitt and Tordella (1980) indicate that elderly migration is an important fraction of the net inmigration to nonmetropolitan areas. Moreover, Heaton et al. (1980) present evidence that the rate of migration to nonmetropolitan destinations is greater among the retired than among the employed. These findings suggest that characteristics other than employment opportunities are the primary determinants of the recent turnaround of elderly migration into nonmetropolitan areas.

Climate stands out as a variable that is particularly important for the elderly. The movement of retired persons to California, Florida, and Arizona represents the dominant streams of interstate migration (Flynn, 1980). Chevan and Fisher (1979) found that climate is a factor in elderly interstate migration, although it is not as strong an influence as employment status, income, and prior lifetime migration. In an analysis of reasons for interstate moves, Long and Hansen (1979) found that 5.4 percent of the total population—but 12.1 percent of those over age 55—cited climate as the reason for moving. Of those who listed climate as the reason for moving, 39 percent were receiving income from pensions or annuities.

Family-related reasons for moving are also more salient among the elderly than the young. Of those aged 20 to 35, 12.2 percent cited family reasons for moving, compared with 17.6 percent for those over age 55 (Long and Hansen, 1979). Assuming some attachment between the elderly and their kin, it is surprising to find that return migration to the State of birth is just as common among the young as among the old (Serow, 1978; Longino, 1979). A partial explanation for this unexpected finding may lie in the relationships between age, length of time away from the place of birth, and the probability of return migration. The probability of return migration decreases the longer the period of separation (DaVanzo, 1982). If there is also a positive correlation between age and the length of the separation period, the controls for length of separation would strengthen the association between age and probability of return migration. Further analysis is needed of the degree to which the elderly are inclined to return to their place of birth or to a community of earlier residence. Information is also needed on the role of kin and other social networks in the return migration process.

Data on the effects of retirement, climate, and family, as well as other variables, support the notion that the elderly are responsive to amenity or quality of life variables in the decisionmaking process. This is not to say, however, that other considerations are to be excluded from explanations of elderly migration.

The decisionmaking typology developed by Wiseman and Roseman (1979; see also Wiseman, 1980) illustrates the diversity of conditions under which old people move. The types of migration most relevant to this paper are amenity migration, return migration, and kinship migration (Wiseman and Roseman, 1979). According to Wiseman and Roseman (1979:334), amenity migration could result from several triggering mechanisms, including ''environmental stress, lessening importance of suburban and urban living as a middle class ideal, income improvements of retired persons, etc.'' Return migration may be similar in many respects to amenity migration, except for the salience of personal contacts in the selection of a destination. The need for assistance may be the primary motive behind kinship migration, or moving closer to family members.

Each of these types of moves seems consistent with conceptions of aging that emphasize tendencies either to retain activity patterns that have been developed in the past or to maintain familiar patterns of living. Further development of these ideas may lead to an integration of migration decisionmaking theories and more general theories of aging.

A Behavioral Migration Model

For those interested in spatial variation, the decisionmaking models, standing alone, are insufficient to explain which types of communities will grow or decline. Fredrickson (1980) has made an important contribution by suggesting ways in which concepts from a behavioral migration model might be applied at the community level. These concepts seem particularly applicable to elderly migration.

The behavioral model assumes that people will not even consider moving until they become dissatisfied with their place of residence (Speare, 1974). Fredrickson (1980) suggests, as a macro-level analog, that the higher the threshold of dissatisfaction in communities the less the outmigration. In the behavioral model, individuals do not consider all possible alternatives, but cease searching as soon as one alternative is encountered. Correspondingly, communities with an "early discovery profile" (i.e., those communities that are likely to be located early in the search process) have a growth advantage. Finally, when the individual has an alternative in mind, a decision for or against moving is based on a comparison between the alternative and the current residence. Thus communities with a "favorable stereotype content" (i.e., a positive public image) have an advantage over communities that have not acquired such a favorable image.

Contributing to favorable views of nonmetropolitan residence are better transportation, improvements in communications, extension of urban amenities into rural areas, and a rising standard of living, all of which have generally lowered the dissatisfaction threshold in urban areas (Fredrickson, 1980). In conjunction with these transformations, tourism has improved the discovery profile of rural areas and has perpetuated the cultural ideal embodied in bucolic settings, however far removed this ideal may be from the day-to-day realities of country living. Thus we gain some insights into the mechanisms whereby individual decisionmaking might alter the pattern of national settlement.

Analysis of elderly migration to nonmetropolitan areas for 1950–60, 1960–70, and 1970–75 corroborates many of the ideas presented above. Presence of amenity related factors (i.e., mild climate and recreational development) has a much greater impact on elderly migration than do economic variables in each of three time periods considered (Heaton et al., 1981). The influence of these amenity variables has remained fairly stable over time, although a slight upturn has been observed in more recent periods. Moreover, amenity variables have a greater impact on elderly than on young migration, while the reverse is true for economic variables. Nevertheless, the temporal change in migration rates and in regression coefficients associating migration with amenity or economic variables are greater for the young than for the elderly, reminding us that an analysis of change in the relative size of the elderly population is incomplete unless behavior of younger people is also taken into account.

THE CONSEQUENCES OF SPATIAL VARIATION IN AGE STRUCTURES

Migration is generally viewed in a positive light because it is associated with opportunities for upward social mobility and, at the macro-level, because it improves economic efficiency by bringing labor supply and demand into balance. These benefits seem less applicable to elderly migration, and at this point, it is appropriate to consider the positive or negative consequences of spatial redistribution of the elderly.

Consequences for Elderly Migrants

The models of migration discussed above imply that migrants benefit from improved quality of life at their destination. Mild winters, peace and quiet, proximity to kin, etc., make life more pleasant. One might go so far as to substitute quality of life for income or job opportunities in an otherwise unchanged economic costbenefit model. From this optimistic view, migration is the mechanism whereby the elderly maximize their level of satisfaction. This is also plausible when migration is induced by negative characteristics at the place of origin, such as an undesirable neighborhood, death of a spouse, or loss of health. From a rationalistic individual perspective, migrants might still be better off than they would have been by remaining at the place of origin.

At present, this view appears to be based more on assumption than on empirical evidence. Fuguitt (1979) reports that about 65 percent of the migrants, young and old alike, to nonmetropolitan areas in the Upper Great Lakes are very satisfied with their community of destination. None of those over age 50 expressed any dissatisfaction. Of course, about 58 percent of those migrants over 50 were also very satisfied with their previous community. Thus, for many elderly, migration resulted in little or no measured improvement in community satisfaction. More extensive research is needed to confirm this finding.

A less sanguine picture may emerge on the nonmigrant side of the coin. Perhaps many elderly people would like to move, but lack sufficient information or resources to make the move. Indeed, we might infer from the general trend toward a concomitant rise in income and increased migration of the elderly that given the information and resources even more elderly people would move. Again, analysis of elderly migration opens a whole range of research questions that are not accessible through standard economic models with their limited emphasis on wages and employment.

Consequences for Communities

Among the consequences to a community that may result from the aging of a population are a shift in the types of goods and services demanded, a possible increase in conservatism, and less rapid social change (Day, 1978). Whether these changes do indeed occur remains to be studied. At the community level, a host of other consequences may be hypothesized. Since various demographic trends could produce an older population, various social consequences are possible, depending on which trends are prevalent. It is doubtful that the spatial variance in fertility and mortality schedules in the United States will change dramatically in the foreseeable future. Therefore, other than changes resulting from existing differences in the age structures, migration remains as the major mechanism whereby spatial differences in age structure will be altered.

It must be noted that elderly outmigration is much more diffuse than elderly inmigration. Although migrants come from a large number of origins, they select only a few destinations (Flynn, 1980). Thus the impact of migration on places of origin is typically less than the impact on places of destination. Moreover, migration from populous areas to sparsely settled areas will have a greater impact on the place of destination than on the place of origin. If 19,000 people were to move from Chicago to northern Wisconsin, for example, a barely perceptible drop in Chicago's population would create rapid growth in the destination communities.

For those places that do experience substantial elderly outmigration, Murphy (1979) suggests three possible benefits: Housing stock is released for younger occupants, demand for welfare services decreases, and inflationary pressures are marginally reduced. However, these ideas are offered as possibilities rather than as empirical generalizations.

For those places that experience substantial inmigration of elderly, a major concern is the potential increase in demand for medical and welfare services. Provision of services could prove particularly costly on a per capita basis in rural areas. In some communities, inmigrants may have higher expectations than residents or demand different types of services, creating conflicts between migrants and residents (Lee, 1980; Murphy, 1979; Ploch, 1978).

The selective nature of migration, however, may mitigate the potential shortage of services. Elderly migrants appear to be healthier, wealthier, and more independent than nonmigrants. For example, migrants to one retirement community had higher morale than nonmigrants, in part because of their higher social standing (Bultena and Wood, 1969). Also, migrants may select destinations where relatives or friends are available to provide some assistance. More generally, migrants from large cities to nonmetropolitan communities do not necessarily need or want many municipal services (Kasarda, 1980). To provide such services regardless of location may be counterproductive.

In some low-density communities with a poorly developed network of social services, an influx of elderly migrants may help provide a population base sufficient to increase the level of services that can be economically provided to all residents (Kafoglis, 1974). As a possible solution to the problem of balancing human welfare needs with taxpayers' willingness to pay, Amos Hawley (personal communication) has proposed a minimum community size, on the basis of cost efficiency, above which public support could be given for human services such as health institutions, libraries, recreation, etc. Residents would have to choose between larger places with more services or low density settings with fewer services.

Of course, in selecting a destination, migrants may take existing services into consideration. Heaton et al. (1981) found that elderly migration in nonmetropolitan areas is less likely than young migration to favor entirely rural counties as destinations. This suggests that a greater need for health, transportation, and other services that are less accessible in rural areas encourages the elderly to choose a residence accessible to urban services. In many areas of high elderly inmigration, contrary to prior expectations, sufficient health facilities and services are available to meet national health standards (Lee, 1980). Further study is needed to determine whether such positive conclusions can be reached for other services.

Beyond providing services, other aspects of community organization may cause conflicts between migrants and long-term residents. The ideal community may be quite different from the perspective of elderly migrants than from the perspective of other residents. For example, where quality-of-life considerations play heavily in the decision to move, migrants may place more importance on preservation of environmental integrity and less on economic expansion (Ploch, 1978). Tax policy can also be a source of contention. The tax assessor in a rural Utah county that has grown dramatically because of elderly inmigration notes that tax reform is becoming an important and controversial issue (personal communication). In the past, ranchers and farmers with extensive landholdings have benefited from a policy that places most of the property tax burden on residential land. Elderly migrants feel that they pay more than their fair share, but have not yet been successful in altering the existing policy. Differing conceptions of the ideal may also create disagreement over such factors as zoning, highway construction, and rent control. On each of these issues, the elderly migrants do not necessarily stand alone, making it difficult to assess the political influence they wield.

In addition, we know little about the communal economic consequences of elderly inmigration. Although migrants tend to be better off than nonmigrants, the elderly on the average are not as well off as the younger population. Moreover, consumption patterns differ between young and old. Shifts in level of income and consumer preferences undoubtedly generate some change in a community, but the degree of change resulting from growth in the elderly population, especially in communities that are small to begin with, deserves greater attention.

It may seem a mild paradox, but growth due to the enhanced potential for voluntary movement among the elderly may result in increased community dependency. The community's economy may become more vulnerable to national decisions regarding transfer payments to the elderly (e.g., Social Security and Medicare). In addition, because changes in age structure resulting from elderly migration will be short-lived unless the migration trend persists, communities need only wait for the duration of the remaining life span of the most recent migrants until the former age distribution is restored. Thus any community specializing as a residence for the elderly must continue to attract migrants to retain this function. A community reacting quickly to an increased need for elderly services may find itself with an excess of facilities and services if migration does not continue.

One important factor with implications for service needs and economic impact centers on the household composition of migrants. Although the household rather than the individual is the unit of consumption, most studies for methodological reasons have examined individual migrants instead of migrant households. When compared with those who move from metropolitan to nonmetropolitan settings, migrants to metropolitan areas are more likely to end up in dependent living arrangements. In contrast, metropolitan-to-nonmetropolitan migrants are apt to be married with the spouse present (Clifford et al., 1982; Longino, 1980b). It would appear that the greatest service burden is being placed on metropolitan areas, although total family income is also greater for metropolitan inmigrants (Longino, 1980b). More detailed analysis is needed to determine what types of services are utilized by what types of households with what levels of income.

A cautionary note against overgeneralization is required. In an analysis of three types of retirement communities, Longino (1980a) demonstrates the diversity of possible effects and illustrates that the relevance of various issues differs according to type of settlement. The three communities considered by Longino include a subsidized planned community, a nonsubsidized planned community, and a de facto retirement community. Migrants to these areas differ in the distance moved, the motives for moving, the way they were recruited, and the types of support systems they build. Moreover, the derived benefits vary by type of community. His findings indicate that decisionmaking models and macrolevel theories such as those discussed above might explain why different types of communities emerge, as well as provide a framework for assessing the consequences of migration, even in those communities that are aging but are not necessarily "retirement communities."

Population Aging Due to Migration by the Young

Migration of young and old often takes place concurrently. Correlations between the young and old migration components of change in the elderly population range between 0.5 and 0.6 for the 1950's, 1960's, and 1970's and, as a consequence, tend to balance each other. For example, in the 1970–75 period, Florida continued to receive a substantial number of elderly inmigrants, but the percentage of elderly remained stable because young people were also moving in. Nevertheless, most communities with declining populations are aging because the young are more mobile and thus have a greater impact on age structure. This trend has been especially noticeable in central cities and remote rural areas.

Untangling the effects of population aging from the overall consequences of the factors that initially led to outmigration is a formidable task. It may prove more fruitful to view population aging as one aspect of the total process of population decline. This process may have both negative and positive consequences.

One of the most obvious outcomes of young outmigration may be to bring balance to a labor market with labor surplus. This would be of little direct benefit to most of the elderly, who are not in the labor force. For the elderly who do work or would like to work, however, outmigration may facilitate their entrance into the labor force, permit upward mobility, or delay the onset of unemployment, particularly where the elderly are at a disadvantage to begin with. Outmigration may also ease competition in the housing market and permit the elderly to obtain better housing or to obtain the same housing at a lower price. Other benefits may also accrue, but until empirical research can document these benefits, skepticism is called for.

The negative consequences of young outmigration, however, probably outweigh the benefits to the elderly left behind. Outmigration signals a decline in the tax base and a potential rise in the tax rate if public services are to be maintained. If outmigration leads to a drop in the total demand for labor, the availability of goods and services could deteriorate in response to the decline in population (Parr, 1966). To make matters worse, those who leave may be the most educated and capable residents, thus draining the area of valuable human resources. The combination of declines in services, increases in tax rates, and loss of human capital may discourage employment growth and may even cause existing firms to move elsewhere (Parr, 1966). A negative spiral could develop that leaves the area in a depressed state.

Although old people on fixed incomes may remain unaffected by unemployment or declines in the wage rate, they bear the brunt of other negative consequences. Being dependent on local services, they are most affected when services decline or terminate. Any increase in tax rates would prove most difficult for those on a fixed income. Moreover, the elderly may be least able to escape these consequences by moving away, because of their location-specific capital. The irony is that older residents generally have more invested in the local area in terms of total public service given and tax dollars paid. Again, however, it is necessary to point out that these comments are speculative; the shortage of accurate generalizable information is serious. We hope that raising the issues will provide motivation for sound research.

CONCLUSION

The character of the elderly population is continuously being modified by the aging and dying of successive birth cohorts. More recent cohorts of old people are retiring at an earlier age, generally have a higher standard of living, and have greater exposure to the world around them. Each of these characteristics suggest that quality-of-life or amenity-oriented migration will gain importance among the elderly. Moreover, in the 1980's, Baby Boom parents will be entering retirement ages, implying that family-oriented moves will persist, if not increase in importance. This potential for greater mobility, in conjunction with the increasing size of the elderly population, underscores the relevance of research on changing spatial distribution of the population. The sections of this paper have outlined current research on aspects of population redistribution and have suggested directions that additional research might take.

The theme of the first section is that in low fertility and low mortality societies, migration is the major determinant of spatial variation in age structure. Fertility, mortality, and aging act to restore spatial homogeneity once migration has occurred, but these processes take several years. Statistics over long periods of time are needed to quantify the impact migration has had on current variations in age structure. Limited evidence suggests that young migration has a greater effect than elderly migration. Recent trends, however, may be reducing the differential importance of young versus elderly migration. Continued monitoring of these trends should prove useful for projecting future distributions of the elderly population.

Because the formal model of spatial distribution places emphasis on migration as the key demographic process inducing change, development of theories to explain elderly migration has been stressed in the second section of this paper. The insufficiency of narrowly conceptualized economic models has been recognized, and some new approaches being developed have been called to attention. At the micro-level, environmental and socialpsychological dimensions of the decisionmaking process are being taken into account, and analogous theories have been suggested on a macro-level. Further development of these types of theories, along with greater attention to the nature of immobility of the elderly, is recommended.

As discussed in the third section, research assessing the consequences of elderly migration for the migrants themselves and for communities of origin and destination is less well-developed. It is generally assumed that migration is a voluntary act that generally improves the well-being of those involved, but there is insufficient evidence to accept or reject this assumption. Several possible consequences, positive and negative, of migration for places of origin and destination have been suggested. The effects of aging of the population may be felt most strongly in low-density settings, regardless of whether outmigration of young or inmigration of the elderly is the cause of the population aging. A preliminary hypothesis is that extensive young outmigration helps create a depressed community and a deterioration in the status of the elderly, whereas elderly inmigration may give impetus to expansion of services and an improvement in the quality of life.

The fact that recent redistribution trends were largely unanticipated gives cause for concern. The lag between the occurrence of trends and the development of models to explain them is a serious threat to the policy relevance of existing models. Nevertheless, these trends have now been detected and intensively analyzed, leaving room for some optimism. Given that current redistribution trends may not remain stable and that the composition of the elderly population is constantly changing, however, new models must be developed, and research on patterns of population distribution must be continued.

REFERENCES

Barsby, S. L., and D. R. Cox 1975. Interstate Migration of the Elderly, Lexington, Mass.: Lexington Books.

Beale, Calvin L. 1969. "Natural decrease of population: the current and prospective status of an emergent American phenomenon." Demography, 6:91–99.

———. 1977. "The recent shift of United Staes population to nonmetropolitan areas, 1970-75." International Regional Science Review, 2:113–122.

Bultena, Gordon L., and Vivian Wood 1969. "The American retirement community: boon or blessing?" Journal of Gerontology, 24:209–217.

Chevan, Albert, and Lucy Rose Fischer 1979. "Retirement and interstate migration." Social Forces, 57:1365–1380.

Clifford, William B., Tim B. Heaton, and Glenn V. Fuguitt 1982. "Residential mobility and living arrangements among the elderly: changing patterns in metropolitan and nonmetropolitan areas." International Journal of Aging and Human Development. Vo. 14, No. 2, pp. 139–156.

Day, L. H. 1978. "What will a ZPG society be like?" Population Reference Bureau, Population Bulletin 33(3), Washington, D.C.

DeVanzo, Julie 1982. "Repeat migration, information costs, and location-specific capital." Population and Environment: Behavioral and Social Issues.

Flynn, Cynthia B. 1980. "General versus aged interstate migration, 1965–1970." Research on Aging, 2:165–176.

Fredrickson, Carl R. 1980. "Towards new theories of aggregate migration behavior." Paper presented at the annual meetings of the Midwest Sociological Society, Milwaukee, Wis.

Fuguitt, Glenn V., and Stephen J. Tordella 1980. "Elderly net migration: the new trend of nonmetropolitan population change." Research on Aging, 2:191–204.

Fuguitt, Glenn V. 1979 "Trends in the net migration of the aged for the nonmetropolitan United States." Present ed to the Inter-University Training Seminar, Midwest Council for Social Research on Aging, Frisco, Colo.

———. 1980. "Components of change in a proportion." CDE Working Paper 80-9, Center for Demography and Ecology, University of Wisconsin, Madison, Wis.

Golant, Stephen M. 1979. "Central city, suburban and nonmetropolitan area migration patterns of the elderly." In S.M. Golant (ed.), The Location and Environment of Elderly Population. New York: Wiley.

Golant, Stephen M., Gundars Rudzitis, and Sol Daiches 1978. "Migration of the elderly from U.S. central cities." Growth and Change, 9:30–35.

Goldscheider, Calvin 1966. "Intrametropolitan redistribution of the older population." Pacific Sociological Review, 9:79–84.

———. 1967. "Differential residential mobility of the older population." Journal of Gerontology, 21:103–108.

Goldstein, Sidney 1976. "Facets of redistribution: research challenges and opportunities." Demography, 13:423–435.

Graff, Thomas O., and Robert F. Wiseman 1978. "Changing concentrations of older Americans." Geographical Review 68:379-393.

Heaton, Tim B., and Glenn V. Fuguitt 1980. "Dimensions of population redistribution in the U.S. since 1950." Social Science Quarterly.

Heaton, Tim B., William B. Clifford, and Glenn V. Fuguitt 1980. "Changing patterns of retirement migration." Research on Aging, 2:93–104.

———. 1981. "Temporal shifts in the determinants of young and elderly migration in nonmetropolitan areas." Social Forces. Vo. 60, No. 1, September, pp. 41–60.

Kafoglis, Madelyn L. 1974. "Economic aspects of the migration of older people." Pp. 88–96 in Carter C. Osterbind (ed.), Migration, Mobility and Aging. Gainesville: University of Florida Press.

Kasarda, John D. (1980). "The implications of contemporary redistribution trends for national urban policy." Social Science Quarterly.

Lee, Anne S. 1980. "Aged migration: impact on service delivery." Research on Aging, 2:243–254.

Lichter, Daniel T., Glenn V. Fuguitt, Tim B. Heaton, and William B. Clifford 1981. Components of change in the residential concentration of the elderly population: 1950–1975. Journal of Gerontology, Vol. 36, No. 4, pp. 480–489.

Long, Larry H., and Kristin A. Hansen 1979. "Reasons for interstate migration." Population Reports, Series P-23, No. 81.

Longino, Charles F., Jr. 1979. "Going home: aged return migration in the United States, 1965–1970." Journal of Gerontology, 34:736–745.

———. 1980a. "Retirement communities." Pp. 391–418 in F.H. Berghorn and D.E. Shafer (eds.), The Dynamics of Aging: Original Essays on the Experience and Process of Growing Old. Boulder, Colo.: Westview Press.

———. 1980b. "Residential relocation of older people: metropolitan and nonmetropolitan." Research on Aging, 2:205–216.

Murphy, Peter A. 1979. "Migration of the elderly: a review." Town Planning Review, 50:84–93.

Parr, John B. 1966. "Outmigration and the depressed area problem." Land Economics, 42:149–159.

Ploch, Louis A. 1978. "The reversal in migration patterns—some rural development consequences." Rural Sociology, 43:293–303.

Serow, William J. 1978. "Return migration of the elderly in the USA: 1955–60 and 1965–70." Journal of Gerontology, 33:288–295.

Speare, Alden, Jr. 1974. "Residential satisfaction as an intervening variable in residential mobility." Demography, 11:173–188.

Stahura, John M. 1980. "Ecological determinants of the aging of suburban populations." Sociological Quarterly, 21:107–118.

Tucker, C. Jack 1976. "Changing patterns of migration between metropolitan and nonmetropolitan areas of the United States: recent evidence." Demography, 13:435–443.

Uhlenberg, Peter 1973. "Noneconomic determinants of nonmigration: sociological considerations for migration theory." Rural Sociology, 38:296–311.

VanEs, J.C., and Michael Bowling 1979. "A model for analyzing the aging of local populations: Illinois counties between 1950 and 1970." International Journal of Aging and Human Development, 9:377–387.

Wiseman, Robert F. 1980. "Why older people move: theoretical issues." Research on Aging, 2:144–154.

Wiseman, Robert F., and Curtis C. Roseman 1979. "A typology of elderly migration based on the decision-making process." Economic Geography, 55:324–337.

Wiseman, Robert F. and M. Virden 1977. "Spatial and social dimensions of intraurban elderly migration." *Economic Geography* 55:324–337.

7

Minority Aging[1]

Kyriakos S. Markides
University of Texas

The area of ethnic minority aging is one of the most underdeveloped in social gerontology. Only recently have researchers probed beyond cross-group comparisons of sociodemographic variables such as income, education, sex, or life expectancy to explore the crucial questions of whether and how ethnicity and minority status affect the process of aging in the United States. Much of this research has concentrated on aging among blacks and more recently Hispanics (mainly Mexican Americans), with other ethnic groups receiving less attention. To date, this research has largely failed to establish the knowledge base and theoretical sophistication necessary for generating testable hypotheses. As Bengtson (1979:14) notes: "Although we may be convinced—indeed take it as a basic premise—that ethnicity is an important dimension in aging . . . we who are converted have not been particularly convincing to our colleagues, or to policymakers . . . possibly because (we) too often focus on ethnicity per se, rather than ethnic strata within the context of other social stratification dimensions." Careful examination of the literature discloses that many conclusions regarding the existence of ethnic or cultural differences are not based on scientific evidence because many studies either lack appropriate data or perform inappropriate data analyses for establishing the existence of ethnic differences.

This review focuses principally on America's two largest ethnic-minority groups—blacks and Hispanics. Most of the limited knowledge in the area is about these two groups. While the broader concept of ethnicity is not ignored, special emphasis is given to how ethnic *minority status* affects the process of

---

[1]In addition to John Santos, the author is grateful to Dianne Fairbank for her critical reading of an earlier version of this paper.

aging, a theme of much current theory. Thus, the undertaking in this, though set within limits, is nevertheless challenging: to outline the literature on blacks and Hispanics that shows how membership in these ethnic minority groups makes aging any different from the majority experience. Although these two groups have distinct cultural backgrounds and social biographies, they also have some characteristics in common by virtue of their disadvantaged minority status. It is these similarities rather than differences that are emphasized here. To the extent that blacks and Hispanics share certain experiences with other minority groups—such as Asians or Native Americans—much of what is discussed will also be relevant to those groups.

New fields of inquiry typically suffer from lack of theoretical integration—perhaps the most critical problem with the field of minority aging. Theoretical developments in the area of minority aging have largely concentrated on a multiple-hierarchy model of stratification in which ethnic-minority group membership is viewed as an aspect of social inequality along with age, sex, and social class (Bengtson, 1979; Foner, 1979). While some speak of triple and even quadruple jeopardies, as in the case of older minority women, most discussion has centered on the hypothesis of "double jeopardy," or the double disadvantage experienced by aged members of minority groups. A diametrically opposed hypothesis commonly referred to as the "age as leveler" hypothesis predicts a decline with age in the relative disadvantage of minority persons since all older people experience similar deprivations regardless of ethnicity. After these two hypotheses are outlined in the next section, empirical findings of research on blacks and Hispanics are evaluated in terms of whether they lend support to either of the hypotheses. The areas of the literature reviewed are income, health, primary group relations, and psychological well-being.

THEORETICAL DEVELOPMENT

Theoretical developments in social gerontology in recent decades have taken place with little, if any, attention to minority aging. One theoretical perspective relevant to minority aging theory is the sociology of age stratification (Riley et al., 1972; Riley, 1976) in which age is treated as a dimension of social stratification. While not directly an outgrowth of this model, current conceptualizations of minority aging are an extension of the stratification perspective in that race or minority status is viewed as an added dimension of inequality along with age, class, and in some formulations, sex. When several of these factors are considered together, we hear of triple, quadruple, or multiple jeopardies characterizing the aged in ethnic minority groups. Since low class, old age, female sex, and minority status are on the lower side of the stratification system, the bottom of the hierarchy is occupied by low class, older, minority women, and the top is occupied by middle or upper class middle-aged or younger white men. Most discussions, however, limit themselves to describing the situation of minority group elderly as one of "double jeopardy," emphasizing the double disadvantage of old age and minority status.

The double jeopardy hypothesis has its origins in the attempts of certain advocacy groups (National Urban League, 1964; National Council on the Aging, 1972) to highlight the relative disadvantage of aged blacks in such important areas as health, income, housing, and life satisfaction. While the concept of double jeopardy was not intended to be a theoretical postulate around which knowledge on minority aging would be organized, it has become the dominant model in the area of research. And although it has not been adequately formulated, double jeopardy is now commonly used to describe the situation of the aged in other minority groups in addition to blacks (Cantor, 1979; Dowd and Bengtson, 1978; Fujii, 1976) as well as in theoretical discussions on the effect of minority status and ethnicity on the process of aging (Bengtson, 1979; Dowd and Bengtson, 1978; Markson, 1979; Varghese and Medinger, 1979). The concept also figures prominently in discussions of minority aging in the rapidly multiplying textbooks in introductory gerontology (Crandall, 1980; Decker, 1980; Hendricks and Hendricks, 1977; Hess and Markson, 1980; Seltzer et al., 1978).

A serious attempt at formalizing a testable double jeopardy hypothesis was made by Dowd and Bengtson (1978) in their study of middle-aged and older blacks, Mexican Americans, and Anglos (or whites) in Los Angeles. The minority aged are said to bear, in effect, a double burden:

> Like other older people in industrial societies, they experience the devaluation of old age found in most modern societies. . . . Unlike other older people, however, the minority aged must bear the additional economic, social, and psychological burdens of living in a society in which racial equality remains more myth than social policy (Dowd and Bengtson, 1978:427).

Dowd and Bengtson go on to suggest that a situation of double jeopardy could be demonstrated if the disadvantage observed at earlier ages were found to widen in old age[2] for minority persons compared to whites.

The double jeopardy hypothesis thus suggests an interaction effect between two stratification systems-age and minority status. It predicts that aging has greater negative consequences for minority persons than for members of the dominant majority (Ward, 1980). While this hypothesis does not have its roots in a scholarly tradition, it has its intellectual counterpart in the mental health and

---

[2]Dowd and Bengtson recognized that the double jeopardy hypothesis should ideally be tested with longitudinal data so that the effects of aging may be separated from cohort effects. Longitudinal data on minority aging, however, are almost nonexistent. In their study, Dowd and Bengtson relied on cross-sectional data while acknowledging their limitations. Additional studies reviewed here for evidence supporting the double jeopardy hypothesis are based on cross-sectional data. Caution thus will be necessary in attributing differences to the effects of aging.

psychological distress literature: the social stress hypothesis as applied to minority groups (Antunes et al., 1974). Here it is suggested that members of minority groups, in addition to bearing the deprivations associated with low social class, must face the added stresses of discrimination and oppression associated with minority status and are thus expected to exhibit higher levels of psychological distress than members of the dominant majority at the same level of social class. This, too, is a double jeopardy hypothesis in that it predicts an interaction effect between two stratification systems: minority status and social class. Both double jeopardy hypotheses may be subsumed under a larger, multiple-hierarchy stratification model which, in addition to minority status, age, and class, includes sex as another dimension of inequality.

The social stress hypothesis is an extension of the social stress interpretation commonly evoked to explain the greater levels of psychological distress in lower classes reported in community surveys and studies of psychiatric epidemiology (Dohrenwend, 1970, 1973; Dohrenwend and Dohrenwend, 1969; Fried, 1975; Kessler, 1979; Kessler and Clearly, 1980). More recent literature in this area is emphasizing that lower class people experience more psychological distress not only because of greater exposure to stressful events, but also, and more important, because they have fewer psychological and social resources for coping with stress (Kessler and Clearly, 1980). Presumably, the same can be said about the suggested relationship between minority status and psychological distress: Members of minority groups experience more distress than members of the dominant majority of similar social class not only because they are exposed to more stresses, but also because they have fewer resources for dealing with these stresses. Moreover, it may be argued that stress can have an even greater effect on the aged and the minority aged in particular since they have even fewer resources for coping with stress. This resource deficit experienced by the aged is even more acute among minority aged: "Not only are the minority aged exposed to greater numbers of stressors, they also have fewer coping resources after a lifetime of financial deprivation, subordination to other groups, and systematic exclusion from access to social and economic opportunity" (Varghese and Medinger, 1979:97).

These propositions rest on the assumption that old age itself constitutes a situation of jeopardy. To what extent this assumption is established by empirical data is not as clear as it might at first appear since the assumption depends on the choice of dependent variable indicating a situation of jeopardy. This brings us to another question: What are the critical variables to be used in evaluating the jeopardy of the minority aged? Four areas are chosen here primarily because they were used as the primary dependent variables in two important recent attempts to test empirically the viability of the double jeopardy hypothesis (Dowd and Bengtson, 1978; Ward, 1980): income, health, primary group relations, and psychological well-being. These indicators of wellbeing or quality of life are areas of great interest to gerontologists. In addition, they provide a useful framework for organizing this discussion of the literature on minority aging.

The literature review that follows is selective rather than exhaustive. It focuses primarily on studies that intentionally or unintentionally, directly or indirectly, provide evidence in support of or opposed to the notion that aging or the onset of old age is more disadvantageous for black Americans or for Hispanic Americans than for the dominant whites. That is, to what extent does the so-called double jeopardy hypothesis accurately depict the interaction between minority status and age? Do the disadvantages of minority persons observed in middle age actually increase with aging or is aging a great leveler of social and racial differences (Kent and Hirsh, 1969; Kent, 1971). After the literature on these questions is reviewed, some discussion of observed discrepancies is offered, along with suggestions for future research.

THE EMPIRICAL EVIDENCE

As noted above, income, health, primary group relationships (family and friends), and psychological wellbeing (e.g., morale, life satisfaction, happiness) are important areas of gerontological concern. The last has been especially important since, in their attempts to offer theoretical formulas for "successful aging," gerontologists have used various measures of psychological well-being as primary indicators of adaptation or adjustment to old age. The other three variables, in addition to being important dependent variables in their own right, have been used as the key independent variables in the successful aging equation: Numerous studies have shown that health, income, and relations with family and friends are consistent predictors of life satisfaction or morale among the aged (Larson, 1978; Markides and Martin, 1979a).

The gerontological literature in these four areas is vast and growing rapidly. Attempts are increasingly being made to sort it out, to synthesize it and generalize about what growing older is like. In much of the empirical literature, however, minority groups have not been included, or inadequate analyses have been made. The following selective review of some of the literature on black and Hispanic aging aims to stimulate further interest, both empirical and theoretical, among researchers in the future.

Income

There is little disagreement in the literature that the income of older people in the United States and other industrial societies is considerably lower than that of middle-aged people. What the literature does not always make clear is the source of this inequality: Is it aging or old age per se, or is it primarily a cohort or generation phenomenon since many of today's elderly worked at unskilled or semi-skilled low-wage jobs that did not provide for adequate pensions, if any at all. Future cohorts of older people are likely to fare better, thus cutting the age differential in income. Given marked increases in real wages in the last three decades or so and a shift to more skilled and white-collar occupations, it is difficult to use cross-sectional data to evaluate the effect of aging on income. Longitudinal analyses are few, despite the fact that income data by age have historically been available in a form amenable to longitudinal analysis.

There is also widespread agreement in the literature that elderly members of ethnic minority groups are socioeconomically disadvantaged compared to elderly members of the majority group. The double jeopardy hypothesis, however, predicts that the disadvantage of the minority persons is greater in old age than in middle age. In their Los Angeles study of Anglos, blacks, and Mexican Americans (aged 45 to 74), Dowd and Bengtson (1978) found empirical support for this prediction: The relative decline in income associated with age was significantly greater for blacks and Mexican Americans than for Anglos even when controls for socioeconomic status, sex, and health were introduced.

Because the findings of Dowd and Bengtson (1978) are based on one city and on cross-sectional data, it is difficult to draw conclusions about the effect of aging on income. A study using a large national sample of blacks and whites (Ward, 1980) found that, with educational and occupational differences controlled, there is some leveling of income differences between the races in old age. Ward feels that this may "reflect the effects of income maintenance policies which benefit older blacks because of their disproportionately low income." Ward's findings are consistent with those of an earlier study using Census data from 1950, 1960, and 1970 (Whittington, 1975), which found that the financial position of blacks compared to whites improved with age. Whittington's study, however, did not include persons 65 years old and over. Whittington's rationale for not including older people in his study is instructive because the results run counter to Dowd's and Bengtson's findings of increasing racial and ethnic disparities in income in old age:

> There are good reasons to expect that beyond age 65 years, the income of Blacks is much closer to that of Whites, although both are substantially reduced. This artificial increase in relative status . . . would be very misleading if included in the analysis. Not only would it portray improvement where none existed but would give more weight to the age variable than it actually deserved (Whittington, 1975:7).

Other available cross-sectional data support Ward's findings of narrowing racial differentials in income with age. Data from a 1978 Current Population Survey, for example, show that families headed by blacks 65 years old and over had an income of $6,066 compared with $9,458 for families headed by whites in the same age group (Administration on Aging, 1980:Table 8). Although this income gap is considerable, it is smaller than that observed in younger age groups, both in absolute dollars and in relative terms: Families headed by blacks (aged 25 to 64) had a median income of $10,880 compared to $18,697 for families headed by whites. The black-to-white ratio, which is 0.58 at this age group, increases somewhat to 0.64 at age 65 and over. The picture is about the same for unrelated individuals: The racial gap declines somewhat in old age with the black-to-white ratio increasing from 0.66 to 0.71. Earlier Current Population Surveys show that a small narrowing of the racial income gap from middle to old age has been consistent over many years (Bureau of the Census, 1979:Table 24). For families headed by persons 65 years old and over, the black-to-white income ratio in 1974 was 0.65 compared to 0.58 for families aged 55 to 64. The corresponding ratios were 0.61 and 0.57 in 1969, 0.65 and 0.55 in 1967, and 0.68 and 0.51 in 1964. If there is any trend in these figures over time, it is one of a small improvement in the position of middleaged blacks compared to Anglos, and little change in the relative position of older blacks compared to older whites. The net effect is a slight decline over the years in the narrowing of the racial income gap with age, indicating that the relative position of older blacks compared to middle-aged blacks is getting somewhat worse, not better. Yet the data still show a relative decline in the racial income gap in old age, a finding consistent with Ward's (1980) data, but not consistent with Dowd's and Bengtson's (1978) findings.

Data on Hispanics are not as readily available as data on blacks. One recent survey (National Center for Health Statistics, 1978) provides added support for a decline in old age of the income gap between both blacks and Hispanics, on the one hand, and Anglos, on the other (see Markides, 1981).

Health

There is little disagreement that aging is accompanied by a progressive though highly variable deterioration of health. Health differences by age observed in cross-sectional analyses are partially due to cohort membership, given the continued improvements in the health of successive cohorts (Fries, 1980). Yet a major share of the differences are undeniably due to aging. That different groups have variant patterns of aging and health decrements is an established premise in gerontology. There is considerable evidence, for example, that aging in the United States is more rapid among blacks than among whites (Morgan, 1968; Jackson, 1980). Measuring health status, however, among the aged or any age group is not a simple matter. According to Shanas et al. (1968:25), ''A person's health may be evaluated by a physician in a physical examination, it may be evaluated by how a person says he feels, and it may be evaluated by how the person behaves.'' While the conflict between the ''medical'' and ''functional'' models of health in old age is not irreconcilable (Shanas and Maddox, 1976), much research on the health of older people is limited to self-ratings of health by the elderly subjects. Research has repeatedly shown that self-ratings correlate moderately with physicians' ratings (Maddox and Douglass, 1973) and to other more or less objective health indexes (Markides and Martin, 1979b), suggesting that older people are fairly realistic about their health. There is good reason to believe that self-ratings are also crude indicators of optimism, morale, or life satisfaction (Friedsam and Martin, 1963; Markides and Martin, 1979a, 1979b). The ambiguous meaning of self-ratings makes them somewhat problematic as indicators of health status; yet both major studies testing the double jeopardy hypothesis (Dowd and Bengtson, 1978; Ward, 1980) used self-ratings as their measures of health.

Dowd and Bengtson found that even with socioeconomic status, sex, and income held constant, older blacks and Mexican Americans in Los Angeles were more likely to report poorer health than were older Anglos.[3] Since the racial and ethnic differences in self-ratings were greater among older persons than among middle-aged respondents, the authors concluded that, as it applies to health, the double jeopardy hypothesis was supported (Dowd and Bengtson, 1978:432).

The data analyzed by Ward (1980) showed that at all ages, blacks gave consistently poorer health evaluations than did whites. However, these differences did not increase nor did they decline with age, supporting neither the double jeopardy hypothesis nor the age-asleveler hypothesis. (For a review of findings on selfratings of health by older Mexican Americans, see Newton, 1980.)

Looking at more objective national data on health, a somewhat different picture emerges. For example, data from the 1976 Health Interview Survey (National Center for Health Statistics, 1978) show that middle-aged and older blacks report considerably poorer health than whites as measured by percent with limitation of activity, days of restricted activity, and bed disability days (see National Center for Health Statistics, 1977, for exact definitions of these terms). However, the increase in the prevalence of poor health from middle age to old age is higher among whites than among blacks. For example, the number of bed disability days per person per year increases from 16.9 among blacks aged 45 to 64 to 18.5 among those aged 65 and over; among whites, on the other hand, the figure increases from 8.0 to 14.6. Thus, although blacks report considerably more disability days than whites at both ages, the gap decreases with age.

The 1976 Health Interview Survey also reported data on persons of Spanish origin. Based on the indicators noted above, Hispanics are much closer in health to the Anglo population than are blacks. For example, similar proportions of Hispanics and Anglos report limitation of activity at both middle age and old age. The number of days of restricted activity and the number of days of bed disability are a little higher among Hispanic persons than among Anglos in middle age, a gap that increases somewhat in old age. While these changes may not be statistically significant, they are in the direction predicted by the double jeopardy hypothesis in contrast to the leveling found in black-white comparisons.

Data on specific health problems provide further evidence that while both middle-aged and older blacks are considerably disadvantaged compared to

---

[3] A study conducted in San Antonio found that, with these variables held constant, older Mexican Americans and Anglos did not differ in their self-ratings (Markides and Martin, 1979b).

whites, the disadvantage is greater in middle age than in old age. Data from 1974 on hypertension, for example, a special health problem of blacks (Jackson, 1978), show that the percentage of blacks who have hypertension rises from 39.1 at ages 45 to 64 to 47.2 at ages 65 and over; the figure for whites goes from 22.7 to 35.3, a substantially larger increase (National Center for Health Statistics, 1980:Table J). Similarly, the incidence of cerebrovascular disease among blacks in 1972 is 2.5 times that for whites at ages 45 to 64, while at ages 65 and over it is less than 1.3 times as great.

Recent National Center for Health Statistics data from 1976 and 1977 show that almost twice as many blacks as whites assess their health as poor at ages 45 to 64 (38.4 vs. 19.3 percent). This ratio declines to 1.53 (44.1 vs. 28.3 percent) at ages 65 and over, again suggesting some leveling of differences, not widening, as found by Dowd and Bengtson (1978). Some leveling is also observed between Hispanics and whites since the Hispanic-to-white ratio declines from 1.47 to 1.29 (National Center for Health Statistics, 1980:Table 1).

In summary, substantial evidence suggests that the health disadvantage of blacks compared to whites is greater in middle than in old age, with some leveling of differences with age. The few data on Hispanics provide no conclusive evidence in support of either leveling or widening of differences with age.

Primary Group Relations

Although it is understandable why the double jeopardy hypothesis would predict negative effects of both race and age on income and health, it is not as clear why this should also take place in the area of primary group relations. Yet both major studies (Dowd and Bengtson, 1978; Ward, 1980) included frequency of interaction with relatives and friends as factors for examining the viability of the double jeopardy thesis. Dowd and Bengtson (1978:433) provide the following brief rationale: "While primary group interaction may not be as critical an indicator of relative status as income or health, it does indicate a source of reward available to the individual in the course of their daily lives that contributes significantly to overall 'quality of life.'"

Dowd's and Bengtson's (1978) findings provide no support for the predictions of the double jeopardy thesis. Mexican Americans and blacks reported higher contact with relatives in middle age than did Anglos, a difference which declined somewhat in old age, though this decline was not statistically significant. On contact with friends and neighbors, Anglos appear to be advantaged compared to the minority, an advantage increasing somewhat with age. However, since there was no noticeable variation by age among the minority respondents on this variable, the situation was not characterized as one of double jeopardy (Dowd and Bengtson, 1978).

Ward's (1980) study found little evidence supporting the notion of double jeopardy in primary group relations among older blacks. Racial differences in interaction with family and friends as well as differences in satisfaction derived from family and friends were generally small and showed no changing patterns with age that supported either double jeopardy or leveling.

The area of family relations of older people is of great importance in social gerontology. There is considerable disagreement and controversy over how supportive the family is of the individual, particularly the older person, among minority groups. In contrast to earlier writings, most writings in the 1970's emphasized the strengths of black families, including the provision of support and meaningful roles for older people (Davis, 1971; Hill, 1978; Jackson, 1970; Wylie, 1971). Yet, as with other minority groups, the supportive role of the family toward the black aged may have been overemphasized by some (see the discussion by Jackson, 1980:137).

The literature on the Mexican American family has had a somewhat different history than that on the black family. In the 1950's and 1960's, it was customary, for example, to describe the Mexican American family as extremely warm and supportive of the individual. Findings of lower incidence of psychiatric treatment were explained in terms of the supportive qualities of the Mexican American family (Jaco, 1957, 1959, 1960). Based on his ethnographic observations in south Texas, Madsen (1969) argued that stress has a more negative effect on the Anglo who experiences it alone, rather than on the Mexican American whose family shares and relieves outside stress. Studies of elderly Mexican Americans in San Antonio (Carp, 1968; Reich et al., 1966) also described the family as extremely warm and supportive of older people. In the late 1960's and early 1970's, a clear shift in the literature is observed. Writers began criticizing earlier studies for presenting a romanticized picture of the Chicano family. Specifically dealing with the place of the elderly in the family, critical reports on the literature were provided by Moore (1971) and by Maldonado (1975). Whereas Moore criticizes the inability of writers to interpret data without stereotypical preconceptions, Maldonado emphasizes the impact of urbanization and modernization in weakening the strength of the extended family.[4] Maldonado (1975) feels that the romanticized stereotype of the place of the elderly in the family may deprive them of needed services. Yet much of the literature continues to report that older Mexican Americans enjoy an advantageous position in the family as compared to older Anglos (Cuellar, 1978; Newton and Ruiz, 1981).

If, as much of the literature suggests, older blacks and Hispanics or other elderly members of minority groups enjoy an advantaged position in the family, then the notion of double jeopardy of minority elderly may not apply to the area of family relations. But what is critical from this theoretical perspective is how the differences, racial or ethnic, change from middle age to old age. Neither literature on family relations nor on relations with friends and neighbors has pro-

---

[4]For discussion of a modernization perspective on older Mexican Americans, see Korte (1981). For a fairly comprehensive and up-to-date review of the literature on the Mexican American family, see Ramirez and Arce (forthcoming).

duced sufficient data for evaluating the double jeopardy versus leveling alternatives. Perhaps what is more important is determining what constitutes an advantage or disadvantage in primary group relations. Greater interaction with kin, for example, may not necessarily imply more satisfying or meaningful family life (Hess and Waring, 1978).

Psychological Well-Being

No other area of research in social gerontology has received as much attention as the area of life satisfaction, morale, or psychological well-being in general. While numerous studies have examined the relationship between age and psychological well-being, the results have been mixed and inconclusive. Some show a small decline in well-being with age (Bradburn, 1969; Edwards and Klemmack, 1973; Neugarten et al., 1961); but when controls for health, socioeconomic status, or other important variables are introduced, the relationship disappears (Edwards and Klemmack, 1973; Kivett, 1976). Still other research has found a positive relationship between age and psychological well-being (e.g., Alston et al., 1974; Bortner and Hultsch, 1970; Clemente and Sauer, 1976; Czaja, 1975; Orchowsky and Parham, 1979; Witt et al., 1980).

The findings on the relationship between race or ethnicity and psychological well-being are as inconclusive as those relating to age. Most studies show that while older blacks and Mexican Americans may score lower than Anglos on various measures of psychological wellbeing, these differences disappear when such variables as socioeconomic status and health are controlled (Clemente and Sauer, 1974; Markides, 1980b; Markides et al., 1980; Spreitzer and Snyder, 1974).

The lack of clear evidence that race or ethnicity or age negatively affects psychological well-being, at least when socioeconomic status and health are held constant, does not provide much support for applying the double jeopardy thesis to this variable. The findings of the two major studies testing the double jeopardy hypothesis corroborate this notion. Dowd and Bengtson (1978) found greater decline with age in "optimism" among Mexican Americans than Anglos, but no significant change in "tranquility" with age. The situation with blacks provided no support for double jeopardy on either component of life satisfaction. Ward (1980) used data from several national surveys to compare blacks with whites in different age groups, and found that seven measures of subjective well-being yielded no patterns either in the direction of double jeopardy or in the direction of leveling. Four measures—Affect Balance Scale, Life Satisfaction Index, an index measuring satisfaction with several domains of life, and a measure of rating life as exciting—showed no changes with age that would support either double jeopardy or leveling. Black disadvantages in global happiness and anomia observed in the younger age group (18 to 39) decline with age. Ward (1980) does not interpret these findings as supporting leveling in old age, however, since they "may . . . reflect the characteristics and experiences of this younger cohort." The only measure of well-being that was in the direction of double jeopardy was a measure of self-esteem, which changed from a small advantage for younger blacks to a small disadvantage in old age. Ward (1980) again warns that "this pattern could be interpreted as a reflection of cohort differences in black pride or system blame, rather than being due to aging effects. Ward's statements underscore the difficulties encountered in evaluating the double jeopardy hypothesis with cross-sectional data.

A somewhat different variable which has been used as an indicator of psychological well-being, though not directly a measure of it, is an older person's perception of aging. Minority group members have repeatedly been found to perceive themselves as reaching old age earlier than Anglos, or to have older age identities (Bengtson, Kasschau, and Ragan, 1977). These differences are, to a large extent, a reflection of socioeconomic disadvantages over a lifetime (Jackson, 1970; Moore, 1971). Yet there is some evidence suggesting that significant ethnic or racial differences in age identifications persist even when the effect of socioeconomic status is held constant (Busse et al., 1970; Markides, 1980a). Since there is good reason to believe that youthful age identities on the part of older people indicate a certain degree of denial of old age, it is possible that the older age identities of minority elderly after socioeconomic status is controlled reflect their relative insulation "from the values of the greater society that, by and large, define old age as an undesirable stage in the life cycle" (Markides, 1980a:665).

When subjective age is defined from the perspective of "awareness of finitude" (Munnichs, 1968), or estimating the time one expects to live, different and quite interesting results have been found. Two independent studies conducted in Los Angeles (Reynolds and Kalish, 1974; Kalish and Reynolds, 1976; and Bengtson, Cuellar, and Ragan, 1977) found that blacks in both middle age and in old age expected to and desired to live longer than whites and Mexican Americans. This is paradoxical given the lower life expectancy of blacks. Reynolds and Kalish (1974:23) suggested that these findings may indicate that blacks may be reluctant to give life up because they worked so hard to "gain a foothold on it." Yet they found this answer unsatisfactory in light of the low expectations and wishes for longevity expressed by Mexican Americans. In addition, there was no evidence that the high expectations and wishes for longevity of blacks reflected greater fear of death or anxiety about the outcome of death (Reynolds and Kalish, 1974: 230; Bengtson, Cuellar, and Ragan, 1977). In a more recent discussion of the matter, Kalish and Reynolds (1976:99-100) suggested the following:

> Given the pressures and the prejudices, the stresses and the discrimination that Black Americans face, their desire to attain a relatively long life, especially in the face of their actuarial life expectancies, is remarkable. While one might patronize these views as unrealistic, to expect to live longer than your allocated time and to

wish to live still longer would appear to reflect optimism and hope, particularly when the surrounding world works toward destruction of the hopes. In these data, we find both resilience and an appreciation of life, undoubtedly supported by religious faith.

Despite their inability to suggest a satisfactory explanation of the phenomenon, Kalish and Reynolds (1976:100) felt that the greater desires and expectations for longevity by blacks are consistent with their low suicide rates in middle and old age (Davis, 1979). They are, however, inconsistent with findings on Mexican Americans, as well as other findings using other measures of subjective or psychological well-being.

Discussion

The double jeopardy hypothesis predicting widening differentials with age between the minority and majority group persons finds mixed support in the empirical literature on blacks and Hispanics. Why do national data on both income and health contradict Dowd's and Bengtson's (1978) Los Angeles findings? One reason may be differences in measurement, sampling, and age-the Los Angeles study only included people up to age 74. In the case of income as noted above, there are good reasons why the income of older members of minorities should be closer to the income of whites at old age than at middle age. Since there is a drop in income with retirement—though not as large as cross-sectional data might suggest (Henretta and Campbell, 1976; Riley and Foner, 1968:82)—we may expect that the relative reduction is lower among minority groups because of their lower incomes in middle age. Although the incomes of the two groups are closer in old age, this does not necessarily mean that the relative economic disadvantage—particularly of blacks—declines. Income figures say little about the other sources of financial security—property, insurance policies, savings— more common among white elderly. One study, for example, showed that older blacks are more dependent on money income than older whites, the latter having greater access to savings and credit (Goldstein, 1971). In addition, greater home ownership by older whites leaves more income for other uses. Although the racial gap in home ownership has declined somewhat in recent years (Hoover, 1981; Jackson, 1980), the disadvantage of older blacks is still large.

While we may accept the above interpretations of why the minority-majority income gap declines in old age for the moment, explaining a decline in the health differentials between blacks and whites (no such pattern is observed with Hispanics) shown in national data presents a greater challenge, unless we use the same logic applied earlier to income. Thus it is possible that the *increase* in old age in the incidence of poor health is lower among blacks because their health is so much poorer in middle age to begin with. There is also another factor here which, while receiving some attention from a methodological standpoint, is receiving virtually no attention regarding its possible effect on racial differences in health: the well-established racial mortality crossover which takes place at about age 75 (Manton and Poss, 1977; Manton et al., 1979; Manton, 1980). That is, the mortality rates of blacks and whites converge gradually in old age and "cross over" at about age 75 so that life expectancy at these advanced ages is higher among blacks than among whites. Attempts to explain this phenomenon in terms of errors in the data have failed to eliminate the crossover (Kitagawa and Hauser, 1973; Manton, 1980; Rives, 1977). Manton (1980:481) discusses the probable reason for the existence of a racial mortality crossover or a crossover between any disadvantaged group with a more advantaged one, as follows:

> The probable basis of such population mechanisms is the effect of differential mortality selection on a heterogeneous population. Specifically it can be shown that, if the individuals in populations are heterogeneous with respect to their endowment for longevity, then a crossover or convergence of the age specific mortality rates of two populations can occur if one population has markedly higher early mortality. The crossover is a result of the differential early mortality which selects the least robust persons from the disadvantaged population at relatively earlier ages so that, at advanced ages, the disadvantaged population has proportionately more robust persons.

Manton's (1980:492) examination of racial crossovers by major causes of death led him to conclude that:

> . . . a larger proportion of Whites survive to advanced age because of better medical treatment and management of the chronic effects of disease. Blacks, on the other hand, would be less likely to survive a disease event at earlier ages so that they would have a proportionately lower prevalence of chronic conditions at advanced ages.

Note that in this last statement, Manton is speaking about chronic conditions at *advanced* ages, after the racial crossover takes place—usually after age 75. The prevalence of chronic conditions among persons 65 years old and over is higher among blacks than whites. Since a sizable proportion of older people are over the age of 75, however, the mortality crossover at this age would lead to fewer overall health problems among blacks 65 years old and over as a group than would be expected in the absence of a crossover. Put another way, the existence of a crossover means a lower increase in health problems among blacks from middle age to old age (65+) than would be observed in the absence of the crossover or than is observed in the white population, as national data show.

This smaller relative increase in health problems from middle to old age among blacks should not be interpreted as indicating an advantage of blacks over whites. On the contrary, it is an indicator of the great disadvantage of blacks relative to whites. The irony in this interpretation is that, other things being equal, any improvements in the relative status of blacks to whites which might reduce higher early mortality (before old age) can be expected to lead to a later mortality crossover, or to the elimination of it altogether. This may also mean an increase in the health disadvantage of older blacks compared to older whites in the future, since more of the less "robust" blacks will be surviving to advanced ages due to better medical care. This increase in the black disadvantage is likely to be greatest after age 75.

A related point should be raised here. Since, as Manton (1980) shows, the mechanism that leads to a racial mortality crossover is greater early mortality that selects the least biologically robust members of the disadvantaged group, it may be presumed that these people are also less likely than the survivors to be robust in an economic sense. If this assumption is correct, the racial mortality crossover may be contributing to the leveling of income differences observed in national statistics. Again, using the logic applied in the previous paragraph, it may be argued that, other things being equal, any reductions in the socioeconomic (and health) disadvantage of blacks compared to whites in middle age will ultimately lead to greater socioeconomic inequality between blacks and whites in old age, especially after age 75.

The existence of a racial mortality crossover is an indication of racial differences in physiological aging under social and environmental conditions in the United States (Morgan, 1968; Jackson, 1980). Thus, following convention, if we arbitrarily assume that old age begins at 65 for whites, blacks and other disadvantaged minority groups are biologically old a few years before 65. That they also become old earlier socially and psychologically is suggested by evidence of their older age identification. If these assumptions are correct, studying racial or ethnic differences in the transition to old age with only chronological age marking such transitions may be inappropriate or, at a minimum, insufficient.

Turning now to the empirical evidence on primary group relations and psychological well-being and how this evidence relates to the predictions of the double jeopardy hypothesis, some brief comments are in order. First, if minority group members are advantaged in terms of family-based supports and roles as much of the literature suggests, speaking of double jeopardy of minority elderly in this area is inappropriate.[5] But as pointed out earlier, the literature has not clarified the extent to which greater involvement with kin on the part of minority aged constitutes an advantage in family relations.

The general lack of support for the predictions of widening differentials with age in psychological wellbeing, reflects the absence of any firm and consistent evidence that either age or race (minority status) are, by themselves, significant predictors of psychological well-being. Since subjective evaluations of life satis-

---

[5]There is some evidence suggesting that the greater involvement of older blacks with their kin has an economic rather than a racial basis (Jackson and Walls, 1978; Ward, 1980).

faction, happiness, or morale are made with important reference groups in mind (e.g., other elderly, other elderly they come in contact with, and earlier ages), it may be unrealistic to expect large differences in such subjective evaluations regardless of how large the differences might be in the objective conditions between age groups or between racial or ethnic groups. This is also why socioeconomic status is such a poor (though usually significant) predictor of life satisfaction or morale (Larson, 1978). Since subjective well-being is so dependent on expectations which are molded, to a great extent, by reference group orientations,[6] it may be inappropriate to use them to indicate the disadvantage of members of ethnic minority groups or older age groups. Otherwise, we run the risk—as most data would suggest-of indicating a lack of disadvantage when one exists, as vast differences in objective conditions resulting from poverty and discrimination would indicate.

To summarize the discussion thus far, the predictions of the double jeopardy hypothesis as currently formulated have not received strong empirical support. While some leveling influences of age might be at work, it is also the case that inappropriate variables (e.g., contact with family or life satisfaction) have been used to measure the disadvantage of older minority members. In addition, conceptualizations of old age in groups with considerably different mortality experiences have been inadequate. Finally, and related, to the extent that early mortality differentially selects the least robust members of minority groups, widening health (and possibly income) differentials in old age (conventionally defined) would be unlikely. This general lack of empirical support for the double jeopardy thesis should not be interpreted to mean that older blacks and older Hispanics are not victims of double jeopardy in the sense that they are subject to discrimination related to both age and minority status.

It is tempting to suggest that race or ethnic stratification is much less important than class stratification as some writers have suggested (Jackson and Walls, 1978; Wilson, 1978).[7] It is also tempting to suggest that age stratification is far less important than social class stratification, as has also been proposed (Henretta and Campbell, 1976; Ward, 1980). Both suggestions may be appropriate. Yet the double jeopardy hypothesis is so poorly conceptualized and articulated-as is the general multiple-hierarchy statification model—that such conclusions may be somewhat premature. Much theoretical work as well as more appropriate empirical investigations are necessary in this important area of inquiry. Finally, if anything should be clear from the above discussion, it is the dynamic nature of the interactive relationship between race or ethnic stratification and age stratification (Ward, 1980:16).

---

[6]It may be pointed out here that reference group explanations have been drawn upon to account for the inability of recent research to show racial or ethnic differences in self-esteem. See Rosenberg (1979), Simmons (1978), and Taylor and Walsh (1979).

[7]Race or ethnic stratification is, of course, important in that it is the major determinant of class stratification, at least as it applies to the disadvantaged ethnic groups. Thus, separating the two stratification systems may be somewhat artificial.

DIRECTIONS OF FUTURE RESEARCH

One problem with research on minority aging and on aging in general is that it is largely limited to studying old age rather than the process of growing old. When younger age groups are included in our samples, aging effects must usually be inferred from crosssectional data. More longitudinal designs are needed in order to discover the dynamics of the interaction between age, minority status, and social class.

Perhaps a most fruitful area of inquiry in minority aging will be the study of racial and ethnic income inequality over the life cycle. Extension of current research (Featherman and Hauser, 1976; Hoffman, 1978; Jiobu, 1976; Kluegel, 1978; Poston and Alvirez, 1973; Rosenfeld, 1980) to include older persons in a longitudinal framework will lead to a better understanding of the relative effects of age, ethnic minority status, and social class. If, as Henretta and Campbell (1976) have suggested, the factors influencing retirement income are similar to those influencing preretirement income, studies that are successful in pointing out the effect of discrimination on the income of minority groups before age 65 can have much to suggest about the impact of such discrimination in old age.

Research in this area may also distinguish racial and ethnic differences in household income from personal or per capita income. Since households headed by older blacks and older Hispanics are typically larger than those headed by Anglos, household data may overstate the average economic well-being of minority persons relative to Anglos because the same income must spread over a larger number of household members (see Bianchi, 1980). Research in this area must also go beyond studying only income inequality by race or ethnicity and examine the total financial situation. A measure of net worth, for example, may be both more accurate and more revealing of racial or ethnic differences in the financial status of older people (Henretta and Campbell, 1978).

Research on the relationship between age, minority status, and health also holds much promise. Of extreme importance here is further research on the racial mortality crossover at advanced ages. Since mortality crossovers have been observed in a great variety of populations around the world (Nam et al., 1978), it is possible that they take place with other American ethnic minority groups and for the same reasons. Though the data are of poor quality, there is evidence, for example, of a crossover between the mortality curves of American Indians and whites (National Center for Health Statistics, 1980). Relevant data are not presently available to investigate a possible crossover between Hispanics and Anglos.

Since deaths from cardiovascular diseases are known to contribute strongly to mortality crossovers (Nam et al., 1978), research must investigate the extent to which blacks (and other minority groups) have shared in the recent decline in mortality from cardiovascular diseases (Stern, 1979).[8] Current trends in

---

[8]Stern (1979) shows that the decline in ischemic heart disease mortality from 1968 to 1976 was somewhat higher among blacks and persons with Spanish surnames than among whites.

cardiovascular mortality by race and ethnicity must be followed closely since they may have consequences for the nature and timing of the racial mortality crossover, and consequently for health differentials between blacks and whites at advanced ages. In addition, any increases in the mortality crossover will have important implications for institutionalization rates of minority elderly, which are currently much lower than among whites.

In the area of family relations, changing demographic trends especially demand the attention of researchers. Recently, for example, Cantor (1979) noted that older blacks appear more involved with their extended kin in northern ghettos than in southern cities such as Durham, N.C. (Jackson, 1971). Since this finding is most likely related to outmigration of younger blacks to the North, research can establish what effect the recent return migration of blacks (Long and Hansen, 1975) will have on extended kin relations of the elderly in both regions.

Migration trends are also important for understanding the relationships of Hispanic elderly with their extended kin. For example, increases in outmigration of younger Hispanics from the Southwest due to rising occupational mobility need to be closely investigated. At the moment, most older Hispanics have many children and grandchildren living nearby (Newton and Ruiz, 1981), and it may be that continued high fertility will assure that some descendents will be around for many years to come. Of more interest may be investigations into the family relationships of older Hispanics who are relatively recent immigrants and likely to be less involved in extended kin relationships. Related to the above, investigations are needed into the effect of continued immigration from Mexico on the overall socioeconomic status of Mexican Americans in relation to Anglos, particularly in old age. Many older Mexican Americans living in the cities of the Southwest are of rural background and from Mexico, a factor thought to lead to difficulties in adjusting to the complex urban industrial society. Are future cohorts of older Mexican Americans going to be different, or will continued immigration of poor Mexican peasants make for little change in the overall socioeconomic disadvantage of older Mexican Americans?

Research on psychological well-being of minority aged may continue, though this area of research holds less promise of much useful knowledge, at least from the perspective of multiple-hierarchy stratification theory. Important contributions may be made by studying the effect of increasing acculturation and assimilation of younger Hispanics on extended family relationships and ultimately life satisfaction of the elderly.

The possibilities and promises of new research on aging among blacks and Hispanics and among other minority groups appear extensive at this time. Despite increased research over the past decade, much more is needed, as this review has shown. Perhaps equally important is the need for theoretical integration. Some progress is being made in specifying the relationships between variables subsumed under the multiple-hierarchy model of stratification (Dowd, 1980; Foner, 1979; Jeffries and Ransford, 1980). Theoretical work along these lines will be extremely useful in helping generate new testable hypotheses in the area of minority aging.

REFERENCES

Administration on Aging 1980. Characteristics of the Black Elderly. Statistical Reports on Older Americans, Number 5. Washington, D.C.: U.S. Government Printing Office.

Alston, Jon P., George D. Lowe, and Alice Wrigley 1974. "Socioeconomic correlates of four dimensions of self-perceived satisfaction." Human Organization 33:99–102.

Antunes, George, C. Gordon, Charles M. Gaitz, and Judith Scott 1974. "Ethnicity, socioeconomic status and the etiology of psychological distress." Sociology and Social Research 58:361–368.

Bengtson, Vern L., 1979 "Ethnicity and aging: problems and issues in current social science inquiry." Pp. 9–31 in Donald E. Gelfand and Alfred J. Kutzik (eds.), Ethnicity and Aging. New York: Springer Publishing.

Bengtson, Vern L., Jose B. Cuellar, and Pauline K. Ragan 1977. "Stratum contrasts and similarities in attitudes toward death." Journal of Gerontology 32:76–88.

Bengtson, Vern L., Patricia L. Kasschau, and Pauline K. Ragan 1977. "The impact of social structure on aging individuals." Pp. 327–354 in James E. Birren and K. Warner Schaie (eds.), Handbook of the Psychology of Aging. New York: Van Nostrand Reinhold.

Bianchi, Suzanne M. 1980. "Racial difference in per capita income, 1960–1976: the importance of household size, headship, and labor force participation." Demography 17:129–143.

Bortner, Raymond W., and David F. Hultsch 1970. "A multivariate analysis of correlates of life satisfaction in adulthood." Journal of Gerontology 32:593–599.

Bradburn, Norman 1969. The Structure of Psychological Well-Being. Chicago: Aldine.

Bureau of the Census 1979. The Social and Economic Status of the Black Population in the United States: An Historical View, 1790–1978. Current Population Reports, Special Studies, Series P-23, Number 80. Washington, D.C: U.S. Government Printing Office.

Busse, Ewald W., Frances C. Jeffers, and Walter D. Orbist 1970. "Factors in age awareness." Pp. 381–389 in Erdman Palmore (ed.), Normal Aging: Reports from the Duke Longitudinal Study, 1955–1969. Durham, N.C.: Duke University Press.

Cantor, Majorie H. 1979. "The informal support system of New York's inner city elderly: is ethnicity a factor?" Pp. 153–174 in Donald E. Gelfand and Alfred J. Kutzik (eds.), Ethnicity and Aging. New York: Springer Publishing.

Carp, Frances 1968. Factors in Utilization of Services by the Mexican American Elderly. Palo Alto: American Institutes for Research.

Clemente, Frank, and William J. Sauer 1974. "Race and morale of the urban aged." Gerontologist 13:106–110.

Clemente, Frank, and William J. Sauer 1976. "Life satisfaction in the United States." Social Forces 54:621–631.

Crandall, Richard C. 1980. Gerontology: A Behavioral Science Approach. Reading, Mass.: Addison-Wesley.

Cuellar, Jose B. 1978. "El Senior Citizens' Club: the older Mexican American in the voluntary association." Pp. 207–230 in Barbara G. Myerhoff and Andrei Simic (eds.), Life's Career-Aging: Subcultural Variations on Growing Old. Beverly Hills: Sage Publications.

Czaja, Sara J. 1975. "Age differences in life satisfaction as a function of discrepancy between real and ideal self concepts." Experimental Aging Research 1:81–89.

Davis, Donald L. 1971. "Growing old black." In U.S. Senate Special Committee on Aging, The Multiple Hazards of Age and Race: The Situation of Aged Blacks in the United States. Washington, D.C.: U.S. Government Printing Office.

Davis, Robert 1979. "Black suicide in the seventies: current trends." Suicide and Life Threatening Behavior 9:131–140.

Decker, David L. 1980. Social Gerontology: An Introduction to the Dynamics of Aging. Boston: Little, Brown.

Dohrenwend, Barbara S. 1970. "Social class and stressful events." Pp. 313–319 in Evan H. Hare and J.K. Wings (eds.), Psychiatric Epidemiology. New York: Oxford.

Dohrenwend, Barbara S. 1973 "Social status and stressful life events." Journal of Personality and Social Psychology 9:203–214.

Dohrenwend, Bruce P., and Barbara S. Dohrenwend 1969. Social Status and Psychological Disorders. New York: Wiley.

Dowd, James J. 1980. Stratification Among the Aged. Monterey, Calif.: Brooks/Cole.

Dowd, James J., and Vern L. Bengtson 1978. "Aging in minority populations: an examination of the double jeopardy hypothesis." Journal of Gerontology 33: 427–436.

Edwards, John N., and David L. Klemmack 1973. "Correlates of life satisfaction: a reexamination." Journal of Gerontology 28: 497–502.

Featherman, David L., and Robert M. Hauser 1976. "Changes in the socioeconomic stratification of the races, 1962–1973." American Journal of Sociology 82:621–651.

Foner, Anne 1979. "Ascribed and achieved bases of stratification." Pp. 219-242 in Alex Inkeles (ed.), Annual Review of Sociology. Palo Alto, Calif.: Annual Review.

Fried, Marc 1975. "Social differences in mental health." In John Kosa and Irving Zola (eds.), Poverty and Health: A Sociological Analysis. Cambridge: Harvard University Press.

Friedsam, Hiram, and Harry W. Martin 1963. "A comparison of self and physicians' health ratings in an older population." Journal of Health and Social Behavior 4:179–183.

Fries, James F. 1980. "Aging, natural death and the compression of morbidity." New England Journal of Medicine 303:130–135.

Fujii, Sharon 1976. "Older Asian Americans: victims of multiple jeopardy." Civil Rights Digest, Fall:22–29.

Goldstein, Sidney 1971. "Negro-white differentials in consumer patterns of the aged, 1960–1961." Gerontologist 11:242–249.

Hendricks, Jon, and C. Davis Hendricks 1977. Aging in Mass Society. Cambridge, Mass.: Winthrop Publishers.

Henretta, John C., and Richard T. Campbell 1976. "Status attainment and status maintenance: a study of stratification in old age." American Sociological Review 41:981–992.

Henretta, John C., and Richard T. Campbell 1978. "Net worth as an aspect of status." American Journal of Sociology 83:1204–1223.

Hess, Beth B., and Elizabeth W. Markson 1980. Aging and Old Age: An Introduction to Social Gerontology. New York: Macmillan.

Hess, Beth B., and Joan M. Waring 1978. "Parent and child in later life: rethinking the relationship." Pp. 241–273 in Richard M. Lerner and Graham B. Spanier (eds.), Child Influences on Marital and Family Interaction. New York: Academic Press.

Hill, Robert 1978. "A demographic profile of the black elderly." Aging 287–88: 2–9.

Hoffman, Saul 1978. "Black-white earnings differentials over the life cycle." In Greg J. Duncan and James N. Morgan (eds.), Five Thousand American Families—Patterns of Economic Progress, Vol. VI. Ann Arbor: Survey Research Center, University of Michigan.

Hoover, Sally L. 1981. "Black and Hispanic elderly: their housing characteristics and quality." In M. Powell Lawton and Sally L. Hoover (eds.), Community Housing Choices for Older Americans. New York: Springer.

Jackson, Jacqueline J. 1970. "Aged Negroes: their cultural departures from statistical stereotypes and selected rural-urban differences." Gerontologist 10:140–145.

Jackson, Jacqueline J. 1978. "Special health problems of aged blacks." Aging 287–88:15–20.

Jackson, Jacqueline J., and Bertram F. Walls 1978. "Myths and realities about aged blacks." In Mollie Brown (ed.), Readings in Gerontology. St. Louis: C.V. Mosby.

Jackson, Jacqueline J. 1980. Minorities and Aging. Belmont, Calif.: Wadsworth.

Jaco, E. Gartley 1957. "Social factors in mental disorders in Texas." Social Problems 4:322–328.

Jaco, E. Gartley 1959. "Mental health of the Spanish Americans in Texas." Pp. 467-488 in Marvin K. Opler (ed.), Culture and Mental Health. New York: Macmillan.

Jaco, E. Gartley 1960. The Social Epidemiology of Mental Disorders. New York: Russell Sage.

Jeffries, Vincent, and H. Edward Ransford 1980. Social Stratification: A Multiple Hierarchy Approach. Boston: Allyn and Bacon.

Jiobu, Robert M. 1976. "Earnings differentials between whites and ethnic minorities: the cases of Asian Americans, blacks and Chicanos." Sociology and Social Research 61:24–38.

Kalish, Richard A., and David K. Reynolds 1976. Death and Ethnicity: A Psycho-cultural Study. Los Angeles: University of Southern California Press.

Kent, Donald P., and Carl Hirsch 1969. "Differentials in need and problem solving techniques among low-income Negro and white elderly." Presented at the 8th International Congress of Gerontology, Washington, D.C.

Kent, Donald P. 1971. "The Negro aged." Gerontologist 11:48–51.

Kessler, Ronald C., and Paul D. Cleary 1980. "Social class and psychological distress." American Sociological Review 45:463–478.

Kessler, Ronald C. 1979. "Stress, social status and psychological distress." Journal of Health and Social Behavior 20:100–108.

Kitagawa, Evelyn M., and Phillip M. Hauser 1973. Differential Mortality in the United States: A Study in Socio-economic Epidemiology. Cambridge, Mass.: Harvard University Press.

Kivett, Vira 1976. The Aged in North Carolina: Physical, Social and Environmental Characteristics and Sources of Assistance. North Carolina Agricultural Experiment Station, Technical Bulletin No. 237.

Korte, Alvin O. 1981. "Theoretical perspectives in mental health and the Mexicano elders." In Manuel R. Miranda and Rene A. Ruiz (eds.), Chicano Aging and Mental Health. U.S. Department of Health and Human Services, U.S. Public Health Service, National Institute of Mental Health, pp. 1–37.

Larson, Reed 1978. "Thirty years of research on subjective well-being of older Americans." Journal of Gerontology 33:109–125.

Long, Larry H., and Kristen A. Hansen 1975. "Trends in return migration to the South." Demography 12:601–614.

Maddox, George L., and Elizabeth B. Douglass 1973. "Self-assessment of health: a longitudinal study of elderly subjects." Journal of Health and Social Behavior 14:87–93.

Madsen, William 1969. "Mexican Americans and Anglo Americans: a comparative study of mental health in Texas." In Stanley Plog and Robert Edgerton (eds.), Changing Perspectives in Mental Illness. New York: Holt, Reinhart and Winston.

Maldonado, David 1975. "The Chicano aged." Social Work 20:213–216.

Manton, Kenneth G. 1980. "Sex and race specific mortality differentials in multiple cause of death data." Gerontologist 20:480–493.

Manton, Kenneth G., and Sharon S. Poss 1977. "The black/white mortality crossover: possible racial differences." Black Aging 3:43–53.

Manton, Kenneth G., Sharon S. Poss, and Steven Wing 1979. "The black/white mortality crossover: investigation from the perspective of the components of aging." Gerontologist 19:291–300.

Markides, Kyriakos S., and Harry W. Martin 1979a. "A causal model of life satisfaction among the elderly." Journal of Gerontology 34:86–93.

Markides, Kyriakos S. and Harry W. Martin 1979b. "Predicting self-rated health among the aged." Research on Aging 1:97–112.

Markides, Kyriakos S. 1980a. "Ethnic differences in age identification: a study of older Mexican Americans and Anglos." Social Science Quarterly 60:659–666.

Markides, Kyriakos S. 1980b. "Correlates of life satisfaction among older Mexican Americans and Anglos." Journal of Minority Aging, Vol. 5, No. 2., pp. 183–190.

Markides, Kyriakos S., Harry W. Martin, and Mark Sizemore 1980. "Psychological distress among elderly Mexican Americans and Anglos." Ethnicity 7:298–309.

Markides, Kyriakos S. 1981. "Health, income and the minority aged: a reexamination of the double jeopardy hypothesis." Journal of Gerontology, Vol. 36, No. 4, pp. 494–495.

Markson, Elizabeth W. 1979. "Ethnicity as a factor in the institutionalization of the ethnic elderly." Pp. 341–356 in Donald E. Gelfand and Alfred J. Kutzik (eds.), Ethnicity and Aging. New York: Springer Publishing.

Morgan, Robert F. 1968. "The adult growth examination: preliminary comparisons of aging in adults by sex and race." Perceptual and Motor Skills 27: 595–599.

Moore, Joan W. 1971. "Mexican Americans." Gerontologist 11:30–35.

Munnichs, J. M. 1968. Old Age and Finitude: A Contribution to Psycho-gerontology. New York: S. Karger.

Nam, Charles B., Norman L. Weatherby, and Kathleen A. Ockay 1978. "Causes of death which contribute to the mortality crossover effects." Social Biology 25:306–334.

National Center for Health Statistics 1977. Current Estimates from the Health Interview Survey: United States—1976. Public Health Service, Vital and Health Statistics, Series 10, Number 119. Washington, D.C.: U.S. Government Printing Office.

———. 1978. Health Characteristics of Minority Groups, United States, 1976. Public Health Service, Vital and Health Statistics, Advance Data, Number 27. Washington, D.C.: U.S. Government Printing Office.

———. 1980. Health United States—1979. Public Health Service. Washington, D.C.: U.S. Government Printing Office.

National Council on Aging 1972. Triple Jeopardy: Myth or Reality. Washington, D.C.: National Council on Aging.

National Urban League 1964. Double Jeopardy: The Older Negro in America Today. New York: National Urban League.

Neugarten, Bernice L., Robert Havighurst, and Sheldon S. Tobin 1961. "The measurement of life satisfaction." Journal of Gerontology 16:134–143.

Newton, Frank 1980. "Issues in research and service delivery among Mexican American elderly." Gerontologist 20:208–213.

Newton, Frank, and Rene A. Ruiz 1981. "Chicano culture and mental health among the elderly." In Manuel R. Miranda and Rene A. Ruiz (eds.), Chicano Aging and Mental Health. U.S. Department of Health and Human Services, U.S. Public Health Service, National Institute of Mental Health, pp. 38–75.

Orchowsky, Stan J., and Iris A. Parham 1979. "Life satisfaction of blacks and whites: a lifespan approach." Paper presented at the Annual Meeting of the Gerontological Society, Washington, D.C.

Poston, Dudley L., Jr., and David Alvirez 1973. "On the cost of being a Mexican American worker." Social Science Quarterly 53:697–709.

Ramirez, Oscar, and Carlos H. Arce (Forthcoming). "The contemporary Chicano family: an empirically based review." In Augustine Baron, Jr. (ed.), Explorations in Chicano Psychology. New York: Praeger, pp. 3–28.

Reich, Julie M., Michael A. Stegman, and Nancy W. Stegman 1966. Relocating the Dispossessed Elderly: A Study of Mexican Americans. Philadelphia: Institute of Environmental Studies, University of Pennsylvania.

Reynolds, David K., and Richard A. Kalish 1974. "Anticipation of futurity as a function of ethnicity and age." Journal of Gerontology 29:224–231.

Riley, Matilda W., and Anne Foner 1968. Aging and Society, Volume I: An Inventory of Research Findings. New York: Russell Sage.

Riley, Matilda W., Marilyn Johnson, and Anne Foner (eds.) 1972. Aging and Society, Volume III: A Sociology of Age Stratification. New York: Russell Sage.

Riley, Matilda W. 1976. "Age strata in social systems." Pp. 189–217 in Robert H. Binstock and Ethel Shanas (eds.), Handbook of Aging and the Social Sciences. New York: Van Nostrand Reinhold.

Rives, Norfleet W. 1977. "The effects of census errors on life table estimates of black mortality." Public Health Briefs 67:867–868.

Rosenberg, Morris 1979. Conceiving the Self. New York: Basic Books.

Rosenfeld, Rachael A. 1980. "Race and sex differences in career dynamics." American Sociological Review 45:583–609.

Sauer, William J. 1977. "Morale of the urban aged: a regression analysis by race." Journal of Gerontology 32:600–608.

Seltzer, Mildred M., Sherry L. Corbett, and Robert C. Atchley (eds.) 1978. Social Problems of the Aging. Belmont, Calif.: Wadsworth.

Shanas, Ethel, Peter Townsend, Dorothy Wedderburn, Henning Friis, Paul Milhoi, and Jan Stehouer 1968. Older People in Three Industrial Societies. New York: Atherton.

Shanas, Ethel, and George L. Maddox 1976. "Aging, health and the organization of health resources." Pp. 592–618 in Robert H. Binstock and Ethel Shanas (eds.), Handbook of Aging and the Social Sciences. New York: Van Nostrand Reinhold.

Simmons, Roberta G. 1978. "Blacks and high self-esteem: a puzzle." Social Psychology Quarterly 41:54–57.

Spreitzer, Elmer, and Elden E. Snyder 1974. "Correlates of life satisfaction among the aged." Journal of Gerontology 29: 454–458.

Staples, Robert 1976. "The Black American Family." In Charles H. Mindel and Robert W. Habenstein (eds.), Ethnic Families in America. New York: Elsevier.

Stern, Michael P. 1979. "The recent decline in ischemic heart disease mortality." Annals of Internal Medicine 91:630–640.

Taylor, Marylee C., and Edward J. Walsh 1979. "Explanations of black self-esteem: some empirical tests." Social Psychology Quarterly 42:242–253.

Varghese, Rahu, and Fred Medinger 1979. "Fatalism in response to stress among the minority aged." Pp. 96–116 in Donald E. Gelfand and Alfred J. Kutzik (eds.), Ethnicity and Aging. New York: Springer Publishing.

Ward, Russell A. 1980. "The stability of racial differences across age strata." Revision of a Paper Presented at the Annual Meeting of the Gerontological Society, Washington, D.C., 1979.

Whittington, Frank 1975. "Aging and the relative income status of blacks." Black Aging 1:6–13.

Wilson, William J. 1978. The Declining Significance of Race. Chicago: University of Chicago Press.

Witt, David D., George D. Lowe, Charles W. Peek, and Evans W. Curry 1980. "The changing association between age and happiness: emerging trend or methodological artifact?" Social Forces 58:1302–1307.

Wylie, Floyd 1971. "Attitudes toward aging and the aged among black Americans: some historical perspectives." Aging and Human Development 2:66–70.

8 Women and Men: Mortality and Health of Older People[1]

Lois M. Verbrugge
University of Michigan

To soothe the feelings of her children when they lost a sibling battle, my mother would say, "Everything will even out by the time you're 80." While this may be true for minor matters like candy bars and checkers games, it is certainly not true for the important matters of health and mortality. Individuals in different demographic and social groupings differ sharply in their chances of reaching older ages (65+) and in their health during later years. The differences are greatest by sex: Men have notably higher death rates at all ages; thus, fewer of them ever reach age 65. And among older men and women, the men appear to have more serious health problems. In contrast, the women have more numerous but apparently milder problems.

Although large sex differences in health and mortality have existed throughout this century, we scarcely know the reasons for them. They emerge from some combination of genetic risks for each sex, from risks acquired during life, and from attitudes that influence symptom perception and curative behavior. Men's overall risks are higher than women's, but we do not know which risks are most important in causing their disadvantage. Will women's favored status continue in coming decades? It is popularly believed that as women participate more in the labor force and adopt lifestyles similar to those of men, their health and longevity will suffer. It is true that if women and men have more similar roles and activities in the future, their health profiles and death rates will be somewhat more similar

[1]In addition to Helena Z. Lopata and George C. Myers, the author is grateful to Berit Ingersoll, Tom Hickey, Edith Gomberg, and Tom Wan for their critical reading of an earlier version of this paper. Jean Kracke provided competent research assistance.

throughout life, including the older ages. But the future may be one of lower mortality for both sexes rather than of increased rates for women.

This paper reviews data on health and mortality of older men and women, and it suggests reasons for the sex differences. The paper is organized in seven sections: population data for older men and women; past, current, and projected mortality for men and women; contemporary sex differentials in the physical health status of older people; differences in older people's use of health services and drugs (medications); plausible explanations for the sex differences in health and mortality; key research questions for testing the explanations; and thoughts about future sex differences in health and mortality of older people.

The paper focuses on physical health and on psychosocial factors that explain sex differences. Mental health is occasionally considered, as a cause or consequence of physical health. Biomedical factors influencing health are sometimes mentioned, but the emphasis is on how people's social and psychological characteristics influence their health status, health behavior, and mortality.

A few definitions are in order. "Health status" refers to measures of illness, injury, and symptoms. It includes individuals' general evaluations of their health, interview reports of health problems, and data from medical examinations. "Health behavior" refers to all curative and preventive actions,[2] relating exclusively to disability (called restricted activity), long-term disability (called functional limitation), health services utilization, drug use (medications), and other preventive health behaviors.

THE POPULATION OF OLDER MEN AND WOMEN

The older population has grown rapidly, both in number and as a percentage of the total population. In 1900, there were 1.5 million women and 1.6 million men aged 65 and over. They were 4.1 percent and 4.0 percent, respectively, of the total female and male populations. The sex ratio was close to parity: 102.0 for people 65 and over and 96.3 for people 75 and over (Table 1).

Women now predominate in the 65 and over age group. In 1979, there were 14.6 million women these ages and 10.0 million men. Older women were 12.9 percent of all females in the United States; the men were 9.4 percent of all males. The sex ratio for older people was 68 men per 100 women. The gap in numbers of men and women widens even more for the very elderly (85 and over), with only 45 men per 100 women.

---

[2]As used here, "health behavior" encompasses Kasl and Cobb's (1966a, 1966b) three terms: health behavior, illness behavior, and sick-role behavior.

TABLE 1
The Population of Older Men and Women, United States, 1900–2050

	Size of older population (millions)			Percent of total population which is 65+ years old			Percent of older population which is 75+ years old			Sex ratio (males per 100 females)			
	Both sexes	Men	Women	Both sexes	Men	Women	Both sexes	Men	Women	65+	65–74	75–84	85+
1900[1]	3.1	1.6	1.5	4.1	4.0	4.1	22.5	22.0	23.0	102.0	104.5	— 96.3 —	
1970	22.4	9.2	13.2	9.8	8.4	11.2	37.8	27.4	39.7	72.0	77.7	65.9	53.2
1979	24.7	10.0	14.6	11.2	9.4	12.9	38.1	33.7	41.1	68.4	77.0	60.4	44.7
2000	31.8	12.7	19.1	12.2	10.0	14.3	45.2	39.7	48.9	66.6	78.6	59.9	39.4
2050	55.5	22.1	33.4	17.6	14.5	20.4	48.0	41.6	52.2	66.0	80.6	61.5	38.8

Estimated population for July 1, 1979

	(millions)			(percent distribution)		
	Both sexes	Men	Women	Both sexes	Men	Women
65+	24.7	10.0	14.6	100.0	100.0	100.0
65–69	8.7	3.9	4.8	35.2	38.6	32.9
70–74	6.6	2.8	3.8	26.7	27.7	26.0
75–79	4.3	1.7	2.6	17.3	16.8	17.7
80–84*	2.8	1.0	1.8	11.3	9.8	12.3
85+	2.3	0.7	1.6	9.5	7.2	11.0
Median Age	72.5	71.8	73.1			

Projected population for July 1, 2000 (Series II)

	(millions)			(percent distribution)		
	Both sexes	Men	Women	Both sexes	Men	Women
65+	31.8	12.7	19.1	100.0	100.0	100.0
65–69	9.2	4.2	5.0	28.9	32.6	26.4
70–74	8.2	3.5	4.7	25.9	27.7	24.7
75–79	6.4	2.5	3.9	10.1	19.7	20.3
80–84	4.2	1.5	2.8	13.3	11.6	14.5
85+	3.8	1.1	2.7	11.8	8.4	14.1
Median Age	74.1	73.1	74.8			

SOURCES: For 1900, Bureau of the Census, Current Population Reports, P-23, No. 311. For 1970, Bureau of the Census, Current Population Reports, P-23, No. 59. For 1979, Bureau of the Census, Current Population Reports, P-25, No. 870. For 2000 and 2050, Bureau of the Census, Current Population Reports, P-25, No. 704.

[1] All figures are for July 1 of the year stated.

141

Future growth of the older population is expected to be substantial. Recent projections made by the Census Bureau show 19.1 million older women and 12.7 million older men in the year 2000. This is a 30 percent increase over 1979 for women and a 27 percent increase for men. In 2000, the sex ratio will be a bit lower than it is now (about 67 men per 100 women) and remarkably low for the very elderly (39 men per 100 women). By 2050, there will be 33.4 million women and 22.1 million men aged 65 and over, with a sex ratio of 66 men per 100 women.

Sex composition of the older population is influenced by several factors during the life spans of birth cohorts: the sex ratio at birth, mortality rates across life, and net immigration. Major events that a cohort experiences can have lasting impact on its sex composition. For example, heavy immigration of young males early in the century has resulted in relatively many men now aged 75 and over. Because of World War II deaths, they will be followed in the next two decades by cohorts with relatively few men. This historical sequence of cohorts will cause some fluctuations in sex ratios and growth rates for the older population in coming years. Disregarding these historical factors, we would expect the sex ratios to drift downward because women's death rates have dropped faster than men's throughout this century and will probably continue to do so for some decades. We would expect the growth rates to decrease slowly because a population ages mainly when fertility rates drop. In the United States, large fertility declines occurred in the first half of this century and, after being interrupted by the Baby Boom, they continued downward. Fertility rates are now low and they are unlikely to drop much farther; thus, the growth rate of the older population ultimately slows down.

Population aging has been a major demographic feature of the 20th century in the United States. The U.S. population will continue to age in the coming decades, but at a slower pace than before. (When the Baby Boom cohorts of the late 1940's and the 1950's become 65 and over, there will be a temporary quickening of this pace, although the overall rate of population aging will continue to decline.) The proportion of the population which is 65+ will continue to rise, and the older population will itself become older (Table 1). Increasingly, the older population will be dominated by women, especially among the very elderly.

Population aging will not continue forever. Projections indicate that if fertility and mortality remain at their current low levels, the population age structure and sex ratios will have become constant by 2050 (Table 1). Even allowing for some fluctuations in fertility and mortality (due to family size preferences, medical breakthroughs, wars, etc.), the population structure will be more stable than it is now. Most population aging will be over, and the older age category will grow at about the same slow rate as the total population.

MORTALITY OF OLDER MEN AND WOMEN

Mortality rates for older men are higher than for older women (Table 2). This is true for all age categories after 65 and for all leading causes of death.[3] Men's disadvantage is largest at the earlier ages (6569), then decreases with advancing age.[4] Older men's death rates are strikingly higher than women's for bronchitis, emphysema, and asthma and for suicide.

Life expectancy figures reflect older men's disadvantage. Using current mortality rates, we can determine how many years a person reaching age 65 can expect to live. Men who are 65 now expect about 14 more years of life, compared to 18 for women (Table 3).

The female advantage appears in every age category after 65. Even at age 85, women can anticipate living 1.4 years more than men who reach that age.

Three aspects of sex mortality differentials are described below in detail: How large contemporary sex differences are for the older population, compared with other ages; trends in sex differences over time for older people; and future sex differences in their mortality.

Males suffer a mortality disadvantage at all ages. Across the entire age span, sex differences are greatest at ages 15–24 and 25–34, when men's mortality rates are more than twice those of women. From age 35, the gap closes substantially and remains relatively constant throughout ages 65–74. After about age 75, sex differences become smaller for "all causes" of death and for most leading causes (Table 2). Apparently, as men and women approach biological limits of human life, their risks of dying become more similar than before. But we must not forget that even near those limits, a man still has less chance of surviving from one year to the next than a woman of the same age.

In this century, mortality rates dropped for both sexes until about 1950. From 1950 to 1970, death rates were relatively stable. Around 1970, they began a sudden and remarkable turn downward. These historical trends have appeared in virtually all age groups of males and females, but during the periods when rates declined, females benefited more than males. Their death rates have dropped faster, resulting in an everwidening gap in life expectancy between the sexes (Table 3).

The 1970's merit special attention as a harbinger of the future. Among the older population, rates dropped for virtually all leading causes; the drop was es-

---

[3]The one exception is diabetes, for which rates are virtually the same for older men and women. This is a recent phenomenon; for many years, women had higher rates than men.

[4]This statement is based on sex ratios (M/F). If we consider sex differences (M-F) instead, we find that the gap widens with advancing age. There is no contradiction: Death rates rise so sharply with advancing age that the absolute differences (M-F) can expand while the relative differences (M/F) shrink.

TABLE 2
Sex Differential in Mortality for the Older Population, United States, 1978

	Older ages			
	65–74	75–84	85+	All ages[1]
Death rates (per 100,000)				
All causes of death				
Males	4185	9385	17259	803
Females	2138	5863	13541	447
Sex ratios (M/F)[2]				
All causes of death	1.96	1.71	1.54	1.80
Diseases of heart[3]	2.14	1.52	1.20	2.04
Malignant neoplasms	1.83	1.93	1.88	1.50
Cerebrovascular				
diseases	1.39	1.14	0.98	1.19
Influenza and				
pneumonia	2.29	1.89	1.52	1.83
Arteriosclerosis	1.63	1.22	1.03	1.28
Diabetes mellitus	1.00	0.92	0.91	1.02
Accidents	2.12	1.74	1.48	2.85
Motor vehicle	2.21	2.50	4.25	2.85
All other	2.15	1.56	1.34	2.85
Bronchitis, emphysema,				
and asthma	3.63	4.71	3.77	2.92
Cirrhosis of liver	2.59	2.30	2.34	2.17
Nephritis and nephrosis	1.65	2.02	1.97	1.59
Suicide	4.19	6.43	9.47	2.98

SOURCES: National Center for Health Statistics, Monthly Vital Statistics Report, Vol. 29, No. 6, Supplement 2, 17 September 1980, and unpublished tabulations from the National Center for Health Statistics.

[1]Age-adjusted. Rates are standardized to the age distribution of the 1940 total U.S. population.
[2]Ratio is male rate divided by female rate
[3]The 10 leading causes of death for people 65+ are listed in rank order. Suicide (rank 11) is also included because of its notable sex differentials.

pecially large for heart diseases and cerebrovascular diseases. (Only malignant neoplasms registered an increase during this period.) The percentage declines for "all causes" and for leading ones were generally greater for older women than older men. Other age groups showed similar trends in the 1970's. Thus, both sexes now have greater longevity than a decade ago, with women having gained slightly more than men.[5]

---

[5]For further discussion of recent trends in sex mortality differentials, see Metropolitan Life Insurance Company (1980) and Verbrugge (1980). Recent trends in mortality for elderly people (85+) are examined by Rosenwaike et al. (1980). The remarkable drop in heart disease mortality in the 1970's is examined in Havlik and Feinleib (1979), Keys (1980), Kleinman et al. (1979), and Stallones (1980). Other good references are Siegel (1979), for long-term trends in mortality of older people, and Myers (1978), for cross-national comparisons of mortality for older people.

TABLE 3
Sex Differentials in Life Expectancy,
United States, 1949–51 to 1978[1]

	Life expectancy at age					
	O	65	70	75	80	85
Males						
1949–51	65.5	12.7	10.1	7.8	5.9	4.4
1960	66.6	17.8	10.2	7.9	6.0	4.5
1970	67.1	13.1	10.6	8.4	,6.6	5.3
1978	69.5	14.0	11.1	8.7	6.9	5.5
Females						
1949-51	71.0	15.0	11.7	8.9	6.7	4.9
1960	73.1	15.8	12.4	9.4	6.8	5.0
1970	74.8	17.0	13.6	10.5	8.0	6.1
1978	77.2	18.4	14.7	11.5	8.9	6.9
Sex difference (F-M)[2]						
1949–51	5.5	2.3	1.6	1.1	0.8	0.5
1960	6.5	3.0	2.2	1.5	0.8	0.5
1970	7.7	3.9	3.0	2.1	1.4	0.8
1978	7.7	4.4	3.6	2.8	2.0	1.4

SOURCES: For 1949-51, Grove and Hetzel (1968). For 1960, Vital Statistics of the United States 1960, Vol. II, Part A. For 1970, Vital Statistics of the United States 1970, Vol. 11, Part A. For 1978, Vital Statistics Report, Vol. 29, No. 6, Supplement 2, 17 September 1980.
[1]Life expectancy is the expected remaining years of life for a person age x.
[2]Difference is female rate minus male rate.

If the decline in mortality continues, men and women will enjoy longer lives in 2050 than now. Current projections are that life expectancy at birth (o eO) in 2050 will be 81.0 years for females and 71.8 years for males. This is an increase of 3.8 years over 1978 for females and 2.3 years for males. The gap between women and men is projected to increase, but at a declining rate. In other words, the biggest gains for women compared with men have already occurred, and future gains will be smaller.

These projections for 2050 indicate what will happen if current mortality trends continue. "Real life" may be quite different. Some demographers think that as women participate more in the labor force and the community, their risks of death will become increasingly similar to men's. If so, the special advantage enjoyed by women in the 20th century will end, and the gap between men's and women's mortality will narrow. Although this scenario is fundamentally different from current projections, it is certainly plausible and possible.

What are the implications of changing social behavior of older men and women? People who live long have endured many insults to their health and survived them. If women do behave "more like men" in their young and middle adult years, their health profiles and mortality risks in old age are likely to resemble those of men, and mortality differentials for the older population should narrow. Yet, as I will discuss later, it is unlikely the sexes will ever have equal rates.

HEALTH STATUS AND DISABILITY OF OLDER
MEN AND WOMEN[6]

With increasing age, resistance to new diseases declines, while chronic conditions developed earlier in life tend to deteriorate; and although acute conditions are less frequent, the recovery period for them is longer. Heart disease, cancer, and hypertension are common companions of old age; three-fourths of older people ultimately die from heart disease, cancer, or stroke. Less life-threatening but prevalent and bothersome are arthritis, digestive disorders, foot and skin problems, and chronic respiratory symptoms. Sensory (vision, hearing, balance) and mental faculties often decline; bones and muscles weaken.

Most chronic diseases are symptomatic before they cause death; thus a period of poor health usually precedes death. Given this sequence, we expect older men to be less healthy than older women, especially from conditions that are leading causes of death. Health data confirm that older men are more seriously ill than older women, but the data also indicate that older women are more frequently ill than men. This is an intriguing difference. Data on subjective perceptions of health status, acute and chronic conditions, and disability for acute and chronic conditions support this conclusion.

Self-Rated Health Status

The majority (78 percent) of noninstitutionalized older people consider their health "excellent" or "good" (Assistant Secretary for Health, 1978). Older people probably compare themselves to age peers, including friends who have died. Thus, their evaluation is more positive than if they compared their health to younger adults or to their own health when younger. Only slightly more older men (32 percent) than women (30 percent) consider their health "fair" or "poor."[7]

If institutional residents were included, reports of poor health would undoubtedly increase. Only about 5 percent of the population 65 and over are in institutions, but these people have poorer health than people outside of institutions (Fillenbaum, 1979). Older women's self-ratings especially would worsen, since a larger percentage of them are institutionalized than older men.

---

[6]This section and the next summarize health data for older men and women. Previous reviews are available in Atchley (1977), Carpenter et al. (1974), Kovar (1977, 1979), National Center for Health Statistics (1971), Riley and Foner (1968), and Shanas and Maddox (1976).

[7]Other studies find similar results (Larson, 1978; Maddox, 1962). How subjective health is related to a number of health problems for older men and women is studied by Ferraro (1980) and Fillenbaum (1979).

TABLE 4
Acute Conditions and Resulting
Disability for Older Men and Women, United States, 1977-78
(Rates per 100 persons per year)

	Men 65+	Women 65+
Acute conditions (rate)[1]	97.3	120.6
Injuries (rate)[2]	16.1	26.0
Percent of injuries sustained at home	50%	63%
Restricted activity days for acute conditions (rate)	988.0	1361.0
Average days per condition	10.2	11.3
Bed disability days for acute conditions (rate)	435.0	559.0
Average days per condition	4.5	4.6
Restricted activity days for injuries (rate)	412.0	827.0
Average days per injury	25.6	31.8
Bed disability days for injuries (rate)	117.0	193.0
Average days per injury	7.3	7.4

SOURCES: National Center for Health Statistics, Vital and Health Statistics Series 10, No. 132 (for July 1977-June 1978), and Series 10, No. 130 (for 1978). See also Series 10, No. 126, for 1977 calendar year.

[1]Acute conditions are counted if they caused restricted activity or required medical attention.

[2]Age-sex specific rates for other types of acute conditions than injuries (infective and parasitic diseases, respiratory conditions, digestive system conditions, all other acute conditions) are available for 1957–58 in Vital Statistics, Series B, No. 6, but not since then.

Acute Conditions and Resulting Disability

Older women have higher incidence rates of acute illnesses and of injuries (Table 4). Most injuries for both sexes occur at home, especially for women. It is therefore no surprise that older women have more days of restricted activity and bed disability for acute conditions in a year. However, an intriguing fact is that older women have more short-term disability *per condition;* that is, they cut down more on usual activities for an acute problem (especially injuries) than men do.

Chronic Conditions and Resulting Disability

Heart disease, hypertension, arthritis, and diabetes are much more prevalent among older people than younger adults. Data from health examinations of the U.S. population show that older women have higher rates than older men for all of these, particularly for hypertension, arthritis, and diabetes (Table 5).[8] In addition, more older women have high serum cholesterol levels (viewed as a risk factor for cardiovascular diseases). However, two important qualifications stand out. First, there are various kinds of heart disease (coronary, hypertensive, rheumatic, etc.). Coronary heart disease is especially life-threatening, and for this, older men have higher prevalence rates. Second, although more women have moderate or severe arthritis, more men suffer from mild arthritis.

The national health examination data also show that women have lower blood hematocrit levels (a sign of anemia). Older men have more serious skin conditions.

Information about chronic conditions is also available from interview surveys and hospital records. These show that older women have higher prevalence rates than men for many more kinds of chronic problems (Table 6).[9] For example, rates of hypertension, arthritis, diabetes, anemia, migraine, sciatica, hypertensive heart disease, varicose veins, digestive and urinary problems, allergies, and orthopedic impairments are higher for women. Most of these are bothersome problems, but seldom causes of death. Also, older women are more likely than men to have several chronic conditions.[10] In contrast, the list of diseases for which men have higher rates is shorter, but it contains most of the leading causes of death for older people: heart conditions (especially coronary heart disease), cerebrovascular disease, arteriosclerosis, pneumonia, and emphysema/asthma.[11] (Men also have higher rates for some problems that seldom cause

---

[8]The data come from national sample surveys which included physical examinations. They are the Health Examination Survey (HES) conducted in 1960-62 and the Health and Nutrition Examination Survey (HANES I) conducted in 1971-74. For HES, the older population includes people aged 65–79; for HANES, 65–74. (Problems with response rates precluded sampling people above these ages.) A table summarizing sex differences in these two surveys for all ages is in Verbrugge (1981a: table 2).

[9]Table 6 is based on data from three surveys: the Health Interview Survey (HIS), Health and Nutrition Examination Survey, and the Hospital Discharge Survey (HDS). They vary in how chronic conditions are queried. HIS has used two formats: One simply asks if a person has had a certain condition in the past 12 months; the other, if a person is limited in activity or mobility by a condition. HANES asks if a doctor ever told the person that he or she had a certain condition and if the condition is still present. HDS provides rates of discharge from short-stay hospitals. It is remarkable that, despite such large differences in how chronic conditions are queried, *sex differences* are usually the same across the three surveys. In other words, for a particular condition, the same sex has higher rates. (However, the levels of those rates vary across the surveys.)

[10]Source: National Center for Health Statistics, Vital and Health Statistics, Series B, No. 11. The data are for 1957–58; there are no more recent figures for the national population.

[11]What about the other leading causes of death? 1) Women have higher morbidity rates for diabetes, but men now have slightly higher mortality rates. 2) Women report more malignant neoplasms and are hospitalized more for them compared with men, but women's death rates are lower. This discrepancy can reflect two things: (a) Women have their cancers diagnosed and treated earlier, so they know about their problems when interviewed. Also, more of women's cancers can be controlled, leaving a female population with cancer experience but lower risk of cancer mortality. (b) Women may be more willing to report cancer than men. 3) No prevalence rates are available for

TABLE 5
Sex Differences in Chronic Conditions and Symptoms for Older Adults
Based on Medical Examinations, United States

KEY:	M	Men have higher morbidity
	F	Women have higher morbidity
	HES	Health Examination Survey 1960–62 (ages 65–79)
	HANES	Health and Nutrition Examination Survey 1971–74 (ages 65–74)

Heart Disease (HES)	
Definitive heart disease	F
Hypertensive heart disease	F
Coronary heart disease	M
Suspect heart disease	M
Hypertension/high blood pressure (HES, HANES)	
Definite hypertension	F
Borderline hypertension	F
Arthritis (HES, HANES)	
Osteoarthritis	F
Mild	M
Moderate or severe	F
Rheumatoid arthritis	F
Skin conditions (HANES)	
Significant skin pathology	M
Needs care ("not now under best care")	M
Symptoms of chronic disease[1] (HES, HANES)	
Mean blood glucose	F
Mean hematocrit	F
Mean serum cholesterol	F
Percent with serum cholesterol of 260 mg/100 ml or more	F
Vision status (HES, HANES)	
Binocular visual acuity—uncorrecte	
Poor distance vision[2]	F
Poor near vision[2]	F
Monocular visual acuity—corrected	
Poor distance vision[3]	F
Hearing status (HES)[4]	
Median hearing level for better ear	
1,000 cycles per second	M
3,000 cycles per second	M
6,000 cycles per second	M
Speech	M

cirrhosis of the liver and nephritis/nephrosis. (In Table 6, they are encompassed in "Other digestive system conditions" and "Diseases of the urinary system," respectively.) 4) Accident deaths result from injuries. Injury rates are higher for older women, but accident mortality rates and hospitalization rates are higher for men. Apparently, women's injuries are less severe and therefore less likely to cause impairment or death. (The data on disability days for injuries-higher for women—are not necessarily contradictory. Women may take better care of themselves for an injury than men do. This would readily account for their higher restricted activity and bed disability per injury.)

TABLE 5 *(contd.)*

Dental status (HES, HANES)	
With one or both arches edentulous	F
Completely edentulous	F
Average DMF score[5]	F
Periodontal disease	M
Should see dentist at early date	M

SOURCES: National Center for Health Statistics, Vital and Health Statistics, Series 11, Nos. 6, 7, 11, 12, 13, 15, 17, 18, 22, 24, 25, 36, 201, 203, 205, 212, 213, 214, 215.

[1]High blood glucose is a sign of diabetes. Low hematocrit is a sign of anemia. High serum cholesterol levels are associated with coronary heart disease.

[2]Poor distance vision is 20/100 or worse. Poor near vision is 14/70 or worse.

[3]Poor distance vision is 20/50 or worse in the better eye.

[4]See also Vital and Health Statistics, Series 11, No. 215, for similar results for HANES.   [5]Sum of decayed, missing, filled, and nonfunctional teeth.

TABLE 6

Sex Differences in Selected Chronic Conditions
for Older Adults Based on Interviews and
Hospital Records, United States

KEY:	M	Men have higher rates
	F	Women have higher rates
	?	Data sources show conflicting results
	( )	A leading cause of death for older people

Neoplasms[1]	
Malignant neoplasms	(F)
Benign neoplasms	F
Endocrine, nutritional, and metabolic diseases	
Thyroid conditions	F
Diabetes	(F)
Gout	M
Diseases of the blood and blood-forming organs	
Anemia	F
Mental disorders	
Epilepsy or chronic convulsions	M
Migraine	F
Sciatica	F
Neuralgia and neuritis	F
Diseases of the circulatory system	
Heart conditions	(M)
Active rheumatic fever and chronic rheumatic heart disease	F
Hypertensive heart disease	F
Coronary (ischemic) heart disease	M
Other heart disease, including heart murmur	F
Hypertensive heart disease without heart involvement (hypertension)	F
Cerebrovascular disease	(M)

continued

TABLE 6 *(contd.)*

Arteriosclerosis	(M)
Varicose veins	F
Hemorrhoids	?
Other circulatory system conditions (e.g., phlebitis, thrombophlebitis)	F
Diseases of the respiratory system	
Pneumonia	(M)
Emphysema	(M)
Asthma	(M)
Chronic sinusitus	?
Diseases of the digestive system	
Peptic ulcer	M
Hernia	M
Other digestive system conditions (e.g., enteritis, colitis, gallstones, hepatitis)	F
Diseases of the genitourinary system	
Diseases of the urinary system (e.g., nephritis)	F
Diseases of prostate	M (only)
Disorders of female reproductive organs	F (only)
Diseases of the skin and subcutaneous tissue	
Eczema, dermatitis, and urticaria	F
Psoriasis and similar disorders	M
Corns and callosities	F
Diseases of nail	F
Diseases of sebaceous glands (e.g., acne)	M
Allergies	F
Diseases of the musculoskeletal system and connective tissues	
Arthritis	F
Rheumatism	M
Displacement of intervertebral disc (slipped disc)	M
Bunion	F
Synovitis, bursitis, and tenosynovitis	F
Accidents, poisonings, and violence	
Fractures	F
Laceration and open wound	M
Impairments	
Visual impairments	F
Hearing impairments	M
Speech defects	M
Complete or partial paralysis	M
Absence of major extremities, fingers, or toes	M
Orthopedic impairments of back, spine, upper extremity, shoulder, lower extremity, hip	F[2]

SOURCES: Data are from the Health Interview Survey, the Health and Nutrition Examination Survey (Medical History Questionnaire), and the Hospital Discharge Survey. The specific source(s) for each condition are shown in Verbrugge (1981a: Table 3). Similar results from a national survey in 1957 are shown in Shanas (1962:8).

[1]Titles are organized according to the International Classification of Diseases.

[2]For some specific sites, men have higher rates. But overall, F > M.

death, for example, gout, peptic ulcer, hernia, psoriasis and sebaceous gland diseases, paralysis, and absence of extremities.) The sex difference for orthopedic problems (higher for women) merits comment: Up to age 65, men have more orthopedic problems; after that age, women do. This is largely due to increased vulnerability of women to injury and impairment from osteoporosis (decrease in bone tissue), which increases sharply after menopause (Gordan and Vaughan, 1977).

What do men and women suffer from most? If we rank the chronic conditions that cause limitations, women are troubled most by arthritis/rheumatism, heart conditions, hypertension, and back/spine impairments. For men, the top problems are heart conditions, arthritis/rheumatism, back/spine impairments, and lower extremity/hip impairments (Bureau of the Census, 1980). These data are based on a question about conditions that have caused major problems in role performance. A more day-to-day perspective comes from asking people what problems have bothered them recently. In 1957, the leading symptoms "in the past four weeks" for older women were general discomforts (not associated with any specific condition), followed by symptoms of circulatory diseases, digestive diseases, and musculoskeletal ailments. For men, the list was general discomforts, then symptoms of circulatory diseases, ear diseases, and musculoskeletal ailments (Shanas, 1962). (More recent data are not available.) These lists are similar to those for limiting conditions, except that for both sexes daily life has many "aches and pains" not due to specific conditions.

The impression that older men have more serious chronic problems is borne out in data on limitations (Table 7). A much larger percentage of older men say they are limited in their major activity. Women, however, report more problems in their secondary activities (clubs, church, etc.), mobility, and personal care activities (bathing, eating, etc.). They have more restricted activity and bed disability days for chronic conditions. And more of them use special aids (cane, walker, wheelchair, special shoes).[12]

The data seem contradictory at first glance, but they are not. For the question about major activity, most older men are asked about problems in having a paid job; most women, about keeping house. For older people, a paid job is probably more physically demanding than housework. (At the very least, a job is less flexible in permitting rests and private time.) Therefore, even if men and women were equally sick, older men would report more limitation in "major activity." Also, regardless of their roles during life, older women may reduce their activities when chronic conditions are at an earlier, milder stage. This would boost women's reports of functional limitations and short-term disability for chronic ailments. That older men report more problems in a major social role while

---

[12]Data on special aids are in Black (1980). Older men are more likely to have an artificial limb or brace—probably a reflection of injuries earlier in life rather than of chronic conditions in older ages.

TABLE 7
Chronic Conditions and Resulting Disability
Among Older Men and Women, United States

	Men 65+	Women 65+
Limitation of activity due to chronic condition (1978)		
Limited in major activity (percent)	43.2%	34.9%
Limited but not in major activity	5.0	7.8
Limitation of mobility due to chronic condition (1972)		
Has trouble getting around alone (percent)	5.4%	6.1%
Needs help in getting around	6.0	7.2
Confined to house	4.9	5.4
Disability days for chronic conditions (1977)[1]		
Restricted activity days (per person/year)	22.8 days	27.6 days
Bed disability days	8.2	11.2
Percent with difficulty in common tasks (1962)		
Walking stairs (percent)	24.0%	35.0%
Getting around the house	4.0	8.0
Washing/bathing	7.0	13.0
Dressing/putting on shoes	7.0	9.0
Cutting toenails	15.0	22.0

SOURCES: National Center for Health Statistics, Vital and Health Statistics, Series 10, Nos. 96, 126, 130; and Shanas et al. (1968) for common tasks items.

[1]Estimated from total disability days (1977) minus disability days for acute conditions (July 1977–June 1978).

women report more trouble in common daily activities reflects their roles and reactions to chronic problems, as well as their levels of real morbidity.

Sensory, Dental, and Nutritional Status

Older women have more vision problems than men, with poorer visual acuity both for uncorrected vision ("glasses off") and corrected vision ("glasses on"). Although women visit ophthalmologists and optometrists more than men do, they still see things less well in daily life.

On the other hand, older men have poorer hearing and dental status. Examinations reveal they have more impaired hearing at all decibel levels and more limitations in daily life from hearing impairments. More older men have periodontal disease and are considered to need prompt dental care. Interestingly, more older women are edentulous (have no natural teeth), and more of their natural teeth have had decay or fillings. It appears that women receive more dental care at earlier ages, whereas older men's current troubles reflect the accumulation of untreated problems which have worsened over time. The data cannot tell us whether men or women are intrinsically more prone to dental problems. They do show that most older women have had problems treated already, but many older men have not.

Older women have poorer nutritional status. They consume less protein, calcium, and iron than recommended, whereas men consume the recommended levels or more (Abraham et al., 1977:53). All three of the nutrients are critical to physical well-being, especially at older ages. In addition, more older women than men are obese (Assistant Secretary for Health, 1978). (For further discussions of nutrition for the older population, see Davis and Randall in this book.)

Comparisons With Other Age Groups

As people age, acute conditions become less frequent for both sexes, and chronic conditions predominate. Generally, older men and women are more similar in their acute conditions and disability than at earlier ages, but they are less similar in chronic conditions and limitation. In middle age, women have notably higher rates of acute conditions than men, partly because of reproductive events. Chronic conditions begin to emerge for both sexes in middle age, with men already showing higher rates for "killer" conditions and more major activity limitations than women.

Discussion

In summary, older women have more acute conditions and more chronic ones; they are bothered more by their chronic conditions, but these diseases are seldom lifethreatening. Older men have higher rates of lifethreatening conditions, which leads to employment restrictions and earlier death. In one sense, older women are "sicker," because their daily lives are more troubled by symptoms; but in another sense, older men are "sicker," because their chronic ailments are more severe and more likely to result in early death. When asked to summarize their health status, older men and women give a similar array of answers—but based on very different health experiences. It is possible that by cutting down activities and accepting limitations for health problems, older women may actually increase their longevity.[13]

---

[13]Recent changes in diabetes morbidity and mortality are suggestive. For years, older women have had notably higher morbidity and mortality from diabetes. Recently, death rates have become about equal for men and women; morbidity rates remain higher for women. Mortality rates have dropped for both sexes, but faster for women. Are diabetic women taking better care of themselves, so their risk of death ultimately becomes less than that of men?

The data suggest that older women accommodate response to health problems earlier and better than older men do. Although women may have more symptoms and chronic problems, their health behavior may reduce the pace of deterioration and enhance life expectancy. Men's relative lack of response to health problems in middle age may ultimately exact a large toll. If older men delay getting medical care when symptoms appear, the chances are reduced of controlling the problem by medication or by changes of habit. And even after diagnosis, older men may be more reluctant than women to respond by changing their behavior; this, too, increases their chances of early death.

Thus, attitudes and behavior towards illness may be very important in explaining sex differentials in shortterm disability, limitations, and death among older people. We know little about how older people cope with acute and chronic problems, and how these reactions ultimately affect their longevity.

We should not forget that the majority of older men and women rate their health "good" or "excellent." Health perceptions are critical to how they feel about life and how they behave. People who perceive their health favorably tend to be happier, more satisfied, more involved in social activities, less tense, and less lonely (Pollock et al., 1980; Tissue, 1972; Wan, 1976). The causal ties among these variables are not fully understood, but even so, it is clear that life is much more pleasant for older people who feel healthy than for those who feel unhealthy. This is true for both sexes.

HEALTH SERVICES USE AND DRUG USE BY OLDER MEN AND WOMEN

Older men and women need more health care than do younger adults. For acute problems and chronic flareups, older people can get medical treatment in familiar ways, often from a physician who has cared for them for years. The same is true for dental problems. However, discontinuities and difficult decisions loom when physical problems become severe and cause limitations. Then older people and their kin must think about institutionalization versus home care.

Because older men are more seriously ill, we might expect them to use more health services and drugs. Indeed, their hospitalization stays are higher. Nevertheless, older women exceed men in utilizing other types of short-term care (visits to physicians and dentists and drug use) and long-term care (institutions and community-based services).

Short-Term Care

Older women tend to make more physician visits per year than do older men (Table 8). Also, the time interval between visits is shorter for women. Visits to other health specialists mirror the sex differences for chronic conditions; older

TABLE 8

Health Services Use by Older Men and Women, United States
(Ages 65+ Unless Otherwise Stated)

	Men 65+	Women 65+
Number of physician visits in past year (per person) (1978)		
Age 65–74	5.5	6.8
75+	6.4	6.4
Number of visits to office-based physicians (1977)	3.8	4.4
Time interval since last physician visit (1978)		
Less than 6 months	65%	72%
6–11 months	12	10
1 year	7	6
2–4 years	10	7
5 or more years	6	4
Never	0	0
Don't know/NA	1	1
Number of dental visits in past year (per person) (1978)	1.0	1.4
Time interval since last dental visit (1978)		
Less than 6 months	23%	25%
6–11 months	8	8
1 year	8	8
2–4 years	15	13
5 or more years	45	44
Never	1	1
Don't know/NA	1	1
Discharges from short-stay hospitals (per 100 persons/year) (1978)		
(Health Interview Survey)	29.7	24.7
Hospital Discharge Survey—non-Federal hospitals		
Age 65–74	34.0	27.9
75+	56.1	49.2
Average length of hospital stay (days per episode) (1978)		
(Health Interview Survey)	10.9	11.3
(Hospital Discharge Survey)		
Age 65–74	10.1	10.7
75+	11.0	11.9

SOURCES: National Center for Health Statistics, Vital and Health Statistics, Series 10, No. 130, and Series 13, Nos. 43, 44, 46.

women see orthopedists, ophthalmologists, optometrists, and podiatrists more often, whereas men see dermatologists more (Carpenter et al., 1974:152). Visits to chiropractors are similar for older men and women. Women appear to have slightly higher use of dental care. For both physician and dental visits, sex differences for older people become smaller with advancing age; by age 75, visit rates are much closer for men and women than before. Most medical and dental care for older people is curative. Although preventive care is important for this age group, little is known about the preventive health services used by older men and women.[14]

Hospitalization stays are higher for older men, but women tend to stay longer for an episode.

How do these patterns of short-term care compare with earlier ages? At all ages, women have more physician visits than men, especially during the child-bearing years. Sex differences are much narrower for children and older people. Women also see dentists more often at all ages, though the frequency of visits declines with age for both sexes and becomes more similar. (Actually, if older men were tending fully to their dental needs, we would expect higher dental visit rates for them than for older women.) From ages 17 through 44, women have much higher hospital discharge rates than men; but when childbirth and other sex-specific conditions are excluded, the sex difference in hospital rates almost disappears. At about age 45, hospitalization rates begin to rise steeply for men; women's rates drop for a number of years but then also rise, though less rapidly than men's. Before age 65, men tend to have longer hospital stays (even when childbirth stays are excluded). This pattern reverses at older ages (65 and older). I shall offer a possible reason in the discussion section of this paper.

Long-Term Care

Long-term care refers to "professional or personal services required on a recurring or continuous basis by an individual because of chronic or permanent physical or mental impairment" (National Center for Health Statistics, 1980). The clientele for long-term care are people with functional limitations—those who have trouble in mobility or transportation, personal care, basic housekeeping activities, and self-management (taking medication, using the telephone). Until recently, long-term care was viewed as synonymous with institutional residence (in nursing or personal care homes, chronic disease hospitals, or mental hospitals). Increasingly, however, home care and other community-based ser-

---

[14]The 1973 Health Interview Survey included questions about preventive services such as electrocardiogram, glaucoma test, chest X-ray, eye exam, and routine physical exam. Unfortunately, data are not published for age-sex groups (National Center for Health Statistics, Vital and Health Statistics, Series 10, No. 110).

vices are available, and data are being gathered about their use by older men and women.[15]

Institutionalization

Most older people who are institutionalized live in nursing and personal care homes, where women constitute the majority of residents. This becomes increasingly true with advancing age (75–84, 85+). For chronic disease hospitals and mental hospitals, older men happen to have higher residence rates, but the proportions of older people in such institutions is low and the sex differences narrow at advanced ages (75+) (Bureau of the Census, 1973).[16]

In the United States, about 5 percent of the population aged 65 and over live in nursing and personal care homes. This figure rises with advancing age; 22 percent of people 85 and over reside in nursing homes. Most residents (86 percent in 1977) are 65 years or older, and 71 percent are women.

Older women in nursing and personal care homes are "sicker" than older men residents. They are less able to take care of their personal needs (e.g., bathing, dressing, toilet, eating); they need more assistance in walking, have poorer vision, and have poorer mental status; they have more chronic conditions and need more nursing care. (Only for hearing status are men residents more disabled than women residents.) One reason for the women's poorer functional status is their older average age (83 for women, 81 for men in 1969), but that is not the only reason, as I will suggest in the discussion section.[17]

In contrast, for younger ages, the men in nursing and personal care homes are likely to be more numerous and sicker than the women residents. The reversal for older people suggests that social factors are important in determining whether to institutionalize a man or woman. Under age 65, disabled men may be difficult for relatives to accept (they are "supposed to be working"), and their wives may have to seek outside employment, leaving no one at home to care for them. At older ages, these job-related factors disappear. Disabled older men are more likely to have a living spouse to care for them than disabled older women, who must find help with other kin or in institutions.

---

[15]For general discussions of long-term care, see Kane and Kane (1980), Office of Management and Budget (1980), and Weissert (1978).

[16]These statements are based on the 1970 Census of Population. Rates for earlier years are reported in Carpenter et al. (1974:141), and some of the sex differences there do not match the 1970 Census. This may have to do with rapid changes in types and numbers of institutions available to older people than to changes in decisions about sending men and women to nursing homes versus other institutions. For the same reason, data for the 1980 Census of Population may show marked changes compared with 1970.

[17]Data sources for the preceding two paragraphs are National Center for Health Statistics, Vital and Health Statistics, Series 12, Nos. 19, 24, and Series 13, No. 43. See also Series 12, No. 22, and Series 13, No. 27. For other data on institutional residents (but not by age-sex groups), see Bureau of the Census, Current Population Reports, Series P-23, No. 69.

Community-Based Care

Most older people with health problems are able to live in the community, given some assistance from kin or social service agencies. Little is known about how many older people obtain long-term care from communitybased sources (e.g., day care away from home, foster homes, hospice care).

We know a bit about home care services, which are the most common kind of community-based care. In 1968, 4 percent of noninstitutionalized people aged 65–74 had some home care; 14 percent of those aged 75 and over received it. Overall, more older women than men received some home care.[18] More recent data will soon be available from the 1979 and 1980 Health Interview Surveys, which asked numerous questions about functional limitations and assistance from formal and informal sources for noninstitutionalized people.

Self-Care

In the past two decades, some older people have developed organizations to promote their well-being and social status through local social activities and political lobbying. At the same time, the "women's movement" and "self-care movement" have grown. Not surprisingly, some organizations have emerged which are devoted solely to older women and to self-care for older people (Butler et al., 1979; Women and Health Roundtable, 1979). The former have questioned the medical establishment's and the drug industry's care of older women, but they have not actively promoted self-care. Older people are strongly attached to the modern health care system, and surveys indicate that they are very satisfied with the care they receive. This minimizes the viability of self-care programs (at least for current cohorts). Organizations for older women and elderly self-care are politically valuable, but they probably influence relatively few older men and women.

Drug Use (Medications)

There are limited data on older people's use of drugs for curative and preventive health care, but the sparse data consistently show that older women use more prescribed and nonprescribed medicines per year than older men. They also use more psychotropic drugs. Higher drug use by women occurs at all ages, not just among older people.[19]

---

[18]Data are published in National Center for Health Statistics, Vital and Health Statistics, Series 10, No. 73.

[19]Data sources on drug use are Bush and Rabin (1976), Mellinger et al. (1974), Parry et al. (1973), Rabin and Bush (1976), and National Center for Health Statistics, Vital and Health Statistics, Series 10, No. 108.

Discussion

In summary, older women use more ambulatory health services than men for both medical and dental care. Older men are hospitalized more often, but they stay fewer days for an episode than hospitalized women. Older women are more likely to receive home care services and to reside in a health institution (especially nursing and personal care homes). They also use more prescription and nonprescription drugs.

How can we explain these differences? Certainly, morbidity is an important factor prompting use of health services and drugs; it represents "need" for care. But many other factors come into play, such as attitudes about health care ("predisposing factors") and access to services and drugs ("enabling factors"). The evidence[20] on attitudes and access factors for older people shows that older people are very satisfied with their medical care (more so than younger people). Few feel that they have unmet health care needs. Older people are eager to comply with physician recommendations about drug therapy and referral to other physicians. They tend to accept medical authority without challenge.

Attitudes about the efficacy of medical care and drugs are important determinants of health behavior. Physician visits, dental visits, and drug use are highly discretionary; people can choose whether or not to utilize them. If older women have more faith in doctors, are more concerned about their health, or perceive symptoms more readily than men, this will encourage their use of health services and drugs. Hospitalization is often another matter, motivated more by the presence and seriousness of a health problem ("need") than by attitudes about benefits of hospital care.

Compared to other age groups, older people tend to have a regular source of medical care, extensive coverage of medical costs through Medicare and Medicaid, and relatively few time constraints. Nevertheless, there are some impediments to seeking care: Older people have fewer financial resources to pay for services not covered by Medicare/Medicaid, travel time to a physician's or dentist's office is longer and often arduous, and office waiting times tend to be longer than at other ages.

Research shows that having a regular source of care (a personal physician) is an important determinant of health care visits.[21] Older women are more likely than older men to have a regular source of care, but they have lower household incomes and wait much longer in offices and clinics. Overall, whether their "access" is better or worse than men's is not clear.

---

[20]Sources for the paragraphs on attitudes and access are Aday et al. (1980), Haug (1979), Kovar and Drury (1978), and Verbrugge (1978).

[21]See Aday (1975), Aday and Anderson (1975), and other references cited in Freeburg et al. (1979, Vol. 3:814-816).

What about access to institutions? Here the critical factors concern availability of home care. An older man is much more likely to have a living spouse, who can provide home care if he is disabled (Shanas, 1979). In contrast, older women are often widowed and have no one willing or able to give longterm care. Institutional residence may be the only solution.

I can suggest three possible reasons for the sex differentials in health services and drug use among older people. These are postulates which are plausible but not yet demonstrated by research.

First, women's higher use of discretionary health services and drugs is related to need, attitudes, and access. Older women are symptomatic more often with acute conditions and chronic flare-ups, and therefore they need more primary care. Also, they are likely to have more positive attitudes about the efficacy of medical care, dental care, and medicine. This comes from health socialization and experiences during childhood and adult years: greater sensitivity to body discomforts, attentiveness to their family's health, and familiarity with the medical care system (e.g., through reproductive care and pediatric care for their children). When they become old, women hold fast to these attitudes and are much more likely than older men to take some action for symptoms; men may try to ignore symptoms and carry on as usual. Having a more regular source of care also boosts women's rates of health care visits.

Women's attitudes can help explain their longer hospital stays. They may be less insistent about going home or may actually ask to stay additional days. Access factors also enter the picture: Women without a spouse have sparser services waiting for them at home, and this prolongs their hospital stays.

Second, in contrast to physician visits, hospitalization rates should reflect need more than health attitudes or access to care. Thus, men's higher rates are compatible with their more serious morbidity. Their chronic conditions lead to more "surprise attacks" (e.g., heart attack and stroke) which necessitate immediate hospital care. In addition, men's conditions may generally be more advanced, which boosts their need for hospital care.

Third, decisions to institutionalize people are largely based on need and access factors. If only needs were operative, we might expect men to have higher rates since they are more seriously ill. But women's needs actually seem to fit better: Living longer, older women accumulate more health problems. Even when not life-threatening, multiple problems take a gradual toll and lead to functional limitations. Thus, an 85-year-old woman will typically have more symptoms and more problems in daily living than an 85-year-old man, but he is more likely to die because his problem is medically serious. The importance of functional limitations is reflected in the health status of institutional residents: Women residents have more limitations than men. Access factors are also critical. Having fewer social and financial resources than men, older women in poor health find it more difficult to stay in the community. Many women become institutional residents in order to secure needed social and health services.

Thus sex differences in health services and drug use by older men and women match their health profiles. Short-term problems (acute conditons or chronic flareups) generate short-term care—more for women. (Recall also their higher rates of restricted activity and bed days.) Serious problems generate hospital care—more for men. Accumulated problems ultimately urge institutional care—more for women. But health attitudes and access also act to increase women's use of ambulatory and institutional services and their use of drugs.

EXPLAINING SEX DIFFERENCES IN HEALTH AND MORTALITY

There are five basic reasons older men and women differ in health status, health behavior, and death rates: inherited risks of illness, acquired risks of illness and injury, illness attitudes and enabling factors, illness behavior, and reporting behavior. Because people often bring health problems into older age from younger ages, we need to consider these factors across the entire life span.

Inherited risks refer here to biological vulnerability to illness because of one's sex. It is believed that males have less resistance to "killer" chronic conditions, so these conditions develop more readily and deteriorate more rapidly for them (Waldron, 1976). Women apparently have some protection from degenerative disease before menopause because of high estrogen levels; but the protection then disappears, and women's rates for "killer" conditions (especially cardiovascular) increase rapidly. Inherited risks probably exert a larger toll on males throughout their lives, even on the hardy ones who survive to very old age.

Men and women tend to differ in their work and leisure activities, lifestyles, and (possibly) levels of stress and reactions to stress. Thus, they are exposed to different acquired risks of illness and injury. The largest differences in roles and activities are at young and middle adult ages. Generally, men have more risks because of their job activities, job-related travel, sports and leisure activities, smoking and drinking behavior, and coping behaviors for stress (often smoking and drinking). In particular, men's smoking behavior is believed to be a key factor in their higher mortality rates (Preston, 1970a; 1970b; Retherford, 1975). Higher alcohol consumption by men is also certainly detrimental. Behaviors in young and middle ages set the stage for chronic conditions that will persist in older ages (65 and over) or cause death before then.

Even at older ages, men may still engage in social activities and lifestyles that elevate their disease risks compared with women. This would increase their chances of developing a new chronic condition and also their chances of having an "old" condition deteriorate. Men's activities may also expose them to more injury risks, but women's more fragile bone structure at older ages makes them actually incur more injuries.

Illness attitudes refer to people's symptom perceptions, assessments of symptom severity, and readiness to take curative and preventive health actions. It is widely believed that women are more sensitive than men to body discomforts, interpret them as illness more often, and are more willing and able to restrict activities, seek medical and dental help, and use drugs. These attitudes predispose women to use more health services and take more time off for illness than men do. In addition, enabling factors, such as access to services and knowledge of services, are important determinants of health behavior. Sex differences in illness attitudes and enabling factors are probably strongest in middle age when women are less likely to be employed and more likely to be attuned to health due to reproductive events and family health care. At older ages, the sex differences in symptom perception, symptom evaluation, and attitudes about health care and health knowledge may persist. Some access factors change: Older women experience more financial and transportation problems in seeking medical care than do older men.

Slowing down for illness and obtaining preventive and curative health care may promote a person's health.[22] These illness behaviors not only help a person recuperate from a current problem, but also enhance resistance to later ones. In addition, frequent medical and dental care increases the chances of early diagnosis and treatment of health problems. Women's greater short-term disability and ambulatory medical care (which imply poorer health at the time they occur) may actually provide long-term health benefits.

Health data are usually collected through personal interviews. If women are more interested in health or have better recall of their health experiences, these reporting behaviors can boost their rates of morbidity and illness behavior compared to men's.

All five factors are involved in explaining sex differences in health status and health behavior, and all except the last help to explain the timing and cause of death.[23] The presence of multiple causal factors (some medical, some psychosocial) helps us see why sex differentials are complex and sometimes appear contradictory. Inherited and acquired risks are generally higher for males, but illness attitudes and reporting behavior tend to boost the morbidity experiences and illness behavior of females. Some access factors encourage health actions for women; others, for men. In the long run, the illness behavior of females enhances their health and reduces their mortality at older ages.

---

[22]Whether curative medical care actually improves health or mainly alleviates symptoms is not known. My statements are therefore presented as hyptheses.

[23]For more detailed discussion of the five factors, see Mechanic (1976), Nathanson (1977), and Verbrugge (1979, 1981a).

RESEARCH ISSUES IN HEALTH AND MORTALITY
OF OLDER MEN AND WOMEN

Sex differences in health and mortality in the older population have scientific, social, and political importance. Scientifically, we would like to know just what it is about gender that has such a profound impact on illness, injury, disability, and death. Socially, men's earlier deaths affect older women's happiness and financial status immensely and are, of course, the ultimate toll for the decedents. Women's longer but more disabled lives are uncomfortable for them and place high demands on kin and social services. Early death and impaired functioning reduce the potential productivity, incomes, social ties, and life satisfaction of older men and women. Policies designed to lengthen lives and reduce the functional limitations of older people must be aimed efficiently and sensitively. Sharp sex differences suggest that public actions must be tailored differently for men and women at young, middle, and older ages.

There are many more speculations than proven explanations about why health and mortality differ so greatly for older men and women. Most of my interpretations are hypotheses rather than statements of fact. Here, I present key questions which deserve scientific study, since the answers can guide public policy for the older population.

Most of the questions here concern attitudes and behaviors in older people which influence health and death. Understanding sex differences at younger ages is also important, since people often bring to old age health problems they developed earlier. For a discussion of research issues that span all adult ages, see Verbrugge (1981b).[24]

Inherited and Acquired Risks

With respect to inherited risks, are males intrinsically less durable than females? Throughout life, are they less resistant to diseases? Are the chronic diseases they develop more likely to worsen than to be controlled? Does cell senescence occur more rapidly in men than in women?[25] These are difficult questions to research, but they are critical to knowing whether equality in health and death is ever possible for the sexes.

---

[24]Since the majority of older people are women, some people say that health issues for the older population are primarily "women's health issues." Because my concern is to understand differences between older men and women, I treat men equally in this section and do not take a "women's health perspective." For a fine discussion of health issues from that perspective, see National Institutes of Health (1979).

Many of the research issues stated here are compatible with the Surgeon General's views on health issues for the elderly (Surgeon General, 1979).

[25]For discussions of cellular aging, see Gelfant and Smith (1972), Hayflick (1980), and Marx (1974).

How important are acquired risks compared to inherited risks in accounting for men's greater mortality? Sex differences in activities and exposures during young and middle adulthood are critical, but let us focus on acquired risks at older ages here. People have fewer roles in old age than in their middle years. They retire from work, often become widowed, and frequently live at some distance from their children. How do role changes affect older people's physical and mental health?[26] What are the important role activities of older men and women, and what risks of illness and injury do these pose? Are the risks from current roles generally greater for men or for women? As young cohorts of men and women adopt more similar lifestyles and roles, will their activities and risks be more similar when they reach older ages too?

Do active roles enhance the health of older people, or is it that only healthy old people are able to engage in active roles? This question expresses the issue of social causation versus social selection. Social causation refers to how roles influence a person's risks of illness and injury. Social selection refers to the phenomemon that healthy people maintain social roles but unhealthy people relinquish them. When we find a relationship between active social roles and good health, we do not know how much this is due to causation or selection. This issue is most important at younger ages (under 65), but it is also important for understanding the link between role loss and poor health among older people. When older employed men and women become ill, do the women leave the labor force sooner than the men? Does employment after age 65 enhance the health of both sexes? Do marriage and close ties with children also promote health?

Illness Attitudes and Enabling Factors

Older people retain many attitudes about illness and health behavior they developed at younger ages, but they also develop new ones as their bodies lose resistance and weaken. We currently have little information on the following questions: Are older women more likely than older men to perceive a discomfort as a sign of illness? For a given perceived symptom, do women consider it more serious than men do? Do older women, more so than men, think that restricting their activities helps to heal acute conditions and alleviate chronic flare-ups? Do women view medical and dental care more favorably than men do? How do older men and women view nonmedical health practitioners (e.g., chiropractors) and home remedies? Do women have a global belief that "doing something about an illness" is good for their health in both the short run and the long run? Do older men believe in stoicism, bravery, and nonpampering for symptoms? How much do older people fear illness, and which illnesses and injuries are most threatening

---

[26]For further discussion of role loss and other stresses in older people's lives, see House and Robbins in this book.

to them? How do older women and men differ in their fears about illness and feelings of vulnerability?

It is especially important for policymakers to know older people's attitudes about long-term care. How do older men and women with severe functional limitations view their options for care? How do they evaluate home care, other community-based care, and institutional residence? Do they voice their preferences to kin and health professionals, and are their opinions considered carefully when decisions about long-term care are made?

How do older men and women differ in enabling factors? What barriers to ambulatory and long-term care do they perceive? What solutions do they themselves propose? What do older women and men know about signs of specific chronic illnesses, good nutrition, and local medical services? Do men generally have less knowledge on these topics? And is lack of knowledge an important factor in delayed care, unmet medical needs, poor nutritional status, and visits to inappropriate sites of care?

Health Status

The data reviewed suggest that older men and women differ in frequency of symptoms and prevalence of severe disease. Do older women truly have symptoms more often? Are men more likely to be unaware of health problems and suffer a ''surprise attack,'' such as a heart attack, hernial obstruction, or respiratory collapse? Among people with a specific chronic condition (such as diabetes), do older men tend to have more severe cases than women? But do older women tend to have more chronic conditions, even though milder ones? Among people with several conditions, what combination of problems do they have? Does this differ for men and women? Do women tend to accumulate conditions which together ultimately cause functional limitations, even though each condition may be rather mild?

What factors underlie self-ratings of ''excellent'' and ''poor'' health for older men and women? How much are the evaluations influenced by the number and type of chronic conditions, acute episodes, functional limitations, social activities, changes in health since middle age, and comparison with health of peers?

Some health problems are so frequent for one sex compared with the other that they can be called ''sex-dominated.'' For example, osteoporosis, arthritis, senile dementia (chronic brain syndrome), depression, and poor vision are especially frequent for older women. Chronic respiratory problems, poor hearing, paralysis/missing extremities, and suicide deaths are especially frequent for older men.[27] These causes of illness and death merit special attention. Why are they

---

[27]For a provocative analysis of self-injury and suicide, see Jarvis et al. (1976).

so much more common for one sex, though both sexes are eligible for them?[28] What is organic and what is social in their etiology?

How important are illness attitudes, access, and knowledge in motivating health behavior for older people? How do these factors compare in importance to "need" (actual levels of morbidity)? Are "predisposing" and "enabling" factors more important determinants for older women than for older men?

Health Behavior

There are abundant questions about older people's behavioral responses to illness and their preventive health care. The following are important for understanding sex differences.

Are older women more likely to have their chronic conditions and dental problems diagnosed earlier (at a less advanced stage)? This issue applies to all ages, but is especially important for older people because recuperative abilities diminish with age.

How do older men and women cope with chronic illnesses and impairments? Do women make accommodations in their roles and daily activities sooner and more easily than men? How do chronic conditions affect older people's moods, feelings about death and illness vulnerability, and social involvement? These are exceedingly important questions, since how older people cope with their health problems is critical to their general well-being.

Whether older people receive appropriate care depends partly on their motivations and effort. Are older men and women equally likely to seek continuous care for health problems? How do older people find appropriate sources of care for physical and mental problems? Do women rely on their friends and kin more, whereas men seek their physician's advice? How fully do older men and women comply with physicians' and dentists' recommendations for drug use, preventive care, and followup care? How frequently do older patients make medication errors, and are errors more common for one sex? How much are these errors due to patient motivation versus insufficient information from physicians and pharmacists?

With respect to long-term care, what factors are taken into account in deciding to institutionalize older men and women? How important are the availability of a spouse, multiple chronic conditions, mental difficulties, functional limitations, and finances? Who is involved in the decision for women and for men? How often do older women and men participate actively in the decision? When they

---

[28]There are also some sex-specific (unique to one sex) problems, such as postmenopausal discomforts for women and prostate troubles for men. These merit medical attention, but they are less interesting for sociological analysis than sex-dominated problems.

become institutional residents, do women adapt more readily and fully than men to the new site? If so, what factors (personal or facility characteristics) account for their better adaptation?

Finally, a very important question which is difficult to study scientifically is whether greater medical care and restricted activity improve women's ability to ward off future acute or chronic conditions. Do they increase their longevity? In other words, do short-term responses to symptoms have long-term benefits? At the moment, we can only guess at the answer.

Provision of Health Care

Do physicians have stereotypic views of older men and women, and do they offer services and followup care based on those stereotypes? How prevalent is physician sex bias in medical care? Does it exist only in certain specialties or for certain health problems (such as lower back pain)?[29] Why are more drugs prescribed for older women, especially psychotropic drugs? Does this sex difference occur both for community-based patients and institutional residents?[30]

Continuous, coordinated medical care is especially needed for older people. A chronic health problem may require different types of services over time, for example, routine checkups, then hospitalization, then physiotherapy. Multiple problems require coordinated care from several medical sources (or holistic care from one). Do older men and women receive comparable continuity and coordination in their medical care? Are comparable physical and social rehabilitation services provided for older men and women after an episode of serious illness or injury? For a comparable episode, do they receive appropriate, comprehensive services so they can return to their desired activities? These questions about the structure of medical care are particularly critical for older women, who have more years to live with their health problems and have multiple problems more often than men.

Public monies now pay for much of older people's health care, and public regulations affect the number and types of long-term care facilities available to them. There are many serious issues about health financing and institutions for older people (DiFederico, 1978; Holahan et al., 1978). In particular, lack of coverage for some common items (prescription drugs, long-term home care, institutional care through Medicare, eyeglasses and hearing aids, dental services, routine exams, foot care) and the lack of intermediate community-based services pose difficulties for many older men and women. The solutions impinge more on

---

[29]There is little scientific research on physician sex bias (Verbrugge and Steiner, 1980), but there is evidence of age bias—a tendency to depreciate the health problems of older people and to offer less care (Butler, 1969; Ford and Sbordone, 1980). If sex bias (against women) also exists, older women have a pernicious double jeopardy when seeking medical care.

[30]For some evidence that institutionalized women are over medicated, see Milliren (1977).

older women than men since they have fewer financial resources for health care while needing more frequent and ultimately more long-term care.

Mortality

Whether brief or prolonged, morbidity precedes and ultimately causes death. When we understand the factors that affect the health of older men and women, we shall understand sex differentials in their mortality too. There should be no "last minute" surprises.

A few intriguing questions about mortality per se merit attention: Are women more likely than men to die from multiple causes? For people who die of multiple causes, what combinations of diseases predominate for men and for women? Are men more likely to die suddenly from a disease attack? Are women more likely to survive such attacks and have several before dying?

THE FUTURE—COHORTS TO COME

The health of older people is dynamic in two respects. First, individuals experience health changes during their lives. Chronic problems that appear in young and middle-aged adults often persist in older ages. Gradually, chronic illnesses and impairments accumulate for older people and cause functional limitations or death. This is an individual level or life-course perspective. We have considered it at length in this paper.

Second, the older population changes its membership over time. New cohorts enter who may differ sharply in economic status, family and marital life, health habits, roles and role attitudes, and health experiences (Riley et al., 1972). For example, people now 75–84 were born around 1900. As children, they had high risks of death from acute conditions. They suffered the Depression in their thirties, which diminished their childbearing and retarded their career development. They had traditional sex roles, with men responsible for family income and women responsible for childrearing and housework. In the year 2000, people of ages 75–84 will be quite different. They fought in World War II and they produced the Baby Boom and economic prosperity after the war. This group too had traditional sex roles during their childbearing years. In 2020, men and women now age 35 will reach the 75–84 age group. They are bearing few children, and they are modifying roles so that job and domestic tasks are more alike for men and women. (This is not a uniform trend for all couples, of course, but the cohort overall is making remarkable changes in sex roles.) Over 60 percent of the women are employed, and many are establishing long-term work careers. This cohort has lived in a generally salutary physical environment, and it is aware of the harmful effects of smoking and heavy drinking.

These three cohorts have experienced a wide variety of health risks, health attitudes, and health behaviors during their lives which should result in different health profiles when they become old. For example, men now 65 and over smoked heavily in middle age; this is reflected in their health problems and diminished longevity compared to older women who smoked little. But coming cohorts of older women will have more smoking experience; they will undoubtedly suffer more respiratory and cardiovascular problems during (and before) old age.

What will contemporary young adults be like when they become the older population? Compared to the current older cohorts, will they have different health problems, make different decisions about health care, and have different mortality rates when elderly? Probably so, but we cannot describe their health profiles for certain. Their behavior in the next few decades is critical. Will young men and women reduce their smoking and drinking, eat moderately, and have sufficient exercise throughout middle age? Will women's increasing participation in the labor force make them happier and healthier, or will it increase stress and exposure to harmful materials, thereby causing poorer health? Current evidence suggests that both men and women are adopting more healthful lifestyles and that women's employment has a beneficial impact on their health (Verbrugge, 1981c). Also, the future may see medical advances for the control of cardiovascular diseases and cancer. All of these factors suggest that death rates will continue their current decline, for both sexes;[31] thus a higher proportion of men and women will reach older ages. However, it is possible that functional limitations will increase in the older population. More people may have illnesses which are controlled but which impede mobility, physical activity, or social activities. (This can occur even if incidence rates for "killer" conditions decrease.)

What will happen to sex differentials in health and mortality? The roles of young men and women are becoming more similar; more women are combining family and job activities, and more men are sharing in domestic responsibilities. This trend toward more similar roles will probably continue for cohorts who are now children. The more similar men's and women's roles are, the more similar their health risks, attitudes, and behaviors are likely to be. Ultimately, this may lead to more similar death rates. I do not think that equal mortality rates will ever occur because women probably do have an intrinsic durability which gives them a longevity advantage even if roles were absolutely identical. But sex differences in health and death should narrow as morbidity and mortality rates fall for both sexes.

In summary, I think the following is a very plausible scenario for the future: As women engage in more social roles, they will be less frequently ill in middle

---

[31]Further declines in overall mortality will be small. This is because most decedents are elderly, and if their chances of surviving one disease improve, they become more vulnerable than before to death from another cause. The topic of "competing risks" has been analyzed by demographers (Keyfitz, 1978; Tsai et al., 1978; see also comments in the American Journal of Public Health, 70(11), 1980).

and older ages. Their rates of acute conditions and shortterm disability will decrease. As working environments and lifestyles improve and as people learn to cope better with the stresses of multiple roles, chronic problems should decrease for middle-aged men and women. Men especially will gain from these changes. Both sexes will enter older ages with fewer life-threatening conditions, or milder cases of them. But by living longer, older men and women will tend to accumulate more chronic troubles, and they may have more functional limitations during their final years. All of these trends lead to more similar health and mortality profiles for older men and women.

These are sweeping forecasts, and we will have to wait many years to see if they are right.[32] Before, then, there is plenty to learn about health, mortality, and their determinants for the current older population and for younger cohorts. Data collection and analysis should take both a short-term and a long-term perspective so that we can document current health status and problems of age groups, and also have cumulative information to understand the cohorts' whole experiences when they finally become the older population.[33]

REFERENCES

Abraham, Sidney, Margaret D. Carroll, Connie M. Dresser,and Clifford L. Johnson 1977. Dietary intake findings, United States, 1971–74.Vital and Health Statistics, Series 11, No. 202. Hyattsville, Md.: National Center for Health Statistics.

Aday, LuAnn 1975. "Economic and non-economic barriers to use of needed medical services." Medical Care 13:447–456.

Aday, LuAnn, and Ronald Andersen 1975. Development of Indices of Access to Medical Care. Ann Arbor: Health Administration Press.

Aday, LuAnn, Ronald Andersen, and Gretchen V. Fleming 1980. Health Care in the United States—Equitable for Whom? Beverly Hills: Sage Publications.

Assistant Secretary for Health 1978. Health, United States, 1978. DHEW Publication No. (PHS) 78-1232. Hyattsville, Md.: National Center for Health Statistics.

Atchley, Robert C. 1977. The Social Forces in Later Life. Belmont: Wadsworth Publishing.

Black, Ethel R. 1980. Use of Special Aids, United States, 1977. Vital and Health Statistics. Series 10, No.135. Hyattsville, Md.: National Center for Health Statistics.

---

[32]Readers may want to think through other scenarios about changes in morbidity and mortality rates and their impact on sex differentials. For example, if women simply mimic traditional male behaviors, they will indeed have greater risks of serious morbidity and mortality. Sex differences will narrow, but unfortunately at higher levels of morbidity and mortality.

[33]It is especially disappointing that most health data show rates for the group 65 and over, without further splits (65–74, 75–84, etc.). With advancing age, health changes very rapidly; so do sex differences. Current practice therefore obscures many important variations. Agencies should routinely report data for more detailed age groups, with sampling errors attached. A promising example is a monograph now being prepared by the National Institute on Aging; it will discuss trends in older people's health, based on Health Interview Survey and Hospital Discharge Survey data, with rates for 65–74 and 75 and over.

Bureau of the Census 1970. 1970 Census of Population. Persons in Institutions and Other Group Quarters. Subject Report PC (2)-4E.

Bush, Patricia J., and David Rabin 1976. "Who's using nonprescribed medicines?" Medical Care 14:1014–1023.

Butler, Robert N. 1969. "Ageism: another form of bigotry." Gerontologist 9:243–246.

Butler, Robert N., Jessie S. Gertman, Dewayne L. Oberlander, and Lydia Schindler 1979. "Self-care, self-help, and the elderly." International Journal of Aging and Human Development 10(1):95–117.

Carpenter, James O., Ray F. McArthur, and Ian T.Higgins 1974. "The aged: health, illness, disability, and use of medical services." Pp. 130–158 in Carl L. Erhardt and Joyce E. Berlin (eds). Mortality and Morbidity in the United States. Cambridge: Harvard University Press.

DiFederico, Elaine 1978. "Health planning and the elderly." Working Paper 5904–13. Washington, D.C.: Urban Institute.

Ferraro, Kenneth F. 1980. "Self-ratings of health among the old and the old-old." Journal of Health and Social Behavior 21:377–383.

Fillenbaum, Gerda G. 1979. "Social context and self-assessment of health among the elderly." Journal of Health and Social Behavior 20:45–51.

Ford, Charles V., and Robert J. Sbordone 1980. "Attitudes of psychiatrists toward elderly patients." American Journal of Psychiatry 137(5):571–575.

Freeburg, Linnea C., Judith R. Lave, Lester B.Lave, and Samuel Leinhardt 1979. Health Status, Medical Care Utilization,and Outcome: An Annotated Bibliography of Empirical Studies (4 volumes). DHEW Publication No. (PHS) 80–3263. Hyattsville, Md.: National Center for Health Services Research.

Gelfant, Seymour, and J. Graham Smith, Jr. 1972. "Aging: noncycling cells an explanation." Science 78 (No. 4059), 27 October: 357–361.

Gordan, Gilbert S., and Cynthia Vaughan 1977. "The role of estrogens in osteoporosis." Geriatrics 32(9):42–48.

Grove, Robert D., and Alice M. Hetzel 1968. Vital Statistics Rates in the United States 1940–1960. PHS Publication No. 1677. Washington, D.C.: National Center for Health Statistics.

Haug, Marie 1979. "Doctor patient relationships and the older patient." Journal of Gerontology 34(6):852–860.

Havlik, Richard J., and Manning Feinleib (eds.) 1979. Proceedings of the Conference on the Decline in Coronary Heart Disease Mortality. NIH Publication No. 1610. Washington D.C.:U.S. Government Printing Office.

Hayflick, Leonard 1980. "The cell biology of human aging." Scientific American 242(1):58–65.

Holahan, John, Judith Feder, Judith Wagner, Robert Lee, Karen Lennox, and Jane Weeks 1978. "Health and the elderly: a policy research agenda for the Administration on Aging." Working Paper 5904–5. Washington, D.C.:Urban Institute.

Jarvis, George K., Roberta G. Ferrence, F. Gordon Johnson, and Paul C. Whitehead 1976. "Sex and age patterns in self-injury."Journal of Health and Social Behavior17:146–155.

Kane, Robert L., and Rosalie A. Kane 1980."Long-term care: can our society meet the needs of its elderly?" Pp. 227–253 in Lester Breslow (ed.), Annual Review of Public Health. Vol. I. Palo Alto: Annual Reviews.

Kasl, Stanley V., and Sidney Cobb, 1966a. "Health behavior, illness behavior, and sick role behavior. I. Health and illness behavior." Archives of Environmental Health 12:246–266.

———. 1966b. "Health behavior, illness behavior, and sick-role behavior: II. Sick-role behavior." Archives of Environmental Health 12:531–541.

Keyfitz, Nathan 1978. "Improving life expectancy: an uphill road ahead." American Journal of Public Health 68:954–956.

Keys, Ancel 1980. Seven Countries: A Multivariate Analysis of Death and Coronary Heart Disease. Cambridge: Harvard University Press.

Kleinman, Joel C., Jacob J. Feldman, and Mary A. Monk 1979. "The effects of changes in smoking habits on coronary heart disease mortality."American Journal of Public Health 69:795–802.

Kovar, Mary Grace 1977. "Elderly people: the population 65 years and over." Pp. 3–26 in Health, United States, 1976–1977. DHEW/HRA 77–1232. Hyattsville, Md.: National Center for Health Statistics.

———. 1979. "Health of the elderly and use of health services." Public Health Reports 92(1):9–19.

Kovar, Mary Grace, and Thomas F. Drury 1978. "Use of medical care services by men and women in their middle and later years." Paper presented at the Gerontological Society meetings, Dallas, November.

Larson, Reed 1978. "Thirty years of research on the subjective well-being of older Americans." Journal of Gerontology 33:109–125.

Maddox, George L. 1962. "Some correlates of differences in self-assessments of health status among the elderly." Journal of Gerontology 17:180–185.

Marx, Jean L. 1974. "Aging research (I): cellular theories of senescence." Science 186, 20 December:1105–1107.

Mechanic, David 1976. "Sex, illness behavior, and the use of health services." Journal of Human Stress 2(4):29-40.

Mellinger, Glen D., Mitchell B. Balter, Hugh J. Perry, Dean I. Manheimer, and Ira H. Cisin 1974. "An overview of psychotherapeutic drug use in the United States." Pp. 333-366 in Eric Josephson and Eleanor A. Carroll (eds.), Drug Use: Epidemiological and Social Issues. Washington, D.C.: Hemisphere Publishing.

Metropolitan Life Insurance Company 1980. "Mortality differentials favor women." Statistical Bulletin 61(2):2-7.

Milliren, John W. 1977. "Some contingencies affecting the utilization of tranqualizers in long-term care of the elderly." Journal of Health and Social Behavior 18:206-211.

Myers, George C. 1978. "Cross-national trends in mortality rates among the elderly." Gerontologist 18 (5, Part 1): 441-448.

Nathanson, Constance 1977. "Sex, illness, and medical care: a review of data, theory, and method." Social Science and Medicine 11:13–25.

National Center for Health Statistics 1971. Health in the Later Years of Life. GPO Stock No. 1722–0178. Rockville, Md. ———. 1980. Long-Term Health Care Minimum Data Set. DHHS Publication No. (PHS) 80–1158. Hyattsville, Md.

National Institutes of Health 1979. The Older Woman: Continuities and Discontinuities. NIH Publication No. 79–1897. Bethesda, Md.: National Institute on Aging.

Office of Management and Budget 1980. Data Coverge on the Functionally Limited Elderly. Report of the Interagency Statistical Committee on Long-Term Care for the Elderly. Washington, D.C.

Parry, Hugh J., Mitchell B. Balter, Glen D. Mellinger, Ira H. Cisin, and Dean I. Manheimer 1973. "National patterns of psychotherapeutic drug use." Archives of General Psychiatry 28: 769–783.

Pollock, John C., Andrew J. Kelly, Kathy Bloomgarden, Peter Finn, and Adam Snyder 1980. Aging in America: Trials and Triumphs. Monticello, Ill.: Americana Healthcare.

Preston, Samuel H. 1970a. Older Male Mortality and Cigarette Smoking—A Demographic Analysis. Population Monograph Series No. 7. Berkeley: Institute of International Studies, University of California.

———. 1970b. "An international comparison of excessive adult mortality." Population Studies 24(1): 5-20.

Rabin, David L., and Patricia J. Bush 1976. "Who's using prescribed medicines?" Drugs in Health Care 3:89–100.

Retherford, Robert 1975. The Changing Sex Differential in Mortality. Westport: Greenwood Press.

Riley, Matilda W. and Anne Foner 1968. Aging and society, Vol. 1: An inventory of research findings. New York: Russell Sage Foundation.

Riley, Matilda W., Marilyn Johnson, and Anne Foner 1972. Aging and Society. Vol. 3: A Sociology of Age Stratification. New York: Russell Sage Foundation.

Rosenwaike, Ira, Nurit Yaffe, and Philip C. Sagi 1980. "The recent decline in mortality of the extreme aged: an analysis of statistical data." American Journal of Public Health 70(10):1074—1080.

174   VERBRUGGE

Shanas, Ethel 1962. The Health of Older People. Cambridge: Harvard University Press.
———. 1979. "The family as a social support system in old age." Gerontologist 19(2):169–174.
Shanas, Ethel, and George L. Maddox 1976. "Aging, health, and the organization of health resources." Pp. 592–618 in Robert H. Binstock and Ethel Shanas (eds.), Handbook of Aging and the Social Sciences. New York: Van Nostrand Reinhold.
Shanas, Ethel, Peter Townsend, Dorothy Wedderburn, Henning Friis, Paul Milhoi, and Jan Stehouer 1968. Old People in Three Industrial Societies. New York: Atherton Press.
Siegel, Jacob S. 1979. Demographic Aspects of Aging and the Older Population in the United States. Current Population Reports, Series P-23, No. 59. Washington, D.C.: Bureau of the Census.
Stallones, Reuel A. 1980. "The rise and fall of ischemic heart disease." Scientific American 243(5):53–59.
Surgeon General and Office of the Assistant Secretary for Health 1979. Healthy People: The Surgeon General's Report on Health Promotion and Disease Prevention. DHEW/PHS 79-55071. Washington, D.C.: Public Health Service.
Tissue, Thomas 1972. "Another look at self-rated health among the elderly." Journal of Gerontology 27:91–94.
Tsai, Shen P., Eun S. Lee, and Robert J. Hardy 1978. "The effect of a reduction in leading causes of death: potential gains in life expectancy." American Journal of Public Health 68:966–971.
Verbrugge, Lois M. 1978. Differentials in Medical Care for Acute Conditions, United States. Biostatistics Technical Report Series, No. 17. Ann Arbor: Department of Biostatistics, School of Public Health, University of Michigan. (Accompanies Vital and Health Statistics, Series 10, No. 129.)
———. 1979. "Female illness rates and illness behavior: testing hypotheses about sex differences in health." Women and Health 4(1):61–79.
———. 1980. "Recent trends in sex mortality differentials in the United States." Women and Health 5(3):17–37.
———. 1981a. "Sex differentials in health and mortality." In Ann H. Stromberg (ed.), Women, Health, and Medicine. Palo Alto: Mayfield Publishing.
———. 1981b. "Women and men's health—research issues for the 1980's." In Proceedings from Conference on "The Sociology of Health Care: Issues for the 1980's." Sponsored by the School of Social Sciences, University of Illinois, Urbana, October 1980.
———. 1981c. "Women's social roles and health." In Proceedings of the Conference on "Women, a Developmental Perspective: a Conference on Research," Bethesda, November 1980. Bethesda: National Institute of Child Health and Human Development.
Verbrugge, Lois M., and Richard P. Steiner 1980. "Physician treatment of men and women patients—sex bias or appropriate care?" Paper presented at the American Public Health Association meetings, Detroit, October.
Waldron, Ingrid 1976. "Why do women live longer than men?" Social Science and Medicine 10:349–362.
Wan, Thomas T.H. 1976. "Predicting self-assessed health status: a multivariate approach." Health Services Research 11:464–477.
Weissert, William G. 1978. "Long-term care: an overview." Pp. 91–109 in Office of the Assistant Secretary for Health, Health, United States, 1978. DHEW Publication No. (PHS) 78-1232. Hyattsville, Md.: National Center for Health Statistics.
Women and Health Roundtable 1979. Roundtable Report 4(4), April. Washington, D.C. (2000 P Street, N.W., Suite 403, 20036).

9

Age, Psychosocial Stress, and Health[1]

James S. House
Cynthia Robbins
University of Michigan

AGE AND STRESS RESEARCH

The study of psychosocial stress and health and the study of aging over the life course are both inherently interdisciplinary, concerned with the interplay of social, psychological, and biological phenomena in determining human behavior and functioning. Research in both fields has progressed from an initial focus on biological and physiological factors to increasing concern with psychological and social elements. This more recent emphasis is necessary and welcome, but there is also a danger that psychosocial researchers will fail to take biological and physiological factors sufficiently into account, just as biological and physiological studies often neglect the psychosocial dimensions of stress and aging. Thus, there is great need for interdisciplinary research that simultaneously considers social, psychological, and biological factors. Such research would be fostered by greater interchange between, and by integration of theory and research in, the areas of stress and aging.

This paper uses a paradigm for stress and health research to analyze the development of health and wellbeing across the life course. Conversely, it examines how age and life-course stage relate to the variables and causal relationships that are central to the study of stress and health. We seek, however, to move beyond recognizing the potential value of bringing into conjunction stress research and

---

[1]In addition to George L. Maddox, the authors are grateful to Toni Antonucci, Linda George, Berit Ingersoll, and Leonard Pearlin for their critical reading of an earlier version of this paper. We are also grateful to Marie Klatt for preparing the manuscript. This paper reflects equal authorship.

aging research in order to specify how this intersection of two research perspectives can provide new theoretical, empirical, and practical insights into health maintenance and disease prevention in adulthood.

A Paradigm for Stress Research[2]

The term "stress" applies increasingly to a general area of research rather than to a clearly defined scientific concept. Figure 1 is one variant of a widely used paradigm for stress research (Levine and Scotch, 1970; McGrath, 1970). This paradigm emphasizes that potentially stressful social or environmental conditions (stressors) do not invariably give rise to particular health outcomes; rather the impact of these conditions depends on how they are perceived and responded to by individuals. Any specific social or environmental condition will be perceived as stressful (e.g., threatening, frightening, overly demanding) by some persons but not by others, depending on the characteristics of the persons and other aspects of their social situations (the conditioning variables in Figure 1).

The perception of stress may lead to somewhat transient behavioral, psychological, or physiological responses (e.g., taking an alcoholic drink, feeling anxious or sad, a rise in blood pressure) and ultimately to more enduring health or disease outcomes (e.g., alcoholism, neurosis, essential hypertension). However, perceived stress produces a particular response only for certain individuals or in certain situations. The more enduring outcomes of a given response depend on how the response affects the precipitating objective conditions and/or perceptions of stress and whether the person is particularly vulnerable (due to previous medical problems, genetic weaknesses, lack of social support, etc.).

Retirement, for example, is a potential stressor; but whether it is perceived as stressful depends on an individual's motivations and abilities to engage in his or her primary occupation versus other activities, the nature of the person's social networks and supports, how and when retirement occurs, etc. Even persons who perceive retirement as stressful manifest various responses and, hence, various health outcomes. Some actively seek to find new activities and directions in life; others may try to deny or repress the perception of stress or alleviate its effects by use of alcohol or drugs; still others may do nothing and lapse into a prolonged state of anxiety or depression. The pattern of responses is a function of the interaction between perceived stress and individual or situational conditioning variables.[3]

---

[2]This section is adapted from House and Jackman, 1979.

[3]Poor health is an outcome in Figure 1, but it may also constitute a potential stressor having social and psychological as well as physical effects. The prevalence of this potential stressor clearly increases with age, and how people respond to or cope with disease and disability is an important issue at the interface of research on stress and aging (Verbrugge, in this book). Our focus here, however, is the role of psychosocial factors in the etiology of health and illness rather than responses to health and illness. Nevertheless, much of our discussion, especially of people's adaptive capacity over the life course, has implications for how people respond to health problems.

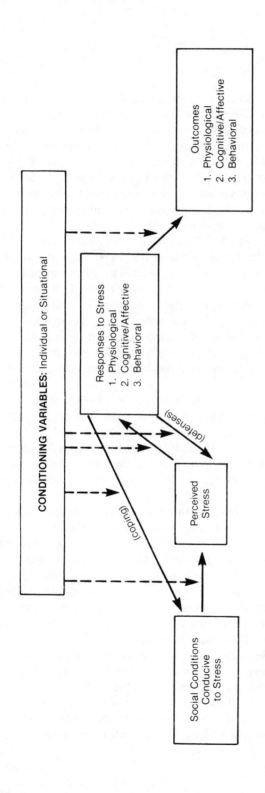

NOTE: Solid arrows between boxes indicate presumed causal relationships among variables. Dotted arrows from the box labeled "conditioning variable" intersect solid arrows, indicating an interaction between the conditioning variables and the variables in the box at the beginning of the solid arrow in predicting variables in the box at the head of the solid arrow.

Age and the Stress Paradigm

Age and life-course stage are conceived as exogenous determinants of the variables in Figure 1. That is, age or life-course stage, as indicated in Figure 2, may be related to: exposure to social conditions conducive to stress, perceptions of stress, short-term responses to stress, enduring outcomes, and each set of conditioning variables. Most notable perhaps is the decline of health with age. Two major unanswered questions are why this occurs and what role psychosocial stress plays. This paper examines whether and to what extent variables in the stress paradigm—especially potential stressors, conditioning variables, and outcomes—are related to age or life-course stage.

Specifically, are exposure to potential stressors (chronic or acute) and availability of conditioning variables related to age or life-course stage in ways that produce "crisis" periods for many individuals—such as the developmental "crises" in parenthood, midlife, and retirement? To what extent do biological or physiological changes associated with aging make people more "vulnerable" to stress, that is, more likely to develop deleterious health outcomes in response to potential stressors or perceptions of stress? Analogously, to what extent do social and psychological conditioning variables associated with aging make people more vulnerable to stress? Do some of these variables also enhance resistance to stress?

Answers to such questions, if available, have substantial practical and scientific implications. Scientific analysis and understanding are worthy goals in their own right; in addition, they form the necessary basis for sound social policies for dealing with problems of stress and aging. If, for example, age or life stage is strongly associated with exposure to psychosocial stressors that can affect future health, the evidence points to a need for social policies targeted at specific ages or life stages.

Also important are the questions of whether age primarily is related to the exposure to stressors or to the capacity to adapt to them, and what specific stressors or adaptive capacities are involved. If exposure to stress is a problem, can such exposure be reduced? If not, can people's ability to adapt to it be improved? If we seek to improve adaptive capacity, we need to know whether to focus on social, psychological, or biological capacities and whether improvements in adaptive capacity in one area can offset decrements in other areas. For example, to what extent can social resources and supports compensate for deficiencies in psychological or biological capacities, and vice versa?

The next two sections address some of these issues by reviewing available evidence from contemporary studies in the United States on the relation of age and lifecourse stage to four of the major classes of variables in Figure 1: 1) health outcomes, 2) potential stressors, 3) perceived stress, and 4) conditioning variables. From this review, we develop a picture of how people respond to stress at various ages, and what implications these responses have for health.

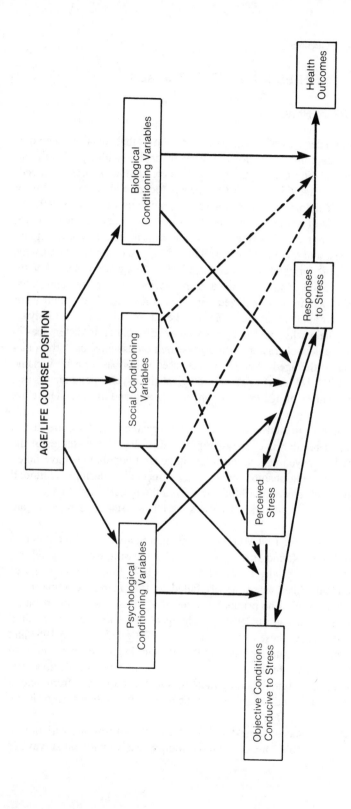

NOTE: Dotted arrows indicate possible. but less plausible conditioning effects.

STRESSORS AND OUTCOMES

Physical and Mental Health Outcomes

Much of the last two decades of research on aging shows that social, psychological, and even physical functioning do not invariably decline with age. Continuity between the early and later parts of the life cycle is greater than is often believed, and most people over age 65 (or even age 70) experience little or no significant decrement in physical, psychological, or social functioning (Maddox, 1979).

This "new" view of aging and the aged has had important implications for research and social policy. Nevertheless, increases in morbidity and mortality remain the strongest and most regular correlates of age, and age is generally the best predictor of most forms of illness and death. Like sex differences in health, however, the association of age with health is more widely recognized and statistically controlled for than it is analyzed. Epidemiologists routinely control for age (and sex) in their analyses of the etiology of health and disease, but rarely do they attempt to explain why age (or sex) is so regularly related to differences in health. The same neglect characterizes most research on psychosocial stress factors in health among the aged. Age is, in fact, used simply as a proxy variable (Maddox, 1979: 120-121) for a variety of biological and psychosocial factors that are the proximate causes of age trends in physical health and disease. These are our focus below.

Variations by age in mental health, other than organic disorders, are not as clear, consistent, or regular as changes in physical health. Some studies of the prevalence of various psychological disorders in general populations have failed to find consistent relationships with age, especially during adulthood (Dohrenwend and Dohrenwend, 1969: Table 2), although at very old ages (beyond 75 or 85) certain mental disorders, such as senile dementia, are pronounced.

Other studies, such as the first Midtown Manhattan Study in 1954 (confined to an age range of 20-59), found strong evidence of increasing psychological impairment with age (Srole et al., 1962). However, a 1974 followup interview of the same respondents (then aged 40-79) failed to find increased impairment (Srole and Fischer, 1980). The original finding, it appears, was a cohort rather than an aging effect. That is, in 1954, people aged 40-59 were more impaired than those aged 20-39. As these two cohorts aged by 20 years between 1954 and 1974, there was no significant increase, on the average, in rates of impairment in either group. The relative disadvantage of the older cohort remained, however. The explanation of the original finding must be sought, it appears, from among the earlier characteristics and experiences of the older cohort rather than from the aging process.

Studies of affective states suggest a similar lack of uniform age variation in mental health. For example, one of the most comprehensive national surveys of quality of life suggests that in cross-section, happiness decreases somewhat with age, but life satisfaction increases over the life course (Campbell et al., 1976). Whether these differences are due to aging or cohort differences remains to be seen. In summary, existing data suggest that people may adapt psychologically to changes over the life course in many respects better than they adapt physically.

Exposure to Potential Stressors

Much stress research focuses on a single stressor, that is, a single event or situation that is potentially stressful, usually some transition in the life course. The key life transitions of young adulthood involve taking on life roles. Within a relatively short time, young adults typically complete their education, enter their jobs or careers, marry, and have their first children (Lowenthal et al., 1975; Rossi, 1979). During middle age, adults face a number of potentially stressful losses. Some of these are concrete and specific—children leave home, parents become ill or die. Other challenges of middle age are more diffuse, but the popularity of books and articles on the "mid-life crisis" (Levinson, 1977-78; Sheehy, 1976; Rubin, 1979) suggests the relevance of the phenomenon at least for some people. Older adults contend with loss events such as retirement, failing health of self and spouse (Fengler and Goodrich, 1979), widowhood (Lopata, 1973; Glick et al., 1974; Parkes, 1972), and institutionalization (Tobin and Lieberman, 1976).

Studies of single transitions have provided valuable insights into the relationships among age, stress, and health. They do not allow us, however, to describe or compare people's total exposure to stress within a given interval of time. A second approach to stress research, the summary of recent life events, allows for such assessments. Changes in life patterns, whether typically positive (marriage) or negative (job loss), require some form of adaptation and are, therefore, potentially stressful. Several checklists exist to measure total exposure to stressful life events. Generally, these events are weighted according to the degree of adjustment they are presumed to require and are then added to arrive at a person's total amount of life stress.

These summated measures of stress have repeatedly been found to correlate negatively with age (Holmes and Masuda, 1974; Dekker and Webb, 1974; Uhlenhuth et al., 1974). Several critics, however, are reluctant to accept the negative correlation as proof that young adults lead the most stressful lives. For example, Rabkin and Struening (1976) suggest that the life events checklists oversample events of young adulthood. George (1980) observes that, although older adults experience fewer life events, the events they do experience—widowhood, retirement, institutionalization—involve major role losses. Of course, the weighting of items is intended to account for the magnitude of events, but a single weight applied to an item for every person checking it can be misleading. For instance, a college student changing apartments and an elderly person entering a nursing home could both receive 20 points for a "change of residence" (Holmes and Rahe, 1967). Furthermore, even the same event (e.g., widowhood) may have quite different meanings and effects at different ages or stages of life.

Further refinement of the life events instruments, however, is likely to provide diminishing returns in our ability to compare people's differing experiences of stress or to predict health and illness. Although change can be stressful, stress should not be equated with change. Most life events are only potentially stressful, their impact conditioned by a host of variables. Not all men experience a mid-life crisis (Nachman, 1979), not all women grieve over the "empty nest" (Lowenthal and Chiriboga, 1972), and some even experience institutionalization with relief (Smith and Bengtson, 1979). Moreover, chronic stress not measured in life events scales can adversely affect physical and mental wellbeing, as is amply documented for occupational stress (House and Jackman, 1979; House, 1974: Frankenhaeuser and Gardell, 1976). Persistent marital strife appears to have more deleterious effects on mental health than does the single event of divorce (Pearlin and Radabaugh, 1980). In addition, cross-sectional studies of recent life events do not provide evidence of the life-course patterns of stressful events for separate cohorts.

By distinguishing among normative transitions, unscheduled events, and role strains, Pearlin and his associates provide a more satisfactory approach to measuring stress exposure. Their method allows for comparison of different age groups, includes both life events and chronic stresses, and covers major life roles. Pearlin and Radabaugh (1980) describe the exposure to stress of men and women in three age categories: under 40, 40 to 55, and over 55.

Normative transitions—life events of an expected, scheduled character (e.g., marriage or job entry)-concentrate in the under-40 category. Young adults are also most likely to experience nonnormative, or unscheduled, transitions (unexpected life events). Only one of these transitions considered by Pearlin and Radabaugh—illness of a spouse—occurs most frequently for adults over 55 (and it might be regarded as more normative at that age). It is today's young adults who are most likely to change jobs, to be promoted on their job, and to divorce or separate from their spouses. Young and middle-aged adults are more likely than older adults to be fired or laid off and to be unemployed for health reasons.

Finally, Pearlin and Radabaugh discuss *role strains*. These are relatively durable problems, frustrations, and conflicts built into the daily roles of people (e.g., economic deprivation, occupational stress, persistent marital conflict). People of all ages experience far more chronic role strains than life transitions. Of the 11 role strains discussed, none is most frequently experienced by the older adults, although one type, lack of reciprocity in marriage, is encountered with similar frequency among all age groups. Occupational strains of overload and depersonalized work relations are most often faced by young adults, while young and middle-aged adults are equally likely to experience inadequate job rewards and noxious work environments. The low degree of occupational strain of older adults is probably due to a combination of their being retired and to their greater satisfaction during their last years of employment. Young adults experience the most marital role strain and also the most economic problems. Middle-aged adults encounter the greatest parental role strain (failure of their children to respect them, to comport themselves acceptably, and to act toward goals).

In summary, it appears from recent studies that young adults may lead the most objectively stressful lives. They seem to experience the most life events and report the most role strain. This may be uniquely characteristic of contemporary young adults, however. Winsborough (1979) finds that recent cohorts of young men move through the progression from schoolboy to married adult much more rapidly than did earlier cohorts.

There are reasons, however, to regard this conclusion as tentative. Methods for measuring the magnitude or impact of life events and other potential stressors are still developing. Pearlin's and Radabaugh's role strain data are limited to people's self reports of their objective life situation, and they neglect one important source of chronic stress associated with old age—failing health. We also know that as people age 1) they are more likely to experience loss events, and 2) the total amount of stress they have experienced increases. It is possible that this accumulation of wear and tear is more consequential for health than is the amount of stress exposure at any single period of time.

Perception of Stress

From survey research, we probably know more about the perception of stress at various ages than we know about actual exposure to potential stressors. A range of cross-sectional surveys reviewed here point to age differences in perception. As some of these are being repeated at subsequent dates, cohort patterns of aging processes will be discernible.

Gurin, Veroff, and Feld (1960) were among the first to explore systematically age differences in the perception of stress. [They reported that the older people are, the less they worry.] More recently, Campbell, Converse, and Rodgers (1976) found that older Americans report greater overall satisfaction with life than do young Americans. In the same study, and again in 1978, people under 30 describe their lives as ''hard'' rather than ''easy'' and ''tied down'' rather than ''free'' more often than do older respondents. In 1978, younger people were also more concerned than older people that they might have a nervous breakdown (Campbell, 1979).

These trends in global perception are generally consistent with the patterns for specific life domains. Several studies have found that older people indicate greater job satisfaction than younger people and perceive less job stress (Gurin et al., 1960; Campbell et al., 1976; House, 1981). Older workers are, however, more likely than younger workers to agree that they would quit their jobs if they did not need the money.

Perceived stress in marital and family life is more closely tied to family life cycle stage (Duvall, 1977) than it is to chronological age per se. Young married adults without children report high satisfaction and low stress. A drop in marital and family satisfaction occurs with the birth of children. Both men and women at this stage report more strain than at any other stage of married life, but the excess of perceived stress is greater for women. Mothers of young children, compared to childless married women the same age, express a greater feeling of being tied down, find life hard rather than easy, are more concerned with financial problems, and more frequently fear they will have a nervous breakdown (Campbell, 1979).[4]

Parenthood exacts a toll on the marital relationship as well. Couples with young children report less overall marital satisfaction, disagree more about spending money, and feel less companionship and mutual understanding in their marriages than do young childless couples. The perception of stress diminishes somewhat when the children enter school, and marital satisfaction improves again when children set out on their own (Glenn, 1975; Lowenthal and Chiriboga, 1971; Schram, 1979; Campbell, 1979). Harkins (1978) reports an improvement in adults' psychological well-being after their children's departure. Campbell finds this as well, and comments: "It is remarkable that this stage of life, often referred to as the 'empty nest,' should have such a lugubrious reputation when it is in fact for most people the most positive period in their married life."

We have thus far presented a rather benign view of aging and perceived stress in the later years. In one important domain, however, old age is associated with an increase in worries and a precipitous decline in satisfaction. This domain is, of course, physical health (Gurin et al., 1960; Campbell et al., 1976; Campbell, 1979).

Like the role strain findings of Pearlin and Radabaugh, the research on life satisfaction does not allow us to distinguish between objective exposure to stressors and the perception of stress. For example, the increase in work satisfaction with age is subject to various interpretations. It is possible that, with age,

---

[4]This emphasis on the perceived stressfulness of the first years of parenthood may seem to contradict Pearlin's and Radabaugh's report of the greatest parental role strain for adults aged 40 to 55. The apparent conflict, no doubt, results from their criteria of parental role strain, unacceptable comportment, failure to act towards goals, and disrespect for parents. These items seem likely to reflect the "sturm und drang" of adolescence to the neglect of the problems younger children can present (e.g., increased housework, fewer nights out, and general demands on time and energy). Although parents of adolescents experience the greatest interpersonal conflict with their children, it is those with small children who find parenthood the most personally taxing.

people either quit odious jobs or are promoted out of them. It is also possible that objective work conditions do not appreciably improve with age, but that workers perceive their jobs as less stressful. This could come about through a lowering of aspirations or by the development of personal resources which enable older workers to view with equanimity situations that would distress younger workers.

This difficulty of interpretation might in part be resolved by examining how the same objective stressors are perceived by people who differ in age. What little evidence exists is provocative. The degree of disruption imposed by certain life events is rated lower by older adults than by younger adults (Horowitz et al., 1974; Masuda and Holmes, 1978). Here the weighting of life events is only hypothetical. What of instances where adults of different ages actually face the same (or a similar) crisis? In three studies of the impact of floods and tornadoes, older adults compared to younger adults reported less stress and physical anxiety, and were less likely to believe they would never recover from the disaster (Bell, 1978: Huerta and Horton, 1978; Kilijanek and Drabek, 1979). At least one stressful life event, unemployment due to a plant closing, was found to create greater perceived stress for older employees (Cobb and Kasl, 1977). This may be the exception that proves the rule, though, for the older workers accurately anticipated they would have a harder time than young workers finding new jobs.

Social psychologists have tended to give a surprisingly gloomy interpretation to this seemingly halcyon fact that, in every important life domain except health, older people report greater satisfaction and less perceived stress. For example, Gurin, Veroff, and Feld (1960) observed that while older adults worry less, they also report less happiness. They concluded that older Americans were passively resigned to their fate. Campbell and his associates also found a combination of high satisfaction and low happiness with advancing age (Campbell et al., 1976; Campbell, 1979). They hypothesized that diminished levels of aspiration in old age account for the finding.

A more positive explanation of these age patterns emphasizes personal control and maturity. To the extent that adults can control their lives, age should be associated with declines in objective stress. Older people have quit jobs they found unrewarding, ended unhappy marriages, and moved to more pleasant homes and neighborhoods. In addition to dropping and changing roles, older adults have adjusted to roles in ways that help them avoid objective stress. For example, through experience, they may learn to get along better with their spouses and coworkers.

Yet objective conditions cannot entirely account for the decline in perceived stress over the life course: The relative composure of older disaster victims testifies to the fact that adults of different ages perceive objectively identical situations differently. Perhaps the resilience of older adults comes from long experience with a variety of stressful life situations. If so, their hard-earned equanimity deserves a less pejorative label than resignation—perhaps maturity or perspective.

Patterning and Cumulation of Stressors

In cross-sectional studies, then, age as a variable is often less strongly associated than the solid variables (e.g., race, sex, income) with exposure to stressors and with health outcomes. If aging is treated as a process rather than a variable, however, attention could be refocused on the patterning and accumulation of stress as people age.

In regard to patterning, the way in which stressful events cluster, order themselves, or relate to the statistical or normative expectations for their occurrence may be consequential for understanding their impact on health. In this sense, the consequences of an event like widowhood (or even a fairly persistent state such as low income or heavy childrearing responsibilities) may vary substantially depending on whether it occurs in close proximity to other events (e.g., job loss), before or after other critical events (e.g., children leaving home), or at an expected (late life) rather than unexpected age (early or middle adulthood). These possibilities have been frequently noted, but rarely studied (cf. Neugarten, 1977; Pearlin and Radabaugh, 1980).

The effects of cumulative exposure to stress over the life course also deserve further attention. Psychosocial stress is one source of the "wear and tear" that constitutes one major explanation of the deterioration of organisms with age (Birren and Renner, 1977:9; Eisdorfer and Wilkie, 1977). We lack, however, the kind of careful longitudinal research necessary to test whether persons with relatively greater cumulative stress over the life course "age" especially rapidly or are especially susceptible to disease.

CONDITIONING VARIABLES

Issues of patterning and cumulation are captured in the stress framework by the notion of conditioning effects. That is, the effect of a given type or level of stress at one age may be conditional on the level or types of stress previously experienced by the person. It is in the consideration of conditioning variables in relation to age that we see the greatest potential for mutual advances in the study of stress and health and the study of aging and human development. Thus let us consider the way in which three major classes of conditioning variables—psychological, social, and biological—vary with age and life-course stage and, hence, can alter the impact of stress on health.

Psychological Conditioning Factors

The attempt to detect and explain age-related changes in psychological functioning or behavior has a long history. There are consistent declines with age in many sensorimotor functions, especially in the speed of response: "One of the most established phenomena of aging is the tendency toward slowness of perceptual, motor, and cognitive processes'' (Birren and Renner, 1977:29). As people age, they tend to become slower and, if forced to react quickly, more error-prone in dealing with behavioral and many cognitive tasks and problems (Rabbitt, 1977; Welford, 1977). Some of this decline in functioning has been associated with physiological deterioration in muscular abilities and in the acuity of major sense organs, most notably eyes, ears, and skin (Fozard et al., 1977; Corso, 1977; Kenshalo, 1977). There is also some evidence that these declines reflect deterioration in central nervous system functioning (Eisdorfer and Wilkie, 1977:267-270).

Memory functions also tend to decline with age (Craik, 1977; Perlmutter, in this book). General intellectual functions show age differences, though "decline with age for many functions may not be seen before ages 50 or 60, and even then the decline may be small" (Botwinick, 1977:603). Again, age differences are most evident in studies involving speeded tests or tasks.

Although perceptual and motor decrements clearly may inhibit the ability of persons to adapt to psychosocial stress, they are not crucial in most situations. Even declines in speed of intellectual, cognitive, and problemsolving activities, as determined largely from laboratory experiments or standardized tests, may not be so critical in adapting to real life situations where quality of response is much more important than speed or quantity. More relevant here are personality dimensions, including coping styles or dispositions, which may influence people's perceptions of objective stressors or their responses to stress. Insofar as these variables have been studied, however, they manifest little consistent and consequential variation with age.

Reviewing research on the relation of age to many individual dimensions of personality (e.g., egocentrism and self-esteem), Neugarten (1977:636) concludes: "In each area, the findings are notably inconsistent from one study to the next, with some but not other investigators reporting age differences," (with one major exception—cross-sectional studies show increases in introversion over the last half of the life course). She also reports that "studies of individual personality dimensions are no more enlightening with regard to the direction of change over time" (Neugarten, 1977:638).

The last few years have seen increased study of the way individuals cope with real life situations. Though still in its infancy, this research does not yet reveal striking age-related differences in the direction of lesser or greater ability to adapt to stress. Pearlin and Schooler (1978) studied the relation to age of over 20 different psychological resources and styles of coping among a large representative sample of persons living in the Chicago urbanized area. With respect to age differences in the efficacy of coping, Pearlin and Schooler (1978:16) conclude:

These results certainly do not support views of aging as a process in which people inexorably become increasingly vulnerable, unable to cope effectively with life-strains. Although there are substantial relationships between age and coping, neither the younger nor the older appear to have any overall advantage in coping effectiveness.

Folkman and Lazarus (1980) measured actual coping behaviors in response to stresses in a small community sample of 100 men and women, aged 45 to 64, who were interviewed about monthly for almost a year. Considering whether coping efforts focused on the problem or on the emotions aroused by the problem, they found "no relationship between age and coping" (Folkman and Lazarus, 1980:235). They suggest that since coping responses are related to the types of stresses experienced (as Pearlin and Schooler found), studies of a broader age range might find changes with age in the frequency of various coping responses as the stresses experienced shift (e.g., from work-related problems in the middle years to healthrelated problems in older age). They rightly emphasize, however, that such changes would not really be a function of personality development.

In summary, extant research reveals little consistent age-related variation in psychological characteristics most likely to affect the perception of, or responses to, psychosocial stress. Some perceptions of stress (e.g., work, marital, and life dissatisfaction) decline with age, perhaps reflecting a growing ability to tolerate or adapt to stress as people move through their middle and later years. These results may, however, merely reflect a decline in the objective stressors associated with age. More importantly, the findings may reflect cohort differences rather than aging over the life course. Given the recency of much psychosocial research on aging and the heavy reliance on cross-sectional differences rather than longitudinal changes, it remains possible that the apparently distinctive attributes of "the aged," both negative and positive, may primarily be characteristics of particular cohorts. As in all aging research, cohort effects may not only spuriously produce the appearance of aging effects, but may also mask them. For example, younger cohorts have more education than older cohorts, and education generally facilitates effective adaptation to stress. Thus, in the Pearlin and Schooler study, controls for education might reveal a clearer tendency for adaptive coping styles to increase with age.

Social Conditioning Factors

Of the many potential social conditioning factors in the stress paradigm, social integration and support have received the most research attention. Previous research suggests that social relationships can reduce stress, improve health, and buffer the impact of stress on health (Back and Bogdonoff, 1967; Lowenthal and Haven, 1968; Cassel, 1970; Nuckolls et al., 1972; Kaplan et al., 1977; Berkman and Syme, 1979; House, 1981). Since all people have some social relationships, and since the supportiveness of such relationships can be enhanced in various ways, the potential for useful application of research in this area is great. The following two questions are important for aging research: 1) How is social support distributed through the life course? 2) Do the effects of social support vary at different stages of the life course?

Aging after middle adulthood is frequently viewed as a series of losses of social roles and relationships (Cumming and Henry, 1961). As people grow older, their children grow up and leave home; they retire; their contact with former coworkers decreases; parents, friends, and spouses die. Social support has been examined because it may protect people from the deleterious health consequences associated with such losses. Raphael (1977) describes an effective application of social support theory in the form of counseling provided to recently widowed women. Lowenthal and Haven (1968) conclude that intimate social relationships buffer against declines in morale and health after age-related social losses. Elderly people low in social support—that is, the single, childless, divorced, and widowed—are more likely to be institutionalized than are those high in social support (Palmore, 1976; Treas, 1977; Shanas, 1979b).

If age is associated with social losses and if social support conditions the relationship between stress and well-being, these two propositions do not explain as much about aging and health as one might imagine or hope. Not all age-related social losses mean a loss of social support. As people age they may relinquish relationships that were not really emotionally important to them (Lowenthal et al., 1975). We need to know more about how substitution of relationships operates with age. Many widowers remarry (Cleveland and Gianturco, 1976), and women who are widowed, although they are far less likely to remarry, may also find and maintain supportive relationships. For example, Lopata (1975) describes "couple companionate relationships" between wives and widows.

Lowenthal and Haven maintain that a single intimate relationship is the critical factor in the morale of the elderly, and few people at any age are completely bereft (Ingersoll and Depner, 1980). Shanas (1979a) discusses the myth of the socially isolated aged, reporting that 95 percent of all people over 65 are community residents, and even among people over 80 only one in eight is institutionalized. Furthermore, according to her data, half of all adults who are 65 and living in the community have an adult child living within 10 minutes of them.

This is not to say that there are not a considerable number of lonely old people who are in poor health. Ethnographic studies of nursing homes and of single occupancy rooming hotels describe the very real predicament of such people (e.g., Stephens, 1976). For many of these, however, their plight in old age is the culmination of a life of marginality (Pilisuk and Minkler, 1980).

Troll (1980) approvingly notes the shift in research emphasis on life course and social networks from a theoretical, pragmatic description to an analysis of the complex processes involved. Since age-related social isolation is rare, an analysis of the effects of various relationships over the life course may be more important than description of the distribution of relationships. As with exposure to stress, the timing and patterning of social support may explain more from a life-course perspective than do exposure levels at various ages. We need more research on people's past histories in relation to their present relationships and adaptation. For instance, Clark and Anderson (1967) conclude that people who have always lived alone fare better than those whose close ties are severed.

From a stress and health standpoint, a person's position in society may be even more critical than position in social networks. In their study of adult development, Lowenthal and her associates consistently found greater variation between men and women than between people at different life stages. Considerable attention is devoted to how social factors such as sex, class, race, and status inconsistency are related to people's exposure and vulnerability to stress (Dohrenwend, 1975; Dohrenwend and Dohrenwend, 1976, 1977; Gove and Tudor, 1977; Pearlin and Schooler, 1978; Kessler, 1979a, 1979b). Some of these factors are known to interact with age in relation to other variables in the stress paradigm. For example, morale in later life correlates more strongly with marital satisfaction for women than for men, whereas physical health relates more strongly to morale in later life among men than among women (Lee, 1978). A life-course perspective might help to elucidate the causal processes behind such statistical interactions.

Biological Conditioning Factors

The strongest and most consistent correlates of age are changes in biological processes of aging and increases in morbidity and mortality. Much of the recent study of aging and human development has attempted to counteract a decrement model of aging in the social, psychological, and even biological spheres. Many beliefs about the severe and steady deterioration of social life and psychological functioning with age have been shown to be exaggerated. Even biological aging proceeds less rapidly, universally, and invariantly than is commonly supposed. Nevertheless, many declines with age in biological functioning and in the ability to avoid or resist noxious environmental agents remain the most widely accepted elements of the aging process (Birren and Renner, 1977; Shock, 1977; Finch and Hayflick, 1977). Although even these biological changes are not yet fully understood, they remain of great importance to understanding the impact of stress and other psychosocial factors on health in a life-course perspective.

Psychosocial stress can be postulated as one potential factor affecting the biological aging process (Eisdorfer and Wilkie, 1977). That is, stress can produce many of the biological and physiological responses characteristic of biological aging—for example, impairment of the immune system and increases in blood pressure. Accumulation of such "wear and tear" over time is one hypothesized cause of biological and physiological deterioration with age.

More important for our present purposes, regardless of the role of stress in producing it, biological aging is likely to make people more susceptible to developing infectious or chronic diseases in response to stress. This interplay between environmental stress and biological aging has been a central concern of many experimental biologists. Thus, Handler (1960) defined aging as "the deterioration of a mature organism resulting from time-dependent, essentially irreversible changes intrinsic to all members of a species, such that, with the passage of time, they become increasingly unable to cope with the stresses of the environment, thereby increasing the probability of death." Handler's definition is really a hypothesis that biological aging processes are potentially strong conditioners of the impact of stress (psychosocial or otherwise) on health. The same hypothesis emerges from literature on social stress and health which emphasizes that stress has broad and relatively nonspecific physiological effects on the body, thus predisposing people to a wide range of diseases (Cassel, 1976). The specific disease developed by any individual depends not on the nature or level of the stress experienced, but rather on other factors (often biological, physical, or chemical) which make a person susceptible to a particular disease at a particular time.

Although the potential interplay between psychosocial and biological factors in the generation of health and disease has been addressed theoretically and in some experimental research (e.g., laboratory studies of the role of stress in accelerating processes of carcinogenesis: Riley, 1975; Solomon et al., 1974), social epidemiological research has given little explicit consideration to the role of age, or biological changes associated with age, in conditioning the impact of psychosocial factors on health and disease. Age and related biological variables are often treated as "control" or "confounding" variables in analyses of the effects of psychosocial variables on health, but seldom do these analyses examine the joint conditioning (i.e., statistical interaction) effects of biological aging and psychosocial stress in producing disease. Such analyses seem to us a priority area for future research on psychosocial factors in health within a life-course perspective.

In their crudest form, such analyses would consider whether age and psychosocial stress combine interactively as well as additively in predicting health and disease. These analyses would be analogous to previous work considering how sex, race, socioeconomic status, and marital status combine additively and interactively in predicting mental health (Kessler, 1979a, 1979b; Pearlin and Johnson, 1977). The analyses would test not only whether effects of age and stress on health are correlated or confounded with each other, but more importantly, whether the impact of stress on health varies by age (or conversely whether the impact of age on health varies by levels of stress to which people are exposed).[5]

---

[5]It is worth noting that the impact of stress on health or disease should not increase with age for all forms of stress or all forms of health. In the case of mental health, people's adaptive capacities probably increase with age. Second, some stresses may become less consequential with age, at least up to relatively old age. For example, Berkman and Syme (1979) find the impact of lack of social connectedness, (e.g., lack of a spouse or close friend and relatives) on mortality to be greatest for their youngest (30-39) respondents. This may reflect a great normative expectation and acceptance of the loss of spouses, friends, and relatives in later life and/or a greater ability to cope with them.

Direct assessments of major age-related biological changes that may predispose people to major infections or chronic diseases would be preferable to using age per se in such analyses. Decrements in the functioning of the cardiovascular and immune systems seem especially important here, since these systems play a major role in the development of the major sources of morbidity and mortality in the middle and later years (Kohn, 1977; Makinodan, 1977). Although research clearly indicates that psychosocial factors can have deleterious effects on the cardiovascular and immune systems (Jenkins, 1971, 1976; Fox, 1978), there is again a lack of attention to the joint or interactive effects on morbidity or mortality of psychosocial stress in conjunction with indicators of cardiovascular or immune functioning. Suggestive evidence comes from research on the type A behavior pattern, which has been found to produce a greater relative risk of coronary disease in persons with high levels of other risk factors of such disease (and, hence, established biological susceptibility) than in persons with low levels of other risk factors (Brand, 1978).

An aging perspective highlights the importance of biological processes and variables as potential conditioners of the impact of psychosocial stress on health. It is in some ways a wonder that, although stress has been shown to affect physical morbidity and mortality generally, almost no effort has been made to examine its effects separately among those who are biologically most susceptible to its deleterious effects.

In summarizing our discussion of age, psychosocial stress, and health, we reemphasize a number of points regarding the state of present knowledge and directions for future research. Although clearly definable life events (considered as stressors) have received considerable attention in stress and aging research, their potential contribution to understanding stress and health over the life course needs further investigation. More enduring stresses such as financial deprivation, lack of social integration, and occupational and familial problems appear equally or more consequential for health.

The level of stress in people's lives—whether measured in terms of life events, enduring stressful conditions, or perceptions of stress—does not appear to increase consistently or markedly by age categories, at least not until quite advanced ages (75 and over). Thus, research on stress and health over the life course should consider psychosociäal factors not only as sources of stress but also as factors that condition the impact of stress on health. How, for example, does the cumulation and patterning of stress affect health? Does experience lessen the negative impact of certain stressors (or do stressful experiences have a cumulative negative effect on health)? The impact on the stresshealth relationship of people's socioeconomic resources, their access to significant and supportive social relationships, and their ability to control events in their lives and of changes (or stabilities) in these factors over the life course are especially promising avenues for future research.

Such research will require appropriately designed collection and analysis of longitudinal data on several cohorts. Such designs enhance our ability to study processes of stress and aging and to identify whether cross-sectional age differences reflect cohort effects or changes in individuals over time.

Finally, there is great need for interdisciplinary research that simultaneously considers social, psychosocial, and biological factors involved in the complex relationships of age, stress, and health. Biological factors, especially cardiovascular and immune functioning, may importantly condition the impact of psychosocial factors on health. Psychosocial factors may similarly act to exacerbate or counteract the impact of deleterious biological forces in the aging process. The interplay of social, psychological, and biological science suggests the great challenge and the great promise of future research on age, stress, and health.

REFERENCES

Atchley, Robert C. 1976. The Sociology of Retirement. Cambridge: Schenkman.

Back, Kurt W., and Morton D. Bogdonoff 1967. "Buffer conditions in experimental stress." Behavioral Science 12:384–390.

Bell, Bill D. 1978. "Disaster impact and response: overcoming the thousand natural shocks." Gerontologist 18:531–540.

Berezin, M.A. 1969. "Sex and old age: a review of the literature." Journal of Geriatric Psychiatry 2:131–149.

Berkman, Lisa F., and S. Leonard Syme 1979. "Social networks, host resistance, and mortality: a nine-year follow-up study of Alameda County residents." American Journal of Epidemiology 109(2):186–204.

Birren, James E., and V. Jayne Renner 1977. "Research on the psychology of aging: principles and experimentation." Pp. 3–38 in James E. Birren and K. Warner Schaie (eds.), Handbook of the Psychology of Aging. New York: Van Nostrand Reinhold.

Botwinick, Jack 1977. "Intellectual abilities." Pp. 580–605 in James E. Birren and K. Warner Schaie (eds.), Handbook of the Psychology of Aging. New York: Van Nostrand Reinhold.

Brand, Richard J. 1978. "Coronary-prone behavior as an independent risk factor for coronary heart disease." Pp. 11–24 in T.M. Dembroski et al. (eds.), Coronary Prone Behavior. New York: Springer-Verlag.

Campbell, Angus 1979. The Sense of Well-being in America: Recent Patterns and Trends. New York: McGraw-Hill.

Campbell, Angus, Philip E. Converse, and Willard L. Rodgers 1976. The Quality of American Life. New York: Russell Sage Foundation.

Cassel, John 1970. "Physical illness in response to stress." Pp. 189–209 in Sol Levine and Norman Scotch (eds.), Social Stress. Chicago: Aldine.

———. 1976. "The contribution of the social environment to host resistance." American Journal of Epidemiology 104(2):107–123.

Clark, Margaret, and Barbara Anderson 1967. Culture and Aging. Springfield: Charles C. Thomas.

Cleveland, William P, and Daniel T. Gianturco 1976. "Remarriage probability after widowhood: a retrospective method." Journal of Gerontology 31(1):99–103.

Cobb, Sidney, and Stanislav V. Kasl 1977. Termination: The Consequences of Job Loss. Cincinnati: National Institute for Occupational Safety and Health.

Corso, John 1977. "Auditory perception and communication." Pp. 536–553 in James E. Birren and K. Warner Schaie (eds.), Handbook of the Psychology of Aging. New York: Van Nostrand Reinhold.

Craik, Fergus I.M. 1977. "Age differences in human memory." Pp. 384–420 in James E. Birren and K. Warner Schaie (eds.), Handbook of the Psychology of Aging. New York: Van Nostrand Reinhold.

Cumming, Elaine, and William H. Henry 1961. Growing Old: The Process of Disengagement. New York: Basic Books.

Dekker, D., and J. Webb 1974. "Relationship of the social readjustment rating scale to psychiatric patient status, anxiety, and social desirability." Journal of Psychosomatic Research 18:145–180.

Dohrenwend, Bruce P. 1975. "Sociocultural and social psychological factors in the genesis of mental disorders." Journal of Health and Social Behavior 16:365–392.

Dohrenwend, Bruce P., and Barbara S. Dohrenwend 1969. Social Status and Psychological Disorders. New York: Wiley.

————. 1974. "Social and cultural influences on psychopathology." Annual Review of Psychology. Palo Alto, Calif.: Annual Review.

————. 1976. "Sex differences and psychiatric disorders." American Journal of Sociology 81:1447–1454.

————. 1977. "Reply to Gove and Tudor's comment on 'Sex differences and psychiatric disorders.'" American Journal of Sociology 82:1336–1345.

Duvall, Evelyn M. 1977. Family Development (5th edition). Philadelphia: J.B. Lippincott.

Eisdorfer, Carl, and Frances Wilkie 1977. "Stress, disease, aging and behavior." Pp. 251–275 in James E. Birren and K. Warner Schaie (eds.), Handbook of the Psychology of Aging. New York: Van Nostrand Reinhold.

Fengler, Alfred P., and Nancy Goodrich 1979. "Wives of elderly disabled men: the hidden patients." Gerontologist 19(2):175–183.

Finch, Caleb E., and Leonard Hayflick 1977. Handbook of the Biology of Aging. New York: Van Nostrand Reinhold.

Folkman, Susan, and Richard S. Lazarus 1980. "An analysis of coping in a middle-aged community sample." Journal of Health and Social Behavior 21:219–239.

Fox, Bernard H. 1978. "Premorbid psychological factors as related to cancer incidence." Journal of Behavioral Medicine 1:45–134.

Fozard, James L., Ernst Wolf, Benjamin Bell, Ross A. McFarland, and Stephen Podolsky 1977. "Visual perception and communication." Pp. 497–534 in James E. Birren and K. Warner Schaie (eds.), Handbook of the Psychology of Aging. New York: Van Nostrand Reinhold.

Frankenhaeuser, Marianne, and Bertil Gardell 1976. "Underload and overload in working life: outline of a multidisciplinary approach." Journal of Human Stress 2(3):35–46.

George, Linda K. 1980. Role Transitions in Later Life. Monterey: Brooks Cole.

Glenn, Norval D. 1975. "Psychological well-being in the postparental stage: some evidence from national surveys." Journal of Marriage and the Family 37 (February):105–110.

Glick, I.O., R.O. Weiss, and C.M. Parkes 1974. The First Years of Bereavement. New York: Wiley.

Gove, Walter B., and Jeanette F. Tudor 1973. "Adult sex roles and mental illness." American Journal of Sociology 78:812–835.

Gurin, Gerald, Joseph Veroff, and Sheila Feld 1960. Americans View Their Mental Health. New York: Basic Books.

Handler, P. 1960. "Radiation and aging." Pp. 199–223 in Nathan W. Schock (ed.), Aging. Washington, D.C.: American Association for the Advancement of Science.

Harkins, Elizabeth Bates 1978. "Effects of empty nest transition on self report of psychological and physical well-being." Journal of Marriage and the Family 40 (August):549–556.

Holmes, Thomas H., and Minoru Masuda 1974. "Life change and illness susceptibility." Pp. 45–72 in Barabara Snell Dohrenwend and Bruce P. Dohrenwend (eds.), Stressful Life Events: Their Nature and Effects. New York: Wiley.

Holmes, Thomas H., and Richard H. Rahe 1967. "The social readjustment rating scale." Journal of Psychosomatic Research 11:213–218.

Horowitz, Mardi J., C. Schaefer, and P. Cooney 1974. "Life event scaling for recency of experience." Pp. 125–133 in E.K. Gunderson and Richard H. Rahe (eds.), Life Stress and Illness. Springfield: Charles Thomas.

House, James S. 1974. "Occupational stress and coronary heart disease: a review and theoretical integration." Journal of Health and Social Behavior 15:12–27.

———. 1981. Work Stress and Social Support. Reading, Mass.: Addison-Wesley.

House, James S., and Mark Jackman 1979. "Occupational stress and health." Pp. 135–158 in Paul I. Ahmed and George V. Coelho (eds.), Toward a New Definition of Health. New York: Plenum.

Huerta, Faye, and Robert Horton 1978. "Coping behavior of elderly flood victims." Gerontologist 18(6):541–545.

Ingersoll, Berit, and Charlene Depner 1980. "Support networks of middle-aged and older adults." Paper presented at the American Psychological Association Annual Meeting, Montreal.

Jenkins, C. David 1971. "Psychologic and social precursors of coronary disease." New England Journal of Medicine 284:244–255, 307–317.

———. 1976 "Recent evidence supporting psychologic and social risk factors for coronary disease" (Parts I and II). New England Journal of Medicine 294:987–994, 1033–1038.

Kaplan, Berton, John C. Cassel, and Susan Gore 1977. "Social support and health." Medical Care 25 (Supplement):47–58.

Kenshalo, Dan R. 1977. "Age changes in touch, vibration, temperature, kinesthesis and pain sensitivity." Pp. 562–579 in James E. Birren and K. Warner Schaie (eds.), Handbook of the Psychology of Aging. New York: Van Nostrand Reinhold.

Kessler, Ronald C. 1979a. "A strategy for studying differential vulnerability to the psychological consequences of stress." Journal of Health and Social Behavior 20:100–108.

———. 1979b. "Stress, social status and psychological distress." Journal of Health and Social Behavior 20:259–272.

Kilijanek, Thomas S., and Thomas E. Drabek 1979. "Assessing long-term impacts of a national disaster: a focus on the elderly." Gerontologist 19(6):555–566.

Kohn, Robert R. 1977. "Heart and cardiovascular system." Pp. 281–317 in Caleb E. Finch and Leonard Hayflick (eds.), Handbook of the Biology of Aging. New York: Van Nostrand Reinhold.

Lee, Gary R. 1978. "Marriage and morale in later life." Journal of Marriage and the Family:131–139.

Levine, Sol, and Norman Scotch 1970. Social Stress. Chicago: Aldine.

Levinson, Daniel J. 1977. "The mid-life transition: a period in adult psychosocial development." Psychiatry 40: 99–112.

———. 1978 The Seasons of a Man's Life. New York: Knopf.

Lopata, Helena Z. 1973. Widowhood in an American City. Cambridge: Shenkman.

———. 1975 "Couple companionate relations: wives and widows." Pp. 73–94 in Nona Glazer Malbin (ed.), Old Family/New Family. New York: Van Nostrand Reinhold.

Lowenthal, Marjorie Fiske, Maida Thurnher, and David Chiriboga and Associates 1975. Four Stages of Life: A Comparative Study of Women and Men Facing Transitions. San Francisco: Jossey-Bass.

Lowenthal, Marjorie Fiske, and Clayton Haven 1968. "Interaction and adaptation: intimacy as a critical variable." American Sociological Review 33(1):20–30.

Lowenthal, Marjorie Fiske, and David Chiriboga 1972. "Transition to the empty nest: crisis, challenge, or relief?" Archives of General Psychiatry 26:8–14.

McGrath, Joseph E. 1970. Social and Psychological Factors in Stress. New York: Holt Rinehart Winston.

Maddox, George L. 1979. "The sociology of later life." Annual Review of Sociology 5:113–135.

Makinodan, Takashi 1977. "Immunity and aging." Pp. 379–408 in Caleb E. Finch and Leonard Hayflick (eds.), Handbook of the Biology of Aging. New York: Van Nostrand Reinhold.

Masuda, M., and T.H. Holmes 1978. "Life events: perceptions and frequencies." Psychosomatic Medicine 40:236–261.

Nachman, Gerald 1979. "The menopause that refreshes." Pp. 306–308 in Peter I. Rose (ed.), Socialization and the Life Cycle. New York: St. Martins.

Neugarten, Bernice L.1977. "Personality and aging." Pp. 626–649 in James E. Birren and K. Warner Schaie (eds.), Handbook of the Psychology of Aging. New York: Van Nostrand Reinhold.

Nuckolls, Katherine B., John Cassel, and Berton H. Kaplan 1972. "Psychosocial assets, life crisis and the prognosis of pregnancy." American Journal of Epidemiology 95:431–441.

Palmore, Erdman 1976. "Total chance of institutionalization among the aged." Gerontologist 16:504–507.

———. 1979b "Predictors of successful aging." Gerontologist 19(5):427–431.

Parkes, C.M. 1972. Studies of Grief in Adult Life. New York: International Universities.

Pearlin, Leonard, and Joyce Johnson 1977. "Marital status, life strains, and depression." American Sociological Review 42 (October):704–715.

Pearlin, Leonard, and Clarice Radabaugh 1980. "Age and stress: Perspectives and problems." In Hamilton McCubbin (ed.), Family, Stress, Coping and Social Supports. New York: Springer.

Pearlin, Leonard, and Carmi Schooler 1978. "The structure of coping." Journal of Health and Social Behavior 19:2–21.

Pilisuk, Marc, and Meredith Minkler 1980. "Supportive networks: life ties for the elderly." The Journal of Social Issues 36(2):95–116.

Rabbitt, Patrick 1977. "Changes in problem solving ability in old age." Pp. 606–625 in James E. Birren and K. Warner Schaie (eds.), Handbook of the Psychology of Aging. New York: Van Nostrand Reinhold.

Rabkin, Judith G., and Elmer L. Struening 1976. "Life events, stress and illness." Science 194:1013–1020.

Raphael, Beverley 1977. "Preventive intervention with the recently bereaved." Archives of General Psychiatry 34:1450–1454.

Riley, V. 1975. "Mouse mammary tumors: alteration of incidence as apparent function of stress." Science 189:465–467.

Rossi, Alice S. 1979. "Transition to parenthood." Pp. 132–145 in Peter I. Rose (ed.), Socialization and the Life Cycle. New York: St. Martins.

Rubin, Lilian B. 1979. Women of a Certain Age: The Midlife Search for Self. New York: Harper Row.

Schram, Rosalyn Weinman 1979. "Marital satisfaction over the family life cycle: a critique and proposal." Journal of Marriage and the Family (February):7–12.

Shanas, Ethel 1979a. "Social myth as hypothesis: the case of the family relations of old people." Robert W. Kleemeier Award Lecture. Gerontologist 19(1):3–9.

———. 1979b "The family as a social support system in old age." Gerontologist 19(2):169–174.

Sheehy, Gail 1976. Passages. New York: E.P. Dutton.

Shock, Nathan W. 1977. "Biological theories of aging." Pp. 103–115 in James E. Birren and K. Warner Schaie (eds.), Handbook of the Psychology of Aging. New York: Van Nostrand Reinhold.

Smith, Kristen Falde, and Vern L. Bengtson 1979. "Positive consequences of institutionalization: solidarity between elderly parents and their middle-aged children." Gerontologist 19(2):555–566.

Solomon, G.F., A.A. Amkraut, and P. Kasper 1974. "Immunity, emotions and stress: with special reference to the mechanisms of stress effects on the immune system." Annals of Clinical Research 6:313–322.

Srole, Leo, Thomas S. Langner, Stanley T. Michael, Price Kirkpatrick, Marvin K. Opler, and Thomas A. Rennie 1962. Mental Health in the Metropolis: The Midtown Manhattan Study. New York: McGraw-Hill.

Srole, Leo, and Anita Kasser Fischer 1980. "The midtown Manhattan longitudinal study vs. 'the mental paradise lost' doctrine." Archives of General Psychiatry 37:207.

Stephens, Joyce 1976. Loners, Losers and Lovers: Elderly Tenants in a Slum Hotel. Seattle: University of Washington Press.
Tobin, Sheldon, and Morton Lieberman 1976. Last Home for the Aged: Critical Implications of Institutionalization. San Francisco: Jossey-Bass.
Treas, Judith. 1977. "Family support systems for the aged." Gerontologist 17: 486–491.
Troll, Lillian E. 1980. "Interpersonal relations: introduction." Pp. 435–440 in Leonard W. Poon (ed.), Aging in the 1980's. Washington, D.C.: American Psychological Association.
Uhlenhuth, E.H., R.S. Lipman, M.B. Baltes, and J. Stern 1974. "Symptom intensity and life stress in the city." Archives of General Psychiatry 31:759–764.
Welford, A.T. 1977. "Motor performance." Pp. 450–496 in James E. Birren and K. Warner Schaie (eds.), Handbook of the Psychology of Aging. New York: Van Nostrand Reinhold.
Winsborough, Halliman H. 1979. "Changes in the transition to adulthood." Pp. 137–152 in Matilda W. Riley (ed.), Aging from Birth to Death: Interdisciplinary Perspectives. Boulder, Colo.: Westview Press.

10

Social Change and Food Habits of the Elderly[1]

Maradee A. Davis
Elizabeth Randall
University of Texas

To approach the topic of aging and nutrition is to confront a complexity of interrelationships. Foods are vehicles for nutrients that in turn function to provide all individuals, including the elderly, with the energy, vitality, and reserve necessary for active social, psychological, and physical performance. Yet inevitable life changes coinciding with the process of aging, such as altered social and family roles, death of spouse and friends, changes in living arrangements, curtailment of mobility, decreased income, and physiological changes, all influence the ability of the elderly to practice sound nutrition.

An understanding of the nutritional well-being of elderly people begins with their nutritional status at younger ages. There is evidence to suggest that nutritional status throughout the life course has implications for the development of specific diseases and disabilities associated with old age. Conversely, disease processes that are prevalent at older ages (such as diabetes, hypertension, cardiovascular disease, renal conditions, and dental problems) require alterations in usual food practices. There is also the possibility that nutritional status may affect the nature and rate of the physiological aging process per se and the concomitant potentials for social and psychological functioning.

This paper addresses the broad topic of the social aspects of aging and nutrition by focusing selectively on food habits and on the potential impact of current trends in family structure, social integration, and gender roles on the food habits of future cohorts of the elderly. Since decisions about food consumption are com-

[1]The authors are grateful to Doris Howes Calloway for critically reading an earlier version of this paper.

monly made within a household context, changes in family structure and gender role may alter the food habits of individuals, including the elderly, across the life course. We review the literature that links the traditional areas of social gerontology with the concerns of research on food habits. The first part of the paper discusses the nature, development, and plasticity of food habits across the life course. The second part reviews literature on the potential effects of current social changes in family structure, social integration, and gender roles on food habits of the elderly. Finally, we suggest directions for future research.

THE DYNAMICS OF AGING AND FOOD HABITS

Food habits are characteristic repetitive behaviors by which individuals seek to meet their physiological need for food within the context of their sociocultural environments and psychological motivations. From this perspective, the term food habits is viewed as inclusive, incorporating actual food consumption, food purchasing, meal patterns, the frequency with which specific foods are consumed, preferences for particular foods, and the value systems underlying food beliefs.

Basic food habits are formed early in life, reflect patterns of past generations, and vary by ethnicity, religion, and social class (Sherwood, 1970; Shifflett and Nyberg, 1978). These patterns are learned, reinforced, and maintained or modified through socialization. Beginning with the first feeding experiences, the child learns to translate basic physiological *hunger* into a culturally patterned *appetite*, simultaneously meeting a variety of social and psychological goals.

Even though food habits are patterned and may tend to be maintained across the life course, these patterns are not immutable. They vary with aging and vary from one cohort to another as society changes.

Cohort Differences

As cohorts move into old age, they bring with them a heterogeneity of food behaviors evolving from the social, cultural, economic, and environmental history of their particular lifelong experiences. This heterogeneity is apparent when we consider the different social and nutritional influences that have affected three cohorts of persons who will be from 55 to 90 years of age in the year 2000.

Many members of the first cohort, those born from 1910 to 1930, grew up in fairly large families that valued the sharing of regular meals. Food prices were relatively low, and technological advances in food processing and national distribution had not been fully realized (Department of Agriculture, 1975). As children or young adults, they experienced the Depression of the 1930's, when indulgent food habits were not encouraged or at times were not even possible. Many were born abroad and came from rural or village backgrounds. Their average educational level is lower than that of more recent cohorts, with possible implications for their selection of foods and their general ability to cope with change. Marriage dissolution rates have been relatively low in this cohort, reflecting greater stability in the family structure. The low fertility rates for this cohort, however, may limit the potential social and economic support they can expect in old age.

By the year 2000, many members of the second cohort, those born between 1930 and 1940, will be of retirement age. Members of this cohort began life in smaller families during the Depression and are themselves a proportionately smaller cohort than those coming before or after. Their adolescence coincided with World War II, but they came to adulthood in a period of unprecedented economic growth and upward mobility. During the Depression and the war, since emphasis necessarily was given to home food production and home processing of fruits and vegetables, many women in this cohort learned selfreliance and became skilled in a variety of methods of food preparation. In their young adulthood, they were exposed to the rapid diffusion of modern kitchen technologies, especially the home freezer, and in mid-adulthood to convenience and fast foods. They were in their twenties and thirties during the 1960's, when the health effects of diet and smoking were publicized, and may have changed their food habits accordingly. In old age, they may expect increased pension benefits and, if current trends continue, a higher proportion may be retiring earlier than the previous cohort. Although many women in this cohort have been homemakers, many will have also joined the work force during middle age.

Those persons in the third cohort, who were born between 1940 and 1950, are members of an extremely large group, some of whom became the activists of the 1960's and joined the "me" generation of the 1970's. They have been exposed to rapid technological and social change and have been raised in an era of "refined" foods, an explosion of fast food technologies, and mass media food promotions (an era in which the consumption of simple sugars rose dramatically while complex carbohydrate intake declined). They also have been influenced by the feminist movements and rapidly changing gender roles, including a greater proportion of women in the work force. They have experienced high levels of family dissolution, have been geographically more mobile, and have lead faster-paced lives. They have been exposed to more options regarding what, when, and where to eat, but the quality of choices they make about food selection may reflect convenience more than nutritional adequacy. They are used to eating on-the-run, to eating out, and to the availability of vending machines.

Higher income and educational levels and possibly earlier retirement will mean that many of the persons who will be aged 50 to 60 in 2000 may already have retired, though they will have some 20 or more years of life ahead of them. Barring dramatic economic change, this cohort will have the means, motivation, and health to pursue a more leisurely lifestyle than have previous cohorts. Because of their continuous adaptation to social and technological change, it would be anticipated that their food habits would be more malleable and changeable than those of previous cohorts. Their habits will also be less predictable, given their exposure to widely differing knowledge and experiences about food preparation and consumption.

What is evident from these three cohorts is that food habits are responsive to pervasive changes in the social structure and that the myriad lifelong experiences and eating habits differ from one cohort to the next.

Age Differences

In addition to cohort differences, there are important questions—so far largely unanswered—about changes in food habits as people age. For such analyses, a major impediment is the inadequacy of existing conceptual models. Theory construction in research on food habits is still at a rudimentary stage. A number of approaches capable of guiding empirical studies have appeared in the recent literature (Ellis et al., 1976; Grotkowski and Sims, 1978; Reaburn, Krondl, and Lau, 1979; Sanjur, 1981; and Sims, 1978), but as yet, these models have not been adequately developed for the task of studying age and nutrition. The limitations in existing conceptual models are evident in the empirical research addressing questions of maintenance and change of food habits across the adult years. One source of difficulty is the disproportionate emphasis placed on the earliest stages in establishing food habits—childhood and the years of rapid growth.

This lack of an adequate conceptualization is reflected in the general inattention to specifying the precise links between social factors and particular food behaviors and to the interactions among variables. For the most part, studies have been descriptive examinations of demographic factors: age, sex, income, and education (Slesinger, McDivitt, and O'Donnell, 1980). The research has generally been cross-sectional, with small selected samples within limited age groups. Therefore, the impact of age per se on food habits has not been examined, nor has there been any attempt to delineate the separate influences of biological, social, and psychological factors. This problem is evident in the following summary of current studies addressing food habits in the adult years.

Although considerable literature is available on the cognitive and cultural components of *food values and beliefs* (Wilson, 1979), the data do not encompass the effects of aging nor focus specifically on the elderly. Nevertheless, there is some indication that many elderly people have changed their food habits in recent years for reasons of beliefs, health, aloneness, and finances (Todhunter, 1976; Brown, 1976), and they also express a willingness to try new foods.

The effects of aging on *food preferences* are similarly poorly defined. The diminished senses of taste and smell in later life alter the sensations derived from foods and may well alter food preferences, as may the widespread problems of poor dentition (Weg, 1978). The classic preference studies conducted by the military (Pilgrim, 1961) found that younger men in the United States Army gave high ratings to beverages, cereals, fruits, and desserts, whereas older enlisted men favored vegetables and soups. Todhunter (1976) reports that beef, green beens, greens, and pork were the favorite foods mentioned most frequently in her study of elderly persons in Tennessee. Only a few respondents could give any reason for disliking a food. Taste and dislike of some vegetables because of texture or because "they disagree with me" were given as reasons for disliking foods.

Some studies of *food purchasing* patterns indicate that access to food stores and income constraints influence purchasing patterns of the elderly (Weg, 1978). However, Hendel's (1969) survey of low-income elderly in a South Minneapolis housing development found that food shopping practices were influenced first by the ability to get to the store and second by the quality and type of food available, with price—back in the 1960's—mentioned as a major consideration by only 11 percent of the sample. There is also a suggestion that because of small families, the need to buy small quantities adds to the problems of selection (Weg, 1978).

Meal patterns are important to nutrition since they affect the distribution of calories within the total daily food intake. The elderly are more likely than younger age groups to eat breakfast (Canadian National Health and Welfare, 1975; Weg, 1978), to consume a greater proportion of total calories and nutrients at breakfast (Slesinger et al., 1980), and to cite breakfast as the favorite meal (Todhunter, 1976). The elderly also tend to skip fewer meals than do younger persons (Slesinger et al., 1980). Different patterns have also been observed between the elderly and younger persons in the quantity and types of between-meal snacks (Canadian National Health and Welfare, 1975). The reasons for such age differences in meal patterns have not been adequately explored.

What evidence is there that actual *nutrient consumption* differs by age? Several national surveys provide some answers. The national Health and Nutrition Examination Survey (HANES I), conducted by the U.S. Department of Health, Education, and Welfare in 1971-74 (Miller, 1973), found that iron, calcium, vitamin A, and vitamin C are the nutrients most frequently consumed in suboptimal amounts by persons 65 to 74 years old (74 was the upper age limit in HANES I) (Abraham et al., 1979). This pattern is not unique to the elderly, since less than optimal amounts of these nutrients are consumed by the U.S. population in general. Obesity, another nutritional problem in the United States, is apparent in the elderly and is most pronounced among women. Despite this situation, low energy consumption was reported for a substantial number of elderly persons, particularly the poor.

Obesity as well as low intake levels of iron among the elderly (aged 60 and over) were recorded in the TenState Nutrition Survey, which was specifically designed to discover nutritional problems among the poor in the United States (Center for Disease Control, 1972). Low intake levels of vitamin C were more common for men than for women. Low vitamin A intake was most marked in the Spanish American population. Riboflavin was reported as being consumed in suboptimal amounts by both blacks and Spanish Americans.

The findings of HANES I are similar to the data now being reported from the 1977-78 Nationwide Food Consumption Survey (NFCS), conducted by the U.S. Department of Agriculture (Rizek, 1978; Hegsted, 1980). This survey can be compared to the 1965-66 Household Food Consumption Survey, also conducted by the U.S. Department of Agriculture (Cronin, 1980). In 1965-66, thiamine and riboflavin were described as limited nutrients for both men and women and vitamin C for men. In the 1977-78 study, the intake of calcium and mean intakes of thiamine, riboflavin, and vitamin C were adequate. Intake of vitamin A, although still suboptimal, improved over the decade. Concern remains for deficiencies in the intake of iron, while the intake of both energy and total fat has decreased.

Changes in the nutritional adequacy of the food habits of the elderly cannot be stated definitively on the basis of these national surveys. Methodological difficulties are inherent in the 24-hour recall as a data-gathering device, in variations across surveys in the standards used for interpreting nutrient intake levels, and in failure to adjust for the common occurrence of illnesses in older persons and for widespread nutrient-drug interactions.

This lack of definitive data on the dynamics of aging and food habits is particularly significant in an era of increasing nutrition and health services. It is hoped that the science base will be improved in the near future, so that steps may be taken to anticipate the nutritional needs of future cohorts of older people. Meantime, an assessment of the impact of current social trends on future food habits would be useful.

TRENDS IN FAMILY STRUCTURE AND GENDER ROLES

Although the physiological need for food exists within the individual, eating is an important psychosocial activity. In our society, the normative social institution responsible for the procurement and consumption of food is typically the family, and eating occurs largely in a family setting. Thus changes in family structure as a result of life-course stage and changing social roles within the family will have effects on the purchase and consumption of food.

Family Structure and Family Stage

Coughenour (1972) and Lewin (1943) both provide theoretical approaches to studying how changes in family structure, function, and roles affect food habits across the life course. Coughenour (1972) has applied Parson's functional prerequisites of the family system, which, although abstract, raise important questions for research. Food consumption is considered to be a *goal directed* social interaction process. *Adaptation* involves defining food needs, accommodating the varying food interests of the family members, incorporating food decisions into related family goals, and applying available resources to the acquisition of food. The numerous meanings attached to food permit the gratification, through foods, of many goals, such as social status, security, good health, and family role performance. The *integrative* factor in food consumption refers to its effect on family cohesiveness and socialization of members into family norms. Food consumption involves a *pattern* of repetitive acts with periods of "latency," or nonconsumption, between them. During these periods, other family activities are undertaken and goals may be reassessed.

Coughenour hypothesized that these functional aspects of food consumption would assume different relative importance at varying stages of the family life cycle. His study design involved 4,000 homemakers who were questioned about activities thought to indicate adaptation, integration, and goal attainment. Results support the existence of the distinct dimensions. As anticipated, adaptive behavior was closely associated with family size, being lowest in the early years of marriage before childbearing begins and highest in families with older children living at home. Family size alone did not account for the adaptive behaviors of older couples, a finding which suggests that some adaptive activities acquired during the childrearing era are retained in later life.

Similarly, integrative activities were lower among young childless couples and older couples and were higher among families with school-age children. This pattern suggests that there is increasing emphasis on the transmission of family norms during the childrearing period.

Homemaker goal gratification from food consumption was found to be highest among young married couples and older couples whose children had left home. Lowest levels of goal gratifiction were detected among homemakers with children aged 6 to 18 in the home. This pattern reflects both an inverse relationship between family size and goal satisfaction and a direct relationship with per capita family income.

Lewin's (1943) "channel theory" (Sanjur, 1981), another theoretical orientation for studying the foodrelated effects of changes in the family across the life course, has as its central premise that most people eat the food presented to them. A study of food habits could thereby be abbreviated by examining how foods come to the table and why. Lewin referred to the routes followed by foods in reaching the consumer as "channels." In the 1940's, the channels proposed were stores, home gardening, roadside purchases, and home processing (baking, canning). Since then, the relative importance of these channels has changed, especially roadside purchases and home processing. Restaurants, school lunch programs, and convenience food outlets now need to be considered as well.

Movement of food into the various food channels of particular families is under the control of human "gatekeepers," in Lewin's terms, the most frequently studied being the homemaker. Knowledge of the cognitive proccesses and value orientations of the gatekeeper is crucial to understanding the food habits of all family members. Amid opposing considerations such as cost versus convenience, adult versus child preferences, and concern for health versus prestige, the gatekeeper makes decisions that govern the entrance of a food into a specific channel.

This model should also be helpful in anticipating the impact of recent changes in gender roles and in family structure. Increasingly, women are choosing to work outside the home, and men are gradually accepting greater responsibility for household tasks. In addition, female-headed households are becoming more common. It is predictable that such social changes will elicit changes in family food consumption practices.

A study of the influence of family life-course phase on *food selection* demonstrates the relevance of family structure to food behaviors (Cross, Hermann, and Warland, 1975). Young single females were found to be strongly interested in saving time. In young families, homemakers were most concerned about food costs and least concerned about caloric and fat consumption, two motivations important to health. Employed homemakers in families with school-age children were also concerned about saving time and about food costs, possibly due to having older children with larger appetites. Older people in general were attentive to caloric and fat consumption and to food costs, and saving time was not a major concern for them. Elderly couples showed greatest concern for nutritive value and were less constrained by food costs. Elderly single women, not unexpectedly, were most strongly influenced by their low incomes.

One structural feature that deserves mention is the increased number of female-headed families at all stages of the family cycle. This family form is strongly related to race and income (Pollitt, Greenfield, and Liebel, 1979; Johnson, 1979). The relatively low income of these units and the high number of children involved pose a major problem for female heads of households: how to ensure adequate nutrition for family members with limited resources of money, time, and skills.

Few studies have addressed this issue, and those that have produced equivocal results. On the one hand, a large-scale study of food behaviors of low-income homemakers in New York State found that urban femaleheaded households of all races purchased more nutritionally adequate diets than did comparable two-parent households (Sanjur et al., 1979:42). On the other hand, studies reported by Hertzler and Vaughan (1979) suggest superior growth rates for children raised in two-parent homes rather than in single-parent homes, with the presence of the father in the home apparently encouraging more nutritionally adequate diets.

Changing Gender Roles

The impact of the marked increase in women who work outside the home on food habits has received moderate attention, notably from food marketers. In 1960, the U.S. Department of Agriculture reported that, as might be expected, households in which the wife was employed outside the home relied more heavily on convenience foods and foods eaten away from home. Subsequent studies highlighting the importance given to efficient use of time by employed women found a similar pattern (Cross, Hermann, and Warland, 1975; Roberts and Wortzel, 1979).

What is particularly intriguing about the topic is that, until definitive empirical data are obtained, the impact of female employment on food practices can be argued, in principle, either to enhance or to inhibit flexibility in food practices. How does use of restaurants or convenience foods compare with selections from supermarket shelves in enhancing exposure to varying foods and food practices? The impact of female employment on food consumption may well be moderated by higher income level and by particular motivations for working. The food expenditure study by Sanjur et al. (1979) documented the function of the wife's employment for elevating low family incomes to a level above poverty, with the obvious potential for improving the nutritional status of family members. Among middleincome and upper-income homemakers, however, employment in pursuit of career satisfaction may have different effects.

An alternative approach would be to examine differences in food consumption in relation to a woman's role orientation, recognizing that a modern orientation may lead to different food choices than a traditional orientation, regardless of employment status. Limited evidence suggests that full-time homemakers are more traditional than women employed outside the home in terms of care and frugality in food shopping (Roberts and Wortzel, 1979). Employed women who are careeroriented have the most modern role orientation, exhibit more impulsive food purchasing, and consume more meals away from home. Employed women who are not strongly career-oriented are more concerned about nutritional quality, but also use more convenience foods (Roberts and Wortzel, 1979). Differences in food preparation motivations have been noted for women who hold contemporary orientations compared with women who hold traditional orientations, independent of age and employment status (Roberts and Wortzel, 1979), with contemporary orientation associated with a rejection of routine and repetitive food preparation and an interest in the creative aspects.

In addition, the entry of married women into the full-time labor force has changed the level of male participation in preparing food and in the gatekeeper role. Consequently, it would be relevant to compare gender differences concerning knowledge about nutrition and motivations underlying food behaviors. Unfortunately, very few adequate studies have examined nutrition knowledge, food beliefs, and shopping behaviors in terms of gender differences. Not surprisingly, one national sample of consumers in 1975 found that men had lower levels of nutrition knowledge than did females (Fusillo and Beloian, 1977). In general, approximately 60 percent of those persons considered to be well-informed were also designated as careful food shoppers, but nutrition knowledge per se did not always lead to careful shopping practices.

Studies concerning the motivations underlying food behavior have focused primarily on women. Research indicates that women's food choices are primarily influenced by personal preferences and those of family members and, to a lesser extent, by the healthfulness and taste of the food (Cosper and Wakefield, 1975). A desire to understand consumer behavior has spawned a number of studies utilizing factor analysis to detect food meanings. One such study (Schutz, Rucker, and Russell, 1975) isolated five factors used by women in classifying foods: high-calorie treats; special meal items; common meal items; refreshing, healthy foods; and inexpensive, filling foods. Such a classification system implies an interest in personal physical appearance, health, economy, and acceptance of food selections by family and/or friends. Comparable data for males are not available.

In respect to the values underlying food selection, those studies that do address gender have identified certain differences (Jellinek, 1973; Reid and Miles, 1977). Wives are especially influenced by nutritive content, convenience, habit, desire to control weight (Schafer, 1979), and health (Yetley and Roderuck 1980). Husbands are especially influenced by taste, appearance, and odor of food (Schafer, 1979), and their selection varies by income (Yetley and Roderuck, 1980). Both spouses attach importance to taste, cost, health, appropriateness of the food, and its novelty (Schafer, 1979). In respect to knowledge of nutrition, however, Yetley and Roderuck (1980) found no statistically significant differences between husbands and wives.

In sum, whether one discusses the increasing participation of males in food selection, the changing roles of women, or changes in family structure, important shifts are occurring in the role of gatekeeper for family food consumption. Such shifts are affecting the food habits and the well-being of older people now and will affect them in the future.

SOCIAL INTEGRATION

If the family, with all its changes, is the primary context for the social organization of food behaviors, what happens to persons who live alone, particularly the elderly? In this section, we examine the effect of social integration on food habits. This examination considers the household, as well as the nuclear family, and the entire issue of social integration versus isolation as they may affect the purchase, preparation, and consumption of food.

Lack of integration into social networks is thought to lead to feelings of alienation, anomie, anxiety, depression, deviant behavior, self-estrangement, and untimely death (Liang et al., 1980). Social integration, conversely, provides a basis for socialization, exchange of information, reciprocity of support, and sharing of goods and services required for individual survival. The importance of social networks in old age has been demonstrated in a number of studies

(Lowenthal and Robinson, 1976; Kahn, 1979; Liang et al., 1980). Yet social integration, if accompanied by strong social control, can also be experienced as a suffocating denial of individuality. Clearly, both social and individual factors need to be addressed simultaneously to understand the balance between interaction and solitude and adaptation, particularly in old age (Lowenthal and Robinson, 1976).

The elderly face a multiplicity of social, economic, environmental, and health changes over which they have little control and which have implications for the nature and extent of their social integration—for example, the trends that have resulted in small family size, high rates of marital dissolution (Glick, 1979), changing gender roles, increased leisure time, changing neighborhoods, residential mobility of offspring, death of friends, and health restrictions. The social integration of many old people is increasingly problematic, both in comparison with younger people and with earlier historical periods.

Several aspects of social integration are relevant to understanding the dynamics of food habits across the adult ages. Social integration and interaction 1) link food habits with social-psychological variables (morale, well-being, depression, loneliness, anxiety, selfesteem), 2) provide access to food sources and reciprocity in serving basic nutritional needs, and 3) facilitate communication and socialization to established or changing food norms.

The gerontological literature, replete with evidence associating social integration to morale, indicates that old people with higher levels of social participation tend to be happier, more satisfied with their lives, and less depressed than do those who are more socially isolated (see Larson, 1978, for a review). To the extent that either social activity or social disengagement influences mood states, they indirectly influence patterns of obtaining, preparing, and consuming food (Fowlie, Cohen, and Anand, 1963; Chinn and Robbins, 1970; Baird and Schutz, 1980). Moreover, social integration reduces the probability of eating alone; when people eat together, their interest in food is stimulated, thus increasing the likelihood of adequate intake (Clancy, 1975). The extent to which social interaction changes with age, therefore, will affect patterns of food consumption.

Living arrangements, particularly the tendency for many elderly widows to live alone, can affect food tastes. On the whole, the youngest, healthiest, and most competent widows maintain independent households, and they are not necessarily cut off from extensive contact with kin, friends, and neighbors. Living alone, however, does mean that an extra effort must be made to seek out companionship for meals, an interpersonal cost that many will feel outweighs potential benefits. The elderly who live alone, in comparison with those who live with someone else, have been found to have less adequate dietary intake (Davidson et al., 1962; Brockington and Lempert, 1966; Monagle, 1967; Cohen, 1974); have less variety in their diets (Reid and Miles, 1977); eat fewer foods requiring preparation (Bransby and Osborne, 1953); and are more likely to skip the evening meal (Slesinger, McDivitt, and O'Donnell, 1980).

Of course, living arrangements are associated with income, gender, marital status, and other characteristics that influence dietary patterns (Guggenheim and Margulec, 1965; Bransby and Osborne, 1953; Guthrie, Black, and Madden, 1972; Cohen, 1974; Reid and Miles, 1977). Yet unfortunately, the studies are limited. There has been no large-scale examination of the relationship between living arrangements and food behavior in a heterogeneous population, allowing for comparisons across age, gender, income, and marital status groupings. Respondents in one study who were defined as "isolates" (living alone, unemployed, and eating solitary meals) had greater difficulty with teeth and gums and consumed a less varied diet and less nutritious foods than the nonisolates (Davidson et al., 1962). Slesinger, McDivitt, and O'Donnell (1980), however, in their study of urban adults, did not find that living alone was negatively associated with the intake of foods from any food group. In other studies, men who live alone were found to have less adequate diets than women who live alone (Monagle, 1967; Brockington and Lempert, 1966; Cohen, 1974). However, there are few males 65 and over who do not live with another family member.

FUTURE RESEARCH DIRECTIONS

This essay has discussed various research efforts focused on the dynamics of changing family structure and function, social integration, and gender roles as they may influence food habits of the elderly. Given the life changes that face the elderly and the varying experiences of different cohorts, it is particularly important that future research examine the process whereby food habits are adapted to changing life circumstances. Such research efforts are dependent upon the development and application of dynamic theoretical perspectives that bring together current social gerontological and food habits research. Both substantive issues and methodological considerations need to be addressed.

Substantive Issues

The influence of men in decisions on food consumption, whether or not they are actively participating in the gatekeeper role, needs to be addressed, as does the impact of the absence of adult males in female-headed households. The consequences of male interest in the sensory characteristics of food rather than in dietary quality are important to pursue as men accept more responsibility for the food choices for themselves and for their family members.

Family changes occurring since the 1960's that may weaken the kin networks of aging parents and the economic hardships faced by many female heads of households (particularly those women seeking to begin to support themselves in middle age) could lead to radical changes in food behavior in adulthood and old age.

Female employment outside the home and its impact on food habits, as discussed in this paper, deserve greater research attention. The implications of this phenomenon for food familiarity, flexibility in food choices, and reliance on preprepared foods are relevant issues for an aging population. If women traditionally have been responsible for including health considerations in a family's food-consumption goals, the question then becomes one of the impact of their changing values on the nutritional status of themselves and other family members. Also relevant for further study is the importance of reduced family size in decision-making and in food-consumption patterns.

In addition to the theoretical approaches of Lewin (1943) and Coughenour (1972), social network analysis (Mitchell, 1969) could be valuable as a framework for research on the dynamics of food habits. For research on food habits, at least four purposes served by the social network have obvious applicability: communication and information, instrumentality and exchange, social and emotional support, and socialization and normative control.

Communication and Information

The structure and durability of social networks can have a direct influence on the amount and type of information about food consumption that is accessible to the individual. Thus we need to know what kinds of food information are exchanged within different types of social networks (e.g., family, friends, retirement community, church, and media). It has been reported, for example, that persons in retirement communities have higher levels of social interaction among age peers than do persons in communities that are not segregated by age (Sherman, 1975a, b; Longino, McClelland, and Peterson, 1980). How might this difference affect food attitudes and behaviors in the two types of settings? We suggest that greater variety and willingness to change habits are characteristic of people who have high levels of interaction.

Instrumentality and Exchange

The instrumentality of the network refers to the achievement of specified goals. The process by which these ends are met usually involves an element of exchange. Of interest to research on food habits is the question of what types of exchange networks at what point in the life course are most influential in the maintenance of healthful food habits. Since an individual must provide for numerous basic survival needs in addition to food, it would also be of interest to explore the interactions, tradeoffs, or exchanges within networks when competing goals are presented.

Social-Emotional Support

The importance of social support, both as a factor influencing morale and well-being and as a buffer against the effects of stressful events, has been emphasized in several recent articles (Kahn, 1979; Cobb, 1979; Leveton, Griffin, and Douglas, 1980). Kahn (1979) proposes the concept of "the convoy of social support" to express the notion that each person moves through life surrounded by a set of significant other persons to whom he or she is linked by an exchange of supportive behaviors. He also suggests two lines of inquiry that are applicable to understanding how food habits change with age: 1) How do convoy characteristics, and the giving and receiving of social support, typically change with age? 2) Are social convoys in old age characterized by increased asymmetry, reduced initiative, increased instability, reduced convoy size, and less receiving of affect and affirmation than in younger years? If we carry these questions a step further, we then ask, how do the changes in convoy characteristics and the giving and receiving of social support influence food patterns and old people's ability to procure, consume, and digest food? Since later adulthood is characterized by significant role changes, lifestyle changes, and frequent deterioration of health, the value of convoys in maintaining appropriate dietary habits may be crucial to survival.

Normative Content and Socialization

The literature on child development has focused on the manner in which children learn new norms and are socialized to becoming members of society. Until recently, however, there has been much less emphasis on the processes of adult socialization, especially with respect to the establishment and maintenance of age-related food norms and ideologies.

For example, studies comparing persons in agesegregated retirement communities with those in nonagesegregated communities indicate that the former are more likely to feel free to pursue "younger" activities because they are not constrained by the expectations of younger age groups. In principle, one might then expect that the age composition of a person's network, as a function of residential patterns, would also have a normative effect on his or her food habits. To the extent that there are "youthful foods" and "aged foods" and age norms for patterns of food consumption, the characteristics of one's network could produce a willingness to depart from earlier food patterns. The mass media also function as an arbiter of food habits. Television, in particular, serves in the role of social companion and socializing agent.

It is sobering to realize that many suggestions we judge to be important "new" areas for future research have, in fact, been proposed as needed areas for research for many years (Gottlieb and Rossi, 1961; Howell and Loeb, 1969). We believe that a number of issues raised over a decade ago bear reiteration:

- It is apparent that foods constitute a complex universe of items. It is likely that one of the most important steps in the development of an understanding of the dynamics of food habits would be to develop a complex set of concepts to differentiate the relevant dimensions of food characteristics. While some attention has been given to the physical components and the psychophysical attributes of foods, additional attention needs to be given to the social-psychological aspects (Gottleib and Rossi, 1961:40).
- There is a need . . . to clearly differentiate (a) generational patterns in selection and eating of foods from (b) changes in eating habits which are age specific. With specific subgroups of aged-, culture-, or generation-based food, use and preparation patterns need to be separated from late life changes in eating habits resulting from such stresses as retirement, widowhood, disease, and age-appropriate food habits (Howell and Loeb, 1969:96).
- Research is needed into the variety of settings within which people wish to eat and what systems of interpersonal interaction are fostered in various settings (Howell and Loeb, 1969:96).
- More research is needed on the dietary habits of the community-based isolated older adult (Howell and Loeb, 1969:96).
- There is a need to talk of ages and stages—the 60 year old is not the same as the 80 year old . . . . Further community research is needed which will describe dietary patterns associated with stages in the late life cycle and the effects of interventions, social or nutritional, at these various stages or later stages (Howell and Loeb, 1969:97).

Methodological Considerations

To treat such substantive issues of food research adequately, studies of sufficient scope and sample size are needed to permit the inclusion and accurate measurement of many of the variables that inevitably shape food behaviors. Statistical techniques capable of detecting interaction effects and capable of supporting longitudinal modeling must be used in future research. Greater attention also needs to be directed towards more valid and reliable measures of food habits than are currently in use. Particular consideration should be given to the effects of chronological age, life-course phase, cohort history, and economic constraints.

Data from four nutrition-related surveys of the U.S. population are currently, or are soon to be, available to researchers for analysis: Health and Nutrition Examination Survey 1971-74 and 1976-79 (National Center for Health Statistics), Nationwide Food Consumption Survey, 1977-78 (U.S. Department of Agriculture), and Supplement to the Nationwide Food Consumption Survey, 1977-78 (Social Security Administration and U.S. Department of Agriculture). These surveys contain information on meal patterns and food consumption as components of the food habits of adults. They are all cross-sectional studies, but do present data on the population at several different points in time.

In summary, the study of aging and food habits in the future could benefit from a systematic application of the emerging sociological theory of age. To understand what nutritional changes may be expected of incoming cohorts of the elderly, it is essential to study the influences of current societal changes that are impinging upon these cohorts. Research focusing on changing family structure, social roles, and social integration offer potential for much exciting and productive research on the dynamics of aging and social change with respect to food patterns. There is a need to move beyond descriptive and univariate studies to research designs that incorporate multivariate analytic approaches and that consider the effects of historical periods and cohort differences on the relationship between aging and food habits. Concurrently, there is a need for methodological development and for refinement of theoretically relevant, valid, and reliable measures of food habits as related to social and family structure, integration, and social networks.

Finally, interdisciplinary perspectives and efforts will be essential to understanding the important interactions of social, psychological, cultural, physiological, and biological influences on aging and food patterns if we are to be successful in meeting the nutritional needs of the elderly.

REFERENCES

Abraham, Sidney, Margaret Carrol, Connie Dresser, and Clifford Johnson 1979. Caloric and Selected Nutrient Values for Persons 1–74 Years of Age. Vital and Health Statistics, Series 11, No. 209. Hyattsville, Md.: National Center for Health Statistics.

Baird, Pamela, and Howard G. Schutz 1980. "Life style correlates of dietary and biochemical measures of nutrition." Journal of the American Dietetic Association 76: 228–235.

Bransby, E.R., and Barbara Osborne 1953. "A social and food survey of the elderly, living alone or as married couples." British Journal of Nutrition 7:160–180.

Brockington, Colin Fraser, and Susanne Martina Lempert 1966. The Social Needs of the Over-Eighties: The Stockport Survey. Manchester: Manchester University Press.

Brown, Esther L. 1976. "Factors influencing food choices and intake." Geriatrics, September:89–92.

Canadian Department of National Health and Welfare 1975. Food Consumption Patterns Report—A Report from Nutrition Canada. Ottawa: Department of National Health and Welfare.

Center for Disease Control 1972. Ten-State Nutrition Survey, 1968–1970. DHEW Publication No. (HSM) 72-8134. Washington, D.C.: Health Services and Mental Health Administration.

Chinn, Austin, and Edith Robbins 1970. "Health aspects of aging." Pp. 209–231 in Adeline Hoffman (ed.), The Daily Needs and Interests of Older People. Springfield, Ill.: Charles C. Thomas.

Clancy, Katherine L. 1975. "Preliminary observations on media use and food habits of the elderly." Gerontologist 15:529–532.

Cobb, Sidney 1979. "Social support and health through the life course." Pp. 93–106 in M.W. Riley (ed.), Aging from Birth to Death. Interdisciplinary Perspectives. AAAS Selected Symposium. Boulder, Colo.: Westview Press.

Cohen, Cyril 1974. "Social and economic factors in the nutrition of the elderly." Proceedings of the Nutrition Society 33:51–57.

Cosper, Barbara, and Lucille M. Wakefield 1975. "Food choices of women: personal, attitudinal and motivational factors." Journal of the American Dietetic Association 66:152–155.

Coughenour, C. Milton 1972. "Functional aspects of food consumption activity and family life cycle stages." Journal of Marriage and the Family, November: 656–664.

Cronin, Frances J. 1980. "Nutrient levels and food used by households, 1977 and 1965." U.S. Department of Agriculture Family Economics Review, Spring:10–15.

Cross, Barbara, Robert Hermann, and Rex H. Warland 1975. "Effect of family life-cycle stage on concerns about food selection." Journal of the American Dietetic Association 67:131–134.

Davidson, Charles S., Jane Livermore, Patricia Anderson, and Seymour Kaufman 1962. "The nutrition of a group of apparently healthy aging persons." American Journal of Clinical Nutrition 10(3):181–199.

Department of Agriculture 1975. That We May Eat. The 1975 Yearbook of Agriculture. Washington, D.C.: U.S. Government Printing Office.

Ellis, James E., John A. Wiens, Charles F. Rodell, and Jerry C. Anway 1976. "A conceptual model of diet selection as an ecosystem process." Journal of Theoretical Biology 60:93–108.

Fowlie, H.C., Cyril Cohen, and M.P. Anand 1963. "Depression in elderly patients with subnutrition." Gerontologia Clinica 5:215–225.

Fusillo, Alice E., and Arletta M. Beloian 1977. "Consumer nutrition knowledge and self reported food shopping behavior." American Journal of Public Health 67:846–850.

Glick, Paul 1979. "The future marital status and living arrangements of the elderly." Gerontologist 19(3):301–309.

Gottlieb, David, and Peter Rossi 1961. A Bibliography and Bibliographic Review of Food and Food Habit Research. Chicago: Quartermaster Food and Container Institute for the Armed Forces Quartermaster Research and Engineering Command, U.S. Army.

Grotkowski, Myrna L., and Laura S. Sims 1978. "Nutritional knowledge, attitudes, and dietary practices of the elderly." Journal of the American Dietetic Association 72:499–506.

Guggenheim, K., and I. Margulec 1965 "Factors in the nutrition of elderly people living alone or as couples and receiving community assistance." Journal of the American Geriatric Society 13(6):561–568.

Guthrie, Helen A., Kathleen Black, and J. Patrick Madden 1972. "Nutritional practices of elderly citizens in rural Pennsylvania." Gerontologist 12: 330–335.

Hegsted, D. Mark 1980. "Nationwide food consumption survey—implications." U.S. Department of Agriculture Family Economics Review, Spring:20–22.

Hendel, Grace 1969. "A study of food behavior of a selected elderly population as related to socioeconomic and psychologic factors." Dissertation Abstracts 29(8-B):2952.

Hertzler, Ann A., and C. Edwin Vaughan 1979. "The relationship of family structure and interaction to nutrition." Journal of the American Dietetic Association 74:23–27.

Howell, Sandra C., and Martin B. Loeb 1969. "Nutrition and aging." Gerontologist 9(3): 1–122.

Jellinek, J. Stephan 1973. "The meanings of flavors and textures." Food Technology, November:47–55.

Johnson, Beverly L. 1979. "Single-parent families." Pp. 571–578 in 1980 Agricultural Outlook. Washington, D.C.: U.S. Senate Committee on Agriculture, Nutrition and Forestry.

Kahn, Robert 1979. "Aging and social support." Pp. 77–91 in M.W. Riley (ed.), Aging from Birth to Death. Interdisciplinary Perspectives. AAAS Selected Symposium. Boulder, Colo.: Westview Press.

Larson, Reed 1978. "Thirty years of research on the subjective well-being of older Americans." Journal of Gerontology 33(1):109–125.

Lewin, Kurt 1943. "Forces behind food habits and methods of change." Pp. 35–65 in The Problem of Changing Food Habits, Bulletin Number 108, Washington, D.C.: National Research Council, National Academy of Sciences.

Leveton, Lauren, Robert Griffin, and Thomas Douglas 1979. "Social supports and well-being in urban elderly." Paper Presented at the 32nd Annual Scientific Meeting of the Gerontological Society, Washington, D.C.

Liang, Jersey, Louis Dvorkin, Eve Kahana, and Florence Mazian 1980. "Social integration and morale: a reexamination." Journal of Gerontology 35(5):746–757.

Longino, Charles F., Jr., Kent McClelland, and Warren Peterson 1980. "The aged subculture hypothesis: social integration gerontophia and self conception." Journal of Gerontology 35(5):758–767.

Lowenthal, Marjorie Fiske, and Betsy Robinson 1976 "Social networks and isolation." Pp. 432–456 in R. Binstock and E. Shanas (ed.), Handbook of Aging and the Social Sciences. New York: Van Nostrand Reinhold.

Miller, Henry W. 1973. Plan and Operation of the Health and Nutrition Examination Survey: United States, 1971–1973. Vital and Health Statistics, Series 1, No. 10a. Rockville, Md.: National Center for Health Statistics.

Mitchell, J. Clyde 1969. "The concept and use of social networks." Pp. 1–50 in Clyde Mitchell (ed.), Social Networks in Urban Situations: Analyses of Personal Relationships in Central African Towns. Manchester: Manchester University Press.

Monagle, J. Edward 1967. "Food habits of senior citizens." Canadian Journal of Public Health 58:504–506.

Parsons, Talcott 1960. "Pattern variables revisited." American Sociological Review 25:467–483.

Parsons, Talcott, Robert F. Bales, and Edward A. Shils 1954. Working Papers in the Theory of Action. New York: Free Press.

Parsons, Talcott, and Edward A. Shils 1951. Toward a General Theory of Action. Cambridge, Mass.: Harvard University Press.

Pilgrim, Francis J. 1961. "What foods do people accept or reject?" Journal of the American Dietetic Association 38:429–443.

Pollitt, Ernesto, D. Greenfield, and Rudolph Liebel 1979 "U.S. needs and priorities on behavioral effects of nutritional deficiencies." Pp. 314–325 in J. Brozek (ed.), Behavioral Effects of Energy and Protein Deficits. Washington, D.C.: U.S. Department of Health, Education, and Welfare.

Reaburn, Janice A., Magdalena Krondl, and Daisy Lau 1979. "Social determinants in food selection." Journal of the American Dietetic Association 74:637–641.

Reid, Dianne L., and J. Elizabeth Miles 1977. "Food habits and nutrient intakes of noninstitutionalized senior citizens." Canadian Journal of Public Health 68(¾):154–158.

Rizek, Robert L. 1978. "The 1977-78 Nationwide Food Consumption Survey." U.S. Department of Agriculture Family Economics Review, Fall:3–7.

Roberts, Mary Lou, and Lawrence H. Wortzel 1979. "New life-style determinants of women's food shopping behavior." Journal of Marketing 43:28–39.

Sanjur, Diva 1981. Sociocultural Perspectives of Nutrition. Englewood Cliffs, N.J.: Prentice-Hall.

Sanjur, Diva, Pam Haines, Sue Travis, Mark Brooks, Beverly Hammons, and Maarten D.C. Immink 1979. "Food expenditures, consumption, and nutrient availability among New York State EFNEP households." Search 9(3):1–58.

Schafer, Robert B. 1979. "The self-concept as a factor in diet selection and quality." Journal of Nutrition Education 11(1):37–39.

Schutz, Howard G., Margaret H. Rucker, and G.F. Russell 1975. "Food and food-use classification systems." Food Technology 29(3):50–64.

Sherman, Susan R. 1975a. "Mutual assistance and support in retirement housing." Journal of Gerontology 30:479–483.

———. 1975b. "Patterns of contacts for residents of age segregated and age-integrated housing." Journal of Gerontology 30:103–107.

Sherwood, Sylvia 1970. "Gerontology and the sociology of food and eating." Aging and Human Development 1:61–85.

Shifflett, Peggy A., and Kenneth L. Nyberg 1978. "Toward a social psychology of food use." Mid-American Review of Sociology 3:17–33.

Sims, Laura S. 1978. "Food-related value orientations, attitudes, and beliefs of vegetarians and nonvegetarians." Ecology of Food and Nutrition 7:23–35.

Slesinger, Doris P., Maxine McDivitt, and Florence O'Donnell 1980. Food patterns in an urban population: age and sociodemographic correlates." Journal of Gerontology 35(3):432–441.

Todhunter, E. Neige 1976. "Life style and nutrient intake in the elderly." Pp. 119–127 in M. Winick (ed.), Nutrition and Aging. New York: Wiley.

Weg, Ruth 1978. Nutrition and the Later Years. Los Angeles: University of Southern California Press.

Wilson, Christine 1979. "Food-custom and nurture." Journal of Nutrition Education 11(4):Supplement 1.

Yetley, Elizabeth A., and C. Roderuck 1980. "Nutritional knowledge and health goals of young spouses." Journal of the American Dietetic Association 77:31–41.

11 Learning and Memory through Adulthood[1]

Marion Perlmutter
University of Minnesota

Age-related changes in adult learning and memory have received considerable attention from experimental psychologists, who traditionally focus on these topics, as well as clinical psychologists, who often treat failing memory among older adults. In general, research issues have been framed within the theoretical models dominant in experimental psychology—that is, associationism in the 1950's and 1960's, and information processing in the 1970's and the early 1980's. Several issues have also emerged from the clinical perspective.

Conceptually, learning and memory can be differentiated. Learning refers to the *acquisition* of information or skill as a result of experience; memory involves the *retrieval* of information or skill learned previously. Experimentally, however, it is difficult, if not impossible, for learning and memory to be separated. For subjects to demonstrate learning, they must have memory, and for memory to be demonstrated, learning must have occurred. Thus, for the purposes of this paper, learning and memory will be considered together. First, research findings concerning age differences in adult learning and memory are described and analyzed. Then, some of the factors that may contribute to the cognitive processes which may explain these differences are discussed.

EVIDENCE OF AGE DIFFERENCES IN ADULT LEARNING AND MEMORY

Information Processing Model and Experimental Methodology

During the last decade or two, information processing models have dominated experimental psychology and its research on learning and memory. Very briefly, learning and memory are viewed as time-based processes that transfer informa-

---

[1]The author is grateful to Jack Botwinick, Fergus I. M. Craik, and Elizabeth Loftus for their critical reading of an earlier version of this paper.

tion within a multistore or multilevel cognitive system. Information is learned or acquired, stored, and retrieved or remembered from sensory, primary, and secondary stores. An important assumption of this perspective is that subjects participate actively in learning and remembering. Indeed, for the information processing researcher, the cognitive activities used in learning and remembering are the central phenomena to be investigated, with possible age differences the focus of developmental research.

In general, research on development and aging has used cross-sectional designs to explore age *differences* in learning and memory skills. Most typically, performance of college students and adults in their sixties has been compared on tasks designed to illuminate cognitive processing. By manipulating particular variables, under highly controlled conditions, experimenters have made inferences about how the constraints on learning and memory vary across age.

Empirical Evidence

Conditioning

Conditioning often is viewed as the simplest form of learning. In classical conditioning, an organism learns to make a generalized response to a signal, and in operant conditioning, an organism acquires an instrumental response to a discriminated stimulus. While quite common before 1960, studies of *classical conditioning* in older adults are rather rare today, although there still are important issues to be resolved about this process. For example, several studies have shown that older adults have greater difficulty acquiring a conditioned eyeblink response than do younger adults (Braun and Geiselhart, 1959; Kimble and Pennypacker, 1963) and that the magnitude of the unconditioned response is significantly correlated with the frequency of conditioned responses (Kimble and Pennypacker, 1963). Thus, it has been hypothesized that over time the eyeblink response becomes habituated, and therefore less susceptible to modification by further conditioning. Moreover, other evidence (e.g., Shmavonian, Miller, and Cohen, 1968, 1970) indicates that on a variety of autonomic measures, old adults have weaker conditioned and unconditioned responses than younger adults. More work is required, however, to confirm this finding.

Other factors also contribute to age differences in classical conditioning. For example, the strength of stimuli is known to have important influences on conditioning and is likely to differ across age, since sensory functioning typically is reduced in older adults. The time parameters chosen in particular experiments might also contribute to conclusions about age-related differences in conditioning, since older adults generally require longer time to encode and respond to stimuli than do younger adults.

Operant conditioning of older adults has not received extensive experimental attention either, although these techniques increasingly are used in a variety of applied settings. Available research points to the efficacy of reinforcement procedures in modifying behavior, even for adults well into their seventies (e.g., Ayllon and Azrin, 1965; Baltes and Zerbe, 1976). Thus, while not all of the parameters of operant conditioning have been documented for older adults, it is already clear that these procedures can be effective in later life. It should be noted, however, that reinforcers that are optimally effective for the young may not always be most effective for the elderly.

Physical Training

Age-related losses in physical skills are welldocumented (e.g., Asmussen et al., 1975; Atomi and Miyashita, 1974; Dehn and Bruce, 1972; Drinkwater et al., 1975; Kilbom, 1971; Profant et al., 1972; Robinson et al., 1976). Such deterioration may provide impetus for learning and compensation. Just as the developing child must learn to cope with rapid growth and hormonal change, the aging adult must learn to adapt to skeletal, muscular, and other organic deficits.

Early studies left doubt about the possibility that *physiological functioning* in older adults could be improved through intervention (DeVries, 1975). Numerous studies since the mid-1960's, however, have demonstrated enhanced aerobic capacity and cardiac functioning following training in both elderly men and women (Adams and DeVries, 1973; DeVries, 1970; Hartley et al., 1969; Kilbom et al., 1969; Saltin et al., 1969; Sidney and Shephard, 1977). Several additional points also emerge from this more recent research. First, those who begin training programs in poorer physical condition show the greatest gains, regardless of age (DeVries, 1970; Kasch and Wallace, 1976). Second, if compared on a percentage basis, older individuals demonstrate gains comparable to younger adults (Adams and DeVries, 1973; DeVries, 1970; Hartley et al., 1969; Saltin et al., 1969; Suominen, Heikkinen, and Parkatti, 1977). Third, although maximal exercise may not be required to obtain improvement in aerobic capacity (DeVries, 1970; Suominen, Heikkinen, and Parkatti, 1977), the type of exercise probably is important. For example, DeVries (1975) argued that the rhythmic exercises (e.g., running, jogging, and swimming) used in most training programs yield optimal results.

Other areas of elderly functioning also show improvement following physical training. For example, improvements have been documented in older adults' skeletal muscle and connective tissue (Suominen, Heikkinen and Parkatti, 1977), fluid intelligence, (Ehsayed, Ishmail, and Young, 1980), conscientiousness and persistence (Young and Ishmail, 1976; Sharp and Reilly, 1975), and health and exercise consciousness (Gutman, Herbert, and Brown, 1977; Sidney and Shephard, 1977; Thomas, 1979). In addition, DeVries (1975) has suggested that physical training may have a greater sedative effect than popular tranquilizers for anxious adults.

It should be evident that older adults show significant improvements in physiological and intellectual performance following physical training and that this improvement is quite comparable to that observed in younger adults. To date, however, few studies have examined the differential efficacy of various types of exercise on elderly functioning (Gutman, Herbert, and Brown, 1977, is an exception). Likewise, the issues of length of time of training for optimal benefits, individual differences in response to exercise programs, and the effectiveness of various presentation methods have not been addressed empirically.

Sensory Adaptation

The detrimental effects of aging on sensory function apparently are universal. For this discussion, only the adaptations that older adults make to deteriorations in sight and hearing are considered. It will be argued that although there are substantial declines with age in the quality of information received from sense organs, older adults learn to compensate for these deficits, at least to some extent.

One of the most common and clearly established agerelated decrements of visual function concerns *dark adaptation* (see Fozard, Wolf, Bell, McFarland, and Podolsky, 1977). It has been found that the rate of dark adaptation slows with age and that the final level of dark adaptation is lower in older adults than in younger adults. An important implication of these changes is reduction of vision during night driving. Yet there has been little research on the adaptation of older adults to night driving conditions, and vision tests for driver's licenses do not include assessments of such skills. Nevertheless, there are several ways in which older adults may accommodate diminished vision associated with reduced dark adaptation. They can learn to look to the lower right corner of the windshield when oncoming headlights are detected rather than looking directly at them, to anticipate problems while driving, and to take advantage of environmental context.

Auditory losses also are common in later adulthood, especially presbycusis, which is loss of hearing for highfrequency sounds (see Corso, 1977). A person suffering from presbycusis may not hear telephones ring, may have difficulty hearing human voices (particularly those of women), and may have problems in interpreting speech intelligibly, since consonants such as F, S, and Z are particularly difficult to hear. Thus loss of hearing associated with presbycusis has implications for both the safety and social communication of older adults. While environmental (e.g., amplification and frequency of signals) and mechanical (e.g., hearing aids) adjustments can reduce the negative impact of hearing loss associated with presbycusis, such aids are not entirely effective. However, older adults learn over time to adapt to some of the limitations of these aids (e.g., overamplification of sudden low-frequency noises). Moreover, older adults who experience hearing loss may compensate by depending more on context and lipreading.

Sensory Memory

The most immediate form of memory—sensory memory-involves retention of information, in relatively uninterpreted form, for very short amounts of time (i.e., not more than several seconds). Although relatively few studies have examined age differences in sensory memory, it is generally assumed that if sensory registration occurs, learning and cognitive difficulties of the elderly lie deeper in the system, rather than in peripheral stages (Craik, 1976; Walsh and Prasse, 1980).

Still, it should be noted that older adults do experience sensory deficits that may be relevant to learning and memory (see Kimmel, 1974). Since higher thresholds of stimulation are required for older subjects to sense and perceive information, some apparent learning and memory deficits may be more appropriately attributed to failures in sensory registration.

Additionally, it should be noted that age-related difficulties in dealing with situations requiring *division of attention* may contribute to learning and memory deficits (Craik and Simon, 1980; Kinsbourne, 1980). It is well-documented that older adults are more penalized than younger adults when they must jointly attend to two input sources, an input source and memory, or memory and response execution (see Craik, 1977). In a series of divided attention studies, Craik (1973) concluded that much of the processing capacity of older adults is taken up by organizing or programming the division of attention, lessening the capacity for processing information. If information processing capacity is reduced in this way, older adults may be forced to process information less deeply, thus accounting for memory deficits.

Verbal Memory

Verbal memory includes representation of the present as well as knowledge about the past. Memory investigators refer to the former, information retained in consciousness, as primary memory and the latter, information retained for much longer periods of time, as secondary memory (Waugh and Norman, 1965). There are at least three reasons for making this conceptual distinction. First, these memory stages have different functions. Primary memory temporarily holds or organizes information; secondary memory is a more permanent knowledge store. Second, some processes, such as retrieval, probably are more central to secondary memory than to primary memory. Finally, the course of development of these two sorts of memory may be different. For instance, it appears that primary memory is relatively unimpaired in the elderly, but that there are age decrements in secondary memory.

Primary Memory. One measure of primary memory is the *recency* portion of free recall—that is, retention of the last few items on a recall list. In most experiments, no age differences in recency have been demonstrated. Even when age differences are observed in overall level of recall, none are evident for the last few serial items (e.g., Bromely, 1958; Craik, 1968).

Another procedure used to evaluate primary memory is the *memory span task,* which assesses the number of items in the longest string that can be reported in correct serial order. Most people can recall approximately seven digits or five words in correct serial order. However, since other estimates of primary memory range only from two to four items (see Watkins, 1974), memory span probably reflects information from both secondary and primary memory. Nevertheless, many investigators find no significant age decrements in digit spans (e.g., Bromely, 1958; Craik, 1968), and others report only slight age decrements (e.g., Botwinick and Storandt, 1974; Taub, 1973).

A similar task, *backward span,* requires subjects to repeat strings of items, but in reverse order. Generally, larger age deficits are found on backward span than on forward span tasks (e.g., Botwinick and Storandt, 1974; Bromely, 1958). Apparently, if reorganization is added to the retention requirement, older subjects become more disadvantaged.

Since number of items recalled may not be the most sensitive index of mnemonic functioning, other techniques have been developed. Anders, Fozard, and Lillyquist (1972) used a *memory scanning* reaction time task to assess age differences in primary memory more precisely. They found that search speed, as well as other basic operations such as decision or response execution, appeared to slow with age. Thus, although the number of items retrieved from primary memory may remain stable throughout adulthood, the speed of search and retrieval is likely to decline.

Secondary Memory. Remembering more items than can be held in primary memory is indicative of secondary memory. It is important to note that this primarysecondary memory distinction is independent of retention interval. That is, even when retention is tested immediately, if the primary memory span has been exceeded, secondary memory contributes to performance, and it is secondary memory that appears to be most impaired by aging (Craik, 1976; Horn, 1976).

The nature of age differences in learning and memory of this more permanent sort has been well-researched. In most of the studies, investigators have assessed age differences in *learning and retention of lists of words.* The overwhelming evidence points to age differences in such verbal learning and memory, with groups of older adults typically performing at statistically lower levels than groups of younger adults. Yet, performance of the oldest subjects almost always is well above chance level, and performance of different age groups invariably overlaps.

Further, the pattern of age differences observed under various experimental conditions differs widely, with several manipulations found to attenuate age differences. Indeed, the differing patterns appear to implicate performance factors as contributors of age differences, leaving open to question the extent to which there are age differences in verbal learning and memory ability per se (see Argrusa, 1978; Arenberg and Robertson-Tchabo, 1977; Botwinick, 1978; Poon, Fozard, Cermak, Arenberg, and Thompson, 1980). For example, age differences in *motivation* have been hypothesized to contribute to the often observed age-related decrements on secondary learning and memory tasks. Typically, it has been assumed that older adults are not as motivated as younger adults, since laboratory tasks may not be meaningful to them. Botwinick (1978), however, has argued that older adults actually are more involved in experimental situations and that they are sometimes inappropriately involved to an extent that depresses their performance. Indeed, psychophysiological studies suggest that older adults may be highly aroused during experimental sessions (Furchgott and Busemeyer, 1976; Powell, Eisdorfer, and Bogdonoff, 1964), and when arousal has been reduced, by drugs or adaptation to the laboratory situation, performance has been found to improve (e.g., Eisdorfer, 1968; Eisdorfer, Nowlin, and Wilkie, 1970).

Older adults also are thought to be more *cautious* than younger adults, a characteristic that often makes them appear to have learned and remembered less than they actually have. For example, while older adults make many errors of omission, they rarely make errors of incorrect responding (e.g., Eisdorfer, Axelrod, and Wilkie, 1963; Korchin and Basowitz, 1957). Moreover, in one study in which omission errors were discouraged by rewarding all responses regardless of correctness, the learning performance of older adults improved more than younger adults (Leech and Witte, 1971).

It also is thought that older adults are more prone to *interference* effects than are younger adults. Unfortunately, as noted by Arenberg and Robertson-Tchabo (1977), methodological difficulties currently make it impossible to evaluate this hypothesis.

Pacing is one factor that clearly has been demonstrated to contribute to age differences in secondary learning and memory performance. In a number of studies in which time available for study and time available for responding have been manipulated, it has been found that older adults are especially disadvantaged by limited time, particularly response time (e.g., Arenberg, 1965; Canestrari, 1963; Eisdorfer, Axelrod, and Wilkie, 1963; Monge and Hultsch, 1971; Taub, 1967). Thus, when sufficient time for response is available, performance of older adults is only slightly worse than that of younger adults. Yet, even when given a long time to respond, older adults perform relatively poorly if they have been rushed during learning. It appears that compared with younger adults, older adults need more time to learn material and to show what they have remembered.

This need for extra learning and response time may be related to limitations in the *spontaneous use of effective cognitive strategies*. Since secondary memory is assumed to involve three major stages of processing (acquisition, storage, and retrieval), a great deal of research has been devoted to isolating the stage at which such processing may be limited. Although it is impossible to totally isolate a stage of processing, certain experimental manipulations allow estimates of deficits at each stage.

1. *Acquisition:* If age deficits in secondary memory are attributable primarily to deficits in *acquisitional processing,* then age difference should not be observed when initial learning has been equated. Indeed, this finding has been obtained in several studies (e.g., Moenster, 1972; Hulicka and Weiss, 1965; Wimer and Wigdor, 1958). But why should older adults require additional exposure to equate acquisition?

Several theorists have hypothesized that various cognitive processes mediate learning and memory. For example, Miller (1956) suggested that items must be *chunked,* Mandler (1967) considered categorical *organization* important, Flavell (1970) argued for verbal *rehearsal,* Paivio (1971) emphasized *imagery,* and Craik and Lockhart (1972) proposed *depth of processing* as a major determinant of learning and retention. In general, instructions to carry out these cognitive operations improve performance of both younger and older adults, but most markedly the performance of older adults. Apparently, older subjects are able to perform these mnemonic operations effectively, but they typically fail to do so spontaneously.

For example, Hulicka and Grossman (1967) and Canestrai (1968) found age-related deficits in use of imagery, but these age differences were attenuated by instructions to use imagery. Similarly, Hultsch (1969, 1971) and Denney (1974) found age-related declines in use of organization that could be modified. Likewise, a rather clear picture emerges from a number of other investigations in which acquisition of younger and older adults' processing has been directed with a wide range of orienting tasks (Craik and Simon, 1980; Erber, Herman, and Botwinick, 1980; Eysenck, 1974; Mason, 1979; Perlmutter, 1978, 1979; Perlmutter and Mitchell, forthcoming; Smith and Winograd, 1978; Till and Walsh, 1980; White, cited by Craik, 1977; Zelinski, Walsh, and Thompson, 1978). This pattern suggests that *encoding ability* probably is less central to age differences in adult memory than is *spontaneous use of optimal encoding operations.*

To reiterate the major points here, the poorer performance of older adults on memory tests of word lists appears to be accounted for by their inefficient *spontaneous use* of encoding strategies. While other cognitive limitations may affect their memory performance on other tasks, list-learning studies provide little evidence of deficits in encoding *abilities* of older adults. Nevertheless, evaluations of encoding that are based only on inferences from memory performance rely upon circular reasoning, and thus are inadequate. Therefore, additional means are required to assess encoding independently of retention.

In one such line of research on the *independent assessment of encoding,* Perlmutter (1979) and Perlmutter and Mitchell (forthcoming) asked subjects to generate free associations to the same words on each of four trials. The processing required to generate free associations was assumed to be similar to that employed when trying to learn lists of words. In some cases, older subjects produced somewhat less common associates than did younger subjects, and older subjects were slightly more variable in their associative productions. In general, however, the results of these association studies agreed with the findings of the memory studies. When directed to carry out associative encoding, the processing by younger and older adults was quite similar.

Another nonmemory paradigm also has been employed to evaluate possible age differences in encoding, independently of the retrieval requirements that can contribute to age differences in recall and even recognition. In particular, reaction-time patterns have been examined. The use of reaction times as a sensitive index of ongoing processing has a long history in cognitive psychology. It has been shown in a variety of procedures that the nature of the semantic relationship between two or more items can inhibit or facilitate reaction times systematically (Meyer and Schaneveldt, 1976). Such reactiontime patterns are thought to reflect activation of semantic knowledge structures, and therefore they can provide an index of processing that is independent of episodic memory performance.

In one such study (Perlmutter and Mitchell, forthcoming), reaction times were recorded as subjects made semantic (animate vs. inanimate) or nonsemantic (upper vs. lower-case type) decisions about target words that were paired with distractors. For both age groups, distractors had little effect on reaction times in the nonsemantic task, but as predicted, reaction times for both groups varied as a function of target-distractor relationship in the semantic task. Thus, the results of this study also suggest that when processing is directed by experimental instructions, younger and older adults encode stimuli similarly.

Thus far, the prevalent type of research on age differences in secondary memory—research on *retention of lists of words*—has been discussed. In general, this research has demonstrated age-related deficits when subjects are left on their own to study stimuli in whatever manner they choose. However, when their study is directed in certain ways, age differences often are attenuated. These findings suggest that an important factor contributing to age differences in memory performance is change in effective strategy use. It appears that effective mnemonic processing is within the repertoire of older adults, although they are less likely to employ it unless they are encouraged.

In recent theoretical statements about memory, a distinction has been made between automatic and effortful processing (Hasher and Zacks, 1979), which are claimed to vary in attentional requirements. Automatic operations are thought to drain minimal energy from the limitedcapacity attention mechanism and not to interfere with ongoing cognitive capacity. On the other hand, effortful operations are thought to require considerable capacity and to interfere with other cognitive activities. Automatic operations appear to develop earlier in life and to reach a level of maximal efficiency sooner than effortful processing mechanisms. Moreover, development across the lifespan is expected to have a greater impact on effortful processes than on automatic processes. The question remains, however, whether there are age-related deficits in *retention of information presumed to be encoded automatically.*

Processes that encode the fundamental aspects of the flow of information, such as the frequency and recency of events, generally are considered to be automatic processes (Hasher and Zacks, 1979). It is assumed that such information is acquired without intention, and thus is not susceptible to alteration by manipulations such as instructions to remember, practice, or feedback concerning accuracy of performance. In a number of studies (e.g., Attig and Hashar, 1980; Kausler and Puckett, 1980; Perlmutter et al., 1981), age differences have not been observed for retention of information assumed to be encoded automatically. In another study, however, Kausler and Puckett (1981) found that intentional encoding instructions significantly affected the performance of older subjects but not younger subjects, pointing to an *age-related decrement in total processing capacity.* This apparent *processing surplus of younger adults* is likely to be an important factor contributing to observed age differences in cognitive function.

2. *Storage:* There is no good evidence of age differences in *storage capacity* (e.g., Wickelgren, 1975). Indeed, present theoretical formulations of learning and memory seem to assume that if material is registered in secondary memory, it is not lost, although it may become inaccessible (Atkinson and Shiffrin, 1968).

3. *Retrieval:* There is considerable research on possible *retrieval* problems of older adults. One method used to evaluate the relative importance of deficiencies in acquisition versus retrieval processes is to *compare recall and recognition* performance. Although recall involves both acquisition and retrieval, recognition generally is assumed to involve mainly acquisition. If memory is conceptualized as the creation of a trace and recollection is determined by appropriateness of information in the retrieval environment, then the difference between recall and recognition resides in differences in the retrieval environment (see Perlmutter and Lange, 1978; Watkins and Tulving, 1975). For recognition, a copy of the encountered stimulus is physically present, while for recall, it must be cognitively retrieved. Thus, if retrieval plays a minimal role in recognition, then age deficits in recognition can be interpreted as reflecting deficits in acquisition or storage. On the other hand, larger recall deficits can be attributed to retrieval difficulties.

Empirical research generally has demonstrated larger age decrements in recall than in recognition. All investigators seem to find fairly large age differences in recall (e.g., Bromely, 1958), but most find small (e.g., Botwinick and Storandt, 1974; Gordon and Clark, 1974) and sometimes insignificant age differences (Craik, 1971) in recognition. In addition, in a single study in which Erber (1974) examined age decrements in recall and recognition, age accounted for 25 percent of the variance in recall but only 10 percent in recognition. Thus, when retrieval demands are minimized, as in recognition, memory disadvantages of older subjects are reduced, but probably not eliminated.

The results of several recall studies also demonstrate that older subjects benefit more than younger subjects from good *retrieval support*. While performance of older subjects is considerably worse than younger subjects on unrelated lists, it is only slightly worse on related lists (Laurence, 1967a). It is possible that when items from a single conceptual category are to be remembered, the category concept serves as a retrieval cue. Moreover, Craik (1968) found that age decrements were related to the size of the pool that the items were drawn from (digits, counties, animals, and unrelated words), and Laurence (1967b) found that age decrements were eliminated when category names were provided at retrieval. Apparently, when adequate retrieval information is available, either by using a limited set of items or by providing retrieval cues, the retention of older subjects is less impaired. These findings add to the interpretation that deficits in effective retrieval contribute importantly to the disadvantage in recall among older adults.

A *repeated trials* recall study carried out by Buschke (1974) provides further evidence of retrieval deficits in the elderly. In this task, subjects were given multiple trials of recall on a 20-word list that was only presented once. The results indicated greater variability in the pool of words older subjects recalled consistently from trial to trial. Apparently, many of the words were adequately acquired and stored, but on some trials, retrieval failures occurred.

In summary, several processing deficits have been demonstrated to underlie the poorer secondary learning and memory performance observed in older adults. Early paired associate learning studies showed that elderly adults suffer from acquisitional deficits. When the level of original learning was equated, age-related retentional differences were eliminated (e.g., Moenster, 1972; Hulicka and Weiss, 1965; Wimer and Wigdor, 1958). Subsequent research has begun to delineate the nature of these acquisitional deficits. Hulicka and Grossman (1967), as well as Canestrari (1968), found that instructing subjects to use mediators diminished age decrements in paired associate learning. Denney (1974) found little clustering by the elderly, and Hultsch found instructions to organize (Hultsch, 1969) and sort tasks (Hultsch, 1971) disproportionally benefited older subjects. A number of investigators (e.g., Craik and Simon, 1980; Erber, 1974; Eysenck, 1974; Perlmutter, 1978, 1979; Zelinski, Walsh, and Thompson, 1978) have studied the effects of various orienting tasks and have found that control of acquisitional processing attenuates age differences. Thus considerable evidence points to age-related deficits in acquisition, although many of these results indicate that the elderly suffer from production deficiencies (Flavell, 1970) rather than inabilities. That is, retentional deficits are reduced when instructions to engage in appropriate acquisitional processing are provided. Moreover, when encoding under controlled conditions has been examined directly (e.g., Perlmutter and Mitchell, forthcoming), age differences have not been observed.

Thus inefficient spontaneous use of effective encoding strategies, rather than encoding ability per se, seems to be implicated as an important contributor to age deficits in the acquisition required for verbal learning and memory.

Several other lines of research have also been described here as indicating further mnemonic deficits in the aged. Investigations of recall and recognition have shown greater age-related deficits in recall than recognition (e.g., Botwinick and Storandt, 1974; Craik, 1971; Erber, 1974), and this finding has been taken to indicate retrieval problems in the elderly. Also, in recall studies in which retrieval support has been manipulated (e.g., Laurence, 1967a, b; Craik, 1968), it has been found that retrieval deficits contribute importantly to age differences; when adequate retrieval cues are provided, age differences are diminished. Finally, a repeated trials experiment (Buschke, 1974) also demonstrated retrieval deficits in the elderly; older subjects evidenced greater variability in the pool of words they recalled consistently from trial to trial. Considerable evidence has accumulated on age-related deficits in retrieval, but questions remain about the mechanisms involved.

Cognitive Skill Training

A number of researchers have attempted to train more complex cognitive skills in older adults. Two studies have demonstrated the modifiability of intellectual functioning (Hoyer, Labouvie, and Baltes, 1973; LabouvieVief and Gonda, 1976), but transfer of training either was nonexistent or limited to closely related tasks. On the other hand, Plemons, Willis, and Baltes (1978) demonstrated modifiability of fluid intelligence skills, as well as transfer of training effects. On a 6-month posttest, however, there was attenuation of the difference between their training group and control group, attributable to practice gains in the control group. This result suggests that practice gains probably were not totally dependent upon the training program.

The durability and transfer of enhanced performance due to training of older adults has been documented in several other domains as well. Sanders and Sanders (1978), for example, found that elderly individuals trained to use an efficient strategy to solve relatively simple identification problems demonstrated better performance on more complicated tasks administered 1 year later. Sterns and Sanders (1980) demonstrated that training of older adults is effective in improving, for at least 6 months, information processing skills needed for effective driving. Similarly, Hornblum and Overton (1976) reported rapid improvement in the performance of older adults on a conservation of surfaces task following a feedback training procedure. Schultz and Hoyer (1976) found that older adults who were given visual-auditory feedback on a perspective-taking task showed performance gains on both an immediate and delayed test, and Zaks and Labouvie-Vief (1980) found that role-playing facilitated older adults' sociocognitive skills.

Learning and Memory in Everyday Life

In contrast to the volume of laboratory studies, relatively little research has examined learning and memory in everyday life. Moreover, the limited research that does exist has not had a developmental focus. Yet, it would seem that the systematic evaluation of real world learning and memory and of age differences in necessary functional skills is essential. At the very least, such an analysis would permit extending and validating current laboratory-based understanding of learning and memory and its development. Moreover, since learning and memory that take place in everyday life tend to be considerably more complex than those tested in most experimental studies, there is some reason to believe that important factors may be missing from current understanding. For example, although it is possible that aging detrimentally influences the micro-mechanisms of learning and memory most heavily relied upon to perform typical experimental tasks, aging may have a more limited adverse effect—or perhaps even a positive effect—on some of the macro-learning and memory styles used in everyday life. Thus information about older adults' everyday learning and memory is greatly needed.

CONCLUSIONS ABOUT LEARNING AND MEMORY THROUGH ADULTHOOD

A great deal of research has examined the learning and memory skills of older adults. In general, agerelated deficits have been observed in performance of laboratory tasks. However, the magnitudes of these group differences often are relatively small, with the performance of older subjects virtually never below chance level. In addition, performance curves of younger and older groups typically overlap to the point where some older adults perform better than some younger adults. Thus, while research consistently indicates that there are age-related deficits in adults' learning and memory, a somewhat moderated perspective of these deficits probably is called for. Even if the observed age differences can be assumed to reflect only age *changes* (which they probably cannot), it appears that, to the oldest age generally included in experimental studies (e.g., 60 to 70), adults' learning and memory performance remains relatively competent. Moreover, although there is some age-related decrement in learning and memory performance, age does not turn out to be a particularly good predictor of performance.

In addition, the relevance of laboratory learning and memory performance to everyday learning and memory situations remains unclear. An assumption of the experimental approach has been that there are basic principles of learning and memory and that these principles can be understood best by experimentally dissecting each relevant factor. Unfortunately, although this approach allows investigators to gain knowledge about the particular variables studied within the confines of the particular situation in which they are investigated, it may not help in assessing the relative importance of these variables (i.e., variance accounted for) in different situations in which other factors also are present. This predicament is especially problematic if the effects of variables are not additive. If variables interact, the main effects from separate experiments may not simply be summed, since estimates of all interaction effects also are needed to account for performance. In essence, then, confidence in the value of findings from laboratory experiments must rest upon subjective assessments of the importance of the variables that have been investigated and on faith that interaction effects have been accounted for adequately. It is essential, therefore, that the relevance of experimental tasks to real world tasks be assessed.

In the meantime, however, some perspective may be gained from recent views of cognition that have stressed the interaction between basic cognitive processes and acquired knowledge (e.g., Chi, 1978; Perlmutter, 1980). It has been found that learning and memory performance is affected by one's familiarity and expertise with material to be learned and remembered, as well as by one's familiarity and expertise with related material. It appears that new knowledge is acquired and retained within old knowledge structures. Thus, when familiar with material to be learned and remembered or with related material, an individual is aided by existing knowledge structures, which provide him or her with something on which to tie the new information. In addition, it appears that with previous familiarity, information can be organized more tightly, and thus assessed more easily.

It is possible, therefore, that the increasing amount and overlearning of information in the knowledge base of older adults permits them to perform many ecologically valid learning and memory tasks as competently as or more competently than younger adults, in spite of less effective learning and memory mechanisms. Although older adults' deteriorating learning and memory mechanisms may lead to increased learning and memory failures, their enriched knowledge bases could permit them to demonstrate learning and memory equal to or better than younger adults, at least on some tasks. Thus, if learning and memory tasks are characterized in terms of the *processes* and *knowledge* required for successful performance, the pattern of age differences in adults' performance may be predicted. To the degree that performance depends upon basic learning and memory processes, younger adults will be favored over older adults; to the degree that performance depends upon acquired knowledge, older adults will be favored over younger adults.

It should be noted, too, that although there has not yet been much systematic developmental research on everyday learning and memory, there is some evidence of effective everyday learning and memory in later adulthood. Therefore, it is believed that an appropriate perspective is to assume that effective learning and memory are lifelong activities. While this perspective seems difficult to dispute, it has not been central to many theoretical or practical considerations of adulthood. Rather, previous conceptualizations of adulthood have tended to view adults as having fixed or declining modes of functioning. Perhaps it has been the recent advent of large numbers of adults—surviving literally 50 or more years of adulthood—that has called this view into question. Still, the full promise of growth and development during adulthood probably has yet to be appreciated. It is hoped that systematic research on possible age limitations, and especially advantages, in everyday learning and memory situations will be forthcoming. While such research is difficult to carry out, it would have extensive theoretical as well as practical implications.

POSSIBLE EXPLANATIONS OF AGE-RELATED DEFICITS IN ADULT LEARNING AND MEMORY

A crucial step for future research is the assessment of cognitive function in everyday situations. Nevertheless, a clarification of the causes of the age differences already documented certainly should be forthcoming. Several factors have been hypothesized, with little empirical validation, as viable explanations of cognitive aging. This section discusses some of these hypotheses.

Age

Age obviously is the focus of developmental considerations of cognitive functioning. It is not so obvious, however, how age should be conceptualized. First, although age is a convenient and exact index of the passage of time, it is also an inexact index of numerous other confounded, and often unrecognized, variables. For example, age is quite predictive of biological state and somewhat less predictive of education, income, lifestyle, and life events. Thus, even if age differentiates individuals in terms of learning and memory skill, it remains unclear what in the age variable actually is relevant. Since some components of the age variable might be more predictive of performance than the conglomerate variable, it is essential that relevant factors be considered individually.

In addition, although age can be used to index passage of time, it is not entirely clear what referent should be used to index age in adulthood. For example, chronological age, which indexes time since birth, is the variable that researchers have investigated. On the other hand, time since completing formal education, or time until death, may actually be more relevant variables. To illustrate, it seems pertinent that younger subjãects in aging studies typically are college students, who routinely face tasks similar to experimental learning and memory tests, while older subjects typically have been out of school for many years and rarely face tasks at all comparable to experimental learning and memory tests. It is likely that the recent experience of younger adults in utilizing learning and memory strategies appropriate for laboratory experiments contributes importantly to the results that are obtained. Thus it may be appropriate to consider age since completing education in such testing, as well as age since birth. Indeed, it would be useful to compare several samples of adults of equal chronological age who differed in time since schooling.

It has also been demonstrated that regardless of age, fairly substantial declines in intellectual performance often are evident several years prior to death. This terminal drop phenomenon (Siegler, 1975) may account for much of the age difference typically reported in studies of cognition. Increasingly older age groups of adults are likely to include large numbers of subjects in the terminal stage. Therefore, it would be useful to carry out post-hoc analyses that excluded subjects tested in the terminal stage. In addition, research designs could include several samples of people who are the same age but who have different life expectancies.

Cohort

It has been argued (e.g., Schaie, 1970, 1973) that age deficits observed in cognitive performance can in part be accounted for by generational or cohort differences. Very briefly, the point is that cohort-specific experiences are completely confounded with the passage of time. Since the passage of time is uniquely experienced by each generation, it is impossible to draw conclusions about age differences that ignore cohort factors, and thus impossible to draw conclusions about the effects of the passage of time that are completely generalizable across cohorts.

This problem is likely to be relevant to considerations of age differences in learning and memory studies. For example, if age is a good predictor of the number of years of education, and if the number of years of education affects learning and memory performance, then random sampling would produce age differences that should be attributed to level of education, rather than to development per se. To determine whether additional factors contribute to age differences, researchers could control for level of education. At a more subtle level, however, cohort effects may produce other less quantifiable influences. For example, it is possible that, over the years, equal amounts of formal education may fail to have an equivalent impact. Fewer years of schooling in today's television-oriented society, for instance, might be sufficient to produce levels of knowledge that are comparable to that which required much longer attendance at school in the past. Alternatively, fewer years of schooling in an earlier, more disciplined era might have produced greater scholarship. Thus, perfect controls for cohort effects are often extremely difficult, if not impossible, to establish.

Expectation

The expectation of decline is another possible explanation of age-related learning and memory deficits. Many stereotypes exist about mental impairment in old age, and some evidence indicates that psychological function can match expectation. Thus the poorer performance of older adults at least partially may be attributable to their fulfillment of an aging role. If this hypothesis is correct, negative correlations between high expectation of learning and memory impairment and learning and memory performance could be predicted. Of course, such correlations would not indicate a causal direction of the relationship, although the lack of such findings would invalidate the hypothesis. A longitudinal analysis of this hypothesis, like other time-dependent hypotheses, surely is called for.

Disuse

Another possible explanation of age-related learning and memory declines involves disuse. It is possible that formerly acquired strategies become functionally less available if they are not used often. Because of disuse, learning and memory strategies may be forgotten, exhibiting deficiencies typical of strategies not wellestablished. It seems likely, for example, that disuse can account for some of the production deficiencies observed in the elderly. Relating individual differences in learning and memory demands to learning and memory skills would permit some assessment of the disuse hypothesis. If learning and memory demands correlate with learning and memory performance, the hypothesis would be supported. Of course, other self-selection factors also could contribute to the relationship.

Depression

Depression has been found to be associated with cognitive deficits (e.g., Miller, 1975; Zelinski, Gilewski, and Thompson, 1980). Moreover, a disproportionate percentage of older adults apparently suffer from depression (e.g., Whanger and Busse, 1975). It is possible, then, that some of the age differences observed in studies of cognitive aging are attributable to a disproportionate number of depressive subjects in the older samples. Separate assessments for depression may be called for.

Biological Changes

Finally, the hypothesis of a biological basis for declines in learning and memory in later adulthood has been quite prevalent (e.g., Albert and Kaplan, 1980; Butters, 1980; Jarvik and Cohen, 1973). This notion suggests that physiological wear and tear, biochemical changes, and poor health reduce an older individual's mental capacities. While there is still little understanding of the exact nature of the relationship between biological and cognitive function, the known age-related changes in both central nervous system function and health certainly cannot be ignored. These factors almost surely are in some way related to cognitive performance. Future research combining biological and psychological assessment is called for.

SUMMARY AND CONCLUSIONS

In this paper, considerable experimental research assessing age differences in learning and memory skills among adults has been summarized. In general, agerelated declines have been noted. However, it is unclear how important these deficits are to learning in everyday life. Some evidence of older adults' effective learning and memory in naturally occurring situations has been documented. Unfortunately, systematic research on possible age limitations and/or advantages in such situations is not available. Identification of how individual differences in older adults relate to learning and memory, as well as documentation of the context, content, activities, and goals of learning and memory in later adulthood, is of utmost importance. Analysis of these issues should provide a richer and more complete theoretical understanding of aging, as well as of learning and memory, and also would be of much practical value. Finally, greater awareness should be given to the changing characteristics of each cohort of older adults, and how their health care and role definitions influence their competence.

REFERENCES

Adams, Gene M., and Hubert A. DeVries 1973. Physiological effects of an exercise training regimen upon women aged 52–79. Journal of Gerontology 28:50–55.

Argruso, Victor M., Jr. 1978. Learning in the Later Years: Principles of Educational Gerontology. New York: Academic.

Albert, Marilyn S., and Edith Kaplan 1980. "Organic implications of neuropsychological deficits in the elderly." Pp. 403–432 in Leonard W. Poon, James L. Fozard, Laird S. Cermack, David Arenberg, and Larry W. Thompson (eds.), New Directions in Memory and Aging. Hillsdale, N.J.: Erlbaum.

Anders, Terry R., James L. Fozard, and Timothy D. Lillyquist 1972. "Effects of age upon retrieval from short term memory, from 20–68 years of age." Developmental Psychology 6:214–217.

Arenberg, David D. 1965. "Anticipation interval and age differences in verbal learning." Journal of Abnormal Psychology 70:419–425.

Arenberg, David D., and Elizabeth A. Robertson-Tchabo 1977. "Learning and aging." Pp. 421–496 in James E. Birren and K. Warner Schaie (eds.), Handbook of the Psychology of Aging. New York: Van Nostrand Reinhold.

Asmussen, E., K. Fruensgaard, and S. Norgaard 1975. "A follow-up longitudinal study of selected physiological functions in former physical education students—after 40 years." Journal of the American Geriatrics Society 23:442–450.

Atkinson, Richard C., and Richard M. Shiffrin 1968. "Human memory: a proposed system and its control processes." In K.W. Spence and J.T. Spence (eds.), The Psychology of Learning and Motivation, Vol. 2. New York: Academic Press.

Atomi, Y., and M. Miyashita 1974. Maximal aerobic power of Japanese active and sedentary adult females of different ages (20–62 years). Medicine and Science in Sports 6:223–225.

Attig, Mary, and Lynn Hasher 1980. "The processing of frequency of occurrence information by adults. Journal of Gerontology 35:66–69.

Ayllon, Teodoro, and Nathan H. Azrin 1965. "The measurement and reinforcement of behavior of psychotics." Journal of Experimental Analysis of Behavior 8:357–383.

Baltes, Margret M., and M.B. Zerbe 1976. "Re-establishing self-feeding in a nursing home resident. Nursing Research 25:24–26.

Botwinick, Jack 1978. Aging and Behavior. New York: Springer.

Botwinick, Jack, and Martha Storandt 1974. Memory, Related Functions and Age. Springfield, Ill.: Thomas.

Braun, H.W., and R. Geiselhart 1959. "Age differences in the acquisition and extinction of the conditioned eyelid response." Journal of Experimental Psychology 57:386–388.

Bromely, D.B. 1958. Some effects of age on short-term learning and memory. Journal of Gerontology 13:298–406.

Buschke, Herman 1974. "Two stages in learning by children and adults." Bulletin of Psychonomic Society 2:392–394.

Butters, Nelson 1980. "Potential contributions of neuropsychology to our understanding of the memory capaci ties of the elderly." Pp. 451–459 in Leonard W. Poon, James L. Fozard, Laird S. Cermack, David Arenberg, and Larry W. Thompson (eds.), New Directions in Memory and Aging. Hillsdale, N.J.: Erlbaum.

Canestrari, Robert E., Jr. 1963. "Paced and self-paced learning in young and elderly adults." Journal of Gerontology 18:165–168.

———. 1968. "Age changes in acquisition." In George A. Talland (ed.), Human Aging and Behavior: Recent Advances in Research and Theory. New York: Academic.

Chi, Michelene 1978. "Knowledge structure and memory development." Pp. 535–553 in R. Siegler (ed.), Carnegie-Mellon Symposium on Cognition. Hillsdale, N.J.: Erlbaum.

Corso, John F. 1977. "Auditory perception and communication." In James E. Birren and K. Warner Schaie (eds.), Handbook on the Psychology of Aging. New York: Van Nostrand Reinhold.

Craik, Fergus I. M. 1968. "Short-term memory and the aging process." In George A. Talland (ed.), Human Aging and Behavior. New York: Academic.

———. 1971 "Age differences in recognition memory." Quarterly Journal of Experimental Psychology 23:316–323.

———. 1973 "Signal detection analysis of age differences in divided attention." Paper Presented at the Meetings of the American Psychological Association, Montreal.

———. 1977 "Age differences in human memory." Pp. 384–420 in James E. Birren (ed.), The Handbook of the Psychology of Aging. New York: Van Nostrand Reinhold.

Craik, Fergus I. M., and Robert S. Lockhart 1972. "Levels of processing: a framework for memory research." Journal of Verbal Learning and Verbal Behavior 11:671–684.

Craik, Fergus I. M., and Eileen Simon 1980. "Age differences in memory: the roles of attention and depth of processing." Pp. 95–112 in Leonard W. Poon et al. (eds.), New Directions in Memory and Aging. Hillsdale, N.J.: Erlbaum.

Dehn, M.M., and R.A. Bruce 1972. "Longitudinal variations in maximal oxygen intake with age and activity." Journal of Applied Physiology 33:805–807.

Denney, Nancy W. 1974. "Clustering in middle and old age: from 30–60, 70–90 years of age." Developmental Psychology 10:471–475.

DeVries, Hubert A. 1970. "Physiological effects of an exercise training regimen upon men aged 52–88." Journal of Gerontology 25:325–336.

———. 1975 "Physiology of exercise and aging." In Diana S. Woodruff and James E. Birren (eds.), Aging: Scientific Perspectives and Social Issues. New York: Van Nostrand Reinhold.

Drinkwater, B.L., S.M. Horvath, and C.L. Wells 1975. "Aerobic power of females, ages 10 to 68." Journal of Gerontology 30:385–394.

Eisdorfer, Carl 1968. "Arousal and performance: verbal learning." In G.A. Talland (ed.), Human Aging and Behavior. New York: Academic.

Eisdorfer, Carl, Joseph Nowlin, and Frances Wilkie 1970. "Improvement in learning in the aged by modification of autonomic nervous system activity." Science 170:1327–1329.

Eisdorfer, Carl, Saul Axelrod, and Frances Wilkie 1963. "Stimulus exposure time as a factor in serial learning an aged sample." Journal of Abnormal and Social Psychology 67:594–600.

Ehsayed, Mohamed, A.H. Ishmail, and Robert J. Young 1980. "Intellectual differences of adult men related to age and physical fitness before and after an exercise program." Journal of Gerontology 35:383–387.

Erber, Joan T. 1974. "Age differences in recognition memory." Journal of Gerontology 29:177–181.

Erber, Joan T., Jim Herman, and Jack Botwinick 1980. "The effect of encoding instructions on recall and recognition memory." Experimental Aging Research 6:341–348.

Eysenck, Michael W. 1974. "Age differences in incidental learning, from 18–30, 55–65, years of age." Developmental Psychology 10:936–941.

Eysenck, Michael W., and M.C. Eysenck 1979. "Processing depth, elaboration of encoding, memory stores, and expended processing capacity." Journal of Experimental Psychology: Human Learning and Memory 5:472–484.

Flavell, John H. 1970. "Developmental studies of mediated memory." In Reese and Lipsitt (eds.), Advances in Child Development and Behavior, Vol. 5. New York: Academic.

Fozard, James L., E. Wolf, Benjamin Bell, R.A. MacFarland, and S. Podolsky 1977. "Visual perception and communication." Pp. 497–534 in James E. Birren and K. Warner Schaie (eds.), Handbook of the Psychology of Aging. New York: Van Nostrand Reinhold.

Furchgott, Ernest, and Jerome K. Busemeyer 1976. "Heart rate and skin conductance during cognitive processes as a function of age." Paper Presented at the Meetings of the Gerontological Society.

Gordon, Sol K., and W. Crawford Clark 1974. "Application of signal detection theory to prose recall and recognition in elderly and young adults." Journal of Gerontology 29:64–72.

Gutman, Gloria M., Carol Herbert, and Stanley R. Brown 1977. "Felden Krais versus conventional exercises for the elderly." Journal of Gerontology 32:562–572.

Hartley, L. Howard, G. Grimby, A. Kilbom, I.A. Nilsson, B.E. Bjure, and B. Saltin 1969. "Physical training in sedentary middle-aged and older men. III. Cardiac output and gas exchange at submaximal and maximal exercise." Scandinavian Journal of Clinical and Laboratory Investigation 24:335–344.

Hasher, Lynn, and Rose T. Zacks 1979. "Automatic and effortful processes in memory." Journal of Experimental Psychology 108:356–388.

Horn, John L. 1976. "Human abilities: a review of research and theory in the early 1970's." In Rosenzweig and Porter (eds.), Annual Reviews of Psychology, Vol. 27. Palo Alto: Annual Reviews.

Hornblum, Judith N., and Willis F. Overton 1976. "Area and volume conservation among the elderly: assessment and training." Developmental Psychology 12:68–74.

Hoyer, William J., Gisela Labouvie, and Paul B. Baltes 1973. "Modification of response speed deficits and intellectual performance in the elderly." Human Development 16:233–242.

Hulicka, Irene M., and Joel L. Grossman 1967. "Age group comparisons for the use of mediators in paired-associate learning." Journal of Gerontology 22:46–51.

Hulicka, Irene M., and Robert Weiss 1965. "Age differences in retention as a function of learning." Journal of Consulting Psychology 29:125–219.

Hultsch, David F. 1969. "Adult age difference in the organization of free recall." Developmental Psychology 1:673–678.

_____. 1971 "Adult age differences in free classification and free recall, from 20–29, 40–49, 60–69, years of age." Developmental Psychology 4:338–342.

_____. 1971 "Organization and memory in adulthood." Human Development 14:16–29.

Hyde, Thomas S., and James Jenkins 1969 "Differential effects of incidental tasks on the organization of highly associated words." Journal of Experimental Psychology 82:472–481.

Jarvik, Lissy F., and Dana Cohen 1973. "A biobehavioral approach to intellectual changes with aging." In Carl Eisdorfer and M. Powell Lawton (eds.), The Psychology of Adult Development and Aging. Washington, D.C.: American Psychological Association.

Johnson, Constance D., and James J. Jenkins 1971 "Two more incidental tasks that differentially affect associative clustering in recall." Journal of Experimental Psychology 89:92–95.

Kasch, Fred W., and Janet P. Wallace 1976. "Physiological variables during 10 years of endurance exercises." Medicine and Science Sports 8:5.

Kausler, Donald H., and James M. Pucket 1981. "Adult age differences in memory for sex of voice." Journal of Gerontology 36.

Kilbom, A., L.H. Hartley, B. Saltin, J. Bjure, G. Grimby, and I. Astrand 1969. "Physical training in sedentary middle-aged and older men: I. Medical evaluation." Scandinavian Journal of Clinical and Laboratory Investigation 24:315–332.

Kilbom, A. 1971. "Physical training with submaximal intensities in women. I. Reaction to exercise and orthostasis." Scandinavian Journal of Clinical and Laboratory Investigation 28:141–161.

Kimble, Gregory A., and H.W. Pennypacker 1963. "Eyelid conditioning in young and aged subjects." Journal of Genetic Psychology 103:283–289.

Kimmel, Douglas C. 1974. Adulthood and Aging. New York: Wiley.

Kinsbourne, Marcel 1980. "Attentional dysfunctions and the elderly: theoretical models and research perspectives." Pp. 113–129 in Leonard W. Poon et al. (eds.), New Directions in Memory and Aging. Hillsdale, N.J.: Erlbaum.

Korchin, Sheldon J., and Harold Basowitz 1957. "Age differences in verbal learning." Journal of Abnormal and Social Psychology 54:64–69.

Labouvie-Vief, Gisela, and Judith N. Gonda 1976. "Cognitive strategy training and intellectual performance in the elderly." Journal of Gerontology 31:327–332.

Laurence, Mary W. 1967. "A developmental look at the usefulness of list categorization as an aid to free recall." Canadian Journal of Psychology 21:153–165.

_____. 1967 "Memory loss with age: a test of two strategies for its retardation." Psychonomic Science 9:209-210.

Leech, Shirley, and Kenneth L. Witte 1971. "Paired associate learning in elderly adults as related to pacing and incentive conditions." Developmental Psychology 5:180.

Mandler, George 1967. "Organization and memory. In Spence and Spence (eds.), The Psychology of Learning and Motivation: Advances in Research and Theory, Vol. 1. New York: Academic.

Mason, Susan E. 1979. "Effects of orienting tasks on the recall and recognition performance of subjects differing in age from 4 to 10 years of age." Developmental Psychology 15:467–469.

Meyer, David E., and Roger W. Schaneveldt 1976. "Meaning, memory structure, and mental processes." Science 192:27–33.

Miller, Glenn A. 1956. "The magical number seven, plus or minus two: some limits on our capacity for processing information." Psychological Review 63:81–97.

Miller, William 1975. "Psychological deficit in depression." Psychological Bulletin 82:238–260.

Moenster, P.A. 1972. "Learning and memory in relation to age." Journal of Gerontology 27:361–363.

Monge, Rolf, and David Hultsch 1971. "Paired associate learning as a function of adult age and the length of anticipation and inspection intervals." Journal of Gerontology 26:157–162.

Paivio, Allan 1971. Imagery and verbal processes. New York: Holt, Rinehart & Winston.

Perlmutter, Marion 1978. "What is memory aging the aging of? From 20–60 years of age." Developmental Psychology 14:330–345.

―――. 1979 "Age differences in adults' free recall, cued recall, and recognition." Journal of Gerontology 34:533–539.

―――. 1980 New Directions in Child Development: Naturalistic Approaches to Children's Memory. San Francisco: Jossey Bass.

Perlmutter, Marion, and Garett Lange 1978. "A developmental analysis of recall–recognition distinctions." In P.A. Ornstein (ed.), Memory Development in Children. Hillsdale, N.J.: Erlbaum.

Perlmutter, Marion, Richard Metzger, Teresa Nezworski, and Kevin Miller 1981. "Spatial and temporal memory in 20 and 60 year olds." Journal of Gerontology 36:59–65.

Perlmutter, Marion, and David B. Mitchell Forthcoming. "The appearance and disappearance of age differences in adult memory." In Fergus I. M. Craik and S. Trehub (eds.), Aging and Cognitive Processes. New York: Plenum.

Plemons, Judy K., Sherry Willis, and Paul B. Baltes 1978 "Modifiability of fluid intelligence in aging: a short-term longitudinal training approach." Journal of Gerontology 33:224–231.

Poon, Leonard W., James L. Fozard, Laird S. Cermack, David Arenberg, and Larry W. Thompson 1980. New Directions in Memory and Aging: Proceedings of the George A. Talland Memorial Conference. Hillsdale, N.J.: Erlbaum.

Powell, Arnold H., Carl Eisdorfer, and M.D. Bogdonoff 1964. "Physiologic response patterns observed in a learning task." Archives of General Psychiatry 10:192–195.

Profant, G.R., R.G. Early, K.L. Nilson, F. Kusumi, V. Hofer, and R.A. Bruce 1972. "Responses to maximal exercise in healthy middle-aged women. Journal of Applied Physiology 33:595–599.

Robinson, S., D.B. Dill, Rod D. Robinson, S.P. Tzankoff, and J.A. Wagner 1976 "Physiological aging of champion runners." Journal of Applied Physiology 41:46–51.

Saltin, L.H., A.K. Hartley, and I. Astrand 1969. "Physical training in sedentary middle-aged and older men. II. Oxygen uptake, heart rate and blood lactate concentration at submaximal and maximal exercise." Scandinavian Journal of Clinical and Laboratory Investigation 24:323–334.

Sanders, Raymond E., and Johnny C. Sanders 1978. "Long-term durability and transfer of enhanced conceptual performance in the elderly." Journal of Gerontology 33:408–412.

Schaie, K. Warner 1970. "A reinterpretation of age related changes in cognitive structure and functioning." In Goulet and Baltes (eds.), Life-Span Developmental Psychology: Research and Theory. New York: Academic.

―――. 1973 "Methodological problems in descriptive developmental research on adulthood and aging." In John R. Nesselroade and Hayne W. Reese (eds.), Life-Span Developmental Psychology: Methodological Issues. New York: Academic.

Schultz, Norman R., Jr., and William J. Hoyer 1976. "Feedback effects on spatial egocentrism in old age." Journal of Gerontology 31:72–75.

Sharp, M.W., and Richard R. Reilly 1975. "The relationship of aerobic physical fitness to selected personality traits." Journal of Clinical Psychology 31:428–430.

Shmavonian, Barry M., L.H. Miller, and Shlomo Cohen 1968. "Differences among age and sex groups in electrodermal conditioning." Psychophysiology 5:119–131.

―――. 1970 "Differences among age and sex groups with respect to cardiovascular conditioning and reactivity." Journal of Gerontology 25:87–94.

Sidney, Kenneth H., and Roy J. Shephard 1977. "Activity patterns of elderly men and women." Journal of Gerontology 32:25–32.

Siegler, Ilene C. 1975. "The terminal drop hypothesis: fact or artifact?" Experimental Aging Research 1:169–185.

Smith, Anderson D. 1980. ''Age differences in encoding, storage, and retrieval.'' Pp. 23–45 in Leonard W. Poon et al. (eds.), New Directions in Memory and Aging. Hillsdale, N.J.: Erlbaum.

Suominen, Harri, Eino Heikkinen, and Terttu Parkatti 1977. ''Effect of eight weeks' physical training on muscle and connective tissue of the M. vastus lateralis in 69-year-old men and women. Journal of Gerontology 32:33–37.

Taub, Harvey A. 1967. ''Paired associates learning as a function of age, rate and instructions.'' Journal of Genetic Psychology 111:41–46.

––––––. 1973 ''Memory span, practice and aging.'' Journal of Gerontology 28:335–338.

Thomas, G.S. ''Physical activity and health: epidemiologic and clinical evidence and policy implications.'' Preventive Medicine 8:89–103.

Walsh, David A., and James J. Jenkins 1973. ''Effects of orienting tasks on free recall in incidental learning: 'difficulty,' 'effort,' and 'process' explanations.'' Journal of Verbal Learning and Verbal Behavior 12:481–488.

Walsh, David A., and Michael J. Prasse 1980. ''Iconic memory and attentional processes in the aged.'' Pp. 153–180 in Leonard W. Poon et al. (eds.), New Directions in Memory and Aging. Hillsdale, N.J.: Erlbaum.

Watkins, Marley J. 1974. ''Concept and measurement of primary memory.'' Psychological Bulletin 81:695–711.

Watkins, Marley J., and Endel Tulving 1975. ''Episodic memory: when recognition fails.'' Journal of Experimental Psychology 104:5–29.

Waugh, Nancy C., and Donald A. Norman 1965. ''Primary memory.'' Psychological Review 72:89–104.

Wickelgren, Wayne A. 1975. ''Age and storage dynamics in continuous recognition memory from 8–10, 19–24, 60–82 years of age.'' Developmental Psychology 11:165–169.

Wimer, Richard E., and Blossom T. Wigdor 1958. ''Age differences in retention of learning.'' Journal of Gerontology 13:291–295.

Young, Robert J., and A.H. Ishmail 1976. ''Personality differences of adult men before and after a physical fitness program.'' Research Quarterly 47:513–519.

Zaks, Peggy M., and Gisela Labouvie-Vief 1980. ''Spatial perspective taking and referential communication skills in the elderly: a training study.'' Journal of Gerontology 35:217–224.

Zelinski, Elizabeth M., David A. Walsh, and Larry W. Thompson 1978. ''Orienting task effects on EDR and free recall in three age groups.'' Journal of Gerontology 33:239–245.

Zelinski, Elizabeth M., Michael J. Gilewski, and Larry W. Thompson 1980. ''Do laboratory tests relate to self assessment of memory ability in the young and old?'' Pp. 519–544 in Leonard W. Poon et al. (eds.), New Directions in Memory and Aging. Hillsdale, N.J.: Erlbaum.

12 Beyond Ageism: Postponing the Onset of Disability[1]

Matilda White Riley
Kathleen Bond
National Institute on Aging

Ageism, a term coined by Robert N. Butler, refers to the stereotyping of people on the basis of age. One important dimension of ageism identifies old age with disability. Many old people do suffer from various disabilities—physiological, psychological, and social-but to equate old age with disability is to be guilty of ageism.

Recent research has demolished three major ingredients of ageism. With reasonable success, it has demonstrated that old age disabilities are *not* 1) universal, 2) necessarily irreversible, or 3) determined solely by biological processes, apart from social and psychological processes. It is time to shift our primary research concern from dispelling false stereotypes about the inevitability of all old age disabilities to understanding those disabilities which are currently widespread and preventing them wherever possible. Looking to the future, we must go beyond ageism. We must build on our knowledge of what is *not* true to gain new knowledge that can be used to prevent, or reverse, the current disabilities of old age. To put this goal into a single phrase, we need to learn how to compress the time between disability and death, to learn how to postpone all kinds of disability up to the end of the human lifespan.

In pursuing this goal, we recognize that scientific demonstration alone cannot dispel public misunderstandings; nor do we propose to substitute a fresh set of overly optimistic false stereotypes for the pessimistic old ones that research has exorcised.

[1]For ideas and criticisms on successive drafts of this paper, the authors express appreciation to: Ronald P. Abeles, Beth B. Hess, Leonard F. Jakubczak, John W. Riley, Jr., Richard L. Sprott, and Richard Suzman. For editorial assistance, they are indebted to Marian Emr of NIA.

In this essay, we first consider how extensive persistence of false stereotypes of aging impedes progress toward our goal of postponing the onset of disability. Next, we review a few evidences suggesting that scientific progress towards such a goal is feasible. Third, we examine how social and psychological research is testing means of reversing existing disabilities, even among older people in long-term care institutions. Finally, we propose an agenda for further biosocial and biobehavioral research directed toward preventing old age disabilities, extending the good middle years, and maintaining health and effective functioning up to the very end of the life course.

REMNANTS OF AGEISM

Despite the advances in scientific understanding, stereotypical views of aging die hard. Resisting the scientific advances, the public, both lay and professional, cling to the notion of aging decline as completely biologically determined. Doctors and old people themselves typically take for granted that, because of aging, older persons are steadily deteriorating biologically, psychologically, and socially.

Anyone who has read the geriatric literature is familiar with the classic diagrams of "age decrements" in physiological functioning (cf. Shock, 1977), which have been widely taught in medical textbooks for many years and are still current today. These diagrams show age curves for such physiological functions as nerve conduction velocity, maximum breathing capacity, and blood glucose levels while fasting. Every one of these functions shows a nearly linear decrease from age 30 to age 80. As we shall presently see, such diagrams perpetuate the stereotype, for they are generally interpreted to mean that, even apart from disease, the ability to function—to respond to stresses over the life course—inevitably declines *because* people are aging.

Unfortunately, many physicians still accept this interpretation uncritically and look on the aging process in stereotypical terms as one of inevitable and universal biological deterioration (Coe and Brehm, 1972). Apparently acting upon this interpretation, many physicians spend less time in office visits with older patients than with younger ones (Kane et al., 1980).

The medical community bears only part of the blame, however. Old people themselves also tend to accept negative stereotypes of aging. When reviewing the literature several years ago (Riley and Foner, 1968), we found that old people take their aches and pains for granted. They seek palliative rather than preventive or corrective treatment. They feel that doctors simply do not understand them and that the disabilities of old age are inevitable and irreversible.

We challenge this oversimplified stereotype, and a great deal of research supports us. Research shows that aging is not entirely fixed or determined by biology. It shows that the biological changes that occur with aging interact with psychological and social processes, resulting in varying degrees of mutability and stability. Human beings do not age as specimens in laboratories. They age in complex, dynamic, and constantly changing societies and in specific human interrelationships that can inhibit or hasten physiological change.

Many of the fallacies which support stereotypes of the aging process arise because these stereotypes are based on data that are cross-sectional rather than dynamic. That is, the classic diagrams of age decrements compare *age differences* between old people and young people at a given time, rather than tracing the same people over time as they age. Thus the cross-sectional data cannot safely be interpreted to refer to the *aging process*.

A simple example illustrates the dangers of interpreting cross-sectional data. Only 38 percent of old people today have completed high school, compared with 66 percent of the middle aged and 84 percent of the young (Bureau of the Census, 1979:144). Obviously, this does not mean that a particular person's educational level (the years of school attended) declines because of growing older. The apparent decline occurs because different cohorts are involved. The cohort of people who are young today have grown up in a society where education is a mass phenomenon—in contrast to the cohort of people who are old today, who grew up in an earlier society when education was far less widespread. Here it is clear that to interpret the age differences in educational level as declines due to aging would support a false stereotype.

Strange as it may seem, many false stereotypes of aging still persist—many of them due to such misinterpretation of cross-sectional age differences. For example, for decades it was believed that intelligence peaks at age 17 and then declines because of aging! This was proved to be a false stereotype when studies showed that more recent cohorts were simply better prepared than their predecessors to perform well on intelligence tests.

What about the classic belief, then, also based on cross-sectional age differences, that physiological functioning inevitably declines because of aging? Is this too a false stereotype, attributable to the fact that different cohorts, who were born and reared in different historical eras, are being compared?

Definitive answers to this question are only now being sought. It is clear that cohorts already old differ markedly from cohorts not yet old in diet, exercise, standard of living, and medical care. Successive cohorts of young people are on the average taller than their parents, and successive cohorts of young women start to menstruate at younger and younger ages. At least one important study (Feinleib et al., 1975) suggests that more recent cohorts are increasingly aware of their own future health and the importance of primary prevention of chronic disease. As part of the Framingham Heart Study, the lives of some 1,600 married couples have been traced for many years. Recently, a parallel study was made of their offspring to compare the parents as they were 22 years ago when they were approximately the *same* ages as their offspring today. In terms of three of the major risk factors in coronary heart disease, the differences between these two cohorts are striking. Compared with their parents, the offspring show lower blood pressure, lower serum cholesterol, and less cigarette smoking. Note that these differences are not due to age, since the ages of parents and offspring are the *same* at the time for which measures in these risk factors are compared. What the differences do suggest is that the cohorts who will be old in the future may be healthier, at least in certain respects, than cohorts already old today.

Such examples indicate why many stereotypes of inevitable aging decline are false. Rather, the data emphasize the fact that aging is mutable, that the ways in which people grow old vary with social conditions. They also disclose the danger implicit in the continuing persistence of the classic stereotype—the danger of giving up in the face of presumably inexorable deterioration, of not learning to live life to the full and to the very end.

EVIDENCES OF FEASIBILITY

Many such studies are beginning to provide evidence that shortening the stage of old age disability may be a realistic goal. Such studies suggest the conditions under which the goal may be approached. Let us consider some of the evidence, both in historical change and in the differing ways that individuals grow old.

Historical Evidences

Current stereotypes of ageism rest not upon history, but upon a short-range view. They focus only upon the most recent cohorts of older people. For these recent cohorts, the stage of old age disability does indeed tend to be protracted—marked by long years of rolelessness, inactivity, and dependency; by chronic disability; and by lingering death. Yet if we take a long-range historical view, it becomes clear that this protracted stage is peculiar to the modern world. It stems from the unprecedented and rapid extension of life expectancy. In earlier cohorts, most members died prematurely before they ever reached disability. It was only a century or so ago that the dramatic "squaring" of the survival curve began—as more and more members of each successive cohort lived out the full lifespan and died more or less at the same time. But as death has been progressively postponed during this past century, other changes have lagged behind. Few new roles have been created to engage the mounting numbers of older people in the family, the household, or the work force. Few efforts have been made to prevent the mounting chronic diseases and impairments of later life—arthritis and heart disease, defects of vision and hearing, faulty memory, and so on. Lives have been extended, but too many have been made miserable by chronic impairment and feelings of uselessness. The survival curve has been squared, but the disability curve has not (cf. Riley in Waring, 1978:36; Fries, 1980).

Today, however, new secular changes are under way that can bring these two curves into closer alignment. (Because we are in the midst of these changes, we often fail to recognize them.) Today, there are clear indications that the role structure is slowly beginning to accommodate the large numbers of elderly incumbents. There are special leisure pursuits for older people, improved income levels, new educational opportunities, and relaxation of mandatory retirement rules. Despite many false starts, there are indications too of new efforts to prevent chronic disease and impairment. There are widespread changes in exercise, nutrition, smoking, driving speed, occupational safety, and preventive care in the family and in the community. As for the future, prediction is hazardous, of course. There are too many unknowns, including unemployment, inflation, international tensions, technological change, intergenerational competition for scarce resources, and shifts in public policy. Yet as each cohort passes through the changing society, it seems likely that older people of the future will be better off than today's older people, not only in health, but also in several economic and social respects.

Insofar, then, as we are able to postpone disability in the future, the current form of protracted old age will appear in a totally new light. Produced by the century-long lag between postponement of death and postponement of disability, today's protracted stage of old age disability will appear as a *historical aberration*, certainly not as the result of natural law, ordained for all time.

Individual Differences

If there is historical evidence that the duration of old age disability is not fixed, there is additional confirmation in the dramatic individual differences among older people. If a protracted stage of disability is far from universal in human history, it is also not universal within any given cohort today. We are no longer satisfied with formulations that homogenize all individual patterns of growing old or with explanations of aging as strictly "normative," as Daniel Levinson and his colleagues (1978), for example, suggest in proposing that every man (*sic!*) must go through such fixed stages as "becoming one's own man" at age 40. We are no longer satisfied to overlook the powerful principle of individual variability. We now recognize that individuals lead the later years of their lives in markedly varied ways. Many have already reached the goal of living a full and healthy life before dying at a ripe old age. Even at the oldest ages, there are some individuals who can see as well, run as far, perform as well on mental tests, and work as full a day as younger people can. These successful older individuals demonstrate that the goal *can* be met.

In addition, these successful individuals provide models for research. We can study them to find out *how* they meet the goal.

NEW KNOWLEDGE FOR REVERSING DISABILITY

Pursuit of our goal requires special research strategies toward better understanding of the aging processes. As long as disability remains a major problem of older people, research must focus immediately on the reversibility of disabling conditions. For the future, a broader research agenda must concentrate on maintaining and enhancing health and effective functioning through prevention and intervention throughout the entire lifespan. To meet both immediate and future objectives, special studies must be designed to probe the linkages between the changing social environment and such potentially preventable or reversible disabilities of old age as memory loss, chronic ill health, sensory deficits, low self esteem, or exclusion from active participation in social and economic roles.

Studies already indicate that certain of the existing old age disabilities can be reversed or alleviated. For example, intellectual decline with aging (when it occurs) can often be slowed or reversed by relatively simple training interventions. Baltes and Willis (1982) have demonstrated that old people's performance on intelligence tests improves with added practice, with instructions about stategies for approaching the problem, and with incentives to increase motivation and attention. Perlmutter (in this book) reviews data showing that physical training improves fluid intelligence, conscientiousness, and persistence; lowers levels of anxiety; and enhances such aspects of physical well-being as cardiac function, aerobic capacity, and the state of muscle and connective tissue. It has also been demonstrated that older people can, and often do, learn to compensate for declines in reaction time, memory, and other age-related deficits by using mnemonic strategies (Poon, Walsh-Sweeney, and Fozard, 1980) or by exercising great care and persistence (Horn and Donaldson, 1980).

Sensory declines in older people can be alleviated in various ways. For instance, Vanderplas and Vanderplas (1980) show that particular styles and sizes of type facilitate reading among many older people whose vision is impaired. Sekuler and Hutman (1980) find that older people—even those with normal visual acuity—often have greater difficulty than younger people seeing large objects in low contrast. Environmental design which provides high contrast can help offset this visual impairment. Moreover, older people can learn strategies for dealing with changes in dark adaptation, as Perlmutter also reports. In addition, research is suggesting ways in which the flavoring or preparation of food can be adapted to age-related changes in taste and smell (Schiffman and Pasternak, 1979) so that proper nutrition may be easier to attain.

Even in nursing homes, research findings indicate that helpless, dependent, and unhappy patients can often recover a degree of functional independence when daily regimens encourage interaction, self-care, and a sense of mastery. Several studies by Rodin (1980), for example, suggest that routines which stimulate independent behavior among nursing home patients can result not only in increased alertness and involvement, but also in improvements in general health and, for one small sample of patients, in reduced death rates.

These scattered examples, slight as they are, begin to indicate how old age disabilities can often be successfully alleviated or even reversed. Research to confirm the early findings and to identify further ways of reversing disabilities must be given high priority. In the meantime, even bolder new research should concentrate on preventing disabilities and maintaining good health and effective functioning throughout later life.

NEW KNOWLEDGE FOR PREVENTING DISABILITY

Of even greater importance than research on how to reverse old age disabilities are studies of how to prevent them from occurring in the first place. The way is open. In 1979, the Surgeon General's *Report on Health Promotion and Disease Prevention* stated that perhaps as much as half of U.S. mortality is due to unhealthy behavior or lifestyle (Department of Health, Education, and Welfare, 1979:9). If continuing changes in behavior and lifestyle can sustain the 20th century triumph of extension of life, surely they can also serve to benefit the added years. Much is already known about certain of the social and behavioral factors that threaten good health as people grow older. The effects of behavior, social relationships, and lifestyle are often cumulative, beginning early in life and leading toward the chronic afflictions of later life. For example (as documented by the Department of Health and Human Services, 1980):

- Smoking has been implicated in many such problems of later life as heart disease, chronic bronchitis and emphysema, various cancers, and stomach ulcers. It is generally recognized as a leading preventable cause of morbidity and death (p. 61).
- Inappropriate consumption of essential nutrients can contribute in complex ways to such disorders as heart disease, adult-onset diabetes, high blood pressure, and possibly certain types of cancer (p. 73).
- Physical inactivity is associated with increased risk of coronary heart disease, whereas continual and extended exercise can constitute a therapeutic regimen for diabetes, musculoskeletal problems, respiratory diseases, and coronary heart disease (p. 79).
- While the nonmedical use of drugs such as tobacco and alcohol tends to decline somewhat with age, the overall use of both prescription and over-the counter drugs increases. Three common practices put the older population at risk of serious health hazards: self-medication, overprescribing by doctors, and the combined use of two or more drugs (p. 67).

Once understood, the social and behavioral factors that control smoking, food consumption, exercise, and drug use should be susceptible to interventive strategies and modification early in life, long before pathology develops.

Clearly, much further research is now needed that goes beyond merely demonstrating this potential—research that specifies the *mechanisms* through which psychosocial aging interacts with biomedical aging, and research that clarifies the social and environmental *conditions* that either promote or undermine health in the later years. Such further research is needed to learn *how* to keep older people well and how to enhance effective functioning and productivity beyond the middle years and into the eighth and ninth decades of life.

We close with a two-item research agenda for the future—easy to set out, but difficult to implement. These agenda items are guided, respectively, by two principles: 1) that aging is lifelong, consisting of interacting biological, psychological, and social processes; and 2) that these aging processes (including biological aging) are influenced by, and in turn influence, social change. For further understanding of these two principles, specific hypotheses must be formulated and examined through carefully designed psychosocial studies, both at the biological interface and at the societal interface. Meeting these dual research needs requires not only innovative research strategies, but also the close collaboration among scholars from different disciplines.

At the *biological interface,* social and behavioral studies are needed to specify how, through what mechanisms, health can be maintained into the later years and the quality of human aging improved. Among the best documented associations between psychosocial factors and diseases of later life, for example, is that between "pattern A behavior" and various of the cardiovascular diseases that affect later life (Krantz et al., 1981). Experiments already under way are examining a cumulative series of hypotheses as to how such specific components of pattern A behavior as competitiveness, time pressure, and suppressed hostility affect various physiological indicators of cardiovascular disturbances (e.g., catecholamine levels in the blood). These experiments, in which, for example, subjects are placed in competitive situations or confronted with hostile opponents, focus directly on *how* particular behaviors can influence particular symptoms of heart disease. They provide just one illustration of the broader potential for identifying biobehavioral mechanisms and social conditions that sustain or restore activity and functioning in the middle and later years. Conversely, there is a need to measure social and individual behavior in response to variations in biological processes. For example, if neuroendocrine secretions (e.g., catecholamine levels) change as people grow older, what effects does this change have on mental abilities or on interpersonal relationships?

Neuroimmunology is another promising new research area at the interface between psychosocial and biological aging. Studies are needed of regulation of the immune system by the brain (Ader, 1981). This system, which protects the body against disease, is integrated with other physiological processes and is known to be involved in the aging process, as evidenced by the increases in autoimmunity and immunodeficiencies with age (Makinodan and Kay, 1980). Moreover, evidence suggests that psychosocial factors may influence immune regula tion. Yet the postulated interactions among behavioral factors, immune changes with aging, and health are still poorly understood. These interactions represent an exciting and important area for study within a developmental psychobiological perspective that extends over the entire lifespan. Such research can provide a foundation for future clinical interventions to maintain physical and mental health far into old age.

At the *societal interface,* we need to know much more about the linkages between individual aging and particular social conditions of time and place. Here again there is suggestive evidence that societal conditions (e.g., fluctuations in the economic cycle) influence the health of individuals; but how? The mechanisms whereby these macrolevel variables are translated into microlevel effects on the individual aging process require specification. Possible models for this type of research are currently being developed (Suzman and Abeles, 1981). The conception of "stress" provides one prototypical model, which postulates both the types of social structural stressors and the psychophysiological processes that result in illness at different ages. Alternative models of linked changes need not rely upon stress as the driving force. For example, social change (e.g., modernization) may result in changes in the lifestyles of individuals (e.g., exposure to new pathogens, dietary changes, changes in risk taking or health behaviors) that may in turn cause psychophysiological changes (e.g., in functioning of the immune system or blood lipid levels) and ultimately affect the individual's health.

As psychosocial research adds new understandings at both the biological interface and the societal interface, the new scientific knowledge can be transferred into practice. Strategies can be developed for teaching people to start young to protect their own old age, for training employers and health care professionals, for restructuring legal and social institutions, for informing public policymakers of the risks over the entire life course that can affect health, performance, and the quality of living in the later years. That social and behavioral understandings can be used effectively is shown by the extraordinary changes in eating, smoking, and exercise made by Americans over the past 20 years. Clearly, people are attempting to control their own health habits.

Only by developing and applying new knowledge can we come closer to the goal, not merely of dispelling ageism, but of actually postponing the onset of disability until the end of the human lifespan. This goal is a radical one—no less, in effect, than to square the disability curve, to align it as narrowly as possible with the survival curve, to allow more and more people to function with full effectiveness up until death. Strenuous research efforts are needed at the frontiers to reach this goal.

REFERENCES

Ader, Robert (ed.) 1981. Psychoneuroimmunology. New York: Academic Press.

Baltes, Paul B., and Sherry L. Willis 1982. "Enhancement (plasticity) of intellectual functioning in old age: Penn State's adult development and enrichment project (ADEPT)." In F.I.M. Craik and S.E. Trehub (eds.), Aging and Cognitive Process. New York: Plenum.

Bureau of the Census 1979. Statistical Abstract of the United States. Washington D.C.: U.S. Government Printing Office.

Coe, R.M., and H.P. Brehm 1972. Preventive Health Care for Adults: A Study of Medical Practice. New Haven: College and University Press.

Department of Health and Human Services 1980. Promoting Health—Preventing Disease: Objectives for the Nation. Washington, D.C.: U.S. Government Printing Office.

Department of Health, Education, and Welfare 1979. Healthy People: The Surgeon General's Report on Health Promotion and Disease Prevention. PHS Publication No. 79-55071. Washington, D.C.: U.S. Government Printing Office.

Feinleib, Manning, et al. 1975. "The Framingham offspring study. Design and preliminary data." Preventive Medicine (4): 518–525.

Fries, James F. 1980. "Aging, natural death, and the compression of morbidity." New England Journal of Medicine 303:130–135.

Horn, John L., and Gary Donaldson 1980. "Cognitive development in adulthood." Pp. 445–529 in Orville G. Brim and Jerome Kagan (eds.), Constancy and Change in Human Development. Cambridge: Harvard University Press.

Kane, Robert, David Solomon, John Beck, Emmett Keeler, and Rosalie Kane 1980 "The future need for geriatric manpower in the United States." New England Journal of Medicine 302:1327–1332.

Krantz, David S., David C. Glass, Richard Contrada, and Neal E. Miller 1981. Behavior and Health: Five Year Outlook on Science and Technology. New York: Social Science Research Council.

Levinson, Daniel J., et al. 1978. The Seasons of a Man's Life. New York: Knopf.

Makinodan, T., and M.M.B. Kay 1980. "Age influences on the immune system." Advances in Immunology 29:287–330.

Poon, L.W., L. Walsh-Sweeney, and J.L. Fozard 1980. "Memory skill training for the elderly: salient issues on the use of imagery mnemonics." Pp. 461–484 in L.W. Poon, J.L. Fozard, L.S. Armak, D. Arenberg, and L.W. Thompson (eds.), New Directions in Memory and Aging: Proceedings of the George A. Talland Memorial Conference. Hillsdale, N.J.: Erlbaum.

Riley, Matilda White, and Anne Foner 1968. Aging and Society I: An Inventory of Research Findings. New York: Russell Sage.

Rodin, Judith 1980. "Managing the stress of aging: the role of control and coping." Pp. 171–202 in Seymour Levine and Holger Ursin (eds.), Coping and Health. New York: Plenum.

Schiffman, S.S., and M. Pasternak 1979. "Decreased discrimination of food odors in the elderly." Journal of Gerontology 34:73–79.

Sekuler, Robert, and Lucinda Picciano Hutmen 1980. "Spatial vision and aging. I: Contrast sensitivity." Journal of Gerontology 35 (5):692–699.

Shock, Nathan W. 1977. "System integration." Pp. 639–665 in Caleb E. Finch and Leonard Hayflick (eds.), Handbook of the Biology of Aging. New York: Van Nostrand Reinhold.

Suzman, Richard M., and Ronald P. Abeles 1981. "Linking societal conditions to the health of individuals." Paper Delivered at the Annual Meeting of the Gerontological Society of America. Toronto.

Vanderplas, J.M., and J.H. Vanderplas 1980. "Some factors affecting legibility of printed materials for older adults." Perceptual and Motor Skills 50:923–732.

Waring, Joan 1978. The Middle Years: A Multidisciplinary View. New York: Academy for Educational Development.

Postword: Where We Are and Where We Might Go

Beth B. Hess
County College of Morris

We enter the 1980's in the wake of several decades of research and activism on behalf of America's elderly. Over the past 20 years, an extensive list of major legislation has been enacted: Medicare, the Older American's Act, the Age Discrimination in Employment Act, and the indexing of Social Security, to name a few of the most prominent. The growth of mass membership in local organizations that focus on the concerns of senior citizens has been phenomenal. Closely linked to these societal-level developments, but following a dynamic process of its own, academic interest in aging and old age has also increased substantially during this period. This book is in many ways a tribute to the breadth and depth of inquiry into old age and aging now being carried out in hundreds of universities, colleges, centers, and institutes. We are today on the threshold of important accomplishments in the areas of research and theory building, as exemplified in this set of papers at the leading edge of this new scientific specialty.

SOME COMMON THEMES

A number of common themes emerge from these essentially independent papers. In most cases, the authors are as much concerned with demolishing erroneous stereotypes as with presenting new evidence. The overriding realization is that many outcomes commonly thought to be attributable to age are actually complex phenomena with multiple origins. The aging organism does not operate in a vacuum, but is engaged in a reciprocal interaction with a particular environment, and is itself the product of life-course experiences during a given slice of history. Physiological aging is only one of many factors that determine the condition and statuses of old people. Moreover, the current condition and status of old people—their resources, needs, and abilities—are not necessarily an accurate guide to the future.

Cohort Analysis and the Life-Course Perspective

These themes reflect two major recent theoretical developments in social science and gerontology. Rejecting psychologistic reductionism and simple functionalist explanations, students of human behavior and aging have increasingly adopted the technique of *cohort analysis* and the perspective of the *life course*. A cohort is a group of individuals who enter a given social system together (usually marked by a particular span of years, e.g., all those born in 1900–05 or all persons entering college in 1950–55) and who then age together across time. Each birth cohort, for example, varies from any other in its size, its composition (race, sex ratio, ethnicity, native birth), and subsequent experiences (fertility, educational attainment, health behavior, etc.). By the time cohort members reach old age, selective mortality and at least six decades of shared history will have produced a unique age stratum. The incomparability of incoming cohorts of old people is a frequent theme in these papers.

Although the specific cohorts chosen for comparison vary from one paper to another, the essential points being made are similar: Those who are old today were born at the turn of the century and before World War I; their socialization experiences, occupational levels, educational attainment, birth rates, mortality risks, and exposure to urban cultures are all very different from those of their children. Other differentiating variables are native versus foreign birth, the probability of having a sibling or parent die while one was a child at home, the likelihood of having an aged relative in the household for a period of time, place of residence, interaction with kin, lifetime earnings, health behavior, political orientation and loyalties, and religious involvement. In all these respects and many others, variations between cohorts may account for more age-related differences than the aging process itself does. Indeed, aging as a biological process is itself influenced by many of these cohort-specific factors. Therefore, we can expect that the timing, incidence, and prevalence of age-related functional declines will vary among successive cohorts.

Another major theme is the realization that the condition of the elderly is rooted in life experiences at earlier ages. This fact is especially obvious when considering health and economic well-being, although much previous work has failed to appreciate fully the lifetime accumulation factor. When comparing retirement incomes among categories of old people—by race, gender, or occupation, for instance—it may appear that earlier discrepancies have been narrowed, surely a misleading conclusion if one fails to measure differences in home ownership and equity, stocks and securities, bank accounts, and other assets. The call for life-course data and longitudinal designs found in these papers, therefore, reflects the recognition that age *differences* found in cross-sectional studies may not be age *changes*. Here, too, cohort differences have explanatory value; for example, educational attainment affects performance on memory tasks, lifetime earnings, health behavior, nutrition, satisfaction in retirement, ability to migrate, and resources for adapting to stress, to mention only a few major variables covered in these papers.

Macrolevel and Microlevel Phenomena

Although it is important to have life-course data for the older age strata, it is essential for many topics that all age categories be taken into account. Macrolevel phenomena can only be understood when the behavior of young and old are considered together. This point is well-illustrated by the dynamics of geographical distribution of old people in which outmigration of younger families has a greater impact on the age structure of a given area than does the movement of older people. The same is true with many other macrosocial variables.

The interplay between macrolevel and microlevel phenomena is another general theme, especially in the treatment of economic variables. For example, population aging (a macrolevel process) affects labor-force mobility and the dependency ratio, which ultimately determine the economic well-being of older individuals. Such societal-level measures as the proportion of people retired or the structure of the Social Security system also affect the microlevel processes of individual retirement decisionmaking and satisfaction with that choice. All too often, researchers have defined the context of later life choices in purely interpersonal terms. As many of the papers in this book demonstrate, however, broader historical patterns and social system characteristics must be introduced into the analysis.

The Influence of Demographic Trends

Along these lines, still another theme reflected throughout this book is the importance of demographic trends, such as the differential effect of fertility rates, on the ways individuals age. No attempt to predict the experience of incoming cohorts of elderly can disregard the relative advantage of Baby Boom parents in terms of family-based support systems, for example. When these parents reach old age at the beginning of the next century, they may strain the Social Security system, but will probably make minimal demands on other publicly funded services. In contrast, their children, who will reach old age toward the middle of the next century, will have few offspring to rely on for care and assistance and hence may generate extraordinary demands upon the social welfare system.

The authors are also sensitive to the many long-term effects of the dramatic increases in life expectancy in this century and the advantages of this increase to women. When coupled with the findings on greater variability among the elderly (compared with other age categories) along a variety of attitudinal, behavioral, and physiological dimensions, these added years mean that the enormous diversity of the older population must be taken into account in any policy initiative. This fact also demonstrates the need for disaggregation of data by 5-year or 10-year birth cohorts. In the areas of health and income (or net worth, to follow the recommendation of several of our authors), this consideration is particularly salient, yet even with these finer chronological distinctions, age itself appears to be an imperfect predictor of performance and capacity.

Objective and Subjective Views

Many of these papers explore the complex links between objective conditions and older persons' perceptions of well-being (in terms of health, life satisfaction, and material status). We have the phenomenon of retired workers who are quite satisfied with their leisure, of blacks whose expectations of longevity exceed those of whites, of the chronically ill who assess their health as good, and of those in stressful situations who manage to cope more successfully than individuals under less objective stress. Two intervening variables are of crucial importance: reference groups and social support systems.

To the extent that older people compare themselves with age peers as reference groups, many conditions will be perceived as "normal" rather than exceptional or unfair. Among retirees, comparisons with age peers who remain in the labor force could be stressful, while comparisons with other retired persons are not; therefore, as more older workers leave the labor force (many before any mandated age), retirement is normalized, and common lifestyles and supportive definitions are developed. Similarly, one's sense of economic well-being depends upon the individual's reference point, whether it is one's own preretirement income or income of others in the retirement cohort. In the matter of health status, such subjective ratings have often proved more predictive of a sense of well-being than have relatively objective measurements. An individual's positive perception of health status affects the behaviors taken in response. There is much in this book to support the frequently cited findings of the late Angus Campbell that satisfaction and happiness need not be related; unhappy people can be satisfied with their situation if the alternatives appear even less satisfactory.

Social Support Systems

Individuals are often insulated from the negative impact of aging (or, indeed, any type of stressor) not only by self-assessments, but also by the availability of others who define the situation in a positive light or who can provide needed services. The mediating effects of such support networks are only recently being systematically explored and appreciated. It would, however, be a mistake to assume that embeddedness in a kinship group is invariably associated either with positive feelings or by positive effects. For example, among ethnic minority groups, the family can sometimes isolate its elderly from needed services. The assumption that families are necessarily wholesome environments for intergenerational living has increasingly been questioned by gerontologists and historians of the family. And today, in many cases, the care of a frail elderly relative can produce unbearable stress on members of both generations (or three generations, if young people are also in the home). This point will undoubtedly receive increasing attention as proposals to shift care from public to private sources are debated. Yet the myth of family devotion remains powerful, and few among us are willing to be known as ungrateful offspring.

Debunking myths is only the first step in understanding, but an essential one. Policy decisions relating to retirement income and family responsibility are too important to be decided on the basis of nostalgia or wish fulfillment. Nor should older people, particularly those in the labor force, continue to be perceived as forgetful or unteachable or unproductive; much evidence is available to illustrate the extreme complexity of these abilities and the great variability with which capacities are maintained or modified with age.

SYNOPSIS OF THE BOOK

This book begins, fittingly, with *Andrew Cherlin's* exposition of the new historical scholarship on the family. It now seems clear that the past was no "Golden Age" of intergenerational solidarity and that the power enjoyed by the elderly was as much a consequence of their control over scarce resources as of filial devotion. Current public programs that support income maintenance and health care for the aged have greatly enhanced the voluntary independence of generations, with both positive and negative consequences that require much fuller investigation. Simplistic arguments about the breakdown of the "extended family" can no longer seriously be maintained. Moreover, since each cohort is characterized by different rates of childbearing, mortality risks, labor force participation of women, and family stability, comparisons with past generations are risky at best and misleading at worst.

Many contemporary trends are worth investigating in terms of their eventual impact on the family relationships of old people: divorce among members of incoming cohorts and among their offspring; sustained low fertility; high remarriage rates, particularly for men; and women's employment outside the home. On the one hand, low fertility reduces the number of possible caretakers in old age; so does divorce. On the other hand, higher levels of education and experience in the labor force should add to the coping powers of elderly women (who compose the great majority of old people). Remarriage can also enhance the resources of older family members. Remarriage among the elderly secures immediate support and relieves the potential burden on offspring, and remarriage of the offspring provides additional kin with whom to establish helping relationships. In other words, the internal structure of families in the future will be considerably more complex than at present.

Further, remarriage may be seen as a means of increasing the supply of grandparents and grandchildren, to the benefit of all concerned. With the possibility that almost one-half of the marriages currently contracted will not survive a full three decades, the importance of remarriage cannot be underestimated. Approximately four of five divorced persons will remarry, at a risk only slightly higher than that for first marriages. However complicated its internal structure, a reconstituted family is a family nonetheless and a resource for its members. Since many grandparents maintain contact with former daughters-in-law and sons-in-law, especially the custodial parent, they may also acquire courtesy kin relationships to the offspring of the second marriage. The potential range of kinship ties is a frequently overlooked factor in analyses of family life in old age.

Family status and support are crucial ingredients of well-being in old age. Of equal (if not greater) importance to morale or life-satisfaction is one's economic situation. It is becoming increasingly obvious that the economic well-being of older people must be examined from a life-course perspective: total lifetime earnings, home ownership, assets and annuities, lifestyle, and personal and interpersonal resources developed over the years. But the economic well-being of any age stratum also depends on the age structure of the society as a whole and the effect this structure will have on the economic sector.

When looking ahead, as described by *Thomas J. Espenshade* and *Rachel Eisenberg Braun,* one must consider the impact of an aging population on labor supply and mobility, on savings and investment for economic growth, and on the cost of supporting nonproducing members of the society. For example, large numbers of older workers can clog channels of upward mobility and, by reducing the wage differentials among workers with different skills, can decrease the motivation of younger employees to upgrade their labor market value. Moreover, if the costs of maintaining an older population in retirement drain capital needed for investment, how can the economic system continue to grow? Must the material well-being of one generation occur at the expense of another's? When considered in juxtaposition to the paper on retirement and the Social Security system, the paper by Espenshade and Braun reminds us of how little we know about the unintended consequences of public policy and how difficult it will be to extricate these questions from a political context.

As a very first step, the phrase "economic wellbeing" must be defined and its components described. Measuring the many factors that compose an individual's economic status is another problem faced by researchers in this area. Even more difficult are the assigning of proper weights to the various factors and accounting for the subjective values placed on different forms of wealth.

Considerations of economic well-being that focus upon individual measures of income, even within a life-course framework, often fail to examine the context of the workplace. We tend to think of business firms as closed systems, operating on economic principles removed from the general flow of births and deaths and aging in society. Perhaps this is why organizational structures are so little studied from the perspective of social gerontology. Yet, as *Harris Schrank* and *Joan Waring* so clearly describe them, work organizations manifest the characteristics of age stratification systems in general, reflecting both the structures of the general society and the particular needs of business firms.

Many types of aging take place within a work organization: Employees grow older, job holders extend their tenure, workers add years of employment, the age composition of the organization changes, and the business firm itself ages. As in the study of any age stratification system, norms that allocate persons of a given age to particular job levels are of utmost importance. Since positions within the firm are carefully graded in terms of organizational rewards—prestige, power, and income-these allocative processes affect the morale and commitment of employees. Maintaining and rationalizing a system of unequal rewards require organizational mechanisms for turnover, promotion, and "cooling out," all in the interests of stability and orderly change in the system.

The fruitfulness of this approach to work organizations is illustrated by Schrank's and Waring's analysis. They describe a fairly consistent pattern in which an individual's organizational age (i.e., the number of years the employee has been with the firm), is negatively related to his or her organizational mobility. A faster rate of promotion among newer than among senior employees could be due to such factors as high turnover among junior members of the firm, the constraints of a hierarchical structure itself, and the greater importance of promotion at the higher levels. Noting that these explanations cannot fully account for the phenomenon, Schrank and Waring propose a "gap hypothesis" whereby the discrepancy between rewards and performance is shifted over time in a fashion that motivates junior members and maintains the commitment of senior employees. Entrants to the firm are placed in positions below their capacity. While they learn the ropes and compete with one another for the next step upward, relatively rapid promotions serve to sort out the more capable and persistent. As the gap between performance and rewards narrows with a person's organizational age, the pace of upward movement slackens, with no loss in the employee's loyalty. Schrank and Waring contend that the gap hypothesis is a more accurate tool of analysis than human capital theory in explaining the age-based patterns of work organizations. At the very least, the age stratification model illuminates aspects of organizational functioning that have long gone unexamined or unexplained.

Retirement is one aspect of economic and personal well-being in later life that has not suffered from a lack of examination or theorizing. As with public perceptions of family life now and in the past, romanticized thinking also surrounds assumptions regarding the virtues of work and activity throughout the life course, but especially in old age. *Anne Foner* and *Karen Schwab* present evidence from major surveys on attitudes toward retirement and work, satisfaction with retirement, and desire to rejoin the labor force. It appears that few older workers are unwilling victims of mandatory retirement rules, that increasing numbers choose to retire even before being eligible for full benefits and pensions, that more would do so if their incomes permitted, and that only a small proportion of older people are looking for employment or work-like activities.

Such findings run counter to the expectations of the Puritan work ethic and the activist (characteristically masculine-oriented) values of our society, as well as the dominant theories in psychology and sociology that predict stressful outcomes of major role transitions, particularly those involving loss of a salient status. The widespread phenomenon of retirement, however, and the secondary industries developed around leisure lifestyles have cushioned the impact of the transition to retirement. Individuals may also resolve cognitive dissonance between expectation and reality by lowering their aspirations and selecting supportive reference groups; that is, "satisfaction" in retirement may have different referents than at earlier stages.

The major problem facing retirees may not be the loss of the work role, but the stability of the Social Security system. In some ways, a tradeoff must be made between higher standards of living in preretirement years (through limitations on family size) and the ultimate consequence of low fertility (shrinkage of the labor force whose payroll taxes pay for the retirement incomes of the elderly). The scenario currently being presented to the public is one of diminishing revenues and higher dependency ratios, with the most favored solution being retaining older workers in the labor force. There are many other possibilities, however, not the least of which is an increase in productivity through the use of automation. Indeed, some labor analysts foresee a future in which the demand for all types of workers will be considerably reduced. In any event, the debate over restructuring of the retirement and Social Security systems should take into account the realities of a disinclination to remain in the labor force by those who have spent four or five decades in relatively repetitive and unsatisfying activities.

At the moment, however, inflationary pressures are leading many workers to postpone early retirement plans. Moreover, public policy in the form of new amendments to the Social Security Act may encourage later retirement rather than earlier retirement—for example, removing limits on income earned without reducing benefits, further lowering the percentage of benefits available at early retirement, raising the age of full entitlement to 70 by the year 2000, and eliminating mandatory retirement provisions altogether. The retirement issue today is far from resolved, and the wishes of workers may prove less important than political and economic processes in its resolution.

Yet another mythical representation of the aged in our society portrays vast hordes of elderly descending upon Florida, Arizona, and southern California. As we learn from *Tim Heaton's* presentation, the flow of older migrants is extremely small compared with that of younger individuals and families who follow the vagaries of the labor market. The migration of younger people rather than the movement of elderly accounts for much of the spatial distribution of the population in the United States. Left behind in rural hamlets and inner cities, the elderly are slightly overrepresented in these two locales and are underrepresented in the developing population centers of the South and West. But not for long. As Heaton describes the effects on populations of aging-in-place and of migration patterns, those areas with a high proportion of old people will grow "younger," while areas such as the suburbs are gradually "aging." The old people in inner cities and small towns will gradually die off, with fewer middle-aged individuals replacing them, while the suburban pioneers of the 1950's are now reaching age 60 or over. The future age composition of such areas will depend on whether younger migrants flow in to take advantage of job opportunities or available housing.

In those areas to which the elderly have migrated, certain changes will take place, though their precise nature and extent are still unresearched. For example, an immediate demand for health and social services is not likely, since migrants tend to be healthier, wealthier, and younger than the older population in general. Over time, however, this situation will surely change, as the migrants age in place. Conflicts between the new and old residents can be anticipated over such issues as tax assessments, school budgets, land use, and provision of services.

As for the future, the advent of better educated and relatively wealthier cohorts of old people, particularly those retiring before mandatory age limits and those who have traveled extensively earlier in life, strongly suggests an increase in elderly migration designed to enhance physical well-being. For the generation of Baby Boom parents, in addition, moves will be made to maximize contact with children. At the same time, there will continue to be numerous elderly individuals and couples for whom migration is financially impossible and who may, thereby, be trapped in dying and decaying locales.

Overall, the current deconcentration of old people—from cities to nonmetropolitan areas—continues a trend that began in the 1950's, preceding the more general and dramatic population shifts of the 1970's away from the Snowbelt States to the Sunbelt and from larger to smaller places. Heaton's paper highlights the causes and consequences of both younger and older migration patterns.

In his paper on minority groups and aging, *Kyriakos Markides* examines the data used to test the "double jeopardy" hypothesis. When compared with their age peers in the dominant group, according to this hypothesis, the minority aged will be more disadvantaged in old age than earlier in life. The reasoning behind the double jeopardy hypothesis is that negative factors accumulate over time and that the effects of age discrimination add to those based on race or ethnicity. The limited support for this hypothesis, despite its apparent plausibility, is largely due to the extreme deprivations experienced by minority group members at all ages; in comparison, the declines in old age experienced by mainstream whites are proportionately greater.

Markides notes the methodological problems overlooked in most tests of the hypothesis and concludes that an accurate assessment of minority status in old age requires a life-course model and appropriate data. The deprivations of later life are rooted in the earlier history of individuals and their birth cohorts. Given the major changes that have taken place in recent decades in the life chances of blacks and Hispanic Americans, it is also possible that new and different patterns will emerge. A further consideration in the case of Hispanics is the extreme variability within that population, not only between Mexican, Puerto Rican, and Cuban subgroups, but also between those who are new immigrants and those who have been acculturated to varying degrees. As for blacks, the growing division on the basis of class must be recognized. As the better educated blacks move into the ranks of the middle class in terms of income and occupation, others are increasingly isolated in the central core of decaying cities.

In almost every respect, the kinds of analyses required for policies directed toward minority elderly have not been performed. This is due in part to inappropriate research designs, in part to public indifference, and also in part to romanticization of the minority family by members of the subgroups themselves as well as the general public. Findings of little support for the double jeopardy hypothesis, or of high levels of kinship interaction, or of optimism and satisfaction should not obscure recognition of the very real disadvantages that characterize the later years as thoroughly as the earlier ones.

In analyzing sex differences in health and mortality in later life, as in racial and ethnic minority differences, it is impossible to understand the data on old age without reference to the entire life course. With gender, moreover, socialization and social role expectations, as well as biologically based vulnerabilities, are additional explanatory factors. Although it now appears clear that males are genetically programmed for shorter lifespans than females, much of the difference in mortality rates by sex is a function of differential health behaviors. One of the major themes of *Lois Verbrugge's* paper is the possibility that women's greater attention to their health at earlier ages accounts for their living longer than men. The paradox of greater morbidity combined with lower mortality for women is partially explained by health behaviors. Female socialization and reproductive experiences lead to enhanced awareness of physical symptoms and greater willingness to do something about them, such as reducing weight or visiting a physician. Men are less apt to take either step, partly because of difficulties in getting away from work and, to some extent, because of the constraints of the male role.

In looking to the future, Verbrugge sees continued extension of life expectancy for both men and women, though at a diminishing rate. For one thing, younger people are adopting more healthful lifestyles (though they may be doing so in more polluted environments). A new emphasis on preventive health care will also serve to reduce excess middle age mortality. As for the gap between male and female mortality rates in old age, Verbrugge acknowledges the possibility that women's entry into stressful occupations could reduce their advantage in life expectancy, but any reduction of the gap will more likely be caused by a reduction in male mortality at the younger levels of old age. Future change in mortality patterns will probably result from changes in the social context and behaviors of men and women rather than from any great medical breakthroughs.

The issue addressed by *James House* and *Cynthia Robbins* is one of the most intriguing in the relatively new field of research often called ''behavorial medicine.'' The relation among social behaviors, psychological predispositions, and health is truly a multidisciplinary area of study, the contours of which are still being mapped. To this intricate web of cause and effect, House and Robbins add the variables of age and life-course stage. How does age, both as a proxy for life-course stage and as a measure of chronological aging with physiological sequelae, affect the number and type of stressors experienced by individuals, their perceptions of stress, the repertoire of responses at their disposal, and the coping resources available to them? In other words, what do age and life-stage information add to our understanding of the relationship between stress and health?

Survey data indicate that younger adults experience a greater number of objective stressors than do older adults and that younger respondents also perceive themselves as more stressed than do older respondents. But it is also true that the elderly experience failing health and a higher lifetime total of stressful events than do younger people. On the one hand, stressors will accumulate throughout the life-course, perhaps indicative of the ''wear and tear'' that leads to decrements in physiological functioning in old age. On the other hand, having coped with so many life events of a stressful nature—both positive and negative—older people have developed superior coping abilities, as evidenced in their lower perceptions of immediate stress. As House and Robbins note, in every important life domain, age is positively related to satisfaction and negatively to perceived stress. The types of dissonance-reducing mechanisms noted with reference to satisfaction in retirement are also cited by House and Robbins: resignation, lowered aspiration, and increased personal control through a lifetime of selective changes (e.g., in employment, in family relationships, and in community involvement). In other words, there are many life-course processes that reduce the negative impact of stress.

Nonetheless, age variations in exposure to stress seem to be less powerful determinants of perception and responses to stressful events—and hence the impact on health—than are other social variables, such as gender, race, and socioeconomic status. Yet age interacts with these social background characteristics to affect the patterning and clustering of life events and the resources with which to cope. The major life transitions, even those associated with loss, appear to be less predictive of health outcomes than was previously thought. In addition, the variable of social network support does not seem to have a uniformly positive effect. Rather, the quality, timing, and patterning of relationships may be more important than quantity, and these are the characteristics of social networks that are often age-related.

Many recurrent sources of stress, such as poverty, isolation, and marital strain, have important consequences for health at all ages. The old, however, must cope with physiological changes that become stressors which affect other health outcomes. The paper concludes with suggestions for the type of research urgently needed to clarify the complex and often recursive relationships among age, stress, and health.

Maradee Davis and *Elizabeth Randall* explore the relatively uncharted territory of age changes in nutrition and food habits. This may be the premiere area in which the effects of aging are obscured by all the other classes of variables encountered by students of aging. First, there are the profound differences among cohorts in ethnicity, early socialization, education, and historical events affecting food preferences and eating habits. Then there are the manifold changes that have taken place in the food industry. These include commercial canning, dehydration, prepared mixes, frozen foods, fast-food outlets, and supermarkets, all of which are typically designed to provide greater convenience in purchasing and meal preparation while also expanding the choice and range of food items available to most consumers. In addition, certain trends have affected the structure of the households that are the primary units of consumption. These include fewer household members (at least since 1960), female labor force participation, temporary dislocations due to divorce, and changing gender roles, to mention the most salient.

Earlier research has focused exclusively on childhood socialization to food preferences, obscuring the great changes that occur across the life course. Similarly, a preoccupation with the woman's role as the family food gatekeeper has limited the collection of data on men as purchasers and preparers of foods, activities which are likely to characterize more adult males in the future.

Today, large numbers of adults live alone. At the younger age ranges, both men and women are maintaining single-person households prior to eventual marriage. Increasing numbers will also become single again following dissolution of a marriage, and many of the women will become heads of families during this period. For them, the number and ages of children are crucial variables in food behavior, within the limits of their reduced incomes. Among the elderly, single-person households are increasingly characteristic of widowed females; it seems reasonable to expect that financial constraints, as well as physical mobility, will determine the food habits of these women. Since food behavior of older women is also responsive to educational level and independent living, incoming cohorts may be very different from those now old.

Nonetheless, people who live alone, particularly those who also eat alone, have food habits that differ from those who share the planning, preparation, and consumption of a meal. Of crucial importance here is the existence and extent of one's social network. Networks often transmit information about food, guide its purchase and preparation, provide companionship during meals, and establish new food habits. To date, however, research linking age and food behaviors lacks both theoretical grounding and methodological sophistication. The research

agenda set by Davis and Randall is a necessary first step to systematic exploration of this topic.

The forgetful old person is a stock comic figure in Western literature, and,
indeed, many elderly people experience difficulties in recall, particularly at advanced ages. Yet we now know that what seemed to be so clear an aging effect is
neither as universal nor as inevitable as was once assumed. *Marion Perlmutter*
details the laboratory data on learning and memory across age categories. Her
careful conclusion is that memory decrements are highly variable among individuals and specific tasks. In addition, the basic ability for recall does not decline as
much as the capacity for spontaneous choice of optimal strategies, at least in the
laboratory tests devised by psychologists. With careful instructions and in a
supportive setting, older persons can learn and respond with levels of accuracy
comparable to younger people.

Laboratory experiments, however, are not necessarily generalizable to "real
life," where older people sucessfully adapt, cope, and devise alternative strategies. Until more longitudinal data and real life behaviors are observed and analyzed, age-related changes in encoding, storage, retrieval, and learning remain
only partly explored. At the moment, according to Perlmutter, age is not a very
good predictor of performance on learning and memory tasks. The process of
decline is too complex, involving interaction among physiological, psychological, and social context variables. Moreover, cohort differences, especially in educational attainment, must be taken into account when assessing the implications
for performance at different age levels. Finally, in many tasks, experience and
prior learning offset the advantages of speed and spontaneity enjoyed by younger
subjects.

It will be a long time, however, before the stereotype of the absent-minded
grandparent is effectively eradicated. Note, for example, the stereotypes about
performance declines among older workers. Such myths serve some functions.
Employers can claim "scientific" support for decisions to cast out older workers. Friends will forgive oversights that would not be excused in younger people.
And many elderly may find their presumed lapses in memory a convenient means
of avoiding responsibility.

The book closes with a paper by *Matilda White Riley* and *Kathleen Bond* that
carries us beyond ageism into the realm of practical programs for enhancing
well-being and productive capacities throughout mature adulthood. Many of the
inevitable decrements currently associated with old age can often be prevented or
postponed through timely intervention and the early adoption of salutary
lifestyles. Research should be aimed toward a foreseeable future when great personal and societal costs of disability, untimely death, and mental deterioration
could be contained or reduced by proper regimens and safe and stimulating
environments.

It is certainly possible that the course of physiological aging can be significantly altered without any of the heralded mystery cures so often hinted at in the
mass media. We do know that health behaviors, like any other, will vary from

one cohort to another and are subject to modification over time. Although it is commonly thought that biological processes follow their own inexorable laws and are the cause of specified behaviors in old age, Riley and Bond illustrate the many ways in which physiological aging is influenced by behavioral and social factors.

Thus, a book that opens with a "sense of history" is brought to a close with a paper that looks ahead to the future and that weaves together the various strands of research in sociology, psychology, and biology. If there is one overriding theme of these papers it is that the links between the age of individuals and the social structure and between objective conditions and individual responses are far from simple. Life-course and cohort considerations make generalizations tentative. And above all, much that had been thought to be an invariable accompaniment of aging is highly modifiable. If social supports protect against the harmful effects of stress, both individual vulnerability and the stressful circumstances can be remedied. If memory tasks require additional time and instructions, these can be provided. If physician visits in midlife enhance life expectancy, these can be encouraged. If early disadvantages lead to cumulative decrements in later life, racial and ethnic differences in life chances could be minimized; so also could social class variation in economic assets and the ability to move to desirable locations.

In other words, there are policy decisions that can affect the course of aging, enhance the lives of old people, and stabilize the social system. All of this has been said many times before. These papers were commissioned to point to new directions for the research required for the policy debates ahead. Ultimately, of course, the use of research findings to guide public discourse is a political issue. The goal of this book is to inform the debate with fresh perspectives from the leading edges.

Author Index

Numbers in *italics* denote pages with complete bibliographic information.